Show Me Mac OS X Panther

Andy Anderson

Steve Johnson

Perspection, Inc.

Que Publishing
800 East 96th Street
Indianapolis, IN 46240 USA

Show Me Mac OS X Panther

International Standard Book Number: 0-7897-3066-9

Library of Congress Catalog Card Number: 2004100880

Printed in the United States of America

First Printing: March 2004

06 05 04 03   4 3 2 1

Que Publishing offers excellent discounts on this book when ordered in quantity for bulk purchases or special sales. For information, please contact:

U.S. Corporate and Government Sales

1-800-382-3419

corpsales@pearsontechgroup.com

For sales outside the U.S., please contact:

International Sales

1-317-428-3341

International@pearsontechgroup.com

Trademarks

All terms mentioned in this book that are known to be trademarks or service marks have been appropriately capitalized. Que cannot attest to the accuracy of this information. Use of a term in this book should not be regarded as affecting the validity of any trademark or service mark.

Apple, the Apple logo, Firewire, iMovie, iTunes, Mac, Macintosh, Mac OS, QuickTime, iCal, iChat, iPhoto, Panther, and Safari are trademarks of Apple Computer, Inc. Microsoft and Windows are either registered trademarks or trademarks of Microsoft Corporation. Other product and company names mentioned herein may be trademarks of their respective companies.

Warning and Disclaimer

Every effort has been made to make this book as complete and as accurate as possible, but no warranty or fitness is implied. The authors and the pub-lishers shall have neither liability nor responsibility to any person or entity with respect to any loss or damage arising from the information contained in this book.

Publisher
Paul Boger

Associate Publisher
Greg Wiegand

Managing Editor
Steve Johnson

Authors
Andy Anderson
Steve Johnson

Project Editor
Holly Johnson

Technical Editor
Holly Johnson

Production Editor
Beth Teyler

Page Layout
Beth Teyler
Joe Kalsbeek

Interior Designers
Steve Johnson
Marian Hartsough

Indexer
Katherine Stimson

Proofreader
Beth Teyler

Team Coordinator
Sharry Lee Gregory

Acknowledgements

Perspection, Inc.

Show Me Mac OS X Panther has been created by the professional trainers and writers at Perspection, Inc. to the standards you've come to expect from Que publishing. Together, we are pleased to present this training book.

Perspection, Inc. is a software training company committed to providing information and training to help people use software more effectively in order to communicate, make decisions, and solve problems. Perspection writes and produces software training books, and develops multimedia and Web-based training. Since 1991, we have written more than 70 computer books, with several bestsellers to our credit, and sold over 4.6 million books.

This book incorporates Perspection's training expertise to ensure that you'll receive the maximum return on your time. You'll focus on the tasks and skills that increase productivity while working at your own pace and convenience.

We invite you to visit the Perspection Web site at:

www.perspection.com

Acknowledgements

The task of creating any book requires the talents of many hard-working people pulling together to meet impossible deadlines and untold stresses. We'd like to thank the outstanding team responsible for making this book possible: the writers, Andy Anderson and Steve Johnson; the project and technical editor, Holly Johnson; the production team, Beth Teyler and Joe Kalsbeek; the proofreader, Beth Teyler; and the indexer, Katherine Stimson.

At Que publishing, we'd like to thank Greg Wiegand for the opportunity to undertake this project, Sharry Gregory for administrative support, and Sandra Schroeder for your production expertise and support.

Perspection

About The Authors

Andy Anderson is a graphics designer and illustrator who has worked with Flash since it was released. A university professor, Andy is a sought-after lecturer in the U.S., Canada, and Europe. The remainder of his time is split between writing graphics and fiction books, and developing graphics, animations, and resource materials for various corporations and seminar companies. His clients include designers and trainers from the U.S. Government, Boeing, Disneyland, and other Fortune 500 companies. He is also the author of 1001 Photoshop Tips and Tricks, Photoshop 7 Studio Workshop, HTML & Web Design, Show Me Adobe Photoshop CS, and Show Me Flash MX 2004.

Steve Johnson has written more than thirty-five books on a variety of computer software, including Microsoft Office 2003 and XP, Microsoft Windows XP, Macromedia Flash MX 2004, Macromedia Director MX 2004, Macromedia Fireworks, and Web publishing. In 1991, after working for Apple Computer and Microsoft, Steve founded Perspection, Inc., which writes and produces software training. When he is not staying up late writing, he enjoys playing golf, gardening, and spending time with his wife, Holly, and three children, JP, Brett, and Hannah. When time permits, he likes to travel to such places as New Hampshire in October, and Hawaii. Steve and his family live in Pleasanton, California, but can also be found visiting family all over the western United States.

We Want To Hear From You!

As the reader of this book, *you* are our most important critic and commentator. We value your opinion and want to know what we're doing right, what we could do better, what areas you'd like to see us publish in, and any other words of wisdom you're willing to pass our way.

As an associate publisher for Que, I welcome your comments. You can email or write me directly to let me know what you did or didn't like about this book—as well as what we can do to make our books better.

Please note that I cannot help you with technical problems related to the topic of this book. We do have a User Services group, however, where I will forward specific technical questions related to the book.

When you write, please be sure to include this book's title and author as well as your name, email address, and phone number. I will carefully review your comments and share them with the author and editors who worked on the book.

Email: feedback@quepublishing.com

Mail: Greg Wiegand
         Que Publishing
         800 East 96th Street
         Indianapolis, IN 46240 USA

For more information about this book or another Que title, visit our Web site at *www.quepublishing.com*. Type the ISBN (excluding hyphens) or the title of a book in the Search field to find the page you're looking for.

Contents

Introduction

Welcome to *Show Me Mac OS X Panther*, a visual quick reference book that shows you how to work efficiently with Mac OS X Panther. This book provides complete coverage of basic and intermediate Mac OS X Panther skills.

How This Book Works

You don't have to read this book in any particular order. We've designed the book so that you can jump in, get the information you need, and jump out. However, the book does follow a logical progression from simple tasks to more complex ones. Each task is presented on no more than two facing pages, which lets you focus on a single task without having to turn the page. To find the information that you need, just look up the task in the table of contents, index, or troubleshooting guide, and turn to the page listed. Read the task introduction, follow the step-by-step instructions in the left column along with screen illustrations in the right column, and you're done.

What's New

If you're searching for what's new in Mac OS X Panther, just look for the icon: New!. The new icon appears in the table of contents so you can quickly and easily identify a new or improved feature in Mac OS X Panther. A complete description of each new feature appears in the New Features guide in the back of this book.

Keyboard Shortcuts

Most menu commands have a keyboard equivalent, such as ⌘+P (Print on the File menu), as a quicker alternative to using the mouse. A complete list of keyboard shortcuts appears in the Keyboard Shortcuts guide in the back of this book.

Step-by-Step Instructions

This book provides concise step-by-step instructions that show you "how" to accomplish a task. Each set of instructions include illustrations that directly correspond to the easy-to-read steps. Also included in the text are time-savers, tables, and sidebars to help you work more efficiently or to teach you more in-depth information. A "Did You Know?" provides tips and techniques to help you work smarter, while a "See Also" leads you to other parts of the book containing related information about the task.

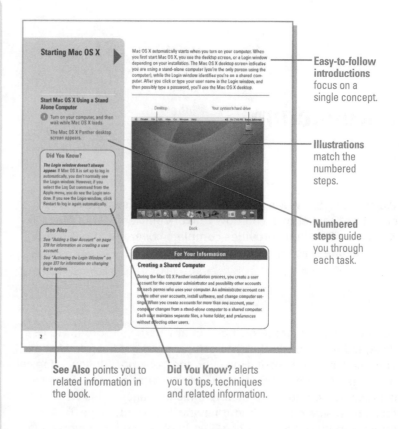

Easy-to-follow introductions focus on a single concept.

Illustrations match the numbered steps.

Numbered steps guide you through each task.

See Also points you to related information in the book.

Did You Know? alerts you to tips, techniques and related information.

Real World Examples

This book uses simple real world examples, which you can follow on your own, to help you learn Mac OS X Panther. For more complex tasks, you can access the example files on the Web, download them onto your computer, and then open or use them in Mac OS X Panther applications and utilities to see how they work. The Mac OS X Panther example files are available online at *www.perspection.com* or *www.quepublishing.com/showme*.

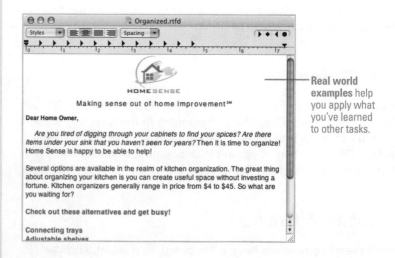

Real world examples help you apply what you've learned to other tasks.

Troubleshooting Guide

This book offers quick and easy ways to diagnose and solve common Mac OS X Panther problems that you might encounter. The troubleshooting guide helps you determine and fix a problem using the task information you find. The problems are posed in question form and are grouped into categories that are presented alphabetically.

Troubleshooting points you to information in the book to help you fix your problems.

Getting Started with Mac OS X Panther

Introduction

Mac OS X Panther is an **operating system (OS)**, a computer program that controls the basic operation of your Macintosh computer and the programs you run. A **program**, also known as an application, is task-oriented software you use to accomplish a specific task, such as word processing, managing files on your computer, or performing calculations.

The **Finder** is part of the Mac OS and starts when you turn on your computer. The Finder displays a menu bar and desktop on your screen that you can use to work with windows, icons, and files. A **window** can contain the contents of a file and the application in which it was created, icons (picture representations of an application or a file), or other usable data. This use of windows and icons is called a **graphical user interface** (GUI, pronounced "gooey"), meaning that you ("user") interact ("interface") with the computer through the use of graphics: icons and other meaningful words, symbols, and windows. A **file** is a collection of information (such as a letter or list of addresses) that has a unique name, distinguishing it from other files. You can use the Finder to open, copy, delete, list, and organize your computer files.

When you turn on your Macintosh computer, the Finder might ask you to log in. Your Macintosh is built to share with other people and work with other computers. If you are sharing your computer with others or accessing other computers over a network, you need to log in (type a user name and password) and log out to switch users or access information. When you're done working on your computer, you should put it to sleep for short periods or shut it down for longer stints.

Starting Mac OS X

Mac OS X automatically starts when you turn on your computer. When you first start Mac OS X, you see the desktop screen, or a Login window depending on your installation. The Mac OS X desktop screen indicates you are using a stand-alone computer (you're the only person using the computer), while the Login window identifies you're on a shared computer. After you click or type your user name in the Login window, and then possibly type a password, you'll see the Mac OS X desktop.

Start Mac OS X Using a Stand Alone Computer

1. Turn on your computer, and then wait while Mac OS X loads.

   The Mac OS X Panther desktop screen appears.

Desktop   Your system's hard drive

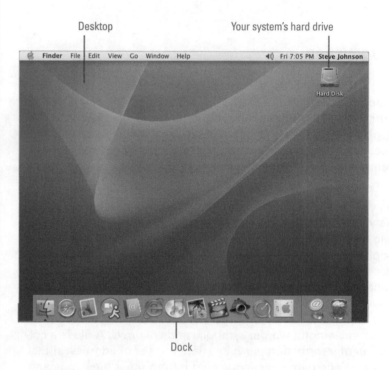

Dock

Did You Know?

The Login window doesn't always appear. If Mac OS X is set up to log in automatically, you don't normally see the Login window. However, if you select the Log Out command from the Apple menu, you do see the Login window. If you see the Login window, click Restart to log in again automatically.

See Also

See "Adding a User Account" on page 378 for information on creating a user account.

See "Activating the Login Window" on page 377 for information on changing log in options.

For Your Information

Creating a Shared Computer

During the Mac OS X Panther installation process, you create a user account for the computer administrator and possibility other accounts for each person who uses your computer. An administrator account can create other user accounts, install software, and change computer settings. When you create accounts for more than one account, your computer changes from a stand-alone computer to a shared computer. Each user maintains separate files, a home folder, and preferences without affecting other users.

Start Mac OS X Using a Shared Computer

1 Turn on your computer and wait while Mac OS X loads.

The Login window opens.

2 Click or type your user name.

3 Type your password. Be sure to use the correct capitalization.

4 Click Log In.

TROUBLE? *If you forget your password, your third attempt to type the password correctly displays your password hint, and a Reset button, where you can use the administrator's master password to create a new password.*

Did You Know?

The password is case-sensitive. Macintosh makes a distinction between uppercase and lowercase letters. Your password should be at least seven characters long, the optimal length for encryption, which is the process of logically scrambling data to keep a password secure.

You can set up your computer to automatically log in (by pass the Login window). Click the Apple menu, click System Preferences, click Accounts, and then select the administrator account. Next, click Login Options, select the Automatically Log In As check box, click the pop-up, and then click an account. Type a password, and then click OK.

You can sleep, restart, and shut down from the Login window. In the Login window, click Sleep, Restart, or Shut Down, and then click the appropriate button or wait 120 seconds.

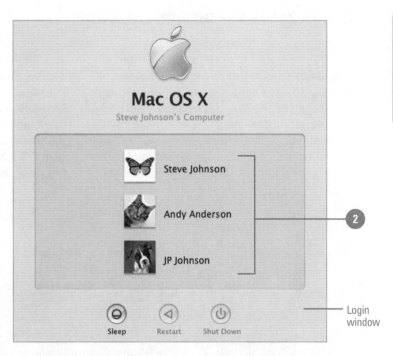

Login window

Exploring the Finder and Desktop

When you first start Mac OS X, you see the Finder desktop, or a log in screen (a way to identify yourself on the computer), depending on your installation. The desktop is an on-screen version of an actual desk, containing windows, icons, files, and applications. You can use the desktop to access, store, organize, modify, share, and explore information (such as a letter or a list of addresses), whether it resides on your computer, a network, or the Internet. The desktop contains icons that represent volumes (such as your Hard Disk to store data), applications, documents, folders, and the Trash. If you upgraded your computer to Mac OS X from a previous version, your desktop might contain many different icons.

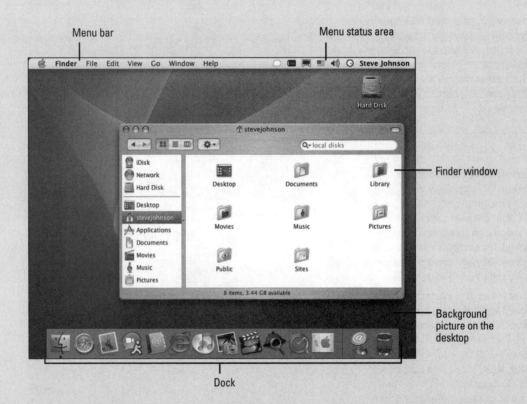

Menu bar

Menu status area

Finder window

Background picture on the desktop

Dock

These icons can also appear a number of different ways depending on your view. When you open an icon, a window or application appears, displaying its contents or an application work environment. The bar at the bottom of the desktop is called the Dock (if it's hidden, point to the bottom of the screen to display it); it allows you to start applications and switch among currently running ones. At the top of the screen is a menu bar, which contain commands you use to perform tasks and customize your environment. At the right end of the menu bar is the menu status area, which displays the time, date, and application related icons, such as the Chat icon, which shows your online status and performs other actions.

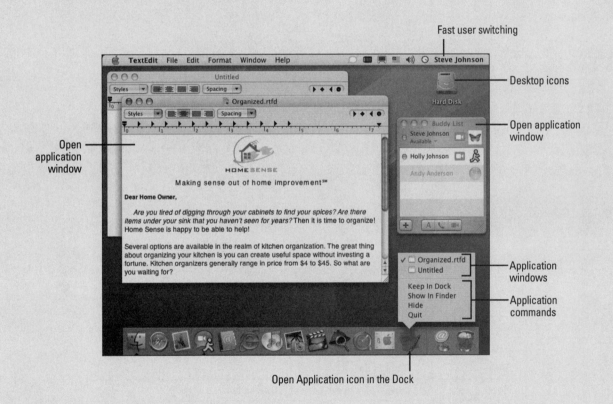

Open application window

Fast user switching

Desktop icons

Open application window

Application windows

Application commands

Open Application icon in the Dock

Using the Mouse

A **mouse** is a handheld input device you roll across a flat surface (such as a desk or a mouse pad) to position the **mouse pointer**, the small symbol that indicates the pointer's relative position on the desktop. When you move the mouse, the mouse pointer on the screen moves in the same direction. The shape of the mouse pointer changes to indicate different activities. However, the pointer usually looks like an arrow pointer in the Finder. Once you move the mouse pointer (the arrow's tip) to a desired position on the screen, you use the mouse button to tell your computer what you want it to do. Macintosh computers typically come with a mouse that contains a single button. However, you can use a mouse with two buttons (left and right), trackball device, or writing tablet to perform the same function. For a two button mouse, the left button performs the same function as the single button.

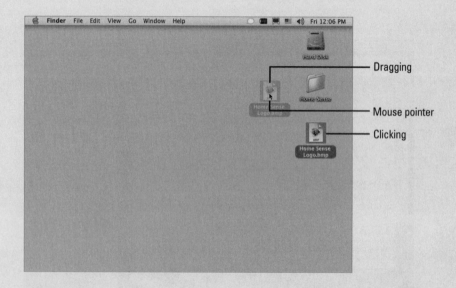

Task	**What to do**
	Basic Mouse Techniques
Pointing	Move the mouse to position it over an item.
Clicking	Press and release the mouse button.
Double-clicking	Press and release the mouse button twice quickly.
Dragging	Point to an item, press and hold the mouse button, move the mouse to a new location, and then release the mouse button.
Pressing	Press and hold the mouse button.

Working with Menus, Toolbars, and Panes

A **menu** is a list of commands that you use to accomplish certain tasks, such as when you use the View menu to open the Customize Toolbar dialog. A **command** is a directive that provides access to an application's features. Each application has its own set of menus, which are on the menu bar along the top of the application window. The menu bar organizes commands into groups of related operations. Each group is listed under the name of the menu, such as File or Help. To access the commands in a menu, you click the name of the menu, and then click the command name. If a menu command is gray, the option is not available at this time; availability depends on what is selected. If a command on a menu includes a keyboard reference, known as a **keyboard shortcut**, such as ⌘+1 for the As Icons command, you can perform the action by pressing and holding the first key, and then

pressing the second key to perform the command quickly. When a menu command is followed by an ellipse (...), a dialog appears when you select it. On a menu, a **check mark** identifies a currently selected feature, meaning that the feature is enabled, or turned on. To disable, or turn off the feature, you click the command again to remove the check mark, or you can select another command (within the menu section, separated by gray lines) in its place. You can also carry out some of the most frequently used commands on a menu by clicking a button on a toolbar. A **toolbar** contains buttons that are convenient shortcuts for menu commands and navigation. A **pane** is a frame within a window, such as a Sidebar, where you can quickly access navigation controls. You can use menus, toolbar buttons, and commands in a pane to change how a window's contents appear.

Pane   Toolbar

Check mark   Keyboard shortcut
Menu   Submenu

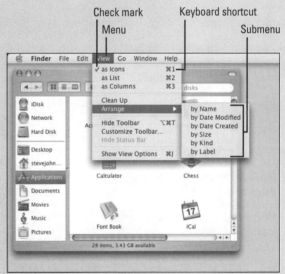

Using Menus for Quick Results

The Finder uses several different types of menus to help you use the commands you need to get the results you want. The Finder uses four types of menus: pull-down, submenu, pop-up, and contextual. The **pull down** menu appears on the menu bar when you click a menu name or status icon in the menu status area. A **submenu** appears when you point to a menu with a triangle. A **pop-up** menu appears in a window or dialog when you click the double arrow. A **contextual** menu appears when you hold down the Control key while you click an item, such as an icon, text, or graphic. A contextual menu displays a list of commands related to the selected item, like the Action pop-up menu. When you click a menu name, the menu stays open. If you don't want to select a menu command, you can click outside the menu or press the Esc key to close it.

Use a Pull Down Menu

1 Point to the name or menu status icon on the menu bar, and then click to open the menu.

2 Point to the menu option you want.

3 If a submenu opens, point to the menu option you want.

4 Click to select the command.

Did You Know?

You can rearrange menu status icons on the menu bar. Press and hold ⌘, and then drag the icon to reposition it.

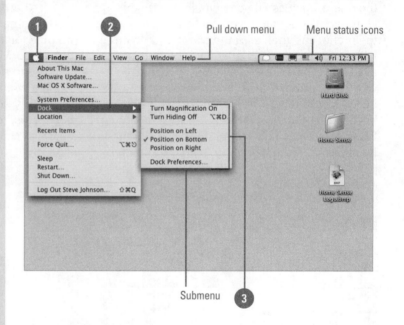

Pull down menu   Menu status icons

Submenu 3

Use a Contextual Menu

1 Point to the item on which you want to act upon.

2 Press and hold down the Control key, and then click to display a contextual menu.

   If you are using a mouse with two buttons, right-click the item.

3 Select the command you want.

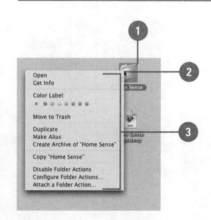

Choosing Dialog Options

The Finder and Mac OS X applications use dialogs to carry out options, provide alert messages, and gather information. A **dialog** is a window that opens when the Finder or an application wants to alert you of an event, or you select a menu command or button followed by an ellipsis. In a dialog, you acknowledge an alert message or select various options, and then provide information for completing the command.

Choose Dialog Options

All dialogs contain the same types of options, including the following:

◆ **Tabs.** Click a tab to display its options. Each tab groups a related set of options.

◆ **Option buttons.** Click an option button to select it. You can usually select only one in a group.

◆ **Check box.** Click the box to turn on or off the option. A checked box means the option is selected; a cleared box means it's not.

◆ **Pop-up menu.** Click the arrow to display a list of commands or options, and then click the one you want.

◆ **Entry field.** Click in the field, and then type the requested information.

◆ **Up and down arrows.** Click the up or down arrow to increase or decrease the number, or type a number in the field.

◆ **Scroll bar.** Drag a slider control to change screen position.

◆ **Preview area.** Many dialogs show an image that reflects the options you select.

◆ **Slider.** Drag a slider control to change a screen position.

◆ **Push button.** Click a button to perform an action or command. A button name followed by an ellipsis (...) opens another dialog.

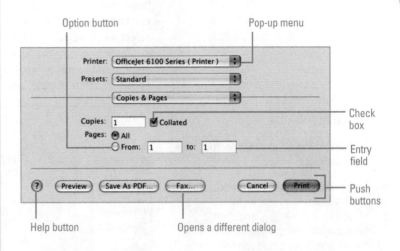

Option button — Pop-up menu — Check box — Entry field — Push buttons — Help button — Opens a different dialog

For Your Information

Navigating and Working in a Dialog

Rather than clicking to move around a dialog, you can press the Tab key to move from one field to the next. You can also use Shift+Tab to move backward. When a field appears with a dark border around it, the text you type appears in the active field. The default button is the one that appears highlighted. You can press the Return key to perform the default button. If you decide not to use options you set in a dialog, you can press the Esc key to perform the Cancel button and disregard the options. Before you can use the keyboard shortcuts, you need to turn on the option. Click the Apple menu, click Preferences, and then click the Keyboard & Mouse icon. Click the Keyboard Shortcuts tab, select the Turn On Full Keyboard Access check box, and then click the Close button.

Working with Icons

Mac OS X uses various icons to graphically represent different items on the desktop, in the Dock, or in a window. The icons represent applications, documents, folders, volumes, and the Trash. **Application icons** are programs you use to create documents. **Document icons** are files you create with applications. **Folder icons** are a storage area for files. **Volume icons** are storage devices, such as hard disks, removable disks, network disks, Internet computers, CDs, DVDs, and iPods. The **Trash icon** (located in the Dock) appears in three different ways: empty, full, and ejecting removable media. On the desktop or within a window, you can select and deselect one or more icons to perform tasks, such as opening, launching, copying, and moving. When you select an icon, the icon graphic and its name become highlighted. Within a Finder window, icons appear in different ways, depending on the window view you select.

Select Icons

◆ **Select an icon.** Click the icon you want to select.

◆ **Select multiple icons by clicking.** Click the first icon you want to select, hold down ⌘, and then click the other icons you want to select within the same window.

   TIMESAVER *Click the first icon, press the Shift key, and then click the last one to select every icon in between.*

◆ **Select multiple icons by dragging.** Position the mouse pointer to the left of the first icon you want to select, drag diagonally across the adjacent icons you want to select, and then release the mouse button.

   A shaded box appears as you drag to indicate the selection area.

◆ **Select all icons.** Click the Edit menu, and then click Select All.

   TIMESAVER *Press ⌘+A to select all icons.*

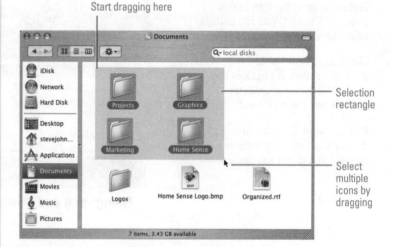

Start dragging here

Selection rectangle

Select multiple icons by dragging

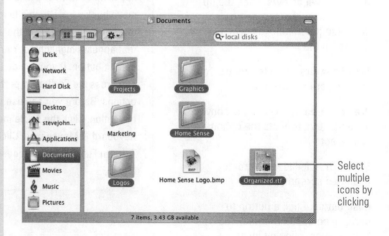

Select multiple icons by clicking

Deselect Icons

◆ **Deselect all icons.** Click a blank area in the window or on the desktop.

◆ **Deselect an icon in a multiple selection.** Press and hold down ⌘, and then click the icon you want to deselect, while keeping the others selected.

Did You Know?

You can quickly open or launch an icon. Double-click the icon to open a window, or open a document, and then launch an application.

Move or Copy Icons

1 To move multiple icons, select the ones you want to move; to copy an icon, hold down the Option key.

2 Point to the icons, and then drag them to the new location.

As you drag, a shaded image of the icon moves along with the mouse pointer.

TROUBLE? *Press the Esc key to cancel the move or copy.*

3 Release the mouse button and the Option key, if necessary.

TIMESAVER *Press ⌘+X to move or press ⌘+C to copy selected icons; and then press ⌘+V to paste them.*

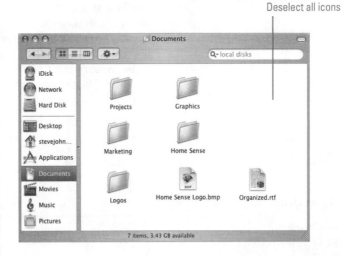

Deselect all icons

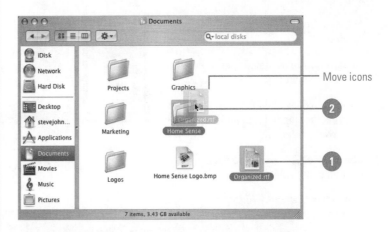

Move icons

2

1

Copy icons

Viewing Windows

A window displays icons and other information in the Finder, and documents in an application. One of the powerful things about the Mac OS is that you can open more than one window or application at once. You can identify a window by its name on the title bar at the top of the window. Before you can work with a window, you need to activate it first. The active window is the one in front with the available buttons (red, yellow, and green) in the upper-left corner. When you're done using a window, you can quickly close it to reduce the clutter on the desktop.

Parts of a Window

Windows in Mac OS X consist of the following parts:

◆ **Close button.** Closes the window.

◆ **Minimize button.** Shrinks the window to an icon in the Dock.

◆ **Zoom button.** Toggles the window size between full and a custom size.

◆ **Title bar.** Displays the name of the window.

◆ **Toolbar Control button.** Toggles the toolbar on and off.

◆ **Toolbar.** Displays buttons and controls for commonly used window commands.

◆ **Size control.** Allows you to set a custom window size.

◆ **Status bar.** Displays information about selected items.

◆ **Sidebar.** (New!) Displays commonly used volumes and folders.

◆ **Column heading.** Displays the names of columns and sorts them (in list view only).

◆ **Search box.** Allows you to find files based on the name.

◆ **Scroll bar.** Displays the content of the window.

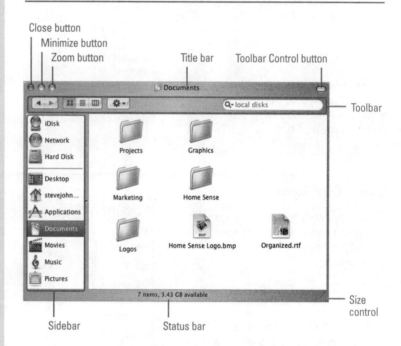

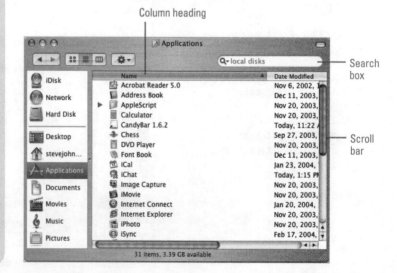

Open and Close a Window

◆ **Open a Finder window.** Double-click a volume or folder icon.

◆ **Open a new Finder window.** Click the File menu, and then click New Finder Window.

◆ **Close a window.** Click the red button to close the window, or hold down the Option key, and then click the red button to close all windows.

TIMESAVER *If you see a dot in the center of the Close button, you need to save your changes.*

Activate a Window

◆ **Activate a window.** Click anywhere on the window, or click the Window menu, and then click the window name.

◆ **Activate and bring all Finder windows to front.** Click the Window menu, and then click Bring All To Front. All open Finder windows that are not minimized are moved in front of application windows.

◆ **Activate and bring a specific application window to the front.** Display the Dock, press (click and hold) an application icon to display a menu, and then select the window you want to make active.

Click to close window   Double-click to open Finder window

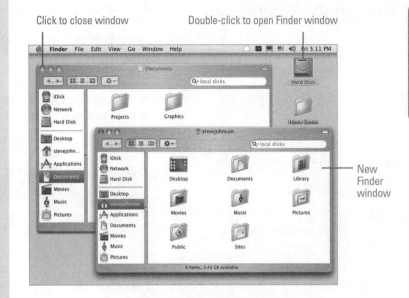

New Finder window

Active window

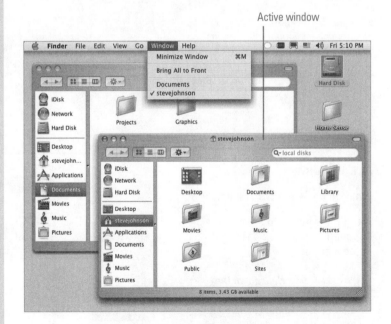

Managing Windows

When you open multiple windows, your desktop can get cluttered with many open windows for the various applications you are using. To organize your desktop, you may need to move it to a different location or change the size of a window. Each window has resize buttons in the upper-left corner to minimize or zoom a window, and a size control in the lower right-corner that you can use to resize the window to a custom size. An icon appears in the Dock for each open window, which you can use to quickly switch between windows or redisplay a minimized window.

Switch Among Open Windows

1 Display the Dock.

2 Press (click and hold) the Finder or an application icon to display a menu.

3 Click the window you want from the menu.

See Also

See "Customizing Exposé" on page 72 for information on temporarily showing and hiding all windows.

Move a Window

1 Point to the window's title bar.

2 Drag the window to a new location, and then release the mouse button.

TIMESAVER *Hold down the* ⌘ *key while you drag the title bar of an inactive window to move it without making it active.*

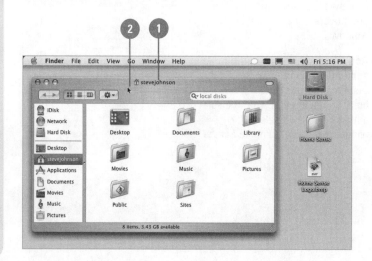

Use Buttons to Resize a Window

All windows contain the same sizing buttons:

◆ **Minimize button (active window).** Click the yellow button to shrink a window as an icon in the Dock, or double-click the title bar.

　TIMESAVER *Press ⌘+M to minimize the active window.*

◆ **Minimize button (all windows).** Hold down the Option key, and then click the yellow button or double-click the title bar to minimize all windows.

◆ **Redisplay minimized window.** Click the window's icon in the Dock or click the Window menu, and the click the window's name.

◆ **Zoom button.** Click the green button to toggle between the smallest possible size that fits on your screen, and the size you set with the size control.

Use the Mouse to Resize a Window

1️⃣ Move the mouse over the size control in the lower-right corner of the window.

2️⃣ Drag the size control until the window is the size you want.

Minimize button
Zoom button

Minimized window

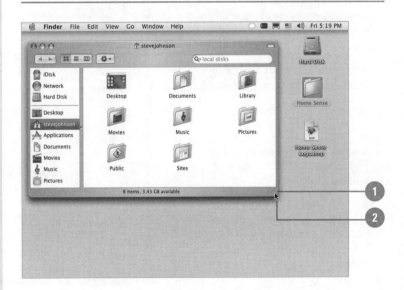

Exposing Windows

When you have multiple windows and applications open at the same time, the screen can get cluttered and make it difficult to work. Exposé (**New!**) lets you quickly move (temporarily) windows out of the way to make it easier to work with windows to find, move, or copy files. You can quickly hide all the open windows to see your desktop, or show all open windows or all open windows in the current application at the same time. When you press any of the Exposé keys quickly, the windows (hidden or shown) stay active using Exposé until you press the key again. However, if you press and hold the keys to use Exposé, the windows return to normal when you release the keys. When you're using Exposé, you can point to a window to see its name and hold the pointer over it or click the window to bring it to the front.

Use Exposé

◆ **Show all open windows at once.** Press the F9 key. When you're done, press the F9 key again.

   For temporary use, hold down the F9 key, and then release.

◆ **Show all open windows in the current application.** Press the F10 key. When you're done, press the F10 key again.

   For temporary use, hold down the F10 key, and then release.

◆ **Hide all open windows (show desktop).** Press the F11 key. When you're done, press the F11 key again.

   All open windows shift to the screen edges to show the desktop.

   For temporary use, hold down the F11 key, and then release.

◆ **Display a window name.** Exposé (F9) all open windows, and then point to a window.

◆ **Activate a window.** Exposé (F9) all open windows, and then click or hold your pointer over a window to bring it to the front and release Exposé.

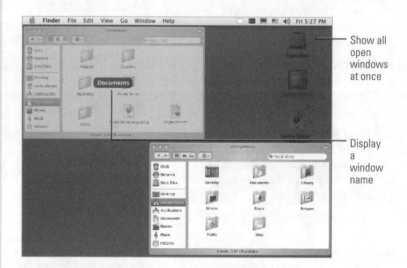

Show all open windows at once

Display a window name

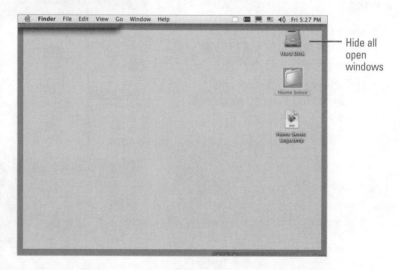

Hide all open windows

Using the Sidebar

The Sidebar (New!) is a panel which appears in the left column of Finder windows, that you can use to quickly access commonly used locations on your computer. The panel appears with two sections. The upper section contains items for volumes attached to your computer, including your hard disk, network, and iDisk. The lower section contains items for folders, including your home folder (labeled with your name), Desktop, Applications, Documents, Movies, Music, and Pictures. You can use the Sidebar to move and copy folders and documents to disks and folders on or connected to your computer, eject removable disks, and burn a CD.

Use the Sidebar

◆ **Display icons.** Click icons in the Sidebar to display contents.

◆ **Move or copy icons.** Drag the folder or document icons from the Contents pane, to the Sidebar icon in order to move or copy them.

◆ **Eject a disk.** Click the Eject button next to any removable disk.

◆ **Burn a CD.** Insert a blank CD or DVD, drag files and folders to it, and then click the Burn button (looks like a beach ball).

Did You Know?

You can change the Sidebar column width. Position the mouse pointer over the divider, click to select, and then drag to change the width.

You can hide and show the Sidebar. Double-click the vertical divider. To show the Sidebar again, double-click the left edge of the window.

See Also

See "Customizing the Sidebar" on page 66 for information on using Finder preferences to customize the Sidebar.

Eject button

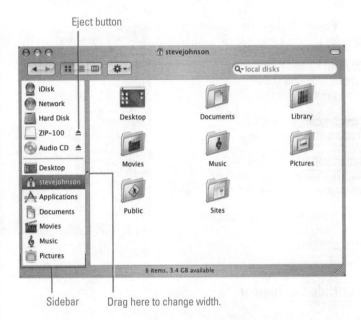

Sidebar   Drag here to change width.

Copy selected item to a disk

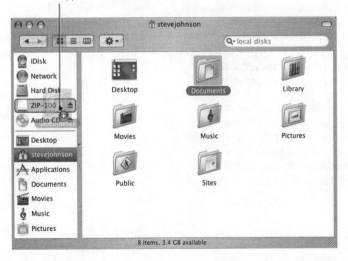

Using Toolbars

The toolbar, in a Finder window, provides easy access to commonly used window commands. You can use the Toolbar Control button three different ways: to hide the toolbar, to display more information in the window, or to show the toolbar to display tools and navigational controls. When you hide the toolbar, the Finder also hides the Sidebar panel and window borders, and moves the status bar to display under the title bar.

Parts of a Toolbar

Toolbars in the Finder consist of the following parts:

◆ **Back button.** Displays the content from the previous window.

◆ **Forward button.** Displays the content from the window before using the Back button.

◆ **View buttons.** Displays the window in different views.

◆ **Action pop-up menu. (New!)** Displays commands for working with a window or selected items.

◆ **Search box.** Allows you to search for a file by name.

Show or Hide the Toolbar

1️⃣ Click the Toolbar Control button in the upper-right corner of the window to toggle between them.

TIMESAVER *Hold down the ⌘ key while you repeatedly click the Toolbar Control button to display various toolbar styles.*

If a double arrow appears at the right side of the toolbar, the window is too small to show all the icons. You can either resize the window, or click the double arrow, and then select a toolbar item.

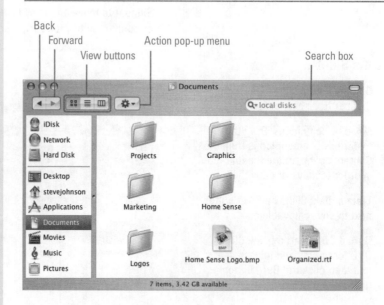

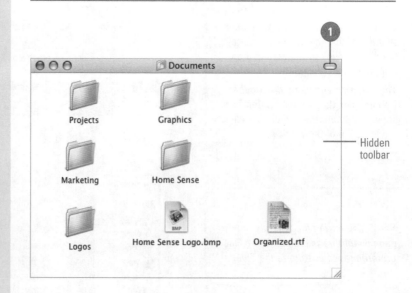

Displaying and Using the Dock

The Dock is a bar at the bottom of the screen that you can use to open frequently used applications and utilities, system preferences, Web sites and the Trash, as well as redisplay minimized applications and Finder windows. If you don't see the Dock at the bottom of your screen, then its automatically hidden. You can change an option in the Dock pane of System Preferences to always display the Dock. The Dock has two sides with a divider line separating the two. The left side is for applications and the right side is for everything else: files, documents, folders, and disks. When you point to an icon, its name appears above it. Document and folder icons in the Dock actually display an image of the contents to make it a little easier to distinguish between them. When you press a folder or disk icon, a list of its contents appears as a menu to quickly display its contents. When you launch an application, it's icon appears in the Dock with a black arrow below it. When you quit an application or window not permanently placed in the Dock, its icon is removed from the Dock. In addition to the predefined icons in the Dock, you can also quickly and permanently add your own icons in the Dock.

Display and Use the Dock

◆ **Display a hidden Dock.** Move the mouse pointer to the bottom or side of the screen.

◆ **Open, launch or redisplay a minimized item.** Click its icon.

◆ **Choose commands for an item.** Press the icon in the Dock, and then click a command.

For example, press an application icon, and then click Keep In Dock to permanently add the icon in the Dock for future use.

Did You Know?

You can turn Dock hiding off and on. Click the Apple menu, point to Dock, and then click Turn Hiding Off or Turn Hiding On.

You can quickly switch between applications in the Dock. Hold down ⌘, and then repeatedly press the Tab key. Release the keys to switch.

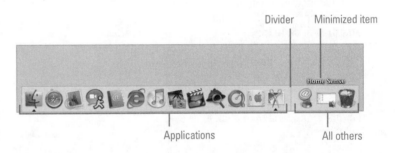

Divider   Minimized item

Applications   All others

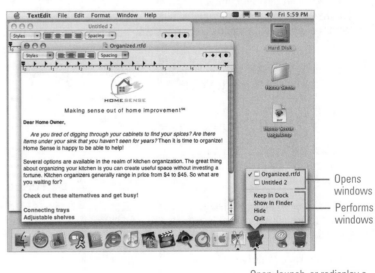

Opens windows

Performs windows

Open, launch, or redisplay a minimized item

Getting Help While You Work

When you have a question about how to do something in Mac OS X, you can usually find the answer with several clicks of your mouse. Mac OS X Help is a resource of information to help you use Mac OS X Panther, which uses the Help Viewer application. The Help Viewer is like an online book with a table of contents, complete with a search feature, and additional links to the Internet to make finding information a little bit easier. You can access help from the Help menu in the Finder as well as many other Mac OS X applications, such as Safari and iChat; you can even switch between the different help libraries using the Library menu (**New!**). If you see the Help button (question mark) in a window or dialog (**New!**), you can click it to get feature related help. If you have an Internet connection, the Help Viewer retrieves online updates to Mac OS X Help content as necessary. For additional help and support information, visit the Apple Computer Web site at *www.apple.com*. Click the Apple - Mac OS X icon in the Dock to quickly access the Mac OS X Web site.

Browse for Help Information

1. In the Finder, or any other application, click the Help menu, and then click Help.

   TIMESAVER *Press* ⌘+*? to open the Help Viewer.*

2. To select another Help, click the Library menu, and then click a help library.

3. Click a link in the Help Viewer window until you find the topic with the information you're looking for.

4. Use the Help toolbar and Go menu to navigation help topics:

   - Click the Home button to return to the first page of the help.

   - Click the Back and Forward button to view previously viewed topics.

   - Click the Go menu to display a list of previously viewed topics, and then click one.

5. Click the Help Viewer menu, and then click Quit Help Viewer.

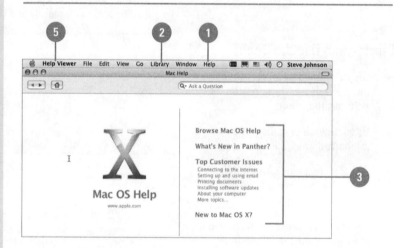

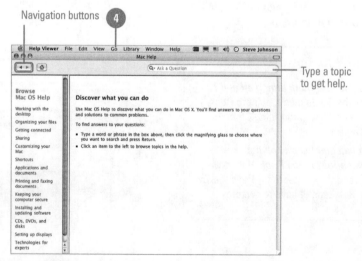

Navigation buttons

Type a topic to get help.

Search for Help Information

1. In the Finder, or any other application, click the Help menu, and then click Help.

2. Click the magnifying glass in the Search box, and then click Search Mac Help or Search All Help.

3. Click in the Search box.

   TIMESAVER *Press the Tab key to quickly go to the Search box.*

4. Type the words you want to find in the help topics, and then press Return.

   A list of matches appears with a Relevance column ranking the results by percentage.

5. Double-click the topic you want to read in the search results list.

6. Use the Go menu or the navigation buttons (Back and Forward) on the Help toolbar to move between help topics.

7. Click the Help Viewer menu, and then click Quit Help Viewer.

Did You Know?

You can start a new search in a new window. Click the File menu, click New, and then perform a new search.

You can print a help topic. Display the help topic in the Help Viewer, click the File menu, click Print, and then click Print again.

You can customize the Help toolbar. Click the View menu, click Customize Toolbar, drag the buttons you want to change on the toolbar, and then click Done.

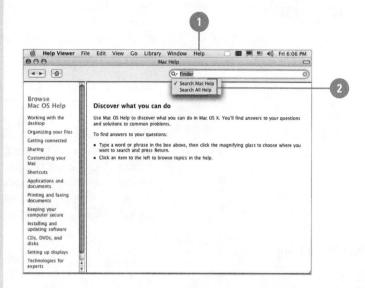

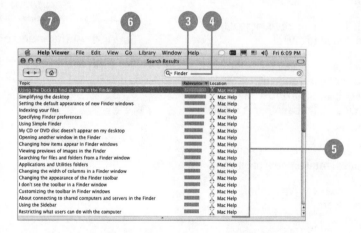

For Your Information

Using Special Character to Help Your Search

If you can't find the information you are looking for using the Search box, you can use special characters "+" (AND), "!" (NOT), and "|" (OR) to refine your help search. For example, typing "finder + desktop" finds both words, typing "finder ! desktop" finds finder, but not desktop, while typing "finder | desktop" finds either finder or desktop. The special characters work like algebra. Still can't find it? Use parentheses with these special characters to group terms, like elementary math problems.

Switching Users

Many users can use the same computer. Their individual Mac OS X accounts allow them to keep their files completely private and to customize the operating system with their own preferences. Mac OS X manages these separate accounts by giving each user a unique user name and password. When a user selects an account and types a password (if necessary), Mac OS X starts with that user's configuration settings and network permissions. When you want to change users, you can logout, which closes all running applications, saves your settings, and signs you off the computer. Or, switch users, which quickly switches between users without having to logout, close applications, and save your current settings. With fast user switching (New!), the name of the current user appears in the status menu area, where you can quickly switch to a new user. If you leave your computer unattended for any period of time, you can set additional security logout options to protect your information.

Fast User Switching

1. Click the *user name* in the upper-right corner of the menu bar.

2. Click the user account to which you want to switch.

   The name grayed out is the current user, and an orange check mark next to a name indicates that another is logged in.

   If required, a Login window opens, requesting a password.

3. If necessary, type your password.

4. Click Log In.

   The computer switches to the new user's desktop (like a box switching sides), which includes the user's home folder, mail, and personal settings.

See Also

See "Setting Fast User Switching" on page 384 for information on enabling Fast User Switching.

Another user logged in.

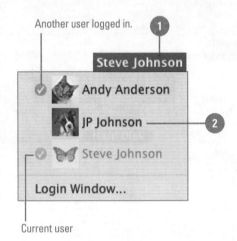

Current user

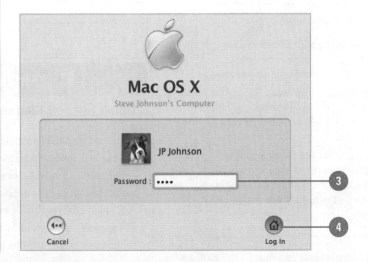

Logout of Your Computer

1. Click the Apple menu, and then click Log Out *user name*.

   TIMESAVER *Press Shift+⌘+Q to log off. If you press the Option key while you select the Log Out menu command, Mac OS X skips the confirmation dialog.*

2. Click Log Out or wait 120 seconds to close all your applications, save your settings, and sign yourself off the computer.

   A Login window appears, displaying user accounts.

3. Click your name.

4. If required, type your password, and then click Log In.

Set Logout Security Options

1. Click the Apple menu, and then click System Preferences.

2. Click the Security icon.

3. Select or clear the Require Password To Wake This Computer From Sleep Or Screen Saver check box.

4. Select or clear the Log Out After *X* Minutes Of Inactivity check box, and then enter the number of minutes you want.

   IMPORTANT *If any dialogs for unsaved documents or open applications appear, your computer will not finish logging you out.*

5. Click the Close button.

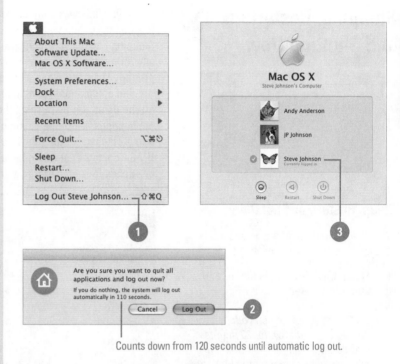

Counts down from 120 seconds until automatic log out.

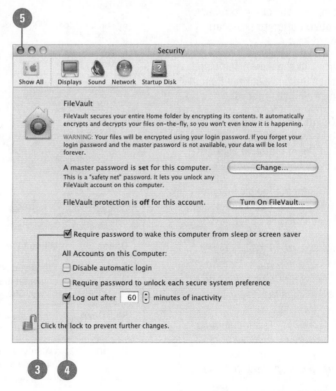

Sleeping, Restarting, and Shutting Down

When you finish working on your computer, you can put your computer to sleep for a little while or shut it down for longer periods of inactivity. Sleeping causes your computer screen to go blank and halt the spinning of your hard disk. Shutting down your computer causes Mac OS X to properly save and close all open files, close all open windows, quit all running applications, and finally, turn off the Macintosh itself. If you turn off the computer by pushing the power switch while Mac OS X or other applications are running, you could lose important data and cause system problems; shutting down correctly avoids these potential problems. If your computer starts to have problems, such as a unusual slow down or applications stop working, try to restart or reset, your computer.

Sleep, Restart, or Shut Down

When you're done working on your computer, do one of the following:

◆ **Sleep.** Click the Apple menu, and then click Sleep.

   IMPORTANT *When your computer is inactive for 20 minutes (the default), Mac OS X automatically puts your computer to sleep.*

   To wake up your computer, click the mouse button or press any keyboard key.

◆ **Restart.** Click the Apple menu, and then click Restart. Click the Restart button or wait 120 seconds.

◆ **Shut Down.** Click the Apple menu, and then click Shut Down. Click the Shut Down button or wait 120 seconds.

   If other users are logged in, type the administrator name and password, and then click Shut Down.

   TIMESAVER *If you press the Option key while you select the Restart or Shut Down command, Mac OS X skips the dialog.*

   TIMESAVER *If your computer has a power key, you can press it to display a dialog with Sleep, Restart, and Shut Down buttons.*

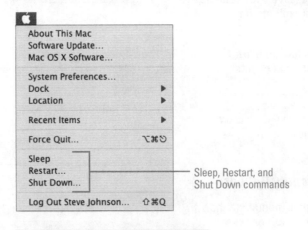

Sleep, Restart, and Shut Down commands

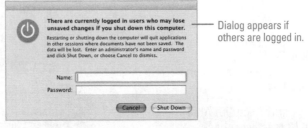

Dialog appears if others are logged in.

Understanding Your Options

Option	When to use it
Sleep	When you want to stop working for a little while, save computer memory, and conserve power (ideal for saving battery life in a PowerBook or iBook portable computer).
Shut Down	When you finish working on your Macintosh and you want to turn off the power to the computer.
Restart	When you have problems and want to reset your computer (clear computer memory and reload system files).

Managing Files and Folders

Introduction

File management involves organizing and keeping track of files and folders. It helps you stay organized so information is easy to locate and use. A **folder** is a container for storing applications and files, similar to a folder in a file cabinet. As with a file cabinet, working with poorly managed files is like looking for a needle in a haystack—it's frustrating and time-consuming to search through irrelevant, misnamed, and out-of-date files to find the one you want.

Finder allows you to organize folders and files in a file hierarchy, imitating the way you store paper documents in real folders. Just as a file cabinet contains several folders, each containing related documents with dividers grouping related folders together, so the Finder file hierarchy allows you to organize your files in folders, and then place folders in other folders. At the top of each hierarchy is the name of the hard drive or main folder. This drive or folder contains several files and folders, and each folder contains related files and folders.

Using the file management tools, you save files in folders with appropriate names for easy identification, quickly and easily create new folders so you can reorganize information, delete files and folders that you no longer need, search for a file when you cannot remember where you stored it, create shortcuts to files and folders for quick and easy access, and compress files and folders to save space.

What You'll Do

Open and View Disks

Open and View Documents

Change the Window View

Arrange Files and Folders in Icon View

Work with Files and Folders in List View and Column View

Go Common or Recent Places

Organize Files and Folders by Color

Search for Files Using the Search Bar

Search for Files Using the Find Window

Create and Rename Files and Folders

Copy and Move Files and Folders

Use Spring-Loaded Folders

Share Files or Folders with Others

Delete and Restore Files and Folders

Get File Information

Create a CD or DVD Using the Finder

Mount and Eject Disks

Opening and Viewing Disks

The desktop is the starting point to access every disk, folder, and file on your computer. When Finder Preferences are appropriately set to display desktop icons, the desktop displays several types of local, removable, and network drives. Drives and folders are represented by icons on the desktop. Each icon graphic represents a different type of disks. Disks are devices that store information used by the computer. The disk with the Mac OS X installed on it is called the **startup disk**, which is typically the hard disk inside your computer. The files related to Mac OS X are stored in the **System folder** on your startup disk. You should not move this folder or make any changes to its contents. Additional Mac OS X related files are stored in the **Library folder**, which stores system and application preference settings and files. Also on your startup disk is an **Applications folder** that contains the complete collection of Mac OS X programs on your computer. You double-click a disk icon, such as your hard disk or a removable disk, on the desktop to open a Finder window, displaying the contents of the disk. Once you open more than one drive or folder, you can use buttons on the toolbar to help you move quickly between folders.

Open and View Disks

1 If you want to view a disk, insert it in your drive.

The removable disk appears on the desktop along with your other drivers, such as your hard disk or a network disk.

2 Double-click the drive icon on the desktop to open it.

3 Double-click a folder icon in the Finder window to open it.

TIMESAVER *The top section of the Sidebar in the Finder window displays the same disk icons found on the desktop.*

4 Click the Back or Forward buttons on the toolbar to return or move to a previously visited window.

TIMESAVER *Hold down* ⌘ *and click a window's title bar to display a folder hierarchy menu.*

5 When you're done, click the Close button.

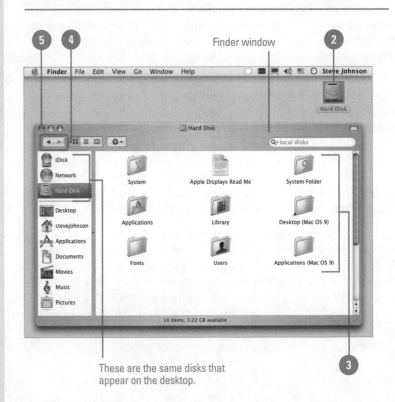

These are the same disks that appear on the desktop.

Did You Know?

You can display disk icons on the desktop. Click the Finder menu, click Preferences, click General, select the check boxes for the disk icons you want to show, and then click the Close button.

You can display icons in the Sidebar. Click the Finder menu, click Preferences, click Sidebar, select the check boxes for the icons you want to show, and then click the Close button.

You can open a disk or folder in a separate window. Click the Finder menu, click Preferences, click General, select the Always Open New Folders In A New Window check box, and then click the Close button.

An uneven CD or DVD may have trouble loading. If your CD or DVD drive seems to make vibrating noises, the disc's weight might be uneven. Sometimes with older drives, the CD or DVD won't load. If it does load, you're fine.

See Also

See "Changing the Window View" on page 30 for information on changing the display of a folder's contents.

See "Mounting and Ejecting Disks" on page 56 for information on using disks, CDs, and DVDs.

Typical Disks on a Computer

Icon	Type Description
	Local A hard magnetic disk (or hard disk) located inside your computer on which you can store large amounts of data. The disk stores all the files on your computer.
	External A hard magnetic disk (or hard disk) connected to your computer using a FireWire or USB plug. The disk provides extra storage.
	Network A hard magnetic disk (or hard disk) connected to your computer over a network. The disk provides extra storage and file sharing.
	iPod A portable hard magnetic disk that plays MP3 music and works with iTunes, which you can also use as a hard disk. The disk provides a compact, bootable hard drive.
	Removable A soft removable magnetic disk on which you can store 100 MB to 500 MB of computer data. Zip drives are not standard on all computers.
	Compact Disc-Read-Only Memory (CD-ROM) An optical disk on which you can read or copy up to 1 GB (typical size is 650 and 700 MB, which holds 74 and 80 minutes of audio) of data. The disc cannot be erased or burned with new data.
	Compact Disc-Recordable (CD-R) A non-reusable disc on which you can burn up to 1 GB (typical size is 650 and 700 MB) of data in multiple sessions. The disc can be burned again with new data until full, but cannot be erased.
	Compact Disc-Rewritable (CD-RW) A reusable disc on which you can read, write, and erase data. Discs come in normal and high-speed formats (typical size is 650 and 700 MB).
	Digital Video Disc (DVD) A disc that holds a minimum of 4.7 GB, enough for a full-length movie. The disc cannot be erased or burned with additional data.
	Digital Video Disc-Recordable (DVD-R) A non-reusable disc on which you can burn up to 4.7 GB of data in multiple sessions. The disc can be burned again with new data until full, but cannot be erased.
	Digital Video Disc-Rewritable (DVD-RW) A reusable disc on which you can read, write, and erase data. The disc holds up to 4.7 GB on each side.
	Flash A memory card the size of a large stamp that holds 128, 256, 512 MB, or greater. Flash drives connect directly into a USB plug and work on any Mac or Windows PC (no software required).

Viewing and Opening Documents

When you open a disk, the Finder window displays the contents of the disk, which includes files and folders containing information and software on your computer. Mac OS X creates a **Users folder** that contains a set of personal folders, known as the **Home folder**, for each user on a shared computer. The Home folder makes it easy to manage the personal and business files and folders you work with every day. The Home folder contains these folders: Desktop, Documents, Library, Movies, Music, Pictures, Public, and Sites. Depending on your previous installation, devices installed, or other users, your personal folders might differ. You can quickly access your Home folder and many other personal folders from the Sidebar. In the Home folder, you can view file information, organize files and folders, and open files and folders. Once you open more than one folder, you can use buttons on the toolbar to help you move quickly between folders.

View and Open Documents

1. Double-click the Hard Disk icon (the startup disk) on the desktop.

2. In the bottom section of the Sidebar, select from the following:

   ◆ Desktop

   ◆ Home (the one with your name)

   ◆ Applications

   ◆ Documents

   ◆ Movies

   ◆ Music

   ◆ Pictures

3. To open a folder, double-click it.

4. If available, drag the scroll box, or click the scroll arrows to view additional documents.

   TIMESAVER *Hold down* ⌘ *and click a window's title bar to display a folder.*

5. To open a document, double-click the file to open it's associated application and the document.

6. When you're done, click the Close button.

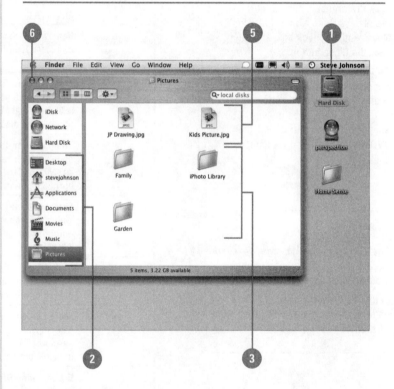

Did You Know?

You can quickly open the Home folder from the desktop. Press Shift+⌘+H. You can also click the desktop background, and then press ⌘+Up Arrow, which is the Enclosing Folder command on the Go menu. Since your Desktop folder is actually in your Home folder, using the command takes you back one folder level.

Your Favorites folder still exists. The Favorites folder from previous versions of the Mac OS is located in the Library folder of your Home folder. The Favorites folder contained links to your favorites files, folders, and Web sites in Microsoft Internet Explorer. If you want to use it, drag the Favorites folder to the Sidebar for quick and easy access.

See Also

See "Changing the Window View" on page 30 for information on changing the display of a folder's contents.

Folders in the Home Folder

Folder	Type Description
Desktop	Each users desktop is mirrored in this folder to keep one separate and maintain the unique custom look and feel.
Documents	A folder designated to store your personal documents and folders.
Library	Each user maintains a personal Library folder, like the main Library folder for Mac OS X, to store your preferences, which includes fonts, e-mail, Internet bookmarks, keyboard layouts, and so on.
Movies	A folder designated to store your movie files; programs, iMovie, use this folder.
Music	A folder designated to store your music files; programs, iTunes, use this folder.
Pictures	A folder designated to store your picture files; programs, iPhoto, use this folder.
Public	A folder where you can place documents and folders that you can share with other users on your computer or a network.
Sites	A folder where you can place Web pages that you can make available on the Internet, known as a **Web server.**

2

For Your Information

Opening a Document with a Different Program

Most documents on your computer are associated with a specific application. For example, if you double-click a document whose file name ends with the three-letter extension ".txt," Mac OS X automatically opens the document with TextEdit, a word processing application. There are situations, though, when you need to open a document with a program other than the one Mac OS X chooses, or when you want to choose a different default program. For example, you might want to open a text document in Microsoft Word rather than TextEdit so that you can take advantage of advanced features. To do this, Control-click the document icon you want to open, point to Open With, and then click the application you want to use to open the document, or drag the file onto the application icon in the Dock.

Changing the Window View

Mac OS X displays the contents of a drive or folder in different ways to help you find the information you're looking for about a file or folder. The available views include Icon, List, and Column. You can change the window view from the View menu, or you can click the View buttons on the Finder window toolbar.

Icon view displays icons, sorted alphabetically in horizontal rows, with the name of the file or folder below each icon. You can also customize the display to include information about the file next to each icon, or a miniature representation of the file or folder. A picture file displays a preview of the image.

List view displays small icons, sorted alphabetically in a single vertical column with the name of the file or folder and additional information, such as size and date, in columns to the right.

Column view displays icons, sorted alphabetically into vertical panes, or frames, which allows you to view information from two different locations. This arrangement enables you to view the file hierarchy of your computer and the contents of a folder simultaneously, making it easy to copy, move, delete, and rename files and folders.

Customize Views

Every window remembers its view settings independently. You might prefer to look at the your Documents folder in List view, but your Applications folder in Column view.

However, you can set view specific options to permanently customize the way you view icons in each view. In Icon view, you can change icon size, show item information or icon preview, label position, arrangement, and background. In List view, you can change file size, date, and status related information. In Column view, you can show icons and the preview column (summary information in the right column). See "Customizing Finder Window Views" on page 62 for more information about the specific options.

Icon view

List view

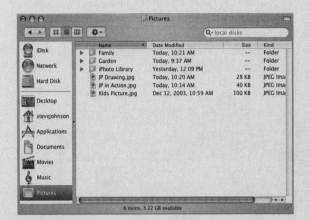

Column view

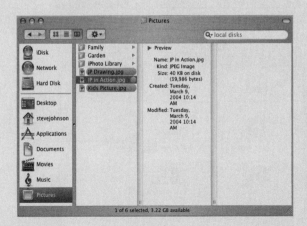

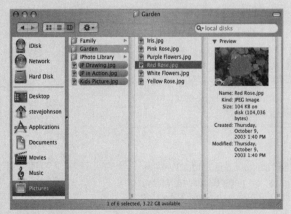

Arranging Files and Folders in Icon View

When you select List view to display your files and folders, you can change the way individual files and folders are sorted by using Arrange menu options on the View menu. You can sort the files by name, date, size, file kind, or color label. You can also have Mac OS X help you clean up your windows by aligning icons to an invisible grid. Each window contains an invisible grid, which icons snap to when called to line up. The Arrange menu options and the Clean Up command are only temporary until you make changes to the window. If you want Mac OS X to automatically keep icons arranged or cleaned up, you need to select appropriate options using the Show View Options command on the View menu.

Arrange or Clean Up Items in Icon View

1. Display the desktop or open the folder you want to arrange.

2. Click the Icon View button on the toolbar.

3. To arrange icons, click the View menu, point to Arrange, and then click the view you want to use:

   ◆ Name

   ◆ Date Modified

   ◆ Date Created

   ◆ Size

   ◆ Kind

   ◆ Label

4. To clean up icons, select the icons you want or deselect all, click the View menu, and then click Clean Up or Clean Up Selection.

See Also

See "Customizing Finder Window Views" on page 62 for information on setting options in Show View Options.

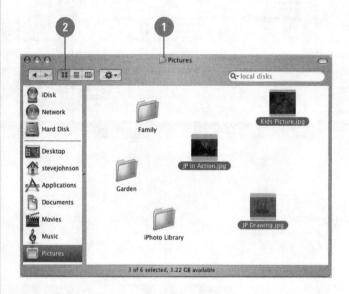

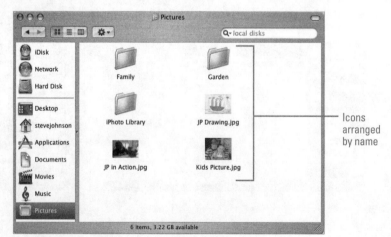

Icons arranged by name

Options for Arranging Files and Folders

Option	Arranges Files and Folders
Name	Alphabetically
Date Modified	Chronologically by their last modification date, with the latest modification date listed last.
Date Created	Chronologically by their creation date.
Size	By size, with the largest folder or file listed first.
Kind	By type, such as all documents created using the TextEdit program.
Label	By color label
Clean Up	Automatically in rows and columns by invisible grid points.

2

For Your Information

Compressing Files and Folders to Save Space

You can compress files and folders into a single file using Stuffit compression software to decrease their size. Compressed folders are useful for reducing the file size of one or more large files, thus freeing disk space and reducing the time it takes to transfer files to another computer over the Internet or network. When a file is compressed, a copy is used in the compression, and the original remains intact. You can uncompress, or extract, a file from the compressed file and open it as you normally would. See "Backing Up and Restoring Compressed Files and Folders" on page 416, and "Opening Compressed Files" on page 415 for more information about compressing and uncompressing files and folders.

Working with Files and Folders in List View

You can display files and folders in a variety of different ways, depending on what you want to see and do. When you view files and folders in List view, a default list of file and folder information appears, which consists of Name, Date Modified, Size, and Kind. If the default list of file and folder details doesn't provide you with the information you need, you can add and remove any file and folder information using Show View Options. If you need to change the way Mac OS X sorts your files and folders, you can use the column header buttons. Clicking on one of the column header buttons (such as Name, Date Modified, Size, or Kind) in List view, sorts the files and folders by the type of information listed in the column. If the columns are not organized in the order you want, you can use the mouse to quickly rearrange columns. If you see an ellipsis in a column, it is too small to display all the information in it. You can drag the column divider to change column sizes all at once or individually.

Show and Hide Folders in List View

1. Open the folder you want to view.

2. Click the List View button on the toolbar.

3. Click the triangle (pointing right) next to a folder in the list.

    TIMESAVER *Select the folder, and then press ⌘+Right Arrow.*

    The folder expands to display an indented list of folders and files from within the folder.

4. Click the triangle (pointing down) next to a folder in the list.

    TIMESAVER *Select the folder, and then press ⌘+Left Arrow.*

    The folder collapses.

Drag to change column width

> ### Did You Know?
>
> *You can quickly show the full text with ellipsis.* Point to the icon's name without clicking for a moment to display a balloon. Hold down the Option key to display it immediately.

Sort Files and Folders by Column in List View

1. Open the folder you want to view.

2. Click the List View button on the toolbar.

3. Click the column header name to sort the file and folder in ascending or decending order.

4. To reverse the column sort, click the column header name again.

Did You Know?

You can add and remove columns in List view. Click the View menu, click Show View Options, select or clear the check boxes you want to add or remove, and then click the Close button.

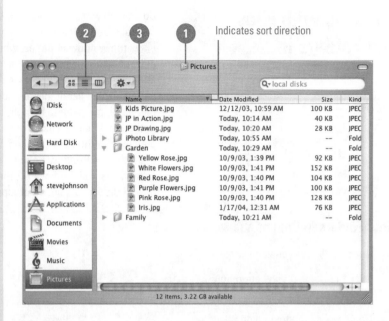

Rearrange and Widen Columns

1. Open the folder you want to view.

2. Click the List View button on the toolbar.

3. To rearrange columns, drag the column header to a new position.

4. To change the width of columns, drag the column divider.

   The width of the column changes and all the columns to the right shift based on the change.

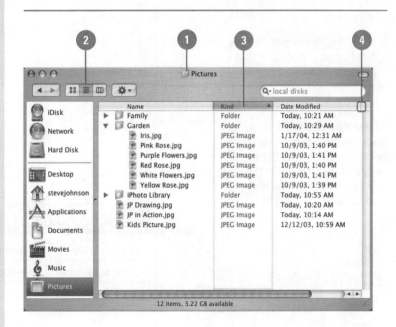

Working with Files and Folders in Column View

Column view makes is easy to display several levels of folders in alphabetical order at the same time within the same window. Column view displays the window in panes, which allows you to view information from different locations making it easy to copy, move, delete, and rename files and folders. When you click a disk or folder in the first pane, the second pane shows a list of all the folders in it. Each time you click a folder in one pane, the pane to its right shows its contents. The other panes slide to the left, in some cases, out of view, which you can scroll back to display them. When you find and click the file you want, the next pane to the right, the **Preview column**, shows a file icon and information about it. If the file is a picture or PDF, the Finder displays the picture or PDF miniature. If the file is a sound or movie, you can play it in the Finder window.

View Folders in Column View

1. Open the folder you want to view.

2. Click the Column View button on the toolbar.

3. Double-click the folder you want to open in a pane.

   The contents of the folder appears in the next pane to the right.

4. To resize a column, drag its right-side handle.

5. Click the file you want to view in the Preview column.

Did You Know?

You can open new windows in Column view. Click the Finder menu, click Preferences, click General, select the Open New Windows In Column View check box, and then click the Close button.

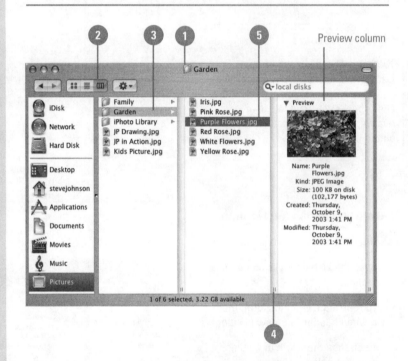

Keyboard Options for Column View	
Option	**Description**
Left or Right Arrow	Jumps one pane to the left or right
Up or Down Arrow	Within a pane, moves up or down to select an item

Going to Common or Recent Places

Mac OS X keeps a list of your most recently used files, folders, and network computers. Instead of navigating through a long list of folders to open a recently used file, you can use the Recent Folders list to find it quickly. If you want to go to a common location, such as your computer, network connections (New!), iDisk (New!), Home folder, Applications folder, Utilities folder, or one you specify, the Go menu makes it quick and easy. After you have opened several folders, you can use the secret folder hierarchy menu in a window's title bar to quickly go backwards through the chain of folders.

Go Places

1. Click the Go menu.

2. Select any of the following:

   ◆ **Common locations.** Click the name of the place.

   ◆ **Recent Folders.** Point to Recent Folders, and then click the name of the folder.

   ◆ **Specific folder.** Click Go To Folder, type a path location, and then click Go. You can use the tilde (~) to indicate the Home folder, "~/Documents/".

3. To go backwards through the folders, hold down ⌘, click the window's title bar, and then click a location from the folder hierarchy menu.

   TIMESAVER Press ⌘+[to go Back a folder; press ⌘+] to go Forward a folder.

4. When you're done, click the Close button.

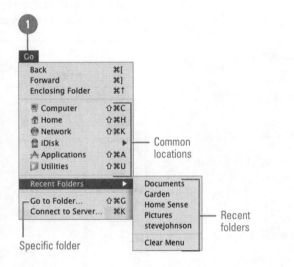

Common locations

Recent folders

Specific folder

Did You Know?

You can quickly open recent applications and documents. Click the Apple menu, point to Recent Items, and then click the recently used application or document you want to open.

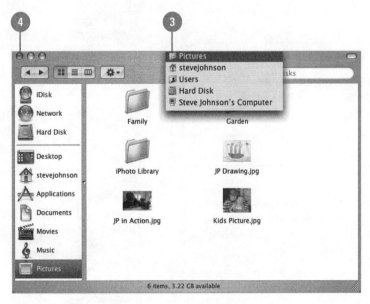

Organizing Files and Folders by Color

Giving an icon or folder a distinctive color can help you organize and find them later. Mac OS X provides seven different colors labels (**New!**) from which to select. The default color label names appear as Red, Orange, Yellow, Green Blue, Purple, and Gray, but you can customize them to suit your own needs and preferences, such as "Final," "In Progress," "Work," "Personal," and "Backup." When you change an icon's color, the icon and name take on the selected color shade. In List or Column view, the entire row takes on the color shade. In List view, you can sort files and folders quickly by color label. Sorting by color label also lets you create alphabetical groups within for color label in a single list. You can also use color labels with the Find command to search for files and folders with a particular color label.

Color a File or Folder Icon

1. Open the folder window with the file or folder icons you want to color.

2. Select the icons you want to color.

3. Click the Actions pop-up, and then click the color label you want.

   TIMESAVER *You can also use the File menu, or Control-click to access the color labels.*

4. When you're done, click the Close button.

See Also

See "Searching for Files Using the Find Window" on page 42 for information on searching for files and folders by color label.

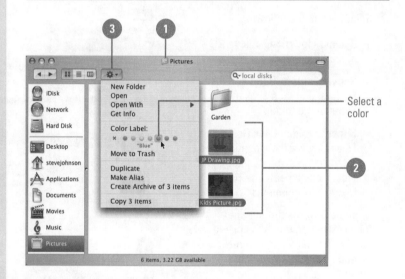

Select a color

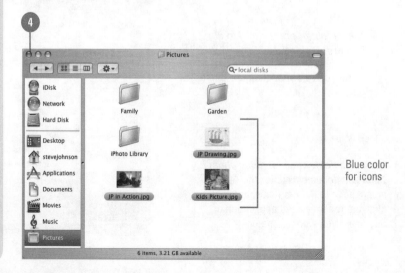

Blue color for icons

Sort a List View by Label

1. Open the folder window with the file or folder icons you want to sort by color.

2. Click the List View button.

3. Click the Label column heading.

   The files and folder are sorted by color. Within each color, the files and folder are sorted in alphabetical order.

4. When you're done, click the Close button.

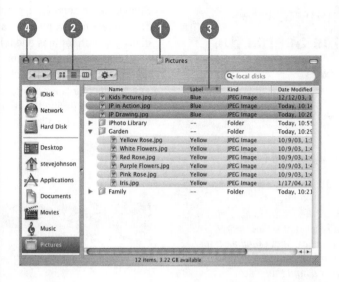

Did You Know?

You need to display the label column before you can sort by color. In List view, click the View menu, click Show View Options, select the Labels check box, and then click the Close button.

Change Color Label Names

1. Click the Finder menu, and then click Preferences.

2. Click Labels.

3. Change the color names with ones that convey more meaning.

   When you go back to List view, instead of seeing the color names, you'll see your new names (such as Personal, Work, In Progress).

4. Click the Close button.

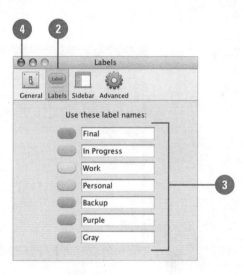

Searching for Files Using the Search Bar

Sometimes remembering precisely where you stored a file is difficult. The Finder window provides a Search bar (New!) that allows you to quickly search for files and folders by name on your local and network disks. The pop-up (magnifying glass) in the Search bar lets you specify where you want to search: Local Disks, Home, Selection, or Everywhere. The results of a search appears in two panes. The upper pane displays the files found during the search. The lower pane displays the location where the selected file is stored on your computer.

Search for Files and Folders

1. Open a Finder window.

   TROUBLE? *If the toolbar isn't available, click the View menu, and then click Show Toolbar. If the Search bar isn't available, click the View menu, and then click Customize Toolbar to add it to the toolbar.*

2. Click the Search bar pop-up on the toolbar, and then select a search location.

   ◆ **Local Disks.** Searches your computer.

   ◆ **Home.** Searches your Home folder.

   ◆ **Selection.** Searches the selected items. If no selection, it searches the current window.

   ◆ **Everywhere.** Searches the disks on or connected to your computer.

3. Type the name or part of the name of the item you want to find.

   As you type, a sprocket icon spins indicating a search is in progress.

4. To pause or cancel a search in progress, click the X button.

   The search results appear during the search.

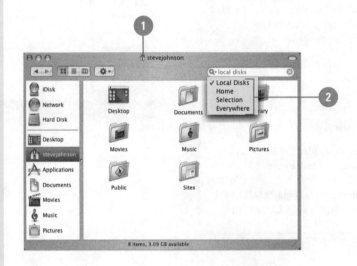

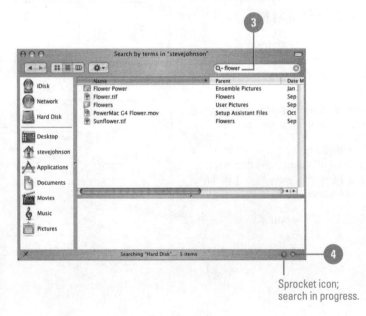

Sprocket icon; search in progress.

Use the Results

◆ **Find the location of a file.** Click a file to display the location is the bottom pane.

◆ **Open a file.** Double-click the file icon.

◆ **Move or delete a file.** Drag the file to a new location or the Trash.

◆ **Rename a file.** Click its name, select the text, and then type a new name.

◆ **Copy a file.** Use the Copy and Paste commands on the Edit menu.

◆ **Sort the result by category.** Click the column header.

◆ **Start a new search.** Change the text in the Search bar, and then press Return.

> **TIMESAVER** *Click the Repeat Search button in the bottom right-corner of the Results window.*

◆ **Close the search.** Click the Close button.

Did You Know?

You can widen the column results to see more details. Drag the dividing line between two column titles at the top of the column.

Click column header to sort.

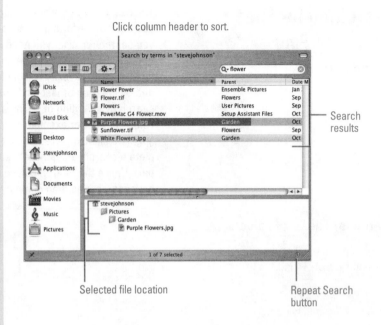

Search results

Selected file location

Repeat Search button

Click to close the search.   Change to start a new search.

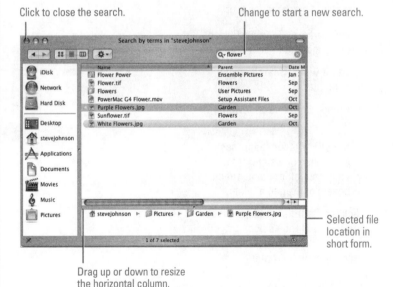

Selected file location in short form.

Drag up or down to resize the horizontal column.

Searching for Files Using the Find Window

The Search bar provides a quick and easy way to search for files, but if you need to perform a more specific search, the Find window can help you search for what you need. The Find window gives you the option to find files or folders by name, location, size, kind, color label, extension, type, creator, visibility (visible files, not hidden one used by Mac OS X), and by creation or last modification date. You can also narrow your search by selecting or typing a specific list of criteria, available in the Find window. For example, you can search for all graphic files with the .jpg extension you created last month that contain *web*. After you complete a search, a separate results window opens (works like the Search bar). Unlike the Search bar, you can change the criteria and perform a new search, and then compare the results between both windows.

Search for Files and Folders

1 In the Finder, click the File menu, and then click Find.

TIMESAVER *Press* ⌘*+F to open the Find window.*

2 Click the Search In pop-up, and then select a search location:

- **Everywhere.** Searches disk on or connected to your computer.

- **Local Disks.** Searches your computer.

- **Home.** Searches your Home folder.

- **Specific Places.** Searches locations you select; select or clear the folder name check boxes; or drag in a folder.

3 Click the Search For Items Whose pop-ups, and then select or type the search criteria; options vary depending on the criteria.

- **Name.** Finds all or part of a file name (capitalization doesn't matter); select another option, such as Contains, Starts With, Ends With, or Is.

- **Content.** Finds words inside your file; handy if you don't remember the name.

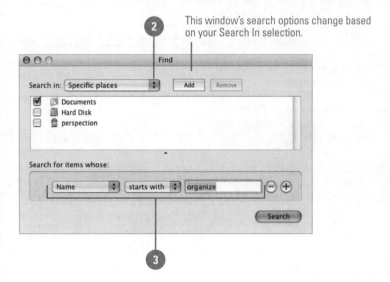

This window's search options change based on your Search In selection.

- ◆ **Date Modified.** Finds files according to the date modified.

- ◆ **Date Created.** Finds files according to the date created.

- ◆ **Kind.** Finds files that are or aren't a certain kind.

- ◆ **Label.** Finds files according to label color.

- ◆ **Size.** Finds files based on size.

- ◆ **Extension.** Finds files according to file extension, such as .txt.

- ◆ **Visibility.** Finds files that are or aren't hidden.

- ◆ **Type.** Find files according to type, such as TEXT; not used much anymore.

- ◆ **Creator.** Find file according to a four-letter code, such as MSWD for Microsoft Word; not used much anymore.

④ To add search criteria, click the Add (+) button, and then specify the criteria you want.

⑤ To remove search criteria, click the Subtract (-) button.

⑥ Click Search to retrieve the files or folders that meet the criteria.

A sprocket icon spins indicating a search is in progress.

⑦ To pause or cancel a search in progress, click the X button.

The search results appear in a separate window.

See Also

See "Searching for Files Using the Search Bar" on page 40 for information on working with the search results.

Use to add or remove folders or disks.

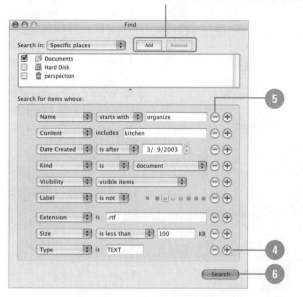

Sprocket icon; search in progress.

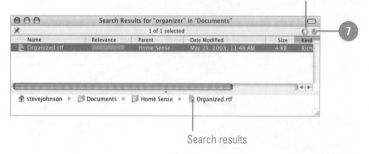

Search results

For Your Information

Indexing Files for a Search

When Mac OS X performs a search on the contents of your files, it needs to index the disk or folder that contains the files to efficiently locate them later. When you perform a search, the Finder automatically creates an index. Instead of creating an index each time you perform a search, you can update the current index for a specific disk or folder. Select the disk or folder you want to index in the Finder, click the File menu, click Get Info, click the Expand button (triangle) for Content Index, click Index Now, and then click the Close button.

Creating and Renaming Files and Folders

The keys to organizing files and folders effectively within a hierarchy are to store related items together and to name folders informatively. Creating a new folder can help you organize and keep track of files and other folders. In order to create a folder, you select the location where you want the new folder, create the folder, and then lastly, name the folder. You should name each folder meaningfully, so that just by reading the folder's name you know its contents. After you name a folder or file, you can rename it at any time.

Create a Folder

1. Open the drive or folder where you want to create a folder.

2. Click the File menu, and then click New Folder.

    TROUBLE? *If the New Folder command is grayed out, you don't have permission to create a folder in the folder. Click the File menu, and then click Get Info to change permissions.*

3. With the new folder name selected, type a new name.

4. Press Return.

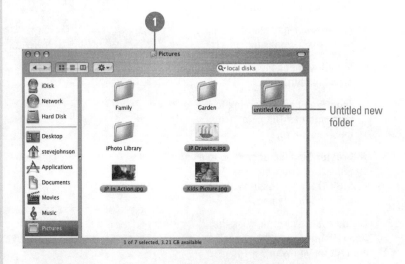

Untitled new folder

Did You Know?

File names can be up to 255 characters. You can use spaces and underscores in names, but you can't use a colon (:). If you are going to use these files on a Windows PC, then don't use the following characters: * : < > | ? " \ or /. It's probably best to keep the name descriptive, but short. This allows you to view the file name in all view settings.

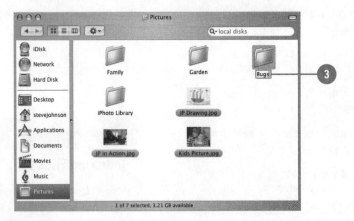

Rename a File or Folder

1. Open the drive or folder with the file or folder you want to rename.

2. Click the file or folder to select it.

3. To erase the entire current name, press Return.

   TROUBLE? *If you can't change the name of a file or folder, you may not have permission to make changes to the item. Click the File menu, and then click Get Info to change permissions.*

4. With the name selected, type a new name, or click to position the insertion point, and then edit the name.

   IMPORTANT *If extensions are showing, changing the name doesn't change the extension as long as the extension stays the same. If you change the extension, the file type changes and you may not be able to open the file with the application in which it was created.*

5. Press Return.

   The file may move to a location based on sort and view.

See Also

See "Showing or Hiding File Extensions" on page 61 for information on file extensions.

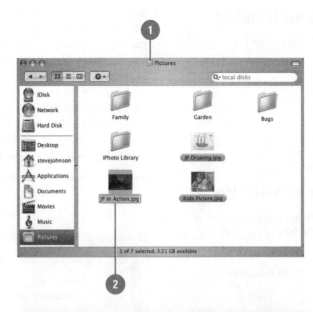

For Your Information

Correcting Your Most Recent Action in the Finder

Everyone makes mistakes and changes their mind at some point, especially when you make changes in the Finder. You can instantly correct your most recent action by using the Undo command (⌘+Z) on the Edit menu. If you change your mind about undoing an action, you can just as easily use the Redo command (⌘+Z) to restore the action you reversed.

Copying and Moving Files and Folders

Sometimes you'll need to move a file from one folder to another, or copy a file from one folder to another, leaving the file in the first location and placing a copy of it in the second. You can move or copy a file or folder using a variety of methods. If the file or folder and the location where you want to move it are visible in a window or on the desktop, you can simply drag the item from one location to the other. Moving a file or folder on the same disk relocates it, whereas dragging it from one disk to another copies it so that it appears in both locations. When the destination folder or drive is not visible, you can use the Cut (to move), Copy, and Paste commands on the Edit menu to move or copy the items.

Copy or Move a File or Folder

1. Open the drive or folder containing the file or folder you want to copy or move.

2. Select the files or folders you want to copy.

3. Click the Edit menu, and then click Cut (to move) or Copy.

   TIMESAVER *Press* ⌘+X *to move or press* ⌘+C *to copy.*

4. Navigate to the drive or folder containing the folder where you want to copy or move the items.

5. Click the Edit menu, and then click Paste.

   TROUBLE? *If you can't copy a file or folder, you may not have permission to make changes to the item. Click the File menu, and then click Get Info to change permissions.*

   TIMESAVER *Press* ⌘+V *to paste.*

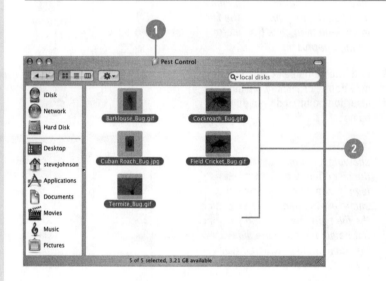

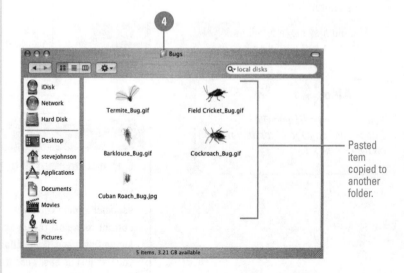

Pasted item copied to another folder.

Copy or Move a File or Folder Using Drag and Drop

① Open the drive or folder containing the files and folders you want to move or copy.

② Drag the selection onto a folder, an icon in the Sidebar, or the desktop.

To copy files and folder, hold down the Option key while you drag.

IMPORTANT *If you pause for a few moments on the destination folder (when spring-loaded folders is turned on) the destination folder automatically opens.*

③ Release the items.

See Also

See "Using Spring-Loaded Folders" on page 48 for information on copy and moving items using spring-loaded folders.

Did You Know?

You need certain permissions to move or copy a file. You need Read Only or Read & Write permissions to the item you want to move or copy. You need Read & Write Only access to the location where you want to place it.

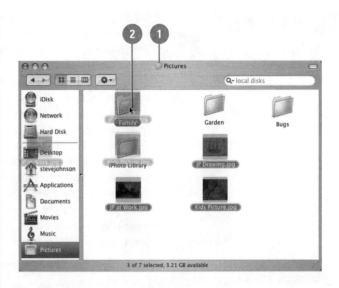

For Your Information

Moving and Copying Items Using Exposé

Exposé can make it easier to move and copy files and folders using drag and drop. To move or copy items between open windows, start to drag the items (hold down the Option key to copy or hold down ⌘+Option to create an alias), press F9 (show all open windows) or F10 (show all open windows in the same application), point to the window where you want to move or copy the item, release F9 or F10, and then drag some more or release the items. A similar process works moving or copying items to the desktop using F11. The Exposé shortcut keys can be changed, so check System Preferences if they are not working properly.

Using Spring-Loaded Folders

When you are moving or copying files and folders around, it can be tiresome to drag a selection to a folder, open the folder, and then continue to drag it to another folder. Spring-loaded folders allows you to drag a file or folder on top of another folder and it springs open to let you continue dragging the selection to another location in one continuous motion. When you drag a selection onto a folder (or even an icon in the Sidebar) and pause for a moment (with the mouse pressed), the window for the folder opens, so you can continue to drag to another folder as desired. You can use Finder Preferences to turn spring-loaded folders on and off, and set the delay setting for the amount of time you want to pause. If you set a long delay or turn off spring-loaded folders, you can press the Spacebar while you drag a selection to open the window immediately. The Spacebar method is useful because windows don't automatically open when you don't want them to, yet you still have the option to use spring-loaded folders when you need it.

Use Spring-Loaded Folders

① Open the drive or folder containing the files and folders you want to move or copy.

② Drag the selection onto a folder or an icon in the Sidebar.

To copy files and folders, hold down the Option key while you drag.

③ Press the Spacebar, or pause for a few moments.

The folder window automatically opens centered on your cursor:

◆ **In Icon view**, the new window replaces the previous window.

◆ **In List view**, a new window opens.

◆ **In Column view**, a new column opens, displaying the new folder's contents.

See Also

See "Customizing the Way Windows Open" on page 60 for information on setting spring-loaded folder options.

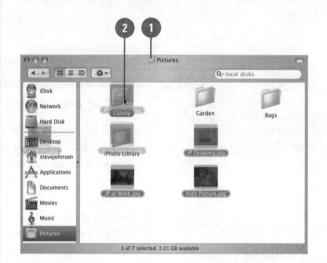

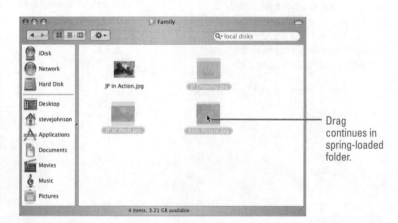

Drag continues in spring-loaded folder.

48

Sharing Files or Folders with Others

Mac OS X maintains a set of personal folders and options for everyone on your computer to make sure the contents remain private, unless you decide to share the contents with others. If you want the other users on your computer, or those connected to your computer over a network to have access to files, you can place those files in the Shared folder that each user can access. The Shared folder is located in the Users folder. It is set up with Read & Write permissions so that all users can open the files in this folder and copy files to the folder. If you want to share files with a specific user on your computer, you can use their Public folder. A Public folder is set up with Read Only permissions that allow others to see and copy it contents, but not change it. Each Public folder is located in the users' Home folder and also contains a Drop Box folder, which is set up with tighter permissions so other people can copy files to a Drop Box, but they cannot see its contents.

Share Files in the Shared Folder or a Public Folder

1. Open the drive or folder containing the files or folders you want to share.

2. Select the files or folders you want to share.

3. Click the Edit menu, and then click Copy.

4. Click the Hard Disk icon in the Sidebar.

5. Double-click the Users folder.

6. Open the folder you want to use to share files:

   - **Shared folder.** Double-click the Shared folder.

   - **Public folder.** Double-click the user name, and then double-click the Public folder.

7. Click the Edit menu, and then click Paste.

8. To use the Drop Box folder in a Public folder, drag the files and folder onto the Drop Box folder.

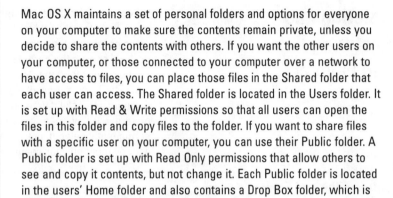

Public folder resides in each users folder.

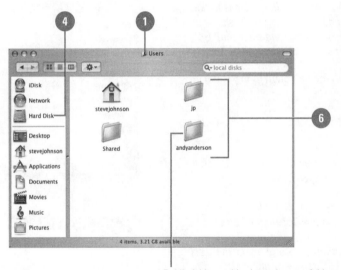

Pasted item in JP's public folder.

Deleting and Restoring Files and Folders

When you organize the contents of a folder, disk, or the desktop, you might find files and folders that you no longer need. You can delete these items or remove them from the disk. If you delete a file or folder from the desktop or from the hard disk, it goes into the Trash. The **Trash**, located on the right side of the Dock, is a temporary storage area for deleted files. The Trash stores all the items you delete from your hard disk so that if you accidentally delete an item, you can remove it from the Trash to restore it. Be aware that if you delete a file from a removable disk, it is permanently deleted, not stored in the Trash. The files in the Trash do occupy room on your computer, so you need to empty it to free up space.

Delete Files and Folders

1. Select the files and folders you want to delete.

   TROUBLE? *If an item is locked, you can't put it in the Trash. Click the File menu, and then click Get Info to unlock it.*

2. Drag the selection to the Trash in the Dock.

   TIMESAVER *Press ⌘+Delete key to delete selected items.*

3. Click the Finder menu, and then click Empty Trash.

   TIMESAVER *Click the Trash icon in the Dock, and then click Empty Trash, or press Shift+⌘ +Option+Delete to empty the trash and skip the warning dialog.*

4. Click OK to confirm the deletion.

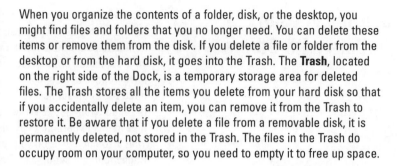

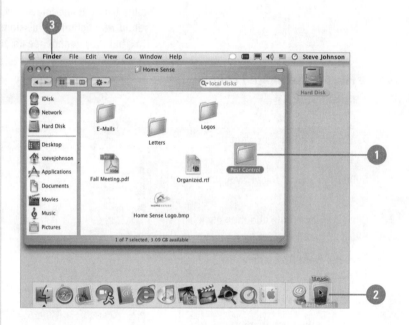

Did You Know?

You can uninstall software using the Trash. There's no uninstall program for Mac OS X. To uninstall a software, drag its folder from the Applications folder to the Trash icon in the Dock.

Restore Files and Folders

1. In the Dock, click the Trash icon.

2. Select the item or items you want to restore.

3. Drag the items back to your Home folder or any other location.

4. When you're done, click the Close button for the Trash window.

Did You Know?

You can undo a deletion. If you accidentally delete a file, click the Edit menu, and then click Undo Delete. Mac OS X remembers your last three actions.

You can still recover deleted files after you empty the Trash in some cases. If you install special data recovery software, you still may be able to recover deleted files.

You can turn off the empty Trash warning. Click the Finder menu, click Preferences, click Advanced, clear the Show Warning Before Emptying The Trash check box, and then click the Close button.

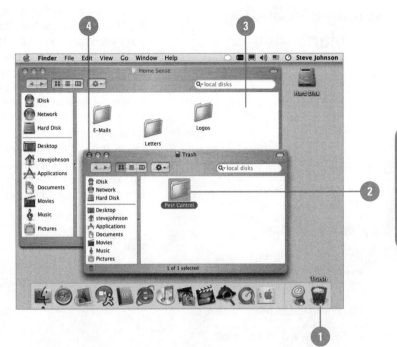

For Your Information

Deleting Files Securely and Forever

If you are selling or giving away your computer, you can securely delete files and folders from your hard disk without any possibility of recovery (New!). Drag the files and folders you want securely deleted into the Trash, click the Finder menu, click Secure Empty Trash, and then click OK to confirm the deletion. Files securely deleted are completely overwritten by meaningless data, which may take a few moments or minutes to complete depending on the size of the files.

Getting and Setting File Information

You can get information about a hard disk, removable disk, network disk, application, folder, or file using the Info window. The Info window displays information about the kind, size, location, date created, and date modified. If you select a disk, the Info window also includes information about format, capacity, available space, and used space. In addition to displaying information, you can also use the Info window to create a stationery file, lock an item, change a files name and extension, determine which application to open a file with, change its ownership and permissions, and write a comment. When you set a file as stationery, the file opens as an untitled copy of the original, so the original file doesn't get changed. If you want to see information for different items without having to close the Info window, you can use Show Inspector to keep the Info window open while you select different items.

Display Info Window

1. Select the files, disks, folders, applications, or alias; don't select anything to get desktop info.

2. Use one of the following methods:

   ◆ **Separate window for each item.** Click the File menu, and the click Get Info.

   A separate Info window appears for each selected item. This is useful for comparing settings and information.

   ◆ **Single window for all items.** Hold down the Option key, click the File menu, and then click Show Inspector.

   A single Info window appears, displaying statistics (by type and size) about the selected items and options common to all the selected items. This is useful for setting the same option for a lot of items, such as locking or unlocking files.

3. Click the expand button (triangle) to display category options, or the collapse button (down arrow) to hide them.

4. When you're done, click the Close button.

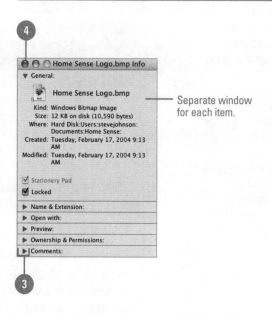

Separate window for each item.

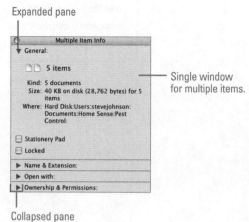

Expanded pane

Single window for multiple items.

Collapsed pane

Set Info Window Options

1. Select the files, disks, folders, applications you want to set.

2. Click the expand button (triangle) for the category in which you want to change options.

3. Change the options you want:

   ◆ **General.** View information about the selected items; create a Stationery Pad (a file opens as untitled); and lock or unlock a file.

   ◆ **Name & Extension.** Read and edit item name and extension; and hide extensions.

   ◆ **Content Index.** Index a disk or folder for better search results.

   ◆ **Memory.** Set memory options for Classic applications only.

   ◆ **Open With.** Specify which application opens when you double-click an icon.

   ◆ **Preview.** Display magnified picture thumbnails or play sounds and movies.

   ◆ **Languages.** Add or remove languages for an application.

   ◆ **Comments.** Add your own comments, which you can display in List view.

4. When you're done, click the Close button.

See Also

See "Setting File Access Permissions" on page 381 for information on setting file permissions and ownership.

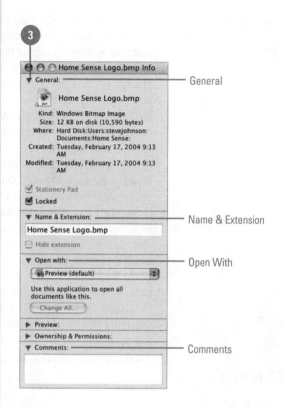

General

Name & Extension

Open With

Comments

Languages

Ownership & Permissions

Creating a CD or DVD Using the Finder

The low cost and large storage size of CDs or DVDs (getting cheaper), and the popularity of recording hardware make using CDs and DVDs an effective approach to some file management tasks. For example, CDs or DVDs are an effective way to back up information or transfer information to another computer without a network or to a Microsoft Windows computer. Before you can create a CD or DVD, you must have blank CDs or DVDs and a CD-RW or DVD-RW drive (also known as a writer or burner), or an Apple SuperDrive installed on your computer. You can copy or write, files and folders to either CD-Rs or DVD-Rs (recordable) or CD-RWs or DVD-RWs (rewritable). With recordables, you can write files and folders only once and read them many times, but you can't erase them. With rewritables, you can read, write, and erase files and folders many times, just like a removable disk. When you write to, or **burn**, a CD or DVD, Mac OS X needs disk space on your hard disk to temporarily store files during the process, so make sure you have free hard disk space available for the size of the CD or DVD. Do not copy more files and folders to the CD or DVD than it will hold; anything beyond the limit will not copy. When the burn is complete, you can use the CD or DVD on a Macintosh or Windows PC appropriately equipped (New!). You can also use other Mac OS X applications with disc burning features, such as iTunes, iPhoto, iDVD, or Disk Utility, to create specialized CDs or DVDs.

Prepare to Burn a CD or DVD

① Insert a blank CD-R, CD-RW, DVD-R, or DVD-RW disc into your drive.

   If you insert a CD-RW disc that you previously recorded, the dialog doesn't appear; you need to erase the disc with Disk Utility before you can burn data on it again.

   TROUBLE? *If the dialog doesn't appear, click the Apple menu, click Preferences, click CDs & DVDs, select the options you want, and then click the Close button.*

② Click the Action pop-up, and then click Open Finder.

③ Type a Name for the disc.

④ Click OK.

   The blank disc appears on the desktop, where you can add and remove files and folders.

To start a multisession CD, open the Disk Utility application. See page 422 for recording details.

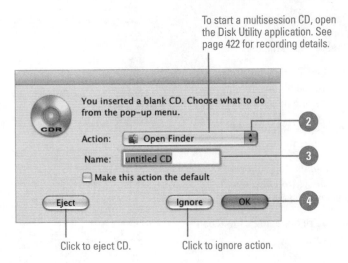

Click to eject CD.   Click to ignore action.

Add and Remove Files and Folders to a CD or DVD

① Open a Finder window.

② Navigate to the files and folders you want to add to the CD or DVD disc.

③ Drag the files and folders to the CD or DVD disc in the Sidebar, and then organize them.

IMPORTANT *If you're using these files on a Windows PC, make sure the file names don't include \ / : * ? " < > |, otherwise you can't open them.*

④ To remove files and folders, click the CD or DVD disc in the Sidebar, or double-click the disc on the desktop, and then drag out the items you don't want.

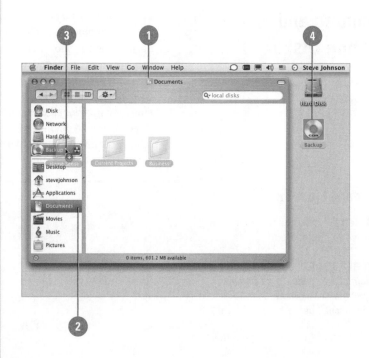

Create a CD or DVD

① If you want, rename the CD or DVD disc just like any other file.

② Use any of the following methods to create a CD or DVD:

◆ **Drag to Trash.** When you drag a disk icon onto the Trash icon in the Dock, it changes to a Burn icon.

◆ **Burn command.** Select the disk icon, click the File menu, and then click Burn. You can also Control-click the disc icon, and then click Burn.

◆ **Sidebar Burn button.** Click the Burn button in the Sidebar.

③ Click the Burn Speed pop-up, and then select a speed.

④ Click Burn.

Burn command on File menu

Sidebar Burn button   Drag to Trash ②

Mounting and Ejecting Disks

When you insert a disk (such as a removable, CD, or DVD), it's icon appears, or **mounts**, in the Computer window, in the Sidebar, and on the desktop (unless you've changed Finder Preferences) for you to open and use. When you no longer need a disk, you eject, or dismount, it from the drive. Mac OS X provides several different ways to eject a disk: drag the disk icon to the Trash (only happens for disks; a little strange, but its old time Mac functionality), select the Eject command, use the Sidebar (New!), or hold down the Eject key. You can also use these methods to remove, or **unmount**, a network or FireWire drive, an iPod, or a disk image from your desktop.

Mount and Eject Disks

① Insert the disk into the appropriate drive to mount the disk.

> **TROUBLE?** *If the computer immediately ejects a CD or DVD, you may need to clean it. Wipe the shiny surface with a soft cloth.*

② Use any of the following methods to eject a disk:

◆ **Drag to Trash.** When you drag a disk icon onto the Trash icon in the Dock, it changes to an Eject icon.

◆ **Eject command.** Select the disk icon, click the File menu, and then click Eject. You can also use Control-click the disk icon, and then click Eject.

◆ **Sidebar Eject button.** Click the Eject button in the Sidebar.

◆ **Eject key.** Press and hold down the Media Eject key in the upper-right corner of your keyboard (if available) for a moment, or press F12.

> **TROUBLE?** *If a CD or DVD doesn't eject, insert a straightened paper clip into the small hole on the front of the drive, or click the Apple menu, click Restart, and hold down the mouse button until it ejects before the restart.*

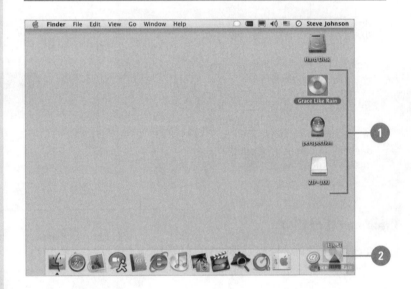

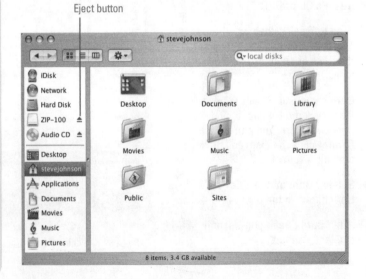

Eject button

Customizing the Finder

Introduction

Finder Preferences allow you to control how you interact with your desktop, windows, and icons. You can access Finder Preferences from the Finder menu. Finder Preferences are grouped into four main areas: General, Labels, Sidebar, and Advanced. The Finder Preferences window is a central location to set Finder related options. However, you can customize the Finder and the desktop in other places too.

In each of the Finder window views (Icon, List, and Column), you can set view specific options to customize the way you view icons. In addition to the predefined items in the Sidebar (the left pane in a Finder window), you can add your own items, including folders, documents, Web Internet Location files, to name a few. The Finder toolbar comes with a few standard buttons, and you can customize to add more. You can use the Customize Toolbar dialog to quickly drag button icons on and off the toolbar. You can set Dock preferences to adjust the Dock size and icon magnification (when you point to one), change the Dock position on the screen, apply a bounce effect to an icon when you launch an application, select a minimization special effect, and make it disappear when not in use.

To save some time, you can create shortcuts to the files, folders, or disks you use frequently, known as Aliases. An **alias** allows you to access the original folder or file from several different places. Exposé lets you quickly move windows out of the way temporarily to make it easier to work with windows in order to find, move, or copy files. If you have novice users who want to use your computer, you can set up a shared user account with Simple Finder, which is a simplified version of the Mac OS X Finder with fewer menus and icons. It's a great way for them to explore, yet keep your data safe.

Understanding Finder Preferences

Finder Preferences allow you to control how you interact with your desktop, windows, and icons. Finder Preferences are grouped into four main areas: General, Labels, Sidebar, and Advanced. You can open Finder Preferences by selecting Preferences from the Finder menu.

The **General preferences pane** allows you to display icons for local and network disks on the desktop, select options for opening new Finder windows, and enable spring-loaded folders and windows. The **Labels preferences pane** allows you to change the name of color labels for Finder items to more meaningful ones, such as work or project, which you can use as search criteria in the Find window. If you accidentally remove a Sidebar icon, you can use the **Sidebar preferences pane** to redisplay Finder specific icons, such as computer, hard disks, iDisk, network, desktop, and applications. The **Advanced preferences pane** provides a few options related to file extensions, an empty the Trash warning, and languages of files for search indexing (cataloging to speed up the searching process).

General

Labels

Sidebar

Advanced

Showing Icons on the Desktop

When you insert a removable disk, a CD, or DVD, or connect to a network server, an icon for the disk automatically appears on the desktop. Depending on your work style, you may or may not want icons to simply appear. You can use Finder Preferences to specify whether icons for hard disks, CDs, and network servers appear on your desktop. Having the icons on the desktop makes dragging them to the Eject icon in the Dock quick and easy, but the icons also add clutter to the desktop.

Show Volume Icons on the Desktop

1. Click the Finder menu, and then click Preferences.

2. Click General.

3. Select or clear the checkmarks for the icons you want to show or hide on the desktop.

    ◆ Hard disks

    ◆ CDs, DVDs and iPods

    ◆ Connected servers (computers attached to a network)

4. Click the Close button.

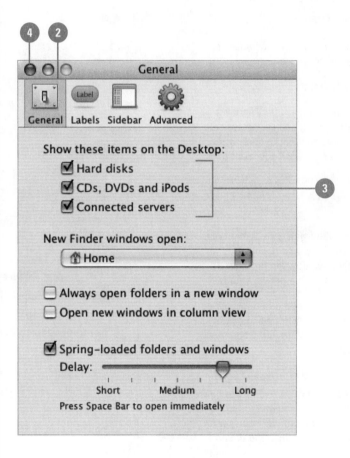

3

Customizing the Way Windows Open

When you create a new Finder window, you can specify options to always open folders in a new window, open new windows in Column view, or use spring-loaded folders and windows. Spring-loaded folders allows you to drag a file or folder on top of another folder, and it springs open to let you continue dragging the selection to another location. Instead of starting and stopping when you move or copy items from one folder to another, you can drag items continuously from folder to folder.

Customize the Way Finder Windows Open

1 Click the Finder menu, and then click Preferences.

2 Click General.

3 Click the New Finder Windows Open pop-up, and then select the window you want to open when you open a new Finder window.

4 Select or clear the Always Open Folders In A New Window check box.

5 Select the Open New Windows In Column View check box, or clear it to open windows in the view selected for the active window.

6 Select or clear the Spring-Loaded Folders And Windows check box. If you select it, drag the slider to adjust the delay.

   TIMESAVER *When you drag an item to a folder with a spring-loaded folder, you can press the Spacebar to open the window immediately without the delay.*

7 Click the Close button.

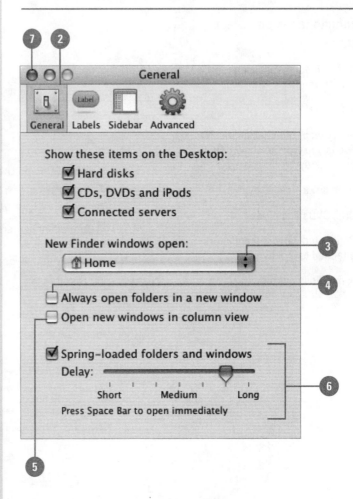

Showing or Hiding File Extensions

A **file extension** is a three-letter suffix at the end of a document's file name that identifies the file type. For Windows operating system users, a file extension determines which application can open a file; the Mac doesn't use it. You might never have seen a document's file extension because your system might be set up to hide it. The file extension for simple text files is ".txt" (pronounced "dot t-x-t"), and many graphic files have the extension ".bmp" or ".jpg". This means that the full name for a text file named Memo is Memo.txt. If you double-click a document whose file name ends with the three-letter extension ".txt," Finder automatically opens the document with TextEdit, a word processing application. If you plan to exchange files with the Windows operating system, then show the file extensions, so Windows recognizes them.

Show or Hide File Extensions

1. Click the Finder menu, and then click Preferences.

2. Click Advanced.

3. Select or clear the Show All File Extensions check box.

4. Click the Close button.

Did You Know?

You can hide or show extensions one icon at a time. Select the icons you want to show or hide, click the File menu, click Get Info, select or clear the Hide Extension check box, and then click the Close button.

You can set an option to show a warning before emptying the Trash. Click the Finder menu, click Preferences, click Advanced, select the Show Warning Before Emptying The Trash check box, and then click the Close button.

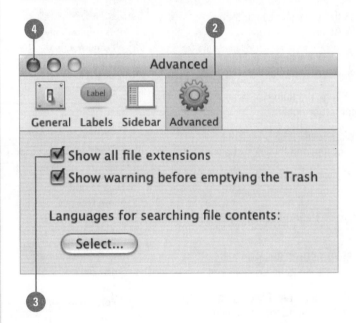

Customizing Finder Window Views

In each of the Finder window views (as Icons, as List, and as Columns), you can set view specific options to customize the way you view icons. For Icon and List views, you can select to apply your changes to the current window or to all Finder windows (a personal default). In Icon view, you can change icon size, label position, arrangement, and background. In List view, you can change file size, date, and status related information. To make the display easier to view, you can display relative dates, such as "Today" and "Yesterday." In Column view, you can show icons and the preview column (summary information in the right column).

Change Icon View Options

1. Open a Finder window.

2. Click the View menu, and then click As Icons.

3. Click the View menu, and then click Show View Options.

4. To change the icon size, drag the slider left or right.

5. To change the icon text size, click the pop-up, and then select a size.

6. Click the label position option (Bottom or Right) you want.

7. Select or clear the following check boxes:

    ◆ **Snap To Grid.** Check to have icons snap to an invisible grid.

    ◆ **Show Item Info.** Check to show item info under the icon name.

    ◆ **Show Icon Preview.** Check to show an image, sound or movie.

    ◆ **Keep Arranged By.** Check and select an arrange option from the pop-up.

8. Click the Background option you want, and any related settings.

9. Click the This Window Only or All Windows option to select where to apply view changes.

10. Click the Close button.

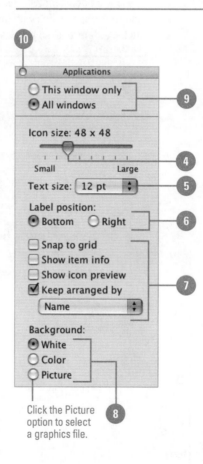

Click the Picture option to select a graphics file.

Change List View Options

1. Open a Finder window.

2. Click the View menu, and then click As List.

3. Click the View menu, and then click Show View Options.

4. Click the Icon Size option you want.

5. To change the icon text size, click the pop-up, and then select a size.

6. Select or clear the check boxes with the information you want to display in list form.

7. Click the This Window Only or All Windows option to select where to apply view changes.

8. Click the Close button.

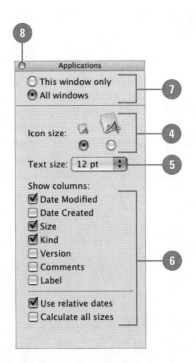

Change Column View Options

1. Open a Finder window.

2. Click the View menu, and then click As Columns.

3. Click the View menu, and then click Show View Options.

4. Click the Text Size pop-up, and then select a point size.

5. Select or clear the Show Icons check box.

6. Select or clear the Show Preview Column check box.

7. Click the Close button.

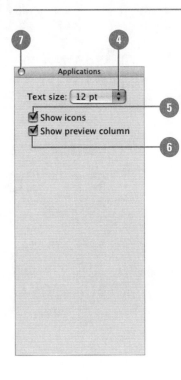

3

Customizing the Toolbar

The Finder toolbar comes with a few standard buttons, but you can add more. You can use the Customize Toolbar dialog to quickly drag button icons on and off. The buttons include Path (navigation pop-up), Eject, Burn, Customize, Separator (designates groups), Space (adds a gap), Flexible Space (adds a gap that expands), New Folder, Delete, Connect, Find, Get Info, iDisk, and Search. If you want the simple look again, you can drag the Default Set of buttons onto the toolbar to reset it. In addition to the button icons in the dialog, you can also drag icons, such as favorite folders, disks, or applications, from the desktop or any Finder folder onto the toolbar. You can also use the ⌘ key to cycle through size combinations of large and small icons and text labels.

Customize the Finder Toolbar

1. Click the View menu, and then click Customize Toolbar.

2. Click the Show pop-up, and then select a display option of Icon Only, Icon & Text, or Text Only.

   TIMESAVER *Control-click the toolbar (without the dialog open), and then click a display option.*

3. Select or clear the Use Small Size check box.

4. To add icons to the toolbar, drag them into place from the gallery.

5. To remove icons, drag them up or down off the toolbar.

6. To rearrange icons, drag them horizontally on the toolbar.

7. To reset the toolbar, drag the default set of items onto the toolbar.

8. When you're finished, click Done.

Did You Know?

You can access buttons that don't fit on a narrow window. You can either resize the window, or click the double arrow, and then select a toolbar item.

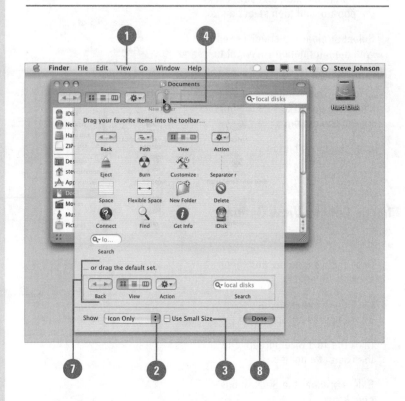

Add, Remove, or Rearrange Icons to the Toolbar

1. Display the icons you want to add to the Finder toolbar in the desktop or any folder window.

2. Drag icons from the desktop, or any folder window, directly onto the toolbar, and then pause before releasing the icon.

   TROUBLE? *If pausing doesn't work, use* ⌘ *while you drag.*

3. To remove an icon from the toolbar, hold down ⌘, and then drag the icon off the toolbar.

4. To rearrange an icon on the toolbar, hold down ⌘, and then drag the icon horizontally on the toolbar.

Change Toolbar Styles

1. Hold down ⌘ while you repeatedly click the Toolbar Control button.

   Each time you click the button, a different toolbar style appears.

Did You Know?

You can change toolbar styles in some applications too. You can also use ⌘ in Mac OS X applications, such as Mail, and many other applications.

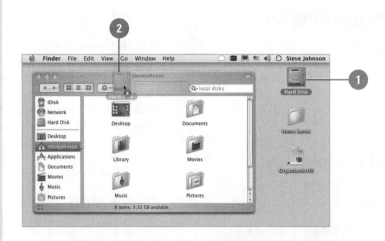

Icon added to toolbar

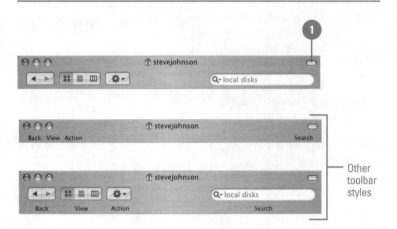

Other toolbar styles

3

Customizing the Sidebar

In addition to the predefined items in the Sidebar (**New!**), you can add your own items, including folders, documents, and Web Internet Location files, to name a few. When you click a volume or folder in the Sidebar, the Finder displays its contents in the window. When you click an application, document, or Web Internet Location file, the item opens in its own application window. If you accidentally remove a Sidebar icon, you can't undo it, but you can redisplay Mac OS X specific items using Finder Preferences. Unfortunately, you have to recreate the ones you added.

Customize the Sidebar

◆ **Add items.** Drag the items to the lower section of the Sidebar.

> **TIMESAVER** *Select an item, and then press* ⌘+T, *or use the Add To Sidebar command on the File menu.*

◆ **Remove items.** Drag the items outside of the Sidebar to detach them.

◆ **Rearrange items.** Drag the items up or down in the list.

◆ **Change the column width.** Position the mouse pointer over the divider between the Sidebar and the window contents, and then drag to change the width.

◆ **Hide and show the Sidebar.** Double-click the vertical divider to hide it. To show the Sidebar again, double-click the left edge of the window.

Add item to Sidebar

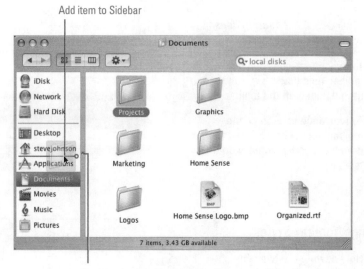

Drag to change column width

Vertical divider   Remove item from Sidebar

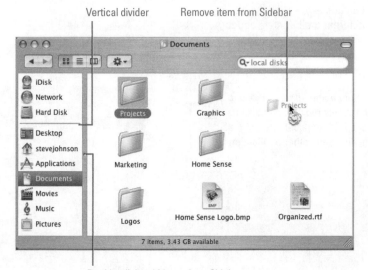

Double-click to hide or show Sidebar

Change Sidebar Preferences

1. Click the Finder menu, and then click Preferences.

2. Click Sidebar.

3. Select or clear the check boxes with the items you want or don't want to see in the Sidebar.

4. Click the Close button.

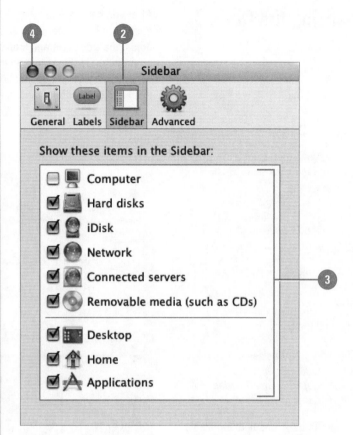

Customizing the Dock ▶

After you have worked with the Dock for a while, you probably want to customize it to better suite your needs. You can set Dock Preferences to adjust the Dock size and icon magnification when you point to one, change the Dock position on the screen, apply a bounce effect to an icon when you launch an application, select a minimization special effect, and even make it disappear when not in use.

Customize the Dock

1. Click the Apple menu, point to Dock, and then click Dock Preferences.

   TIMESAVER *Control-click the divider in the Dock to quickly display the Dock submenu.*

2. Select the Dock options you want to adjust:

   ◆ **Dock Size.** Drag slider to change the Dock size.

   TIMESAVER *Position the pointer on the divider in the Dock, so it turns into a double-headed arrow, and then drag to size it.*

   ◆ **Magnification.** Check to enable it, and then drag the slider to magnify the icons when you point to them in the Dock.

   ◆ **Position On Screen.** Click the Left, Bottom, or Right option.

   ◆ **Minimize Using.** Click the pop-up, and then select an animation effect.

3. Select the Animate Opening Applications check box to have the application icon bounce when you launch an application.

4. Select or clear the Automatically Hide And Show The Dock.

   This changes when you select the Turn Hiding On menu command.

5. Click the Close button.

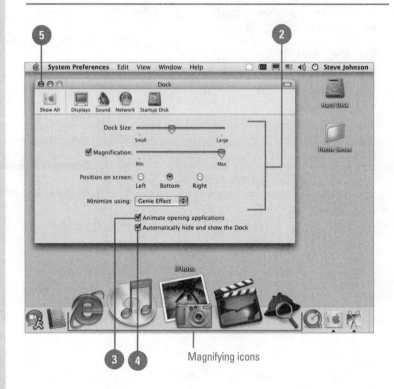

Magnifying icons

Add, Remove, and Rearrange Items in the Dock

◆ **Add an item.** Drag an icon from a Finder window to the Dock, and then position application icons to the left of the divider line and all other icons to the right.

◆ **Add an open application item.** Open the application, display the Dock, press the application icon, and then click Keep In Dock.

◆ **Open a document using an application item.** Drag the document icon to the application icon in the Dock.

◆ **Move an item.** Drag the icon to the position you want in the Dock.

◆ **Remove an item.** Drag an icon out of the Dock.

> **TROUBLE?** *If you delete an application or document from your computer with an icon in the Dock, the Dock icon changes to a question mark, which you can remove.*

Did You Know?

You can slow down the minimization of a window or application (a cool genie effect). Shift-click a window's Minimize button. The window collapses into the Dock about one-fifth the usual speed. You can also Shift-click the icon in the Dock to slowly unminimize the window. Unfortunately, you can't speed it up.

Add an item

Add an open application

Open a document

Move an item

Remove an item

Open a folder

3

Creating Aliases

It can take you a while to access a file or folder buried several levels down in a folder. To save some time, you can create shortcuts to the items you use frequently. **Aliases** are shortcuts that point to a folder or file. An alias allows you to access the original folder or file from several different places. When you create an alias to a folder or file, the icon includes a little arrow in the lower-left corner. You can't make an alias for an application. However, you can add an application into the Dock, which acts like an alias. When you double-click an alias icon, a folder opens with the contents of the original folder or a document opens using it's associated application. If you delete an alias of a folder or file, the original folder or file is not deleted, just the alias.

Create an Alias

1. Open the Finder window with the icon in which you want to create an alias.

2. Select the icon.

3. Click the File menu, and then click Make Alias.

    TIMESAVER *Hold down ⌘+Option, and then drag a file or folder to create an alias.*

    The alias icon appears in the Finder window.

4. If you want, rename the alias icon, and then press Return.

5. Drag the alias icon to the desktop or another folder.

Did You Know?

You can quickly find the original file or folder of an alias. Select the alias file or folder, click the File menu, and then click Show Original. You can also press ⌘+R.

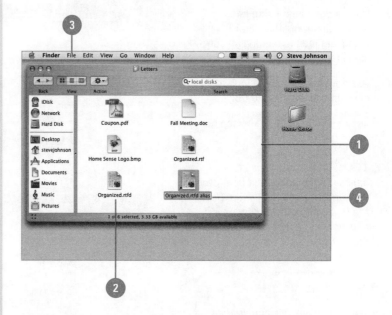

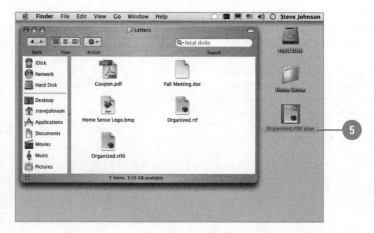

Create an Alias with the Title Bar

1. Open the application and document in which you want to create an alias.

2. Position the mouse pointer on the icon next to the document title in the title bar.

3. Drag the icon to the desktop, or on a folder or disk.

Did You Know?

You can drag the Title bar icon onto an application Dock icon. If you want to open a document created in one program (say TextEdit), and you want to open it up in another program (say Microsoft Word), you can drag the Title bar icon of a document in TextEdit to the Microsoft Word icon in the Dock to open it.

You can drag an alias icon into the Dock. Drag the alias icon into the Dock on the right side. When you release the mouse, the icon appears in the Dock.

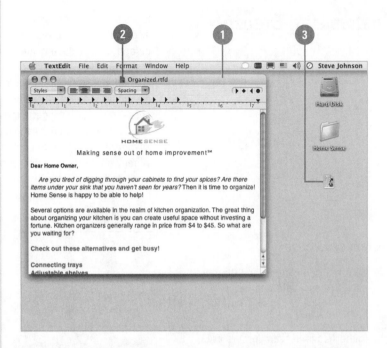

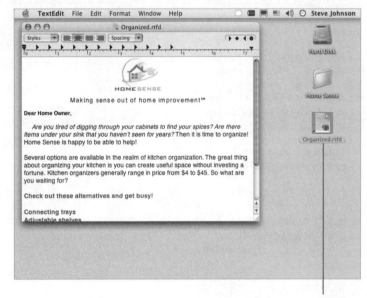

Alias for TextEdit document

Customizing Exposé

Exposé (**New!**) lets you quickly move windows out of the way temporarily to make it easier work with windows to find, move, or copy files. The default way to move windows with Exposé is to use keyboard function keys. However, these function keys might already be taken by other applications, or your computer. You can customize Exposé to move window in three ways: screen corners, keyboard, and mouse. Using screen corners, you can trigger Exposé when you point to one of the screen corners, which you can customize to display different windows. Using the keyboard pop-ups, you can change the Exposé keyboard shortcuts. When you display the pop-ups, you can press other modifier keys, such as Shift, Option, Control, or ⌘ to create a new shortcut. If you have a mouse with two buttons, you can change options to trigger Exposé with your mouse.

Customize Exposé

1 Click the Apple menu, and then click System Preferences.

2 Click the Exposé icon.

3 In the Active Screen Corners area, click the pop-ups for the corner you want to use, and then select an option:

- ◆ **All Windows.** Select to show all open windows at once.

- ◆ **Application Windows.** Select to show all open windows in the current application.

- ◆ **Desktop.** Select to hide all open windows and show desktop.

4 In the Keyboard area, click the pop-ups for each Exposé operation, press a keyboard modifier (Shift, Control, Option, or ⌘) if you want, and then select a keyboard.

5 In the Mouse area, click the pop-ups for each Exposé operation, and then select a mouse button.

6 Click the Close button.

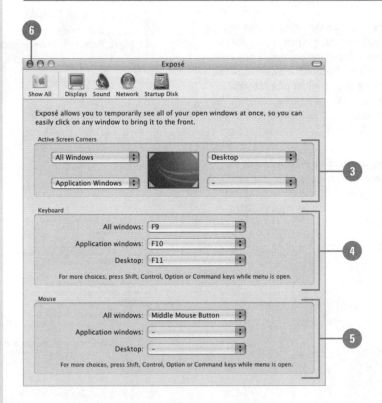

Using Simple Finder

If you have novice users who want to use your computer, you should set up a shared user account with Simple Finder. **Simple Finder** is a simplified version of the Mac OS X Finder with fewer menus and icons, and allows limited access to the items on your hard disk. The Dock contains only three folders: Documents, My Applications, and Shared. The Documents folder provides a place for users to save their documents, while the My Applications folder provides access to the applications you select for them in Accounts Preferences. If you want to share documents with them, they can access the items in the Shared folder.

Set Up the Simple Finder

1. Click the Apple menu, and then click System Preferences.

2. Click the Accounts icon.

3. Click the user account for the person, or click the Add button (+) to create one.

4. Click the Limitations tab.

5. Click the Simple Finder tab.

6. Select or clear the applications and options you want using the Allow All, Uncheck All, or Locate buttons, to enable or disable for the account.

7. Click the Close button.

Did You Know?

You can get administrative access while logged in to Simple Finder. Click the Finder menu, click Run Full Finder, and then type your name and password. When you're done, click the Finder menu, and then click Return To Simple Finder.

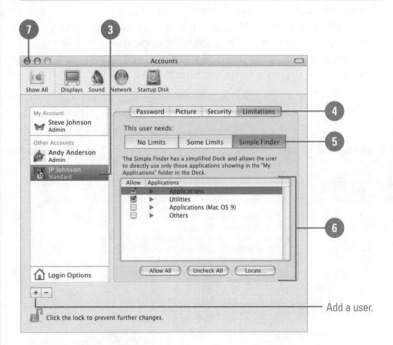

Add a user.

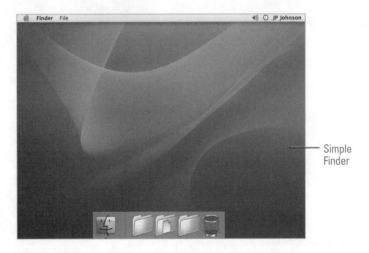

Simple Finder

Tinkering Around

Like with every operating system, there are things you want to do, but just can't with the current version. That's where third-party programs and utilities come in to do the job. TinkerTool provides access to several secret Mac OS X Panther features that were either not made available to the average user or available only for development purposes. TinkerTool is a free utility that allows you to add a drop shadow to your Dock, change the minimize effect, control placement of scroll bars, and substitute fonts throughout the system (dialogs, title bars, menu bars, and help balloons, etc.) to name a few. The changes you make with TinkerTool only apply to the current user and don't affect the settings of other users on a shared computer. If you're not satisfied with the changes, you can use the Reset panel to restore your system back to the way it was before you started making changes. You can download the utility application from *www.downloads.com* or other similar Web sites; so check it out!

Finder options

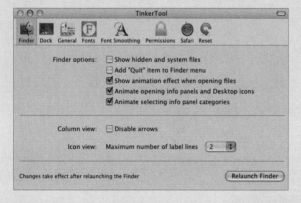

Dock options

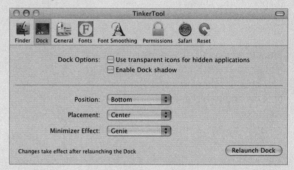

General options

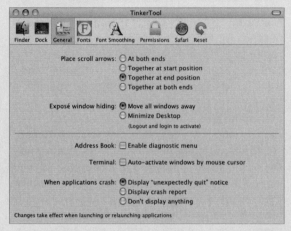

Fonts options

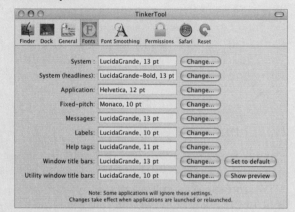

Permissions options

Safari options

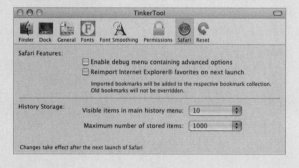

3

Customizing Other Ways

Other third-party developers have come up with some wonderful tools that you can use to do things you currently can't with Mac OS X Panther. Some are free, while others charge a small fee. You can download these utilities at *www.downloads.com* or other similar Web sites.

Replace Finder Icons

CandyBar is a utility that lets you quickly, easily, and safely change the default icons in Mac OS X. You can customize everything from the look of the Finder toolbar and folders to the Trash can. You can now attach an author's name, e-mail, and URLs to iContainers, a set of icons into a single file. You can even save your current icon scheme to an iContainer to quickly switch among custom-created sets. Candy-Bar is also integrated with Picadex, an icon organizer.

Automatic Maintenance

Macaroni is a utility that handles regular maintenance for Mac OS X, including the Mac OS X repair-privileges process and Unix-style maintenance. From cleaning up old temp files and installer logs, to removing language-specific localized files from applications, Macaroni's automatic clean-up routines are sure to recover and save valuable disk space. You can schedule maintenance tasks to run in the middle of the night when you're asleep (be sure to leave your computer turned on) or you can run them when you want them to happen. Macaroni remembers the schedule for you, running these maintenance tasks on a regular basis. After you install Macaroni, you can access and change Macaroni settings in System Preferences. However, you really don't need to do anything; Macaroni has done it for you. Simply, install it and forget about it!

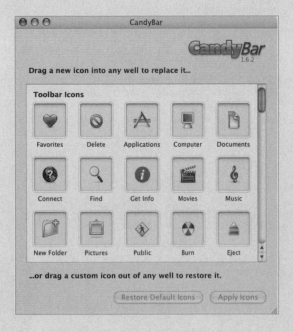

Setting System Preferences

Introduction

System Preferences allows you to customize various parts of Mac OS X, such as the appearance of your desktop, your computers date and time, the way CDs and DVDs start up when you insert them, or use speech recognition to convert a spoken voice into commands or electronic text. If you have an ink device on your computer, you can use System Preferences to improve the recognition of ink to text. You can access System Preferences from the Dock or the Apple menu. Many applications also have their own preferences, which you can access from the application menu within the application.

Where Did They Go?

If you are familiar with Mac OS 9, you may be wondering what happened to a few system utilities, such as Control Panels, Control Strip, Chooser, and the System Folder. Instead of Control Panels, Mac OS X consolidates all of you computer settings into System Preferences. Instead of the Control Strip, Mac OS X uses menu status icons on the right side of the menu bar, which you can turn on and off using preference icons in System Preferences. Chooser settings are available in the Print & Fax pane in System Preferences and the Printer Setup Utility is in the Utilities folder. The System Folder goes by the name System and you can no longer change the contents of the folder. The customizable parts of the System Folder are now available in the Home folder for each computer user. Mac OS X no longer uses system extensions. If you are using Mac OS 9 and need system extensions, you can install them in the Extensions folder in the Mac OS 9 System Folder and use the Classic icon in System Preferences to customize settings.

What You'll Do

Understand System Preferences

View System Preferences

Lock and Unlock Preference Settings

Change Appearance Options

Set Up the Desktop

Set Up Screen Savers

Set the Date and Time

Change International Options

Set Universal Access Options

Save Energy

Select a Startup Disk

Change the Way a CD & DVD Starts

Set QuickTime Options

Control Sound

Recognize Your Speech

Let Mac Do the Talking

Set Ink Preferences

Understanding System Preferences

System Preferences allow you to customize system wide settings for various aspects of Mac OS X Panther and your computer. The System Preferences window is organized alphabetically or by categories: Personal, Hardware, Internet & Network, and System. Each category contains preference areas within Mac OS X that you can change to customize the way the operating system works. Only an administrator can change system settings that affect everyone who uses the computer.

Personal

Appearance. Change the look and feel of buttons, selected items, and scroll bars. *See page 82.*

Desktop & Screen Saver. Change the desktop background or select a visual screen effect to hide your desktop, or protect others from using your computer when you're not using your computer. *See pages 84-85.*

Dock. Change the location of the Dock, adjust the size of icons, set magnification, or hide the Dock. *See page 68 in Chapter 3.*

Expose'. Set keyboard shortcuts or mouse positions to show or hide all your windows at one time. *See page 72 in Chapter 3.*

International. Change your computer to read or write with different languages. *See page 88.*

Security. Protect your computer and the information on it. *See page 385 in Chapter 16.*

Hardware

Bluetooth. Control how to send and receive files between your computer and other Bluetooth devices. (Available only if Bluetooth is enabled). *See page 412 in Chapter 17.*

CDs & DVDs. Set startup options when you insert a CD or DVD. *See page 95.*

Displays. Set the screen size, resolution, color settings, and the screen arrangement when using multiple screens. *See page 440 in Chapter 19.*

Energy Saver. Set the computer to sleep and conserve power, and schedule automatic shutdown and startup. *See page 92.*

Ink. Set the computer to write text using a graphics tablet and stylus, recognize the ink, and turn it into words. (Available only if a graphics tablet or ink device is installed.) *See page 104.*

Keyboard & Mouse. Change the speed of your mouse or keyboard, and customize universal keyboard shortcuts or application specific shortcuts. *See pages 435-437 in Chapter 19.*

Print & Fax. Add a printer, monitor print jobs, set up to receive faxes, and share printers and a fax modem with other users. *See page 166 in Chapter 7.*

Sound. Change computer sound volume, effects, and sound input or output devices. *See page 98.*

Internet & Network

.Mac. Create an online .Mac account and set options to access .Mac, iDisk, and your .Mac mail. *See Chapter 11, page 263.*

Network. Create and manage network and Internet connection settings. *See Chapter 17, page 431.*

QuickTime. Change settings for playing QuickTime movies on the Internet, change your Internet connection speed, and set the file open association with QuickTime. *See page 96.*

Sharing. Set services for Personal File Sharing, Personal Web Sharing, and Printer Sharing; adjust firewall settings to protect your computer from access over the Internet; and share your Internet connection with others. *See Chapter 17, page 391.*

System

Accounts. Set up accounts, access privileges, and log in and out settings to share your computer with others. *See Chapter 16, page 375.*

Classic. Set Mac OS 9 options to turn the Classic environment on or off, and manage Classic extensions, sleep settings, and utilities. *See Appendix A, page 469.*

Date & Time. Set your computer's date, time, and time zone, or use a network time server. *See page 86.*

Software Update. Set a schedule or options to check for updates automatically on the Internet. *See page 417 in Chapter 18.*

Speech. Set the computer to speak the text on the screen or use spoken commands to control your computer. *See page 100.*

Startup Disk. Select the disk or drive you want to use to start up you computer. *See page 94.*

Universal Access. Set options for the visual or hearing impaired to make it easier to use the computer keyboard, mouse, and screen. *See page 90.*

Adding or Removing Third-Party System Preferences

In addition to the System Preferences included with Mac OS X, you can add other System Preferences developed by other companies, known as third-party system preferences. To install a third-party preference, download or drag the preference to your hard disk, double-click its icon, and then follow the on-screen instructions. To uninstall a third-party preference, use the method provided by the developer, or hold down the Control key, click the Preference icon in the System Preferences window, click Uninstall, and then follow the on-screen instructions. For an example, *see page 76 in Chapter 3.*

4

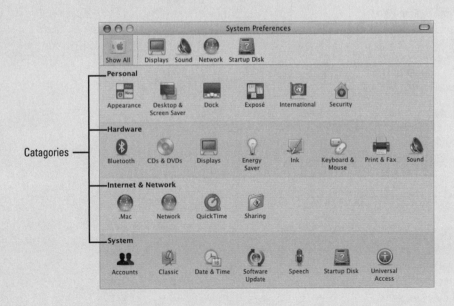

Catagories

Viewing System Preferences

System Preferences are organized into categories by default. Each category contains a set of icons, which you can open to set customization options in preference panes for different aspects of the Macintosh operating system. You can also view the icons in the System Preferences window alphabetically, depending on your preference. Simply click a preference icon to open it, and then make the changes you want. The preferences take effect when you quit or close System Preferences.

View System Preferences

1 Click the Apple menu, and then click System Preferences or click the System Preferences icon in the Dock.

2 To change preference organization, click the View menu, and then click Organize By Categories or Organize Alphabetically.

3 To open a preference, click the icon.

TIMESAVER *Press the first letter of the preference's name to select the icon, and then press the Spacebar to open it.*

4 To switch to another preference, click the View menu, and then click the one you want to open.

TIMESAVER *Click the Show All button on the toolbar to show all the preference icons.*

5 When you're done, click the System Preferences menu, and then click Quit System Preferences, or click the Close button.

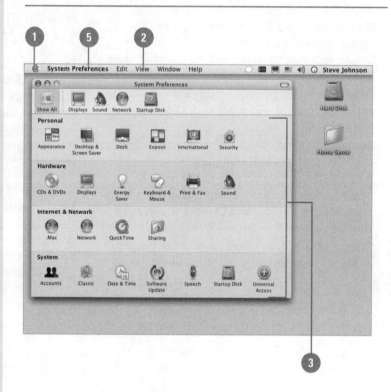

Did You Know?

You can customize the System Preferences toolbar. To add a button to the toolbar in System Preferences, drag an icon to the toolbar. To remove a button, drag it out of the toolbar.

Locking and Unlocking Preference Settings

Some preference panes are locked for security reasons. If preference settings are all grayed out, the preference pane is locked to prevent non-administrators from making changes. Check the Lock icon at the bottom of System Preferences. If the Lock icon is locked, you need an administrator name and password to unlock it and make changes. If you log in as an administrator, the Lock icon is unlocked, unless you set a security option to have the preference panes stay locked. When you close the preference pane, it locks automatically.

Unlock a Preference Pane

1. Click the System Preferences icon in the Dock.

2. Click the preference pane icon (such as Security) that you want to lock settings.

3. Click the Lock icon.

4. To unlock, type an administrator name and password.

5. Click OK.

6. Click the Close button.

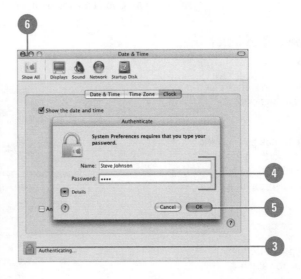

Set Preference Panes to Lock

1. Click the System Preferences icon in the Dock.

2. Click the Security icon.

3. If settings are grayed out, click the Lock icon, type an administrator name and password, and then click OK.

4. Select the Require Password To Unlock Each Secure System Preference check box.

5. Click the Close button.

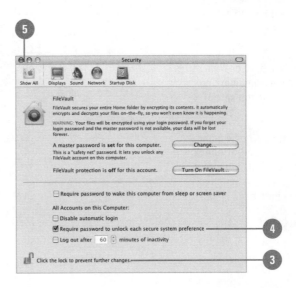

4

Changing Appearance Options

The Appearance pane in System Preferences allows you to change the look and feel of Mac OS X in a few areas. You can change the color scheme for buttons, menus, and windows, and the highlight color for text and lists. Or if you're not comfortable using the scroll bars, you can change the way scroll bars work and the placement of the scroll arrows (New!). If your text looks blurry or jagged, you can adjust the font smoothing, known as **anti-aliasing** (New!), style to fix it (after you log out and back in). As you open files and applications, Mac OS X keeps a list in the Recent Items submenu in the Apple menu. In the Appearance pane, you can set the number of recent items that appear in the menu.

Change the Appearance Color and Scroll Bars

1. Click the System Preferences icon in the Dock, and then click the Appearance icon.

2. Click the Appearance pop-up, and then select a color. If you select Other, the Color Picker palette appears so you can select a color.

3. Click the Highlight Color pop-up, and then select a color.

4. Click the At Top And Bottom or Together option to set the placement of scroll arrows.

5. Click the Jump To The Next Page or Scroll To Here option to select an operation when you click in the scroll bar.

6. Select the Use Smooth Scrolling check box to avoid slight jumping when you click inside the scroll bar.

7. Select the Minimize When Double Clicking A Window Title Bar check box to make it easier to minimize a window instead of using the small yellow Minimize button.

8. Click the Close button.

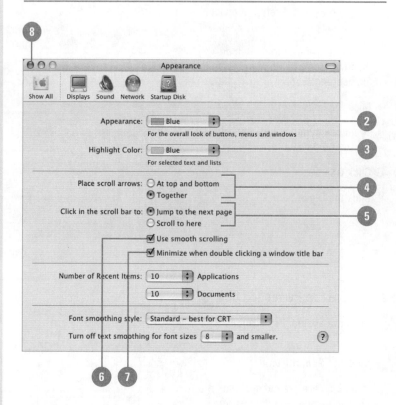

Smooth Fonts

1. Click the System Preferences icon in the Dock, and then click the Appearance icon.

2. Click the Font Smoothing Style pop-up, and then select a style:

   ◆ Standard - Best For CRT (cathode ray tube, old TV style)

   ◆ Light

   ◆ Medium - Best For Flat Panel (laptops and desktop Macs)

   ◆ Strong

3. Click the Turn Off Text Smoothing For Font Sizes pop-up, and then select a font size.

   All text in the font size or smaller is not smoothed, which makes it easier to read.

4. Click the Close button.

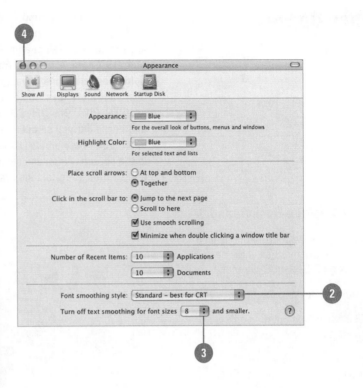

Change Number of Recent Items

1. Click the System Preferences icon in the Dock, and then click the Appearance icon.

2. Click the pop-ups for the Number Of Recent Items, and then select a number.

3. Click the Close button.

Did You Know?

You can clear the Recent Items sub-menu. Click the Apple menu, point to Recent Items, and then click Clear Menu.

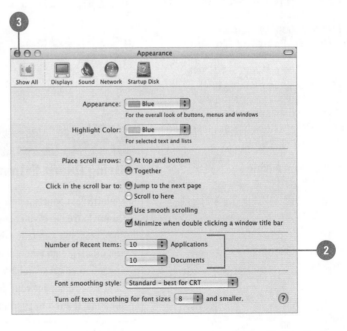

4

Setting Up the Desktop

The desktop **background**, or wallpaper, is a picture that serves as your desktop's backdrop, the basic surface on which icons and windows appear. You can select a background picture from the ones provided with Mac OS X (which includes Apple Background, Nature, Abstract, or Solid Colors) or select one of your own in the Desktop & Screen Saver pane in System Preferences. You can select pictures in a variety of formats (such as JPEG, PICT, GIF, TIFF, PDF, or PSD) from your own Pictures folder, another folder you select, or even an iPhoto folder (Photo Library, Last Import, or iPhoto album (**New!**)), and then select options to make them fit to the screen. When you select a picture from a folder, you can display all the pictures at certain intervals in alphabetical or random order.

Select a Desktop Background

1. Click the System Preferences icon in the Dock, and then click the Desktop & Screen Saver icon.

2. Click the Desktop tab.

3. Click an image category folder in the left column.

4. If you click Choose Folder, navigate to and select a folder, and then click Choose.

5. Select a thumbnail.

6. If you're using your own pictures, click the pop-up, and then select a picture fit option: Fill Screen, Stretch To Fill Screen, or Tile.

7. To show all the pictures in a folder, select the Change Picture check box, select an interval from the pop-up, and then select the Random Order check box or clear it for random order.

8. Click the Close button.

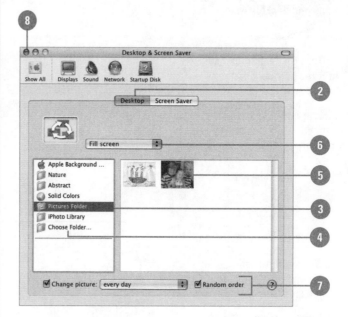

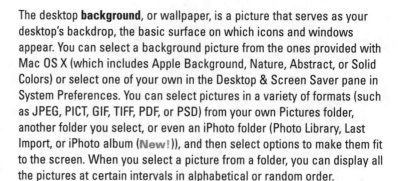

For Your Information

Using Quartz Extreme Enhanced Graphics

Mac OS X supports a new accelerated graphics technology called **Quartz Extreme**. If you have a supported graphics card installed on your computer, you can take advantage of faster window resizing and scrolling, cross-fading when changing desktop pictures, and a cube-rotation animation when switching users. To find out if your computer supports Quartz Extreme, set your desktop to change background pictures every 5 seconds. If each background fades into the next, then you have it.

Setting Up Screen Savers

In the past, you needed a screen saver (a continually moving display) to protect your monitor from screen burn in. Those days are gone with the emergence of new display technology. Screen savers are more for entertainment than anything else. When you leave your computer idle for a specified wait time, a screen saver displays a continuous scene, such as an aquarium, until you move your mouse to stop it. If a security option is set in the Security pane in System Preferences, your computer requires a password when you wake from a screen saver. You can select a screen saver from the ones provided with Mac OS X, or select a folder with pictures (all saved in the same format) or a published slideshow from a .Mac account online, which gets downloaded to your computer.

Set Up a Screen Saver

1. Click the System Preferences icon in the Dock, and then click the Desktop & Screen Saver icon.

2. Click the Screen Saver tab.

3. Select a screen saver in the list, using any of the following methods:

   ◆ Click a screen saver, such as Flurry or Abstract.

   ◆ Click Pictures Folder, and then select one, or click .Mac to use pictures from a slideshow.

   ◆ Select the Use Random Screen Saver check box to use a different screen saver each time one is activated.

4. Click Options, select the check boxes you want, (type the member name for a .Mac slideshow), and then click OK.

5. Drag the slider to determine when the screen saver starts.

6. To activate the screen saver with your mouse pointer, click Hot Corners, specify the options you want in the corner you want it.

7. Click OK.

8. Click the Close button.

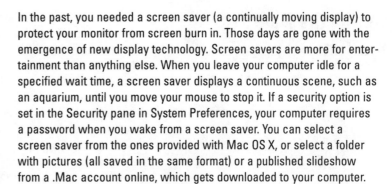

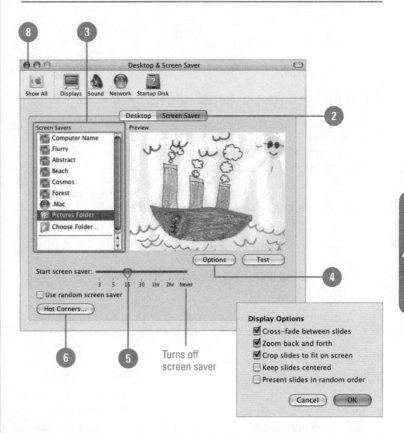

Turns off screen saver

Setting the Date and Time

The date and time you set on your computer is very important. When you save a file or send and receive an e-mail, your computer uses the date and time you set in the Date & Time preference pane. You can set the date and time manually, or if your computer is connected to the Internet, you can have a time server set it automatically. If you have a full time Internet connect, such as DSL or cable, use the time server, otherwise you should set it manually. To make sure your files and e-mail times are not off by a few hours, you need to set your time zone. You can also set the date and time to display as a digital (12:05 PM) or analog (round face with hands) clock in the menu bar or in a window, or have the computer speak, announcing the time (New!) at certain intervals.

Set the Date and Time

1. Click the System Preferences icon in the Dock, and then click the Date & Time icon.

2. Click the Date & Time tab.

3. To set the time automatically over the Internet, select the Set Date & Time Automatically check box, and then use the pop-up to select a time server.

4. To set the date and time manually, use any of the following methods:

    ◆ Select the individual date and time fields, and then enter a number, or use the up and down arrows.

    ◆ Click a date in the calendar and drag the hands on the clock.

    TROUBLE? *Click Revert to reset the date and time.*

5. Click Save.

6. Click the Time Zone tab.

7. Click the part of the map closest to your location.

8. Click the Closest City pop-up, and then select the closest city to your location.

9. Click the Close button.

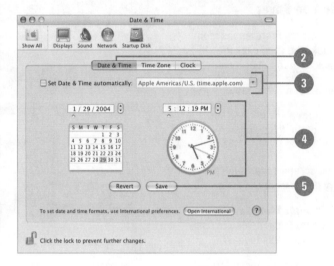

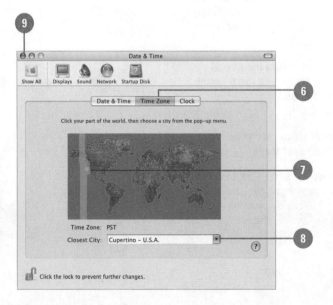

Show and Hear the Date and Time

① Click the System Preferences icon in the Dock, and then click the Date & Time icon.

② Click the Clock tab.

③ Select the Show The Date And Time check box.

④ Select the view in (Menu Bar or Window) and view as (Digital or Analog) option you want.

⑤ Select or clear the following check boxes:

◆ **Display The Time With Seconds.** Check to add seconds to the time (Menu Bar).

◆ **Show AM/PM.** Check to show AM or PM.

◆ **Show The Day Of The Week.** Check to show the day of the week (Menu Bar).

◆ **Flash The Time Separators.** Check to show a blinking colon.

◆ **Use A 24-Hour Clock.** Check to show military time (18:00 instead of 6:00 PM)

◆ **Transparency.** Drag to set for date and time in a window.

⑥ To speak the time, select the Announce The Time check box, click the pop-up, and then select an interval.

To change the computer voice, click Customize Voice.

⑦ Click the Close button.

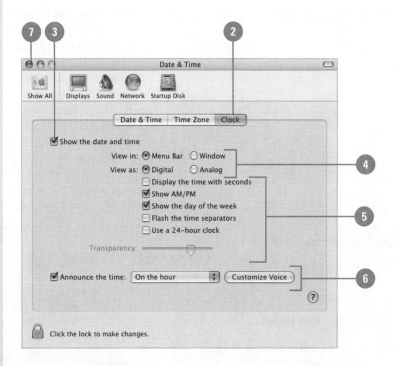

Window view

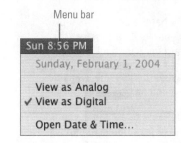

Menu bar

For Your Information

Using the Menu Bar Clock

When you display the clock in the menu bar, the time appears in analog form or as a clock icon with the current time. If you want to know the date, click the clock. A menu drops down displaying the complete date. The menu also allows you to switch between digital and analog clock types and open the Date & Time pane in System Preferences.

4

Changing International Options

The International pane in System Preferences gives you options to use different languages for menus, dialogs, and the keyboard, as well as write text in other languages. The language you write can be different from the language for menus, dialogs, and the keyboard. The Language tab allows you to select a language (**New!**) that you use in application menus and dialogs, and write in an application. The Formats tab allows you to select international formats for dates, times, numbers, and measurement units. The Input Menu tab provides you with a list of languages that you can select a keyboard layout (**New!**), which lets you type in other languages. If you're not familiar with the keyboard layout, you can use the Keyboard Viewer to show you what keys to press to display the keys you want in the input menu language. To make language selection easier, you can add the Input menu to the menu bar.

Set Input Menu Options

1. Click the System Preferences icon in the Dock, and then click the International icon.

2. Click the Input Menu tab.

3. Select the check box next to the language(s) you want to use.

4. To see what the characters look like on your keyboard, select the Keyboard Viewer check box.

   The Keyboard Viewer is available on the menu bar in the Input Menu.

5. Click Options, select the keyboard shortcut or text matching options you want, and then click OK.

6. To change input menu languages from the menu bar, select the Show Input Menu In Menu Bar check box.

7. Click the Close button.

   TIMESAVER *Press* ⌘+ *Spacebar to switch between the two most recent keyboard layouts. Press Option+⌘+Spacebar to cycle down the list of keyboard layouts.*

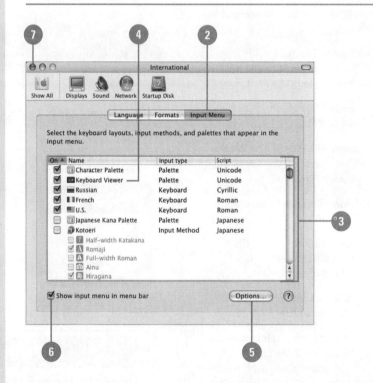

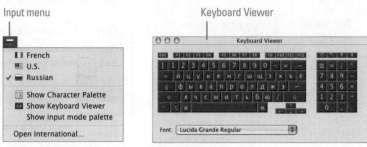

Input menu

Keyboard Viewer

Set International Date, Time, and Number Formats

1. Click the System Preferences icon in the Dock, and then click the International icon.

2. Click the Formats tab.

3. Click the Region pop-up, and then select a region. If necessary, select the Show All Regions check box to display your region.

4. For Dates, Times, and Numbers formats, click Customize.

5. Specify the formats you want, and then click OK.

6. Click the Close button.

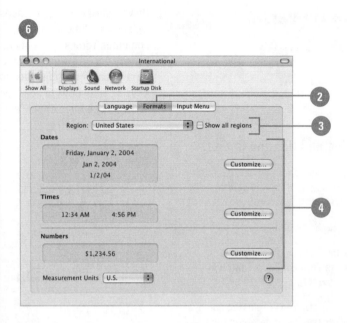

Change Language Options for Menus and Dialogs

1. Click the System Preferences icon in the Dock, and then click the International icon.

2. Click the Language tab.

   A list of available languages on your computer appears.

3. To add or remove languages, click Edit, select or clear the check boxes, and then click OK.

4. Drag the language you want to the top of the list.

   If an application can't support the first language, it tries to use the second one, and so on.

5. Click the Close button.

   Changes take place the next time you launch the Finder or an application.

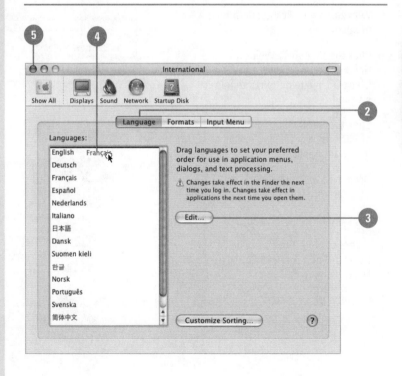

4

Setting Universal Access Options

Universal Access preferences make it easier for a person with a disability, such as difficulty seeing or hearing or controlling a mouse, to use a computer. You can set options to have the screen flash when alert sounds occur, switch the screen to black and white for more visual contrast, zoom in on the screen to make images larger to see, use Sticky Keys or Slow Keys to help control the keyboard, and use Mouse Keys to make mouse functionality available on the numeric keypad.

Set Seeing and Hearing Options

1. Click the System Preferences icon in the Dock, and then click the Universal Access icon.

2. Click the Seeing tab.

3. Click the Turn On Zoom button or click the Turn Off Zoom button (a toggle switch).

    Press ⌘+Option++ (plus) to zoom in, or press ⌘+Option+- (minus) to zoom out.

    With zoom on, click Zoom Options to customize.

4. Click the Switch To White On Black button or click the Switch To Black On White button (a toggle switch).

5. Click the Set Display To Grayscale or click the Set Display To Color button (a toggle switch).

6. Drag the slider to enhance the contrast as necessary.

7. Click the Hearing tab.

8. Select or clear the Flash The Screen When An Alert Sound Occurs check box.

9. Click the Close button.

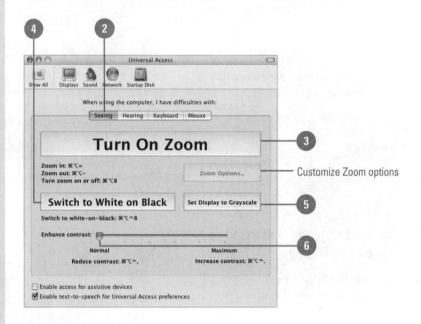

Customize Zoom options

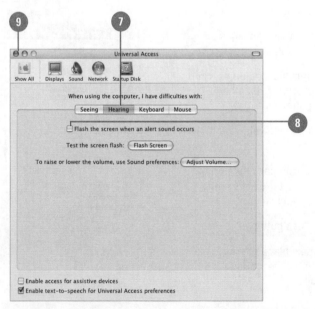

90

Set Keyboard Options

1. Click the System Preferences icon in the Dock, and then click the Universal Access icon.

2. Click the Keyboard tab.

3. To press a group of modifier keys as a sequence, select the On option (Sticky Keys), select or clear the Beep When A Modifier Key Is Set check box, and then select or clear the Display Pressed Keys On Screen check box. If so, white symbols appear when you press a modifier key.

4. To make the keyboard respond more slowly, click the On option (Slow Keys), drag the Acceptance Delay slider, and then select or clear the Use Click Key Sounds check box.

5. Click the Close button.

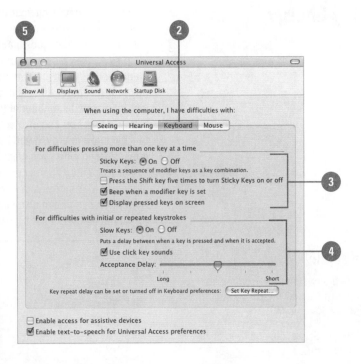

Set Mouse Options

1. Click the System Preferences icon in the Dock, and then click the Universal Access icon.

2. Click the Mouse tab.

3. Click the On option (Mouse Keys).

   Press 5 on the numeric keypad to click an item on the screen. Press 0 to press and hold, and then press 5 again to release, press and hold.

4. Drag the Initial Delay slider to set how quickly the pointer starts moving when you press a key.

5. Drag the Maximum Speed slider to set the maximum speed the pointer moves.

6. Click the Close button.

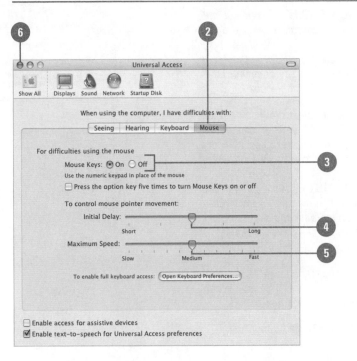

Saving Energy

When you're not using your computer, you can save energy by putting it to sleep. When you put your computer to sleep, the power mode is set to low and the screen goes black to save energy. Your computer is still running, so it takes less time for it to wake up. You can use the Sleep command on the Apple menu to put your computer right to sleep, or you can put your computer and display to sleep automatically when it has been idle for a specific amount of time or when you schedule it at a regular time interval. You can also set the hard disk to sleep whenever possible to save more energy. If you have an iBook or PowerBook, it automatically goes to sleep when you close the lid. You move your mouse or press a key to wake it up. If a security option is set in the Security pane in System Preferences, your computer requires a password when it wakes from a sleep. You can also schedule a computer restart or shutdown, at a regular time interval, or a restart after a power failure.

Set Sleep Options

1. Click the System Preferences icon in the Dock, and then click the Energy Saver icon.

2. Click the Sleep tab, and then click Details, if necessary.

3. Drag the slider to set a time interval before sleep mode starts.

   IMPORTANT *To prevent your computer from sleeping, drag to Never to turn off sleep mode, and then clear the Put The Display To Sleep When The Computer Is Inactive For check box.*

4. Select or clear the Put The Display To Sleep When The Computer Is Inactive For check box. If so, drag the slider to set a time interval.

   TROUBLE? *If the sleep time is less than the screen saver time, then increase the sleep time or click Screen Saver to change it's time.*

5. To conserve energy, select the Put The Hard Disk(s) To Sleep When Possible check box.

6. Click the Close button.

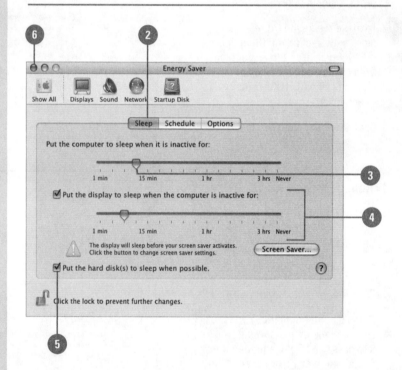

Set a Sleep, Startup, or Shut Down Schedule

1. Click the System Preferences icon in the Dock, and then click the Energy Saver icon.

2. Click the Schedule tab, and then click Details, if necessary.

3. Select or clear the Start Up The Computer check box. If so, select an interval from the pop-up, and then set a time.

4. Select or clear the bottom check box. If so, select an operation from the first pop-up menu, select an interval from the second pop-up, and then set a time.

5. Click the Close button.

Set Wake and Power Failure Restart Options

1. Click the System Preferences icon in the Dock, and then click the Energy Saver icon.

2. Click the Options tab, and then click Details, if necessary.

3. Select or clear the Wake When The Modem Detects A Ring check box.

4. Select or clear the Wake For Ethernet Network Administrator Access check box.

5. Select or clear the Allow Power Button To Sleep The Computer check box.

6. Select or clear the Restart Automatically After A Power Failure check box.

7. Click the Close button.

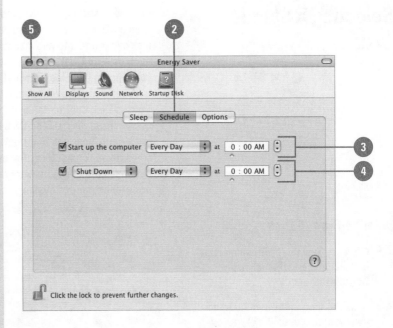

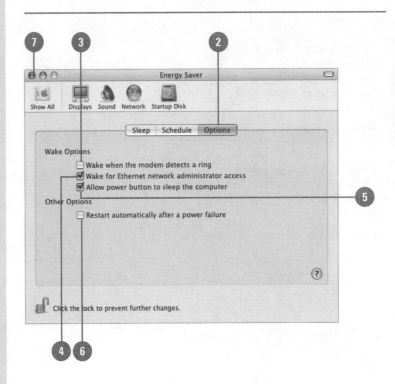

Selecting a Startup Disk

Instead of starting from your local hard disk, you can start your computer from a CD, a network volume, another disk or disk partition (a single hard disk separated into two distinct areas), or another operating system, such as Mac OS 9. Starting your computer with Mac OS 9 is useful when you want to use older applications that are not compatible with Mac OS X. When you start your computer in Mac OS 9, you need to use the Startup Disk Control Panel in the Apple menu to switch back to your Mac OS X startup disk. If Mac OS 9 is not available in the Startup Disk preference pane, your computer only starts in Mac OS X, which happens on some newer computers. However, you can still run most Mac OS 9 applications in the Classic environment, which you can start using the Classic preference pane in System Preferences.

Select a Startup Disk

1. Click the System Preferences icon in the Dock, and then click the Startup Disk icon.

2. Click the icon of the system folder you want to use as the startup disk.

3. Click Restart.

   TIMESAVER *Hold down the Option key while you restart your computer, select a startup disk, and then click Restart.*

See Also

See Appendix A, "Using the Classic Environment," on page 469 for information on starting your computer with Mac OS 9.

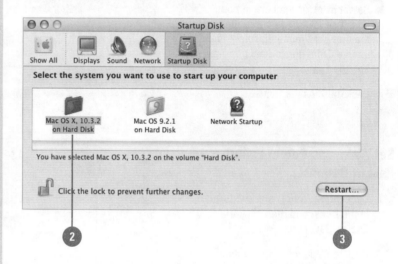

Changing the Way a CD or DVD Starts

When you insert a CD or DVD into your computer, Mac OS X automatically performs an operation, such as opening iTunes and playing an audio CD. You can change what happens when you insert a CD or DVD in the CDs & DVDs preference pane in System Preferences. You can have Mac OS X open a dialog to ask you what to do, ignore it, run a script, or open an application, such as iTunes, iPhoto, iDVD, or Finder, to burn or play a disc. If you ignore a CD or DVD, the disc doesn't show up on the desktop or in a Finder window.

Change CD or DVD Start Settings

1. Click the System Preferences icon in the Dock, and then click the CDs & DVDs icon.

2. Click the pop-ups for each type of CD or DVD, and then select a startup option:

   ◆ **Ask What To Do.** A dialog appears that asks you what to do with the disc.

   ◆ **Open an application.** Select Open Finder, Open *application name* or click Open An Application to select one.

   Mac OS X automatically opens the application you select.

   ◆ **Run Script.** Select and schedule a script to run.

   ◆ **Ignore.** Nothing happens.

3. Click the Close button.

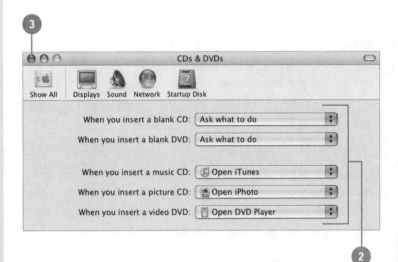

Did You Know?

You can change Finder preferences to show CDs or DVDs on the desktop. Click the Finder menu, click Preferences, click General, select the Removable Media check box, and then click the Close button.

Setting QuickTime Options

The QuickTime pane in System Preferences affects the way your Macintosh plays back movies from the Internet using the QuickTime plug-in or from your local drive using QuickTime player. You can change Plug-In options to automatically play streaming video over the Internet, Connection options to adjust your connection speed, and Update options to make sure you have the latest version of the QuickTime software. The QuickTime pane also provides a music option to select a music synthesizer for playing back MIDI files, but you only have one choice. The Media Keys options provide special passwords for unlocking movies so you can watch them, but this feature is rarely used.

Set Plug-In Streaming Options

① Click the System Preferences icon in the Dock, and then click the QuickTime icon.

② Click the Plug-In tab.

③ Select the Play Movies Automatically check box to start playing streaming movies as soon as they begin to download. (instead of waiting for the download to complete before starting.)

④ Select the Save Movies In Disk Cache check box if you plan to replay the same movie many times in the same session.

⑤ Click the Close button.

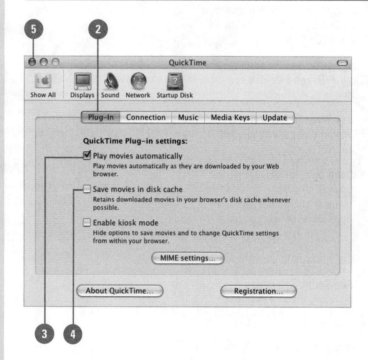

Set Connection Options

1. Click the System Preferences icon in the Dock, and then click the QuickTime icon.

2. Click the Connection tab.

3. Click the Connection Speed pop-up, and then select a connection speed that matches your Internet connection hardware.

   TROUBLE? *If you're not sure, check with your ISP.*

4. If available, select the Allow Multiple Simultaneous Streams check box to playback multiple streaming movies.

5. Click the Close button.

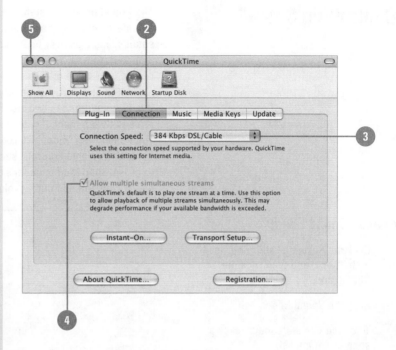

Set Update Options

1. Click the System Preferences icon in the Dock, and then click the QuickTime icon.

2. Click the Update tab.

3. Click an option to update or install QuickTime software or install new 3rd-party QuickTime software.

4. To update or install QuickTime software now, click Update Now.

5. Select the Check For Updates Automatically check box to get announcements when an update happens.

6. Click the Close button.

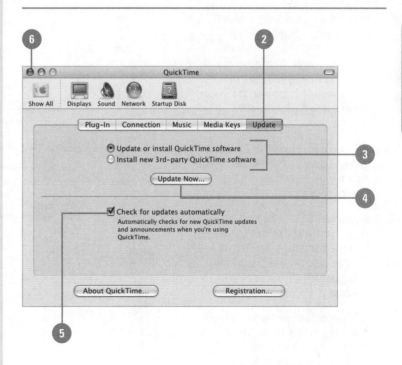

Controlling Sound

The Sound pane in System Preferences allows you to adjust input, output and alert volumes, change input and output sound devices, change alert sounds, and play user interface sound effects, such as when you drag an icon to the Trash. You can use an input device, such as a microphone, to record your voice or give spoken commands and an output device, such as built-in or external speakers, to play music, words, and other sounds. If your computer has two stereo speakers, you can adjust the sound balance between them. If you don't want to hear sound from your speakers, you can turn on Mute, just like on your TV or stereo. If you use applications with volume controls, such as iTunes, the volume can only be equal to or less than the computer's output volume. To make volume control easier, you can add output volume to the menu bar.

Change Sound Effects

1. Click the System Preferences icon in the Dock, and then click the Sound icon.

2. Click the Sound Effects tab.

3. To change an alert sound, click a sound from the list.

4. Drag the Alert Volume slider to adjust the alert volume, which is relative to the output volume.

   TIMESAVER *Hold down the Option key while you drag the main speaker volume on the status menu bar to adjust the alert volume.*

5. To play sounds when you perform certain actions in the Finder, select the Play User Interface Sound Effects check box.

6. If you have volume keys on your keyboard, clear the Play Feedback When Volume Keys Are Pressed check box to disable the feedback option, which allows you to use the keys to change the volume.

7. To change output volume from the menu bar, select the Show Volume In Menu Bar check box.

8. Click the Close button.

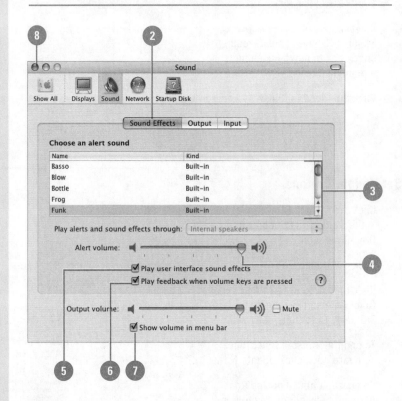

Volume on menu bar

Set Sound Output Options

① Click the System Preferences icon in the Dock, and then click the Sound icon.

② Click the Output tab.

③ Select a device for sound output.

Options vary depending on the output sound device.

④ Drag the Balance slider to adjust the sound for the left and right speakers.

⑤ Drag the Output Volume slider to increase or decrease the volume, or select the Mute check box to turn speaker sound off.

⑥ Click the Close button.

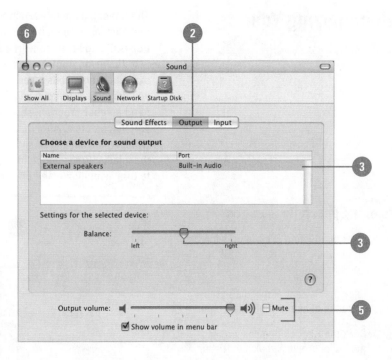

Set Sound Input Options

① Click the System Preferences icon in the Dock, and then click the Sound icon.

② Click the Input tab.

③ Select a device for sound input.

Options vary depending on the input sound device.

④ Drag the Input Volume slider to increase or decrease the volume.

The input level meter displays the sound level coming from the selected sound device.

⑤ Click the Close button.

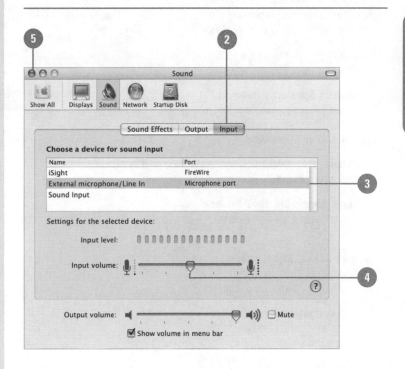

4

Recognizing Your Speech

The Speech pane (**New!**) in System Preferences allows you to initialize and customize speech recognition on your computer. **Speech recognition** is the ability to convert a spoken voice into commands or electronic text. However, Apple's speech recognition only does half the job; it only executes commands listed in the Speakable Commands window, which you can add or remove in groups, such as menu bar commands. You need another program, such as iListen (*www.macspeech.com*) to convert voice to text. After you turn on speech recognition, the Feedback window (a small circle microphone) appears, displaying the Esc key in the middle. Press and hold or press the Esc key, which you can change, to turn listening on and off. Now you can speak your commands.

Enable Speech Recognition

1. Click the System Preferences icon in the Dock, and then click the Speech icon.

2. Click the Speech Recognition tab, and then click the On/Off tab.

3. Click the Recognition pop-up, and then click Apple Speakable Items.

4. Click the On option to display the Feedback window. To remove the window later, click the Off option.

5. Click a button or select the options you want:

   ◆ **Turn On Speakable Items At Login.** Check to enable speech recognition when you start or log in to your computer.

   ◆ **Helpful Tips.** Click to display tips about speakable items.

   ◆ **Open Speakable Items Folder.** Click to open the Speakable Items folder.

   ◆ **Play Sound.** Select a sound to play when your computer recognizes a spoken command.

   ◆ **Speak Confirmation.** Check to have your computer repeat the command it heard.

6. Click the Close button.

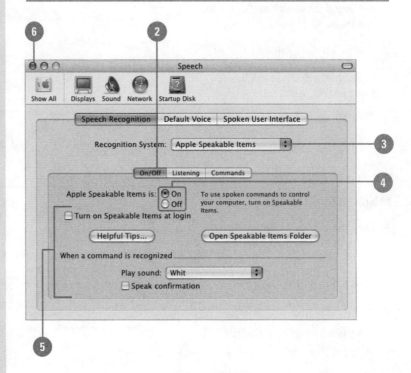

Select Listening Options and Commands

1. Click the System Preferences icon in the Dock, and then click the Speech icon.

2. Click the Speech Recognition tab, and then click the Listening tab.

3. To change the listening key, click Change Key, enter a new key, and then click OK.

4. Click an option to listen while the listening key is pressed or while listening is turned on (by pressing the listening key).

   If you select the second option, you can type a name and use the Name pop-up to specify whether the name must be spoken before each command.

5. Click the Commands tab.

6. Select or clear the check boxes with the groups of commands you want to enable or disable.

7. Click the Close button.

Use Speech Recognition

1. Hold down the listening key or press it to turn listening on.

2. To display a list of commands, click the Feedback window triangle, and then click Open Speech Commands Window.

3. Say the name if necessary, and then say a command.

   Recognized commands appear above the Feedback window, while feedback appears below.

4. Release or press the listening key to turn listening off.

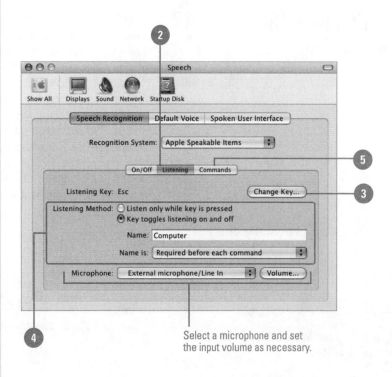

Select a microphone and set the input volume as necessary.

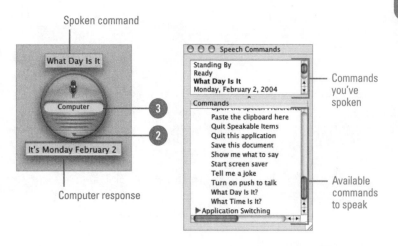

Spoken command

Computer response

Commands you've spoken

Available commands to speak

4

Letting Mac Do the Talking

Your Macintosh can speak to you as well as listen. Mac OS X can read aloud what appears on your screen, such as typed text, alert messages, window items, menus, and other interface items. It speaks using a synthesized voice (**New!**), such as Pipe Organ, Cellos, or Junior. Some voices, such as Pipe Organ, are based on a song and sing the voice. You can use the Speech pane in System Preferences to select a default voice, set talking alert options for when alerts appear on the screen, and other spoken options for the user interface. Instead of just showing you, the Mac can tell you when an application needs your attention, such as when your printer is out of paper, or read buttons, icons, tabs, dialog options, and selected text in e-mails and documents when you point to it as well as read select text when you press a keyboard shortcut.

Set the Default Speaking Voice

1. Click the System Preferences icon in the Dock, and then click the Speech icon.

2. Click the Default Voice tab.

3. Select one of the voices in the Voice list.

   The computer speaks so you can hear the voice, and a description of the voice appears on the right.

4. To change the speed at which the voice speaks, drag the Rate slider.

5. To hear the select speaking voice at the current rate, click Play.

6. Click the Close button.

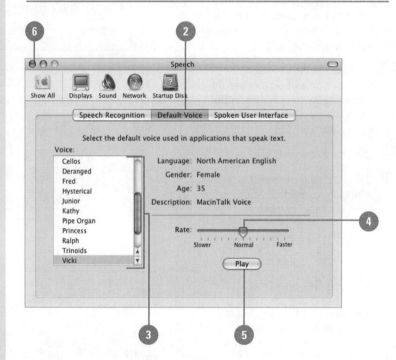

Set Spoken User Interface Options

1 Click the System Preferences icon in the Dock, and then click the Speech icon.

2 Click the Spoken User Interface tab.

3 Select the alert options you want:

◆ **Speak The Phrase.** Check to speak a certain phrase when an alert appears. Use the pop-up to select a phrase.

◆ **Speak The Alert Text.** Click to read the contents of an alert dialog. Use the pop-up to select an alert voice.

◆ **Wait Before Speaking.** Drag to set the delay between the alert and the computer speaking.

◆ **Demonstrate Settings.** Click to display a sample of the alert.

4 Select the other spoken items options you want:

◆ **Announce When An Application Requires Your Attention.** Check to verbally announce when an application needs your attention, such as your printer is out of paper.

◆ **Text Under The Mouse.** Check to read text that appears under your mouse pointer when you point to a menu, button, or other interface item.

◆ **Selected Text When The Key Is Pressed.** Check to read any text you select when you press a key combination. In the dialog, press a keyboard shortcut or stop speaking selected text, and then click OK.

5 Click the Close button.

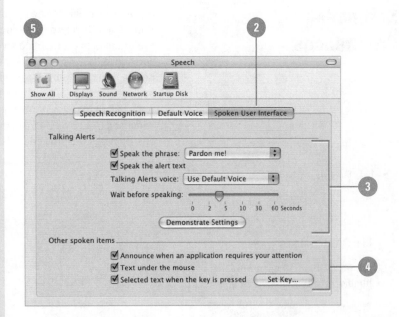

Setting Ink Preferences

If you have an ink device on your computer, you can use System Preferences to improve the recognition of ink to text. You can adjust Ink Preferences to your writing style, either widely or closely spaced, and to see how quickly your writing pen cursor changes back into a clicking device. You can improve recognition by adding words it may not know, such as names (like a custom dictionary for spell checking). As you write, Ink recognizes certain gestures or shapes, which get performed as commands, such as Undo, or pressed as keys, such as Delete or Space. The Gestures tab provides a list of gestures that you can turn on and off.

Set Ink Preferences

1. Click the Apple menu, and then click System Preferences.

2. Click the Ink icon.

3. Click the On or Off option to turn handwriting recognition on or off.

4. Click the Settings tab.

5. Specify the options you want:

   ◆ **My Handwriting Style Is.** Drag slider to set spacing.

   ◆ **Allow Me To Write Anywhere.** Check to use Anywhere mode.

   ◆ **Language.** Click to select a ink writing language.

   ◆ **Ink Pad Font.** Click to select a default recognition font.

   ◆ **Show Ink Window.** Check to use Ink Pad mode.

   ◆ **Show Ink In Menu Bar.** Check to add the Ink menu commands to the menu bar.

6. Click the Gestures tab.

7. Select or clear the check boxes to turn gesture actions on and off.

8. Click the Word List tab.

9. Use the buttons to add or change uncommon words you use.

10. Click the Close button.

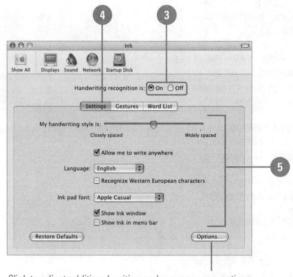

Click to adjust additional writing and mouse usage options.

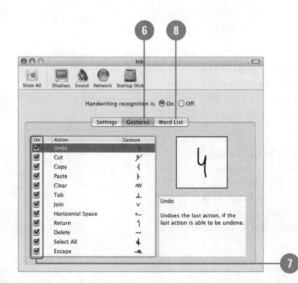

Using Mac OS X Applications

Introduction

Now that you know how to work with the graphical elements that make Mac OS X Panther work, you're ready to work with applications. An **application** is software you use to accomplish a specific task, such as word processing or managing files on your computer. Panther comes with several small applications and utilities that are extremely useful for completing basic tasks, such as creating a written document or performing basic calculations. Panther not only comes packaged with quite a few new applications, such as Font Book and iChat AV, it also has enhanced many of the old favorites such as: Address Book and Chess. Its suite of applications let you organize your workflow and create sticky notes. You can even edit and create digital media for use on the Internet, CD, or burn it onto a DVD. In addition, Panther makes setting up and communicating over the Internet easier than ever. And, if you happen to own an iSight (Macintosh Web camera), Panther helps you communicate with other iSight owners using audio and video.

If you deal with a lot of fonts, Panther comes packaged with a font management system second to none. And, if that's not enough to get you going, Panther comes equipped with AppleScript. **AppleScript** lets you write your own mini applications to help with repetitious tasks. Panther's applications are powerful tools for organization, gaming, controlling digital media, and Internet communication, just to name a few.

What You'll Do

Use Mac OS X Applications

Launch and Quit Applications

Switch Between Applications

Create and Edit an Address Book

Manage an Address Book

Add an Image to an Address Book

Play Chess

Perform Calculations and Conversions

Capture Images with a Digital Camera

Capture Screen Shots with Grab

Preview Images and PDF's

Play DVD and QuickTime Movies

Create Sticky Notes

Manage Fonts with Font Book

Activate, Deactivate, and Customize Fonts

Understand AppleScript Basics

Use Ready-Made AppleScripts

Write and Record AppleScripts

Using Mac OS X Applications

Mac OS X comes with several accessories, built-in applications that, while not as feature-rich as many applications sold separately, are extremely useful for completing basic tasks. A frequently used list of Mac OS X applications is provided here. However, you can view a complete list of installed applications in the Applications folder on your hard disk drive. The Applications folder also contains a Utilities folder with additional application tools you can use to perform specialized functions, which are detailed more in later chapters.

Frequently Used Mac OS X Applications	
Program	**Description**
Address Book	Stores names, addresses, and other contact information
AppleScript	Automates tasks using a programming language
Calculator	Performs arithmetic calculations
Character Map	Inserts special characters from installed fonts
DVD Player	Plays sound, music, and video
Font Book	Installs, previews, and manages fonts and font collections
iCal	Keeps track of calendar appointments
iChat	Sends and receives instant messages to online contacts
Image Capture	Transfers images from your camera to your computer
iMovie	Creates movies using audio and video files
iPhoto	Organizes and shares digital photo collections
iSync	Compares information on your computer and devices and updates them to be the same
iTunes	Plays digital sound files
Mail	Provides e-mail, newsgroup, and directory services
Preview	Views, rotates, resizes, crops, and converts image files (JPG, GIF, TIF, PSD, PICT, PNG, BMP, and SGI)
QuickTime Player	Plays media located on your computer, a CD, or Internet
Safari	Displays Web (HTML) pages
Stickies	Creates notes for reminders, lists, and messages
Sherlock	Finds information available from Web services
TextEdit	Creates, edits, and displays text, Rich Text Format, and Word documents

Launching Applications

All of the Macintosh OS X Panther applications are automatically loaded during the installation of the operating system, and appear on the hard drive within the Applications folder. When you open the hard drive, you'll have the choice of viewing the file as icons, as file names (with information), or as file names in columns. Regardless of what view you choose to launch a Mac application, simply locate the desired application in the open window, and then double-click the application to load.

Launch an Application

1 Double-click the hard drive icon on your desktop.

2 To change views, click a view button, such as View By Columns.

3 Click the Applications folder.

4 Scroll up and down to view the available applications by name.

5 Double-click on the application name, or application icon, to launch.

Did You Know?

You can quickly launch an application from the Dock. Point to the bottom of the desktop to display the Dock, and then click the application icon you want to launch. Unless the Finder places the application in the Dock by default, you need to add the application to it.

See Also

See "Customizing the Dock" on page 68 for more information on adding an application to the Dock.

See "Viewing Windows" on page 12 and "Managing Windows" on page 14 for more information on working with the view of a Macintosh window.

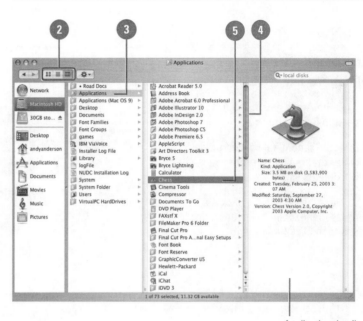

Application details are displayed.

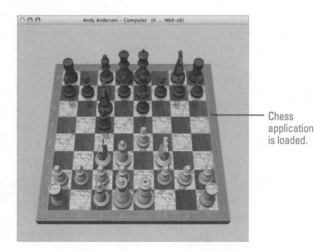

Chess application is loaded.

5

Opening Applications and Files

As you open applications and files, their names are kept in the Recent Items submenu in the Apple menu for easy access the next time you want to open a specific application or file. The Mac OS has always allowed you to double-click a document icon to launch the application used to create it and the document itself. If the Mac OS doesn't know what application created it (and gives you an error message), you can use drag and drop in the Dock to help you open the document. You can drag a document icon in the Dock on an application icon. If the application can possibly open it, the application icon becomes highlighted. Release the icon to open the application and the document.

Open Recently Used Applications and Files

1. Click the Apple menu, and then point to Recent Items.

2. Click the recent application or file under the Applications or Documents listing.

3. To clear the recent list, click the Apple menu, point to Recent Items, and then click Clear Menu.

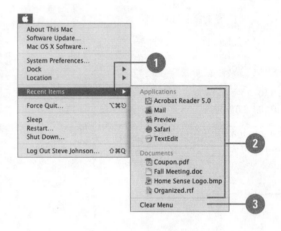

Open Applications and Files

◆ Double-click the document icon.

◆ Drag the document icon to the application icon in the Dock, either the one that created the document or one that will accept it.

   NOTE *Hold down Option+⌘ while you drag a document icon into the Dock to force all applications to accept the icon. However, an error message may result.*

See Also

See "Changing Appearance Options" on page 82 for information on changing the number of recent items.

Double-click to open.   Blank icon; no association.

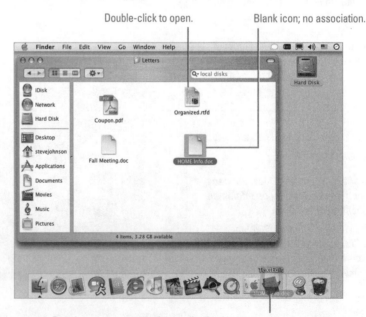

Drag icon onto an accepting application icon to open.

Quitting Applications

When you're done working with an application, you should exit, or close it, to conserve your computer's resources. If an application stops responding while you work, Mac OS X provides you with the option to end the task. When you end a task, you'll probably lose any unsaved work in the problem application. If the problem persists, you might need to reinstall the application or contact product support to fix the problem.

Quit an Application

1. Click the application menu.

   In this case, the Chess menu.

2. Click Quit *application name*.

   TIMESAVER *Press* ⌘+*Q to quit an application.*

3. If necessary, click Save to save your changes.

Quit an Application That is Not Responding

1. Click the Apple menu, and then click Force Quit.

   TIMESAVER *Press* ⌘+ *Option+Esc to force a quit.*

2. Click the application name you want to force a quit.

3. Click Force Quit.

4. Click Force Quit again to confirm you want to force a quit.

5. Click the Close button.

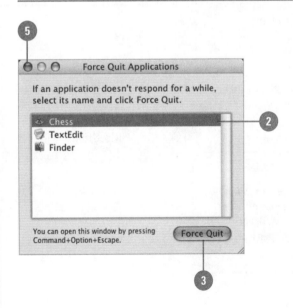

Switching Between Applications

The Dock is initially located at the bottom of the desktop and is most often used to launch an application or switch from one application to another. When you launch an application, it's icon appears in the Dock with a black arrow below it. If an application is not available in the Dock, you can hide any open applications to display the desktop, open your hard disk, and then launch the application you want. If you arrange open application windows so that they are visible, you can switch among them simply by clicking in the window in which you want to work.

Hide and Show an Application

1 Click the application menu.

In this case, the Chess menu.

2 Click Hide *application name* to hide the application.

TIMESAVER *Press ⌘+H to hide the application.*

3 Point to the bottom of the screen to display the Dock. You'll see the hidden application in the Dock.

4 To show the application, click the application icon in the Dock.

Hide Other Applications

1 Click the application menu, and then click Hide Others.

TIMESAVER *Press Option+ ⌘+H to hide all other applications.*

Did You Know?

You can bring forward an application and its windows and hide all other applications. Hold down Option+ ⌘, and then click the program icon in the Dock.

110

Switch Between Applications

Mac OS X provides several ways to switch between applications:

◆ Click a visible window in the other application.

◆ Display the Dock, and then click an application icon to show (black triangle below icon) or launch the application.

◆ Press and hold down ⌘, and then repeatedly press the Tab key to highlight the Dock icon of an open application (**New!**). (Use Shift+⌘+Tab to move backwards) Release both keys when you reach the one you want to open.

To leave without switching applications, press the Esc key.

TIMESAVER *Press ⌘+Tab once to open the application you used most recently. This is very useful when you are switching between two applications.*

◆ Press F11 (use Exposé) to hide all open windows, double-click the hard disk icon, open the Applications folder, and then double-click an application icon.

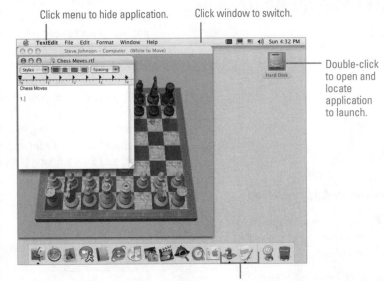

Click menu to hide application.   Click window to switch.

Double-click to open and locate application to launch.

Click icon in the Dock to switch.

Did You Know?

You can quickly switch between windows within an application (including the Finder). Repeatedly press ⌘+~ (the Tilde key to the left of the number 1 key) to cycle through open windows in the application. Release both the keys to display the window you want.

5

Creating an Address Book

When you work with Panther's enhanced Address Book, you have the ability to create cards of information. Each card can hold all the information you want to keep on a contact, no matter how many phone numbers and e-mail addresses a particular friend, or company might have. In addition, you can add a picture with a drag and a drop. Panther's new Address Book, comes packaged with a bunch of enhancements such as: label generation, change of address notification, synchronization with Microsoft Exchange servers, view iChat Buddy status, and even the ability to use speech recognition to look up and search the Address Book database (**New!**). Creating an Address Book involves launching Address Book, and then working through the simple setup procedures.

Create an Address Book

1. Open the Applications folder, and then double-click the Address Book icon.

2. Click the Add Group button (+) to add a group.

3. Give the new group a descriptive name, and then press Return.

4. Click the Add Name button (+) to add a new card.

5. Type a Name, and then using the Tab key, type a Company Name (if necessary).

Did You Know?

You can access the Address Book application in the Dock. Once you've opened the Address Book from the Applications folder, the icon is placed in the Dock.

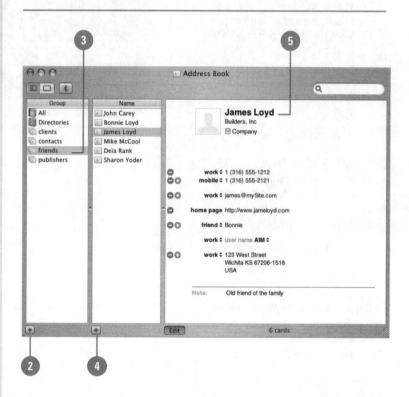

6　Click in the individual card fields to add information such as: Phone number, e-mail address, home address, Internet home page, and Instant Messaging user name (a .Mac or AIM screen name).

If you enter an IM or AIM user name, you can view iChat Buddy status while browsing contacts in the Address Book.

7　If necessary, click the Remove button (-), located to the left of some of the data fields to remove that field.

8　Click in the Note field to add specific text notes.

9　If necessary, click on the Field pop-up to change the field name.

10　Repeat steps 4 thru 9 to add additional address cards.

11　Quit Address Book.

Did You Know?

You can archive your Address Book data. If your Address Book data is important, you can back up the data in case of a catastrophic failure. Open the Address Book application, click the File menu, and then click Back Up Database. The file name comes with the date of the backup. All you have to do is select where you'd like to save the backup, and then click the Save button. To restore the data click the File menu, and then click Revert To Database Backup. Select the file with the correct date, and then click Open. A warning message appears informing you of the Revert operation. Click OK to revert back to your Database Backup file.

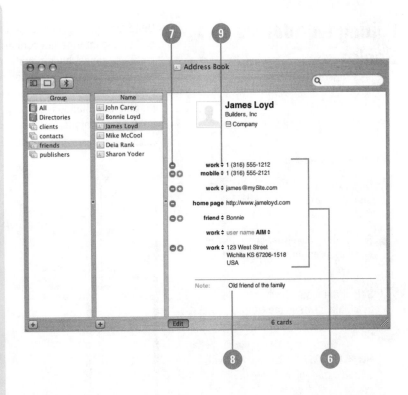

For Your Information

Importing Contacts into Address Book

Address Book creates and reads vCards, the standard method of exchanging data between applications. If you have vCards in another application, such as an e-mail application, you can import or export addresses with Address Book. To create a vCard, drag an address card out of the Address Book window. You can drag individual vCards in and out of the Address Book window. To import a set of vCards, click the File menu, point to Import, click vCards, select the file that contains the exported addresses, click Open, and then click OK (if you're updating contact information, click Review Duplicates (New!) to reconcile any conflicts). To see the last batch of addresses you added to Address Book, click Last Import in the Group column.

5

Editing an Address Book

Once a contact is placed within the Address Book, it's a simple matter to edit or add information concerning a contact. The Address Book automatically saves the information as you change it, so there's no need to stop and save your work. Editing or updating an Address Book contact involves the same skills learned in creating a contact, with the exception that the information is already there, so all you need to do is edit, add, or delete the contact.

Edit an Address Book

1 Open the Applications folder, and then double-click the Address Book icon.

2 Select the Group that contains the contact or contacts you want to modify.

3 Select the Name from the available cards in the Group.

4 Click Edit.

IMPORTANT *The Edit button is a toggle button, and once it's clicked, you'll be in edit mode for any selected name.*

Did You Know?

The Address Book application remembers your location. When you open the Address Book, it loads the Group that you had last used.

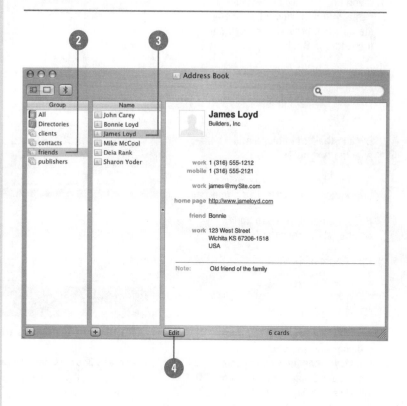

5. Click in any of the fields to edit the existing information.

6. Click the Remove button (-) to remove a specific data piece.

7. Click the Add button (+) to add an additional data piece.

8. To remove a contact from the list, select a contact in the Name column, press the Delete key, and then confirm your delete.

9. Quit Address Book.

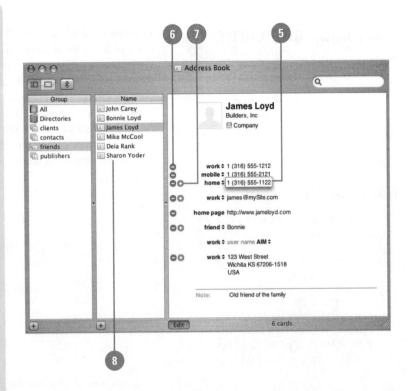

Did You Know?

You can undo mistakes in the Address Book. If you accidentally delete a contact, don't worry, just click the Edit menu, and then click Undo Delete Record. The Address Book comes equipped with multiple undos.

For Your Information

Printing from the Address Book

Address Book makes it easy to print a mailing list or print labels. The expanded Print dialog provides options to select a printing style and specify the specific fields from the Address Book you want to include in the printing (**New!**). To print a mailing list or labels from Address Book, click the File menu, click Print, select a printer from the pop-up, select Lists or Mailing Labels from the Style pop-up, select a paper size from the pop-up, select an orientation, select or clear the attributes (fields) to display the information you want (such as phone, e-mail, address, Instant Messenger, photo, job title, etc.), select a font size from the pop-up, specify the number of copies, preview the results in the left pane, and then click Print.

Managing an Address Book

Any address book, even Panther's, can quickly become a confusing mess of unorganized data. Unlike paper address books, Panther's can create a very organized system... if you know what to do. For example, you should create logical groups, and then use obvious naming conventions for each contact. You can name your groups by family, school, work, community service, kids sports teams just to name a few. Panther's Address Book has many features that helps you manage your groups and the contacts you create. You can even use the vCard format to exchange contact information between various programs (New!).

Manage an Address Book

1️⃣ Click the Address Book menu, and then click Preferences.

2️⃣ Click General to organize the viewable screen.

3️⃣ Make any of the following changes: Display Order, Sort By, Address Format, Font Size, Notify People When My Card Changes, and Synchronize With Exchange (New!).

4️⃣ Click Template to organize the card data screen.

5️⃣ Make any of the following changes:

- ◆ Work, Mobile phone numbers
- ◆ Email and Homepage information
- ◆ Names
- ◆ Work address

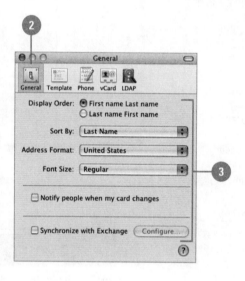

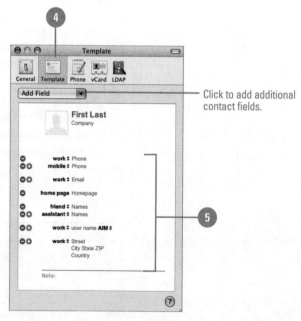

Click to add additional contact fields.

Did You Know?

You can let the Address Book read a contact to you. (New!) Control-click your mouse in the contact window, point to Speech, and then click Start Speaking. To end the audio, Control-click, point to Speech, and then click Stop Speaking.

6　Click Phone to set the format for the phone number entry.

7　Click the Formats pop-up, and then select a format for your phone numbers.

8　Click vCard to set the preferences for vcards.

9　Make any of the following changes:

   ◆ vCard Format

   ◆ Enable Private 'Me' Card

   ◆ Export Notes in vCards

10　Click LDAP to set up directory connections to automatically search for information on network directory servers.

11　Select an LDAP connection.

12　Quit Address Book.

Did You Know?

You can move contacts in your Address Book. Open the group, and then drag the contact from the open group to the new group.

You can exchange contacts in your Address Book with other Mac users. Select a contact, click the File menu, and then click Export vCard.

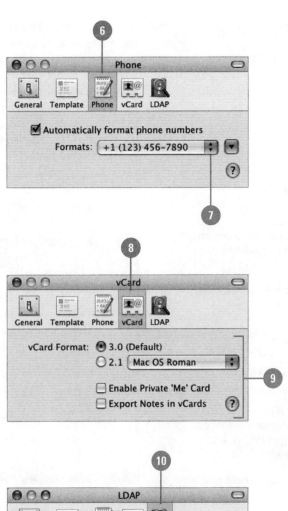

Add LDAP connection

Adding an Image to an Address Book

It's not unusual for an address book to grow quite large. Over time, you'll add more and more addresses and occasionally delete old ones, until you have dozens even hundreds of contacts listed in your address book. Sometimes, identification requires more than just a name or an address, so Apple gives you the ability to add an image to a contact. Maybe it's to help associate a face with a name, or just be reminded (visually) of a special someone—whatever the reason, adding an image is as simple as opening the file containing the image, and dragging it into the photo box for the selected contact.

Add an Image to an Address Book

1. Open the Applications folder, and then double-click the Address Book icon.

2. Select the Group which contains the contact.

3. Select the Name of the contact that you want to add the image to.

4. Drag the image into the active contact.

   Address Book opens an image placement dialog which lets you resize the image to fit in the allocated space.

5. Drag the slider left or right to resize the image.

6. Click Set to add the image to the contact.

7. Quit Address Book.

Did You Know?

You can add instant pictures to an address contact. Double-click the photo box, and then click the Take Video Snapshot button. If you have a Web cam attached to your computer, you can then take an instant snapshot based on anything the camera sees.

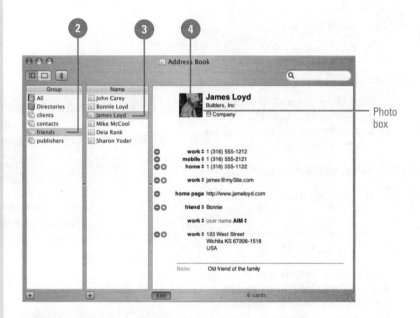

Photo box

Click to use your Web cam.

Playing Chess

CHECKMATE, oh how I love to hear those words, or at least when I'm the one saying them. Computers aren't just for business proposals, worksheets, and documents. We all know that there are thousands of games available for computer systems, but one of the most challenging games in the world is available as soon as you load Panther. Chess is available in the Applications folder and ready for you to play on your own screen. Panther has beefed up the program, giving you more options, and even making it quite a challenge to those who have moved beyond the beginner stage.

Play Chess

1. Open the Applications folder, and then double-click the Chess icon.

2. Click and drag a piece. For example, the white King's pawn at E2 to E4.

3. Black responds with a move.

4. Click the Moves menu, and then click Take Back Move, Show Hint, or Show Last Move.

5. Click the Chess menu, and then click Preferences. Select from the following options:

   ◆ Click the Board pop-up to select a new playing surface.

   ◆ Click the Pieces pop-up to select different playing pieces.

   ◆ Select the Speech check boxes to use voice recognition software to call your moves.

   ◆ Drag the Computer Plays slider to increase or decrease the computer's playing skills.

   ◆ Select the Show Move In Title check box to display the current move in the Title bar.

6. Click the Close button.

7. Click the Game menu, and then select a game option, such as New Game or Save Game.

8. Quit Chess.

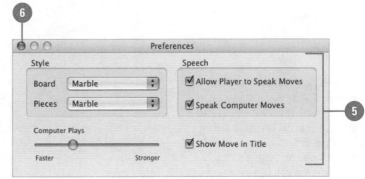

Performing Calculations and Conversions

Panther comes with a great tool to help you perform common calculations and to do complex conversions (New!). The Calculator application has been around for a long time, however, Panther gave it a new interface, and a few powerful features, that just might make you want to reacquaint yourself with an old friend. If you're like most people, you probably have a dozen calculators laying about your home and office. If you're tired of all the mess, then take a look at Panther's idea of a calculator. Not only does it help you add 2 + 2; it helps you convert miles into kilometers or the Euro dollar into American currency. The Calculator application gives you the ability to perform conversions on everything from currency to volume, from temperature to speed, and more.

Work with the Calculator

1. Open the Applications folder, and then double-click the Calculator icon.

2. Click the buttons on the calculator to perform standard calculations.

3. Click the View menu, and then click Show Paper Tape, to display a Paper Tape dialog, which shows all of your calculations.

4. Click Clear to clear the tape, or click Recalculate Totals to have the calculator refigure the total.

5. Click the File menu, and then click Print Tape to have a paper copy of your calculations.

6. Click the View menu, and then click Advanced to have access to a scientific calculator.

7. Quit Calculator.

Did You Know?

You can use the keyboard with the Calculator. If you have a 10-keypad, instead of trying to click the calculator buttons, just use the keypad. Panther instructs the Calculator application to read the keypad objects, and display the results in the calculation window.

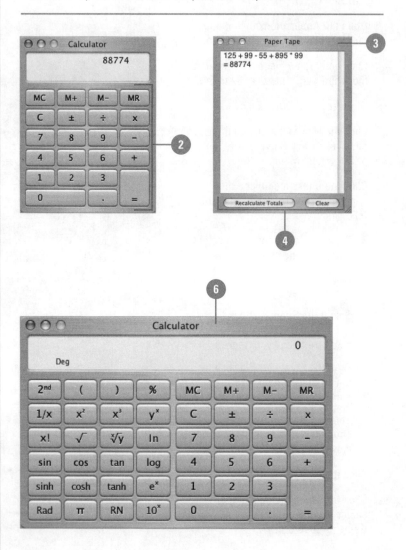

Work with Conversions

1. Open the Applications folder, and then double-click the Calculator icon.

2. Enter a value into the calculation window.

3. Click the Convert menu, and then click Currency. If you need to change the convert type, click the Convert pop-up and make your change.

4. Click the From and To pop-ups to select currency countries.

5. Click Update Currency Rates to access the latest exchange rate (requires an Internet connection).

6. Click OK.

    The conversion results display in the calculation window.

7. Quit Calculator.

Did You Know?

You can save calculation results in memory. Click the M+ (memory add) button to save a calculation result or to add a calculation result to the value residing in memory. At any time during the calculation, if you want to use that result, click the MR (Memory Recall) button and the number reappears. In addition, you can use the M- (memory subtract) to subtract a displayed result from the value in memory, or the MC (memory clear) button to clear out the memory.

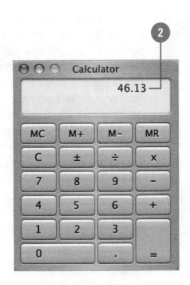

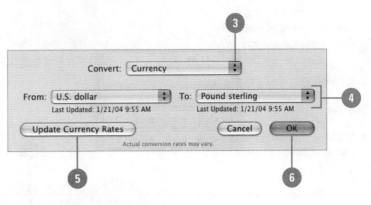

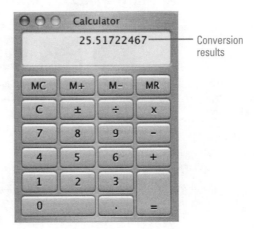

Conversion results

5

Capturing Images with a Digital Camera

Panther has provided you a way to directly access your digital camera and organize your images. Just plug in your digital camera or scanner directly, and import your pictures from any application that supports Services and Rich Text Format (most digital cameras and scanners). The Image Capture application lets you download all or selected contents from your digital camera, crop images to a variety of sizes, and even delete unwanted pictures from your camera. You can even use Image Capture to build a Web page, complete with individual thumbnails of your photos. Just click Build Web Page from the Automatic Task pop-up on the toolbar. Image Capture automatically generates the Web page and stores the images in the Pictures folder on your hard drive (**New!**).

Capture Images with a Digital Camera

1. Plug a digital device into your computer.

2. If necessary, open the Applications folder, and then double-click the Image Capture icon.

3. Click the Download To pop-up, and then select where to store the images.

4. Click the Automatic Task pop-up, and then select from the tasks.

5. Click Options, select from the available options, and then click OK.

6. Click Download All to move all the images from the digital device to the folder on your hard drive.

7. Click Download Some, and then select the images (hold down ⌘ to select more than one).

8. Click Rotate Left, Rotate Right, or Delete buttons to adjust or delete.

9. Click Download.

10. Quit Image Capture.

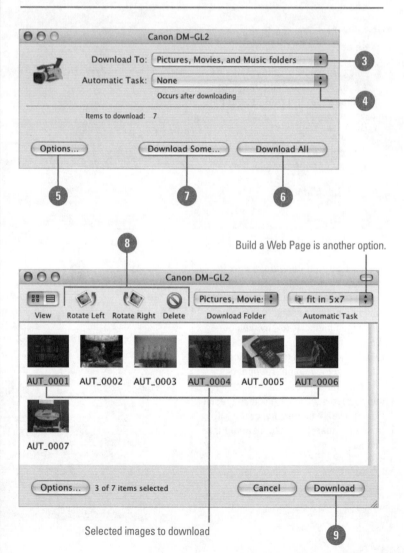

Build a Web Page is another option.

Selected images to download

122

Capturing Screen Shots with Grab

If there is something on your computer screen, such as an error dialog, window, or desktop, that you want to capture as a picture to show someone, you can use a built-in utility called Grab to get the job done. Grab is useful for taking pictures of different parts of the screen, like the ones in this book. This may not be a tool you'll use everyday (unless you are a computer trainer or book author), but it may come in handy one day.

Capture Screen Shots with Grab

1. Display the screen you want to capture.

2. Open the Applications folder, double-click the Utilities folder, and then double-click the Grab icon.

3. Click the Capture menu, and then select the command with the method you want to use:

   ◆ **Selection.** Drag to select a capture area.

   ◆ **Window.** Click the Choose Window button, and then click a window.

   ◆ **Screen.** Click a screen.

   ◆ **Timed Screen.** Click the Start Timer button, display a screen, and then wait 10 seconds.

4. Click the File menu, and then click Save As.

5. Select the drive and folder in which you want to save the file.

6. Type a name for the file, and then click Save.

7. Quit Grab.

Did You Know?

You can show a pointer in a screen capture. Click the Grab menu, click Preferences, click a pointer type or the blank one for no pointer, and then click the Close button.

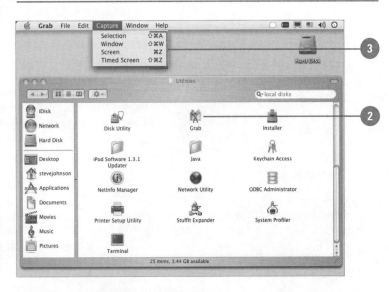

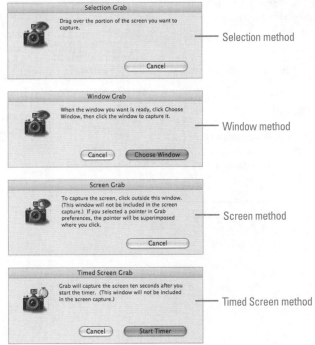

Selection method

Window method

Screen method

Timed Screen method

5

Previewing Images and PDF's

Need a quick way to view images, or possibly a Portable Document File (PDF)? No problem, Panther's built-in PDF viewer, Preview, lets you quickly view graphics and PDF files with the click of a button. In fact, once you've opened a PDF document file, Preview lets you perform an indexed search, select text and copy it to the clipboard, even view FAX documents using its built-in FAX support (New!). In addition, if you open an EPS (Encapsulated PostScript) or a PostScript file, Preview converts the file into the PDF format. The Preview application works to open any images or documents which are not identified by another program. For example, double-clicking on a Photoshop document file (.psd) would open the image in Photoshop. However, if you double-click on a graphic file from your digital camera, chances are it would open in the Preview application. And the same would be true of a PDF document, if you owned Adobe Acrobat, or the Acrobat Reader application. If you want to open one or more images in the Preview application regardless of file type, then you must open them using the Preview File Open command.

Preview Images and PDF's

1. Open the Applications folder, and then double-click the Preview icon.

2. Click the File menu, and then click Open.

3. Select one or more files to open from the available images or documents.

4. Click Open.

Did You Know?

The Preview application gives you the ability to move an image directly to the printer. Select the image, click the File menu, and then click Print.

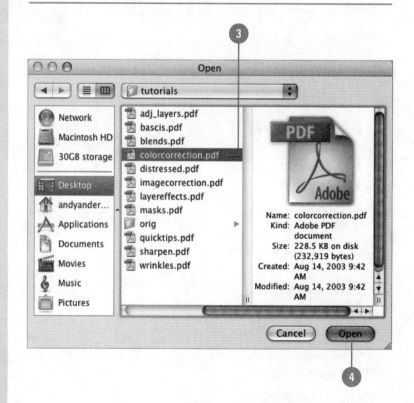

124

5. Click the Drawer button to expand or collapse the thumbnail page view of the images.

6. To move between pages in a PDF document, click the Back or Forward buttons.

7. To move directly to a specific page within a PDF document, type a page number, and then press Return.

8. To move up or down through the list of displayable images, click the Page Up or Page Down buttons.

9. To increase or decrease the viewing size of the image, click the Zoom In or Zoom Out buttons.

   The Zoom function does not impact the printing size of the image.

10. To select a portion of the image click to choose a Selection tool button, and then drag within the image.

11. To copy the selected area to the clipboard, click the Edit menu, and then click Copy.

12. Quit Preview.

Did You Know?

You can open multiple file types in Preview. Select the items you want to open regardless of the type, and they'll open in the Preview application.

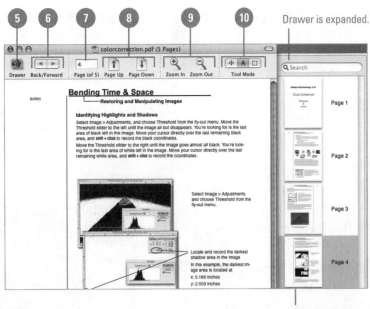

Drawer is expanded.

Thumbnail view of PDF.

For Your Information

Using PDFs

The PDF (Portable Document File) format is the way to save and move documents between computers and operating systems. Do you need to send a document to several people, and you're not sure if they're using a Macintosh or Windows machine? Do you want the document to be viewed exactly as you created it? Then the PDF format is the way to go. Adobe's Portable Document File has literally swept the computer industry (Mac, Windows, and UNIX); allowing you to combine text and graphics into a format that can be viewed by literally anyone who has the Preview application (on Macintosh), or the Adobe Acrobat Reader application (available free from *www.adobe.com*). As a matter of fact, the Acrobat Reader is shipped with every computer, regardless of model or operating system.

5

Playing DVD Movies

Okay, it's time to break out the popcorn and soda, because the new and improved DVD player in Panther is here. Using the DVD player, you can access a movie chapter by chapter, freeze the action, move forward and backward through the movie, and even play a movie in slow motion frame-by-frame. You can even watch your video in full screen mode while you work on another display. In addition, the new Panther DVD Player offers close captioning (**New!**). All that translates into a great viewing experience—sounds like a winner to me.

Play DVD Movies

1. Insert a DVD into the DVD drive of your computer.

2. The DVD player automatically loads the movie.

3. Select from the following Movie Player options:

   ◆ Click the Left, Right, Up, Down, or Return buttons to navigate.

   ◆ Click the Previous or Next Chapter buttons to move between movie chapters.

   ◆ Click the Play/Pause or the Stop button to play/pause or stop the movie.

   ◆ Click the Eject button to stop the movie and eject the DVD.

   ◆ Click the Title or Menu buttons to view the movie title or menu.

   ◆ Drag the volume control to raise or lower the volume.

   ◆ Open the Options panel, and then select between Slow Motion, Step Frame, Return, Sub Title, Audio, or Angle.

4. At the top of the window, click the Video menu, and then select between the various viewing options.

5. To exit the movie without using the controller, press ⌘+Q.

Movie Player

Navigate

Volume Control

Slow Motion   Step Frame

Sub Title

Options panel

Audio

Previous; Hold to Fast Rewind

Play & Pause

Stop

Next; Hold to Fast Forward

Return   Angle

Playing QuickTime Movies

QuickTime 6 now features 3GPP, which is considered the standard for creating, delivering, and playing multimedia over high-speed wireless networks. Apple is the first to offer this feature, and it allows users all over the world to share 3GPP content with others via both computers and mobile devices. Besides fully supporting the 3GPP, QuickTime works with the MPEG4 format, giving you access to movie clips and high quality images. In addition, QuickTime delivers several performance enhancements, including DV encoding and decoding improvements, providing greater efficiency throughout the DV workflow for users of Final Cut Pro, iMovie, and other QuickTime-based applications. And if it's file support you're after, the latest version of QuickTime supports: MIME type handling, improved automatic detection of streaming transport, direct playback of .amr, .sdv, Flash 5, DVC Pro PAL, JPEG 2000, Applescript, and more than 100 other media types such as DV, MP3, and JPEG.

Play QuickTime Movies

1. Open the Applications folder, and then double-click the QuickTime Player icon.

2. If you're connected to the Internet, the QuickTime window displays an advertisement.

3. Click the movie controls to Play, Pause, Rewind, and Stop the movie.

4. Click the QuickTime button to gain access to other QuickTime options.

5. Click the File menu, and then click Open to load individual QuickTime (or other formatted) movies or URLs.

6. Click the Movie menu, and then select from the available options.

7. Quit QuickTime Player.

Did You Know?

You can export movie files into different formats, as well as work with various compression settings for audio and video, when you upgrade to ***QuickTime Pro.*** *Click the QuickTime Player menu, point to Preferences, and then click Registration.*

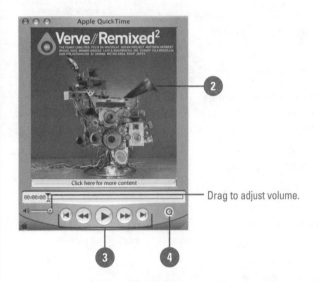

Drag to adjust volume.

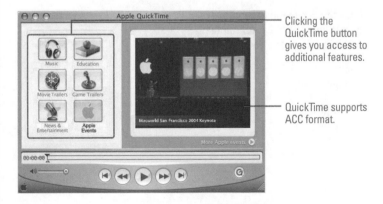

Clicking the QuickTime button gives you access to additional features.

QuickTime supports ACC format.

5

Creating Sticky Notes

The Sticky Notes application is not new to Panther, however it does give you the ability to tack notes onto your desktop; where they stay until removed. Just think, no longer do you need to worry about the sticky note on your monitor losing it's "stick" and falling off. With Panther, you can use your desktop the way Apple intended—to help with everyday life. Once you create a sticky note, you can change the color of the note, change the color and size of the text, or even have your sticky note talk to you by turning on the speech mode through the Edit menu.

Create Sticky Notes

1 Open the Applications folder, and then double-click the Stickies icon.

When you first open the Stickies application, you'll see 3 pre-written stickies notes.

2 Click the File menu, and then click New Note.

3 Type the text into the note area.

4 To increase or decrease the note size, drag the lower-right corner of the sticky note.

5 Click the Font menu, and then select from the font options.

6 Click the Note menu, and then select between Floating Windows or Translucent Windows.

7 To change the color of the selected note, click the Color menu and make your change.

8 Click the File menu to import or export notes, archive your notes, and to print or save your notes.

9 Click the Close button to quit without saving.

10 Quit Stickies.

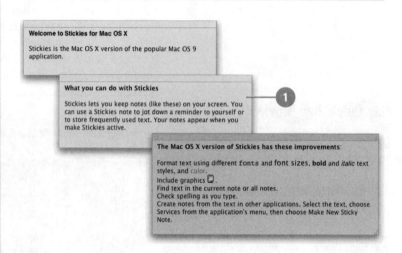

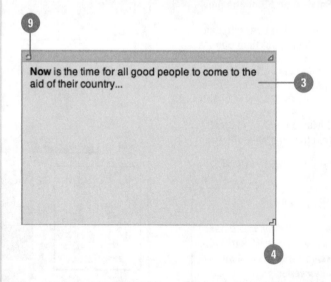

Managing Fonts with Font Book

Most of us have fonts…a whole lot of fonts and Panther adds to it. There are a lot of font management programs floating around, but Panther's Font Book application (**New!**), not only meets the needs of the most demanding font aficionado, but also comes packed with great features. For example, you can organize your fonts into specific user-defined folders, and then activate those folders, or specific fonts within the folder without having to restart your application. In addition, Font Book gives you a window to view the font, and change its viewing size on the fly.

Manage Fonts with Font Book

1. Open the Applications folder, and then double-click the Font Book icon.

2. Click the File menu, and then click New Collection.

3. Click the File menu, and then click Add Fonts.

4. Select the fonts you want to add to the New Collection (active folder), and then select:

   ◆ For Me Only

   ◆ For All Users Of This Computer

   ◆ For Classic Mac OS

5. Click Open.

6. Select a collection from the Collection column, and then click on a font to view a sample.

7. To increase or decrease the view of the font in the window, drag the view slider up or down.

8. To copy a font, click and drag a font from the Font window into another Collection.

9. If necessary, type search criteria to locate specific fonts.

10. To remove a font from a Collection (this does not delete the file from the hard drive), select a font and then press the Delete key.

11. Quit Font Book.

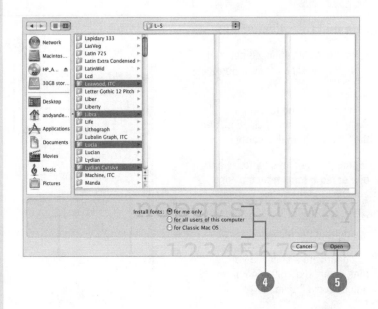

Activating, Deactivating, and Customizing Fonts

Once you've created a series of font collections, it'll be necessary to instruct the Font Book application (**New!**) as to what fonts you want to use, and what fonts you want to turn off. It's important to understand that fonts consume memory on your computer. For example, if you have hundreds of fonts active (and that's not unusual), it takes more RAM memory to maintain those fonts; even if you're not using them. That's where font management comes into play. Using Font Book, you can decide what fonts you need, and what fonts can be retired, or disabled, for the remainder of the work session.

Activate and Deactivate Fonts

1 Open the Applications folder, and then double-click the Font Book icon.

2 To activate all the fonts in the Collection, select a Collection, and then click the Enable button.

3 To activate selected fonts, select one of more fonts from the Font column, and then click Enable.

If a font is disabled, it says Off to the right of the font.

4 To deactivate a collection or a font, select the collection or font, and then click Disable.

IMPORTANT *The Enable button is a toggle, when a font is active, it displays the word Disable, and when a font is disabled it displays the word Enable.*

5 Quit Font Book.

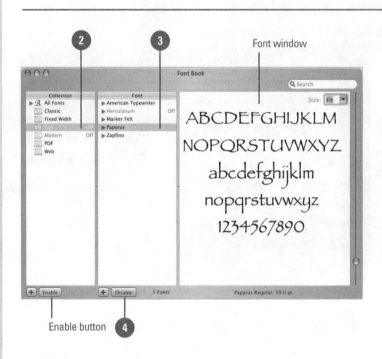

Font window

Enable button

Did You Know?

You can access more fonts from the Internet. Open your browser search engine and type **Free TrueType Fonts** to access all kinds of free fonts.

Customize Fonts

1. Open the Applications folder, and then double-click the Font Book icon.

2. Select the font you want to customize.

3. Click the Preview menu, and then click Custom.

4. Control-click your mouse in the font window, point to Font, and then select from the following customizing options:

   ◆ **Show Fonts.** Lets you adjust the font; including color, size and drop shadow.

   ◆ **Bold.** Changes the font into bold.

   ◆ **Italic.** Changes the font into italic.

   ◆ **Underline.** Adds an underline to the font.

   ◆ **Outline.** Converts the font to outline.

   ◆ **Styles.** Lets you create and manage groups of fonts using styles.

   ◆ **Show Colors.** Lets you change the color of the selected font.

5. Make any changes to the font, and then close any open dialogs.

6. Quit Font Book.

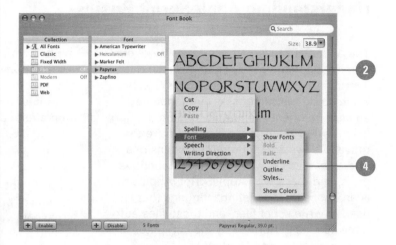

Text Strikethrough
Text color
Underline
Document color; opens Show Colors dialog

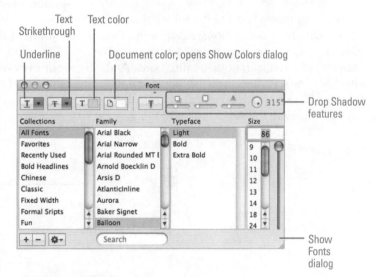

Drop Shadow features

Show Fonts dialog

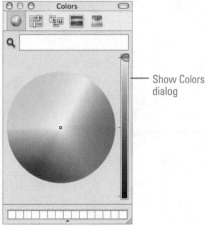

Show Colors dialog

Understanding AppleScript Basics

The AppleScript language is your way of communicating with your operating system; instructing it to perform specific tasks. Who wants to do the same tasks over and over again... no one. For example, adding the .jpg extension to 150 graphic files that have to move to a system that requires extensions. There is an easier way to perform repetitive tasks, and that's with AppleScript. **AppleScript** is an English-like scripting language that is used to write script files, and those files automate actions performed by the computer (like adding an extension 150 times).

ActionScripting is more than a language that repeats recorded actions; AppleScript can make decisions based on user-interaction or by analyzing data, documents, or situations. And with Mac OS X Panther and the AppleScript Studio, you can create powerful Mac OS X applications with the Aqua look-and-feel

written entirely in AppleScript. AppleScript is an automation language that helps us get thought the mundane tasks of working on a computer and that's more than worth the time and effort spent in learning AppleScript.

AppleScript provides shortcuts for complex tasks such as naming files, resetting preferences, or connecting to the Internet, and the AppleScript Studio comes bundled with dozens of pre-written scripts that can immediately help you with your daily computer tasks. In addition, the automated workflow gives consistency, and speed to any Macintosh project. Since more can be accomplished in the same amount of time, you become more efficient— all through the power of AppleScript. To create your own AppleScripts, open the AppleScript editor, and type the script using precise language limitations.

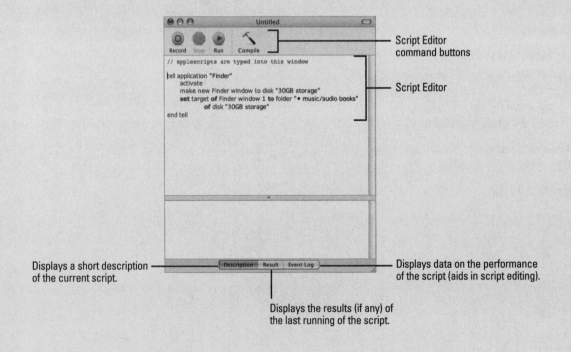

Displays a short description of the current script.

Script Editor command buttons

Script Editor

Displays data on the performance of the script (aids in script editing).

Displays the results (if any) of the last running of the script.

Using Ready-Made AppleScripts

You can use AppleScript right away, by working with AppleScripts created by the friendly folks at Apple. To gain access to the ready-made scripts, open the Applications folder, select the AppleScript folder, and then select Example Scripts, or do it the easy way by activating the built-in Script menu. When you activate the Script menu, the Script icon appears on the right side of the menu bar and is available whenever you open an application. For example, you could click the Scripts icon, point to Printing Scripts, and then click Convert To PDF.

Use Ready-Made AppleScripts

1 Open the Applications folder, double-click the AppleScript folder, and then double-click the Install Script Menu icon.

2 Open an application such as Microsoft Word or Adobe Photoshop.

3 Click the Scripts icon.

4 Point to a script category.

5 Select a script option.

6 Quit the application.

7 To remove the Scripts icon, double-click the Remove Script Menu icon in the AppleScript folder.

8 Click the Close button.

Did You Know?

You can remove the AppleScript menu from the Mac desktop menu. Open the Applications folder, point to the AppleScript folder, and then double-click the Remove Script Menu application.

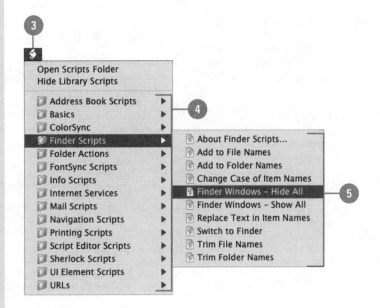

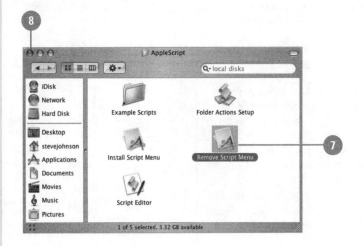

Writing and Recording AppleScripts

Anyone can write AppleScripts. All it requires is the Script Editor application available with Panther, and knowledge of the AppleScript language. The AppleScript editor lets you type script directly into the editor window, or you can click the Record button, and then perform some Mac operation, as the editor records each step as you work. There are many places where you can go to increase your AppleScript understanding; however, point your browser to *http://www.apple.com/applescript/,* and then click the Resources link to access current resources dealing the creative techniques for AppleScript.

Write and Record AppleScripts

1. Open the Applications folder, point to the AppleScript folder, and then double-click the Script Editor icon.

2. Type the Script directly into the Script Editor window.

3. Click the Record button to record within the active script.

4. Click the Run button to run the active script.

5. Click the Stop button to stop the running of the active script.

6. Click the Compile button to create a version of the active script.

7. Click the File menu, and then click Save, or Save As to save the script using a unique name and location.

Did You Know?

You can create AppleScript beyond the capabilities of the Script Editor Application. The AppleScript Studio is a solution for creating total applications, using the aqua interface and all the other elements associated with the Macintosh operating system. Point your browser to *http://www.apple.com/applescript/,* and then click the AppleScript Studio link for more information.

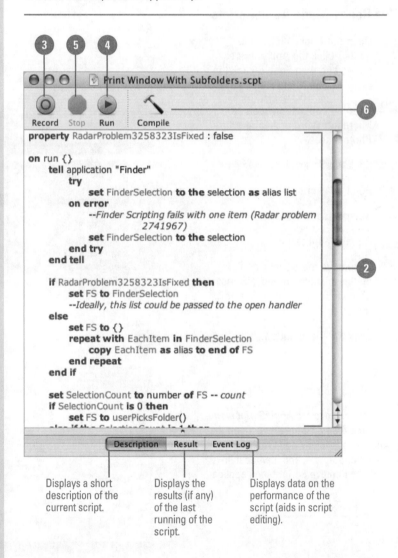

Displays a short description of the current script.

Displays the results (if any) of the last running of the script.

Displays data on the performance of the script (aids in script editing).

Working with Documents

Introduction

Mac OS X Panther comes with a word processing application, called TextEdit, you can use to create basic documents. TextEdit is designed especially for working with text, so it's a snap to create and edit letters, or any other word-based communication. TextEdit contains all the tools and features you need to produce interesting documents that say exactly what you mean, and have the look to match.

TextEdit is a versatile word-processing application. You can use TextEdit to view, create, and edit documents containing multilingual text, graphics, movies, and other document files. If you are working with HTML code (document as they appear in a Web browser), TextEdit makes the perfect editor. If you have speakers connected to your Macintosh, you can hear documents read aloud by your computer. When you're done working with a document, you can save it in multiple formats, such as plain text, Rich Text Format (RTF), and Microsoft Word.

Tools, such as the Spelling Checker, help you present your thoughts accurately, clearly, and effectively. When your text is complete, you can quickly add formatting elements, such as bold type and special fonts, to make your documents look professional. Each document contains styles that have common design elements, such as coordinated fonts, sizes, and colors, as well as, page layout designs. Apply the existing styles for headings, titles, body text, and so forth. Then modify the template's styles, or create your own to better suit your needs. Make sure you get the look you want by adding emphasis using italics, boldface, and underline, changing text alignment, adjusting line and paragraph spacing, setting tabs and indents, and creating bulleted or numbered lists. When you're done, your document is sure to demand attention and convey your message in its appearance.

What You'll Do

Create and Open a Document

Edit Text

Recognize Handwriting Ink

Make Corrections

Change Text Wrap

Check Spelling

Find and Replace Text

Format Text

Display Rulers

Set Paragraph Tabs and Indents

Change Character Spacing

Change Line Spacing

Apply and Create a Style

Insert Special Characters

Add Pictures, Movies, or Files to a Document

Save and Close a Document

Set TextEdit Preferences

Creating and Opening a Document

A **document** is a file you create using a word processing program, such as a letter, memo, or resume. When you start TextEdit, a blank document appears in the work area, known as the document window. You can type information to create a new document and save the result in a file, or you can open an existing file (using the Sidebar and List or Column view (New!)) in various formats, and save the document with changes. You can also add pictures, movies, and files in your documents.

Create a Document

1. Open the Applications folder, and then double-click the TextEdit application.

    If TextEdit is already open, click the File menu, and then click New.

2. To change the file format, click the Format menu, and then click Make Plain Text or Make Rich Text.

3. Type your text.

4. Press Return when you want to start a new paragraph.

5. When you're done, save and close the document.

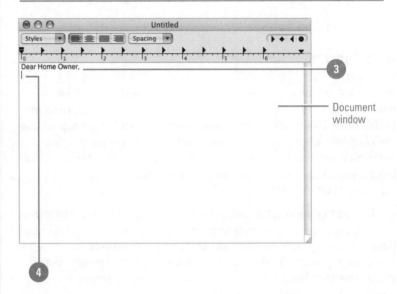

Document window

See Also

See "Saving and Closing a Document" on page 158 for information on saving a document.

See "Setting Up Page Options" on page 168 for information on selecting paper size, orientation, and printer scaling and format.

Did You Know?

You can set the file format for all new documents. Click the TextEdit menu, click Preferences, click the Plain Text or Rich Text option, and then click the Close button.

For Your Information

Understanding Document Formats

You can open and edit plain text, HTML (HyperText Markup Language, which displays Web pages in a browser), Rich Text Format (RTF), Rich Text Format Directory (RTFD), and Microsoft Word files in TextEdit. However, you can only save files in the plain text, RTF, and Word format. Plain text files use the file extension **.txt**, RTF files use **.rtf**, and Word files use **.doc** (New!). If you add graphics to an RTF file, the file extension changes to **.rtfd**. The RTF and Word formats can include formatting, pictures, and other embedded files, while the plain text format can only include nonformatted text. In a plain text document, you cannot change preset tabs and font styles and colors are not saved. Since Microsoft Word is a full featured word processing application, not all Word features, such as tables, are supported in TextEdit.

Open an Existing Document from Within an Application

1. Click the File menu, and then click Open.

2. Select the hard drive and the folder in which you want to open the file.

   TIMESAVER *Click the Where pop-up to select from a list of recent places you already visited.*

3. Click the document you want to open.

4. If the document contains one or more languages, click the Plain Text Encoding pop-up, and then select Unicode (for multiple languages) or a specific language.

5. If you want to open a HTML document or create a plain text document, select the Ignore Rich Text Commands check box.

6. Click Open.

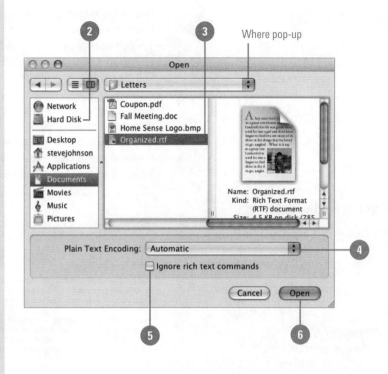

Where pop-up

Open a Recent Document

1. Click the File menu, and then point to Open Recent.

2. Click the recently opened document you want to re-open.

Did You Know?

You can remove all recently used documents from the Open Recent sub-menu. Click the File menu, point to Open Recent, and then click Clear Menu.

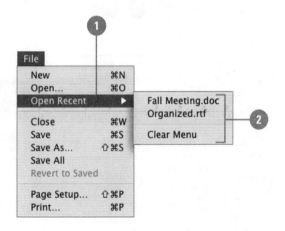

Editing Text

One of the advantages of using a word processing program is that you can edit a document or change the contents without re-creating it. In the TextEdit work area, the mouse pointer changes to the I-beam pointer, which you can use to reposition the insertion point (called navigating) and insert, delete, or select text. Before you can edit text, you need to highlight, or select, the text you want to modify. Then you can delete, replace, move (cut), or copy text within one document or between documents even if they're different programs. When you cut or copy an item, it's placed on the Clipboard, which stores only a single piece of information at a time. You can also move or copy selected text without storing it on the Clipboard by using drag-and-drop editing.

Select and Edit Text

1. Open a document, and then move the I-beam pointer to the left or right of the text you want to select.

2. Click, and then drag the pointer to highlight the text.

   TIMESAVER *Double-click a word to select it; triple-click a paragraph to select it.*

3. Perform one of the following editing commands:

   ◆ To replace text, type your text.

   ◆ To delete text, press the Delete key.

Insert and Delete Text

1. Click in the document to place the insertion point where you want to make the change.

   ◆ To insert text, type your text.

   ◆ To delete text, press the Delete key.

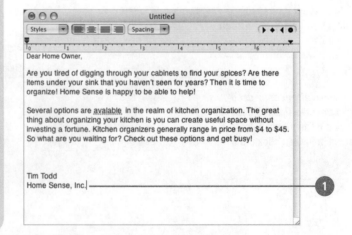

Move or Copy Text

1. Select the text you want to move or copy.

2. Click the Edit menu, and then click Cut or Copy.

   TIMESAVER *Press ⌘+X to cut or press ⌘+C to copy.*

3. Click where you want to insert the text.

4. Click the Edit menu, and then click Paste.

   TIMESAVER *Press ⌘+V to paste.*

Move or Copy Text Using Drag and Drop

1. Select the text you want to move or copy.

2. Point to the selected text, and then click and hold the mouse button.

   If you want to copy the text to a new location, also press and hold the Option key. A plus sign (+) appears in the pointer box, indicating that you are dragging a copy of the selected text.

3. Drag the selected text to the new location, and then release the mouse button (and the Option key, if necessary).

4. Click anywhere in the document to deselect the text.

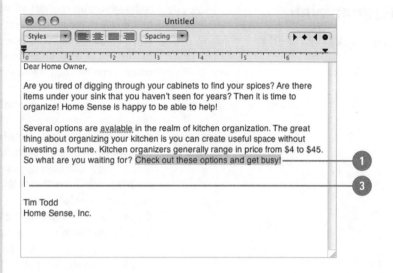

6

Recognizing Handwriting Ink

Although typing information into an document or e-mail through the keyboard is fast and efficient, you may find that you need to enter information in handwritten form, known as **ink**. Programs that accept ink, such as TextEdit or Mail, provide handwriting recognition to help you convert handwriting into text. Before you can insert handwritten text into a document, you need to have an ink device, or a handwriting tablet, such as Wacom, attached to and installed on your computer. With handwriting recognition turned on in the Ink pane in System Preferences, you can write in two ink modes: Anywhere or Ink pad. Anywhere mode is useful for writing in a word processing document. As you write in Anywhere mode, your ink strokes appear in a yellow lined translucent overlay. As the Mac recognizes the writing, it converts the ink to text, inserts it in the open document, and erases it from the overlay. When you need to use the mouse, you need to turn off Anywhere mode. Ink pad provides a floating window in which you can use the stylus to write ink and to perform commands as the mouse. Using ink can be tricky at first, but over time you'll get the hang of it.

Insert Handwritten Text Anywhere into a Document

1. Open a program, such as TextEdit, that accepts ink.

2. Turn on handwriting recognition (Ink icon in System Preferences).

    The Ink toolbar appears.

3. Write your text in the yellow lined overlay. After recognition, the text that you write appears in the document.

4. To turn Anywhere mode off to use the mouse, click the On/Off button on the Ink toolbar.

5. When you're done, turn off handwriting recognition, and close any open documents.

See Also

See "Setting Ink Preferences" on page 104 for information on turning hand-writing recognition on and off, as well as other options.

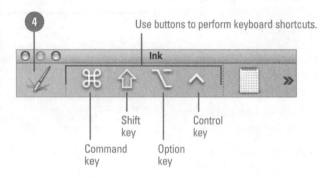

Use buttons to perform keyboard shortcuts.

Command key
Shift key
Option key
Control key

Recognized text

Insert Handwritten Text Using the Ink Pad

1. Open a program, such as TextEdit, that accepts ink.

2. Turn on handwriting recognition (Ink icon in System Preferences).

   The Ink toolbar appears.

3. Click the Show Ink Pad button on the Ink toolbar.

4. Click the A button to input text, or click the Star button to create a drawing.

5. Write your text or draw with the pen in the Ink Pad window.

   TROUBLE? *If Ink makes a mistake, hold down the Option key, tap the word, and then select a transcription option.*

6. Use the Ink toolbar buttons (Command, Shift, Option, or Control) to perform keyboard shortcuts.

7. Click Send to have your text or drawing pasted into the open document behind it.

8. When you're done, turn off handwriting recognition, and close any open documents.

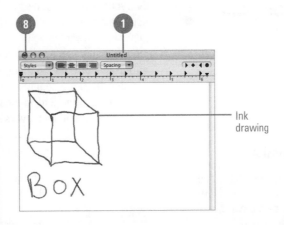

Ink drawing

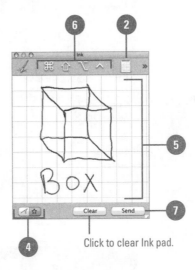

Click to clear Ink pad.

Did You Know?

You can recognize gestures in Ink pad.
As you write, Ink recognizes certain gestures, or shapes, which get performed as commands, such as Undo, or pressed as keys, such as Delete or Space. A list is available on the Gestures tab in the Ink pane in System Preferences.

For Your Information

Speaking Text in a Document

TextEdit can speak all or part of the text in a document. To speak text in a document, deselect all text to speak the entire document or select the text you want to hear, click the Edit menu, point to Speech, and then click Start Speaking. To make the speaking stop, click the Edit menu, point to Speech, and then click Stop Speaking. The voice you hear is set in the Speech pane of System Preferences. To change the sound of the computer's voice, click the Apple menu, click System Preferences, click Speech, click the Default Voice tab, select a voice, and then click the Close button.

6

Making Corrections

Everyone makes mistakes and changes their mind at some point, especially when creating or revising a document. With TextEdit you can instantly correct typing errors by pressing a key. You can also reverse more complicated actions, such as typing an entire word, formatting a paragraph, or creating a chart. If you need to undo several actions, you can use the Undo command multiple times. With the Undo command, if you change your mind, you can just as easily use the Redo command to restore the action you reversed.

Undo or Redo an Action

◆ Click the Edit menu, and then click Undo to reverse your most recent action, such as typing a word, formatting a paragraph, or creating a chart.

   TIMESAVER Press ⌘+Z to undo.

◆ Click the Edit menu, and then click Redo to restore the last action you reversed.

   TIMESAVER Press ⌘+ Shift+Z to redo your undo.

   NOTE The Undo and Redo commands may change based on the action that was last performed (such as typing or dragging).

Click to undo
Click to redo

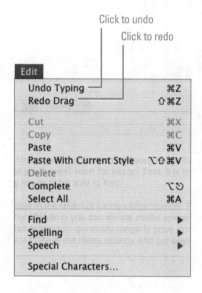

Edit	
Undo Typing	⌘Z
Redo Drag	⇧⌘Z
Cut	⌘X
Copy	⌘C
Paste	⌘V
Paste With Current Style	⌥⇧⌘V
Delete	
Complete	⌥⎋
Select All	⌘A
Find	▶
Spelling	▶
Speech	▶
Special Characters...	

Correct Typing Errors Using the Keyboard

To Delete	Press
One character at a time to the left of the insertion point	Delete
One word at a time to the left of the insertion point	Option+Delete
Selected text	Delete

Changing Text Wrap

By default, TextEdit wraps lines of text based on the width of the window. If you change the width of the window, the lines of text get shorter or longer. If you widen the window, the text gets smaller. When you print the document, TextEdit reduces the font size of the text to match the printed document to what you see on the screen, which might not be the results you want to achieve. To avoid this, you can change the text to wrap to the paper size. TextEdit uses the paper size and orientation you set in Page Setup, to determine the point in which the text line wraps.

Change Text Wrap

1 Click the Format menu, and then click Wrap To Page or Wrap To Window.

When you change the text wrap to Wrap To Page, a rectangle appears in the window indicating the margins of the document.

See Also

See "Setting Up Page Options" on page 168 for information on changing the paper size.

Did You Know?

You can set your text to be hyphenated. Hyphenation prevents ugly gaps and short lines in text. Click the Format menu, and then click Allow Hyphenation. To turn hyphenation off, click the Format menu, and then click Disallow Hyphenation.

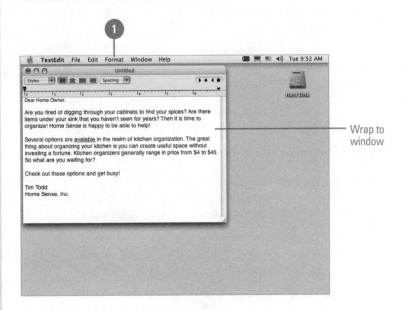

Wrap to window

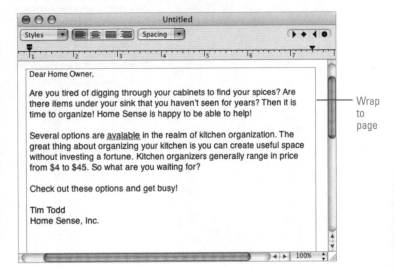

Wrap to page

6

Checking Spelling

As you type, a red wavy line appears under words not listed in TextEdit's dictionary (such as misspellings or names) or duplicated words (such as *the the*). You can correct these errors as they arise or after you finish the entire document. Before you print your final document, use the Spell Checker to ensure that your document is error-free.

Correct Spelling and Grammar as You Type

① Control-click a word with a red dotted underline.

② Click a substitution, or click Ignore Spelling to skip any other instances of the word.

Did You Know?

You can add a familiar word to your dictionary. Control-click the wavy line under the word in question, and then click Learn Spelling. The wavy line disappears and you've added the word or name to the dictionary.

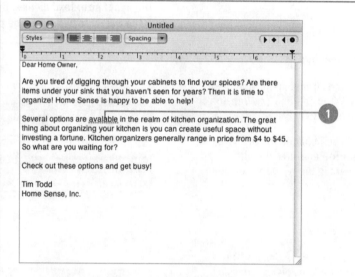

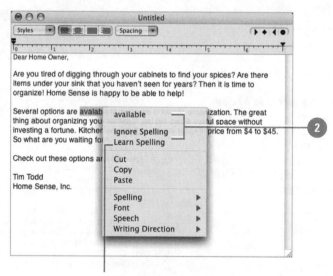

Click to add a word or name to the dictionary.

Correct Spelling

1. Click at the beginning of the document or select the text you want to correct.

2. Click the Edit menu, point to Spelling, and then click Spelling.

   As it checks each sentence in the document or your selection, TextEdit selects misspelled words or problematic sentences and provides appropriate alternatives.

3. If necessary, click the Dictionary pop-up, and then select a dictionary.

4. Select an option:

   ◆ Click a suggestion, and then click Correct to make a substitution.

   ◆ Click Ignore to skip the word.

   ◆ If no suggestion is appropriate, click in the document and edit the text yourself. Click Find Next to continue.

   ◆ Click Learn or Forget to add or not add the word to the dictionary.

   The Spell Checker will beep when the process is done.

5. Click the Close button to return to the document.

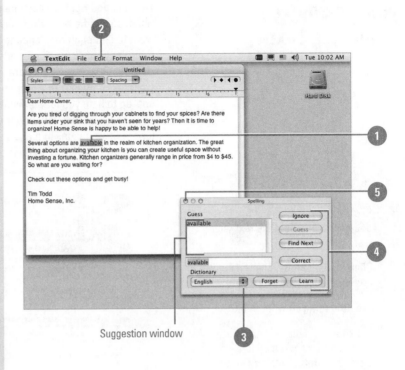

Suggestion window

Finding and Replacing Text

The Find and Replace commands (**New!**) make it easy to locate or replace specific text or formulas in a document. For example, you might want to find each reference to a individual or company name in a long report to verify that it's properly used. Or you might want to replace all references to a special character in your document with another one. If you only know part of a word you want to find, you can use the Contains pop-up to help you locate what you're looking for. If you are looking for a case sensitive text with upper and lower case characters, turn off the Ignore Case option. To make sure you check the entire document no matter where you start, turn on the Wrap Around option.

Find Text

1. Click at the beginning of the document, or select the text you want to find.

2. Click the Edit menu, point to Find, and then click Find.

3. Type the text you want to find.

4. Click the Contains pop-up, and then select a search option: Contains, Starts With, or Full Word.

5. Select other options:

    ◆ **Ignore Case.** Check to ignore upper and lower case characters.

    ◆ **Wrap Around.** Check to wrap back to the beginning of the document.

6. Click Next until the text you want to find is highlighted.

    You can click Next repeatedly to locate each instance of the text.

7. If a message box appears when you reach the end of the document, click OK. Otherwise, the computer will beep when the Find is complete.

8. When you're done, click the Close button.

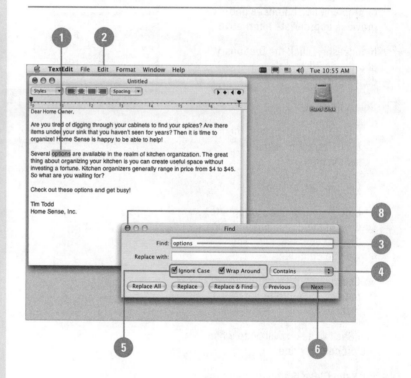

Replace Text

1 Click at the beginning of the document, or select the text you want to replace.

2 Click the Edit menu, point to Find and then click Find.

3 Type the text you want to find.

4 Type the text you want to replace.

5 Click the Contains pop-up, and then select a search option: Contains, Starts With, or Full Word.

6 Select or clear the Ignore Case and Wrap Around check boxes.

7 Click Next to begin the search and find the next instance of the search text.

8 Click one of the Replace buttons:

◆ **Replace All**. Click to substitute text throughout the entire document.

◆ **Replace**. Click to substitute the replacement text.

◆ **Replace & Find**. Click to substitute the replacement text and find the next instance.

You can click Next to locate the next instance of the search text without making a replacement.

9 If a message box appears when you reach the end of the document, click OK. Otherwise, the computer will beep when the process is done.

10 When you're done, click the Close button.

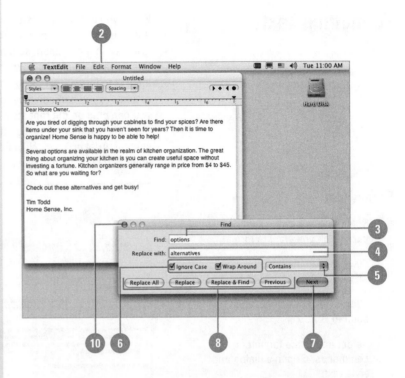

For Your Information

Summarizing the Contents of Documents

If you have a long document, such as a report or Web page, you can use Apple's Summarize service to create a summary of the contents (actually the statistically relevant sentences or paragraphs). To create a summary, select the text you want to summarize in the document, click the *Application name* menu (such as **TextEdit**), point to Services, and then click Summarize. Select the Sentences or Paragraphs option to specify how you want to make the summary document, drag the Summary Size slider to expand or condense the summary, and then click the Close button. Click Save, name the summary, select a location, and then click Save. If the application you are using doesn't support the Summarize service, copy and paste the text you want to use into TextEdit, which does support the service. To save the file as a TextEdit document, click the File menu, and then click Save As.

Formatting Text

When you are working with Rich Text Format (RTF) and Word Format documents, you can change the format or the appearance of text and graphics in a document so that the document is easier to read or more attractive. A quick and powerful way to add emphasis to parts of a document is to format text using bold, italics, underline, or color. For special emphasis, you can combine formats, such as bold and italics. In addition, you can change the font style and size. A **font** is a set of characters with the same typeface or design that you can increase or decrease in size, such as Arial or Times New Roman. Font size is measured in points; one point is 1/72 of an inch high.

Format Text

1 Select the text or click in the paragraph you want to format.

2 Click an alignment button: Left, Center, Justify, and Right.

3 Click the Format menu, and then point to Font.

4 Select any of the formatting commands to open a dialog and style text:

◆ **Show Fonts.** Click to change multiple text formatting options at the same time.

◆ **Show Color.** Click to change text color.

Select any of the formatting menu individual commands:

◆ Bold

◆ Italic

◆ Underline

◆ Outline

◆ Bigger (font size)

◆ Smaller (font size)

5 Click in the document to unselect the newly formatted text.

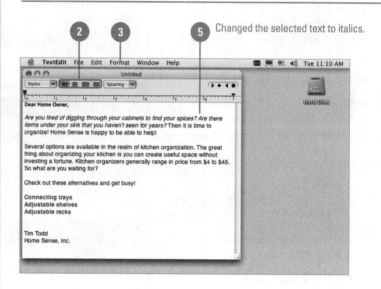

Changed the selected text to italics.

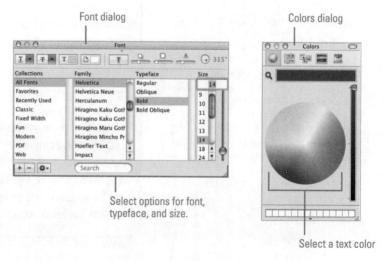

Font dialog

Colors dialog

Select options for font, typeface, and size.

Select a text color

Displaying Rulers

The TextEdit ruler does more than just measure. The horizontal **ruler** above the document shows the length of the typing line and lets you quickly adjust left and right margins, indents, and set tabs. You can hide the ruler to get more room for your document. When you press Return to start a new paragraph, TextEdit continues to use the same ruler settings. As you work with a document, ruler settings change. Instead of resetting ruler settings each time, you can copy and paste them.

Show and Hide the Ruler

① Click the Format menu, point to Text, and then click Show Ruler.

TIMESAVER *Press* ⌘+R *to show or hide the ruler.*

A check mark next to the command indicates the ruler is shown. A non check mark indicates the ruler is hidden.

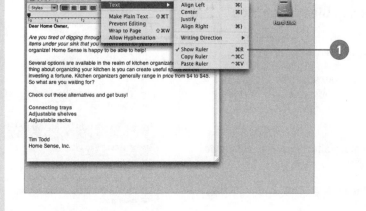

Copy and Paste the Ruler

① Click in the line to place the insertion point or select the lines with the ruler settings you want to copy.

② Click the Format menu, point to Text, and then click Copy Ruler.

TIMESAVER *Press Control+* ⌘+Z *to copy ruler.*

③ Click in the line to place the insertion point or select the lines in which you want to paste the ruler.

④ Click the Format menu, point to Text, and then click Paste Ruler.

TIMESAVER *Press Control+* ⌘+Z *to paste ruler.*

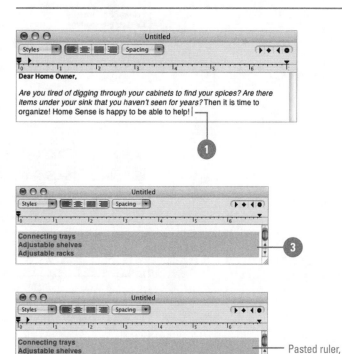

Pasted ruler, same as step 1.

6

Setting Paragraph Tabs

Tabs set text or numerical data alignment in relation to the edges of a document. A **tab stop** is a predefined stopping point along the document's typing line. Default tab stops are set every half-inch on the ruler, but you can set multiple tabs per paragraph at any location. Each paragraph in a document contains its own set of tab stops. The default tab stops do not appear on the ruler, but the manual tab stops you set do appear. Once you place a tab stop, you can drag the tab stop to position it where you want. If you want to add or adjust tab stops in multiple paragraphs, simply select the paragraphs first.

Create and Clear a Tab Stop

1. Select the text or click in the paragraph you want to format.

2. Drag a tab stop from the tab stop palette above the ruler or one already on the ruler where you want to set it.

3. To move a tab, drag the tab stop to position it where you want.

4. To clear a tab stop, drag it off the ruler.

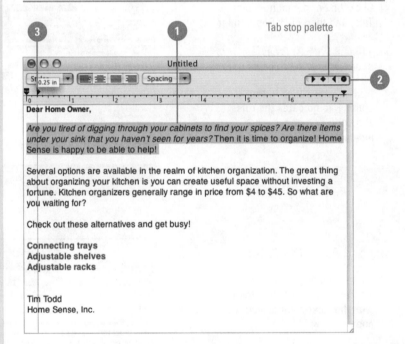

Tab stop palette

Tab Stops

Tab Stop	Name	Description
▶	Left tab stop	Aligns tab text to the left
◆	Center tab stop	Aligns tab text to the center
◀	Right tab stop	Aligns tab text to the right
●	Decimal tab stop	Aligns numbers to the decimal point

Setting Paragraph Indents

When you indent a paragraph, you move its edge in from the left or right margin. You can indent the entire left or right edge of a paragraph or just the first line. The markers on the ruler control the indentation of the current paragraph. The ruler has three markers. The top rectangle, called the **paragraph indent marker**, controls where the first line of the paragraph begins. The bottom triangle, called the **left indent marker**, controls where the remaining lines of the paragraph begin. The triangle on the right side of the ruler, called the **right indent marker**, controls where the right edge of the paragraph ends.

Change Paragraph Indents

Select the text or click in the paragraph you want to format.

◆ To change the left indent of the first line, drag the Paragraph Indent marker.

◆ To change the indent of the second and subsequent lines, drag the Left Indent marker (under the Paragraph Indent marker).

◆ To change the left indent for all lines, drag the Left Indent marker, and the Paragraph Indent marker to the same point.

◆ To change the right indent for all lines, drag the Right Indent marker.

As you drag a marker, the dotted guideline helps you position the indent accurately.

Paragraph Indent marker

Left Indent marker

Right Indent marker

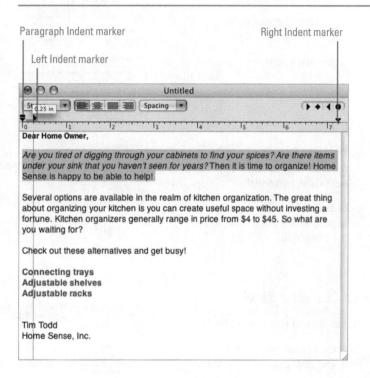

6

Changing Character Spacing

Kerning is the amount of space between each character that you type. Sometimes the space between two characters is larger than others, which makes the word look uneven. You can expand or condense the spacing to create a special effect for a title, or re-align the **baseline** (**New!**), which is the position of characters to the bottom edge of the text—this is helpful for positioning the copyright or trademark symbols.

Change Character Spacing

① Select the text you want to format.

② Click the Format menu, point to Font, and then point to Kern.

③ Click any of the following options:

◆ **Use Default.** Uses default kerning.

◆ **Use None.** Removes kerning.

◆ **Tighten.** Moves the characters together slightly; you can repeat the command.

◆ **Loosen.** Moves the characters slightly apart; you can repeat the command.

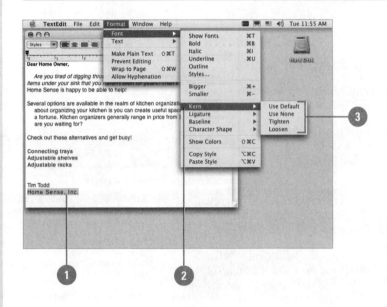

Change Character Baseline

① Select the text you want to format.

② Click the Format menu, point to Font, and then point to Baseline.

③ Click any of the following options:

◆ **Superscript.** Moves the text above the level of normal text.

◆ **Subscript.** Moves the text below the level of normal text.

◆ **Raise.** Moves the text up only a little bit; you can repeat the command.

◆ **Lower.** Moves the text down only a little bit; you can repeat command.

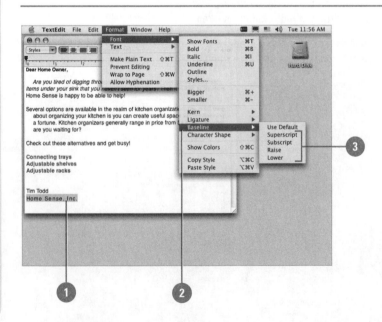

Changing Line Spacing

The lines in all TextEdit documents are single-spaced by default, which is appropriate for letters and most documents. But you can easily change your document line spacing to double or you specify to allow extra space between every line. This is useful when you want to make notes on a printed document. Sometimes, you'll want to add space above and below certain paragraphs, for headlines, or indented quotations to help set off the text. To set specialized line spacing setting, use the Other command on the Spacing pop-up (New!). You can select options for line height, inter-line spacing, and paragraph spacing. **Line height** is the distance from the top of a line to the top of the line below it; **inter-line spacing** is the distance from the bottom of a line to the top of the line below it;, and **paragraph spacing** is the distance from the bottom of a paragraph to the top of the first line in the paragraph below it.

Change Line Spacing

1. Select the text you want to change.

2. Click the Spacing pop-up on the ruler, and then select a spacing option:

   - Click Single or Double to apply single line space or double line spacing.

   - Click Other, specify the exacting options you want, and then click OK.

Did You Know?

You can insert and remove a page break. Click the Format menu, and then click Wrap To Page (if necessary) so the page break can be visible. Click to place the insertion point where you want the page break, press Control+Q, and then press Control+L. To remove a page break, place the insertion point below the page break, and then press Delete.

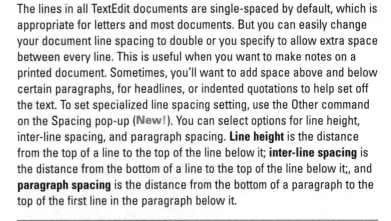

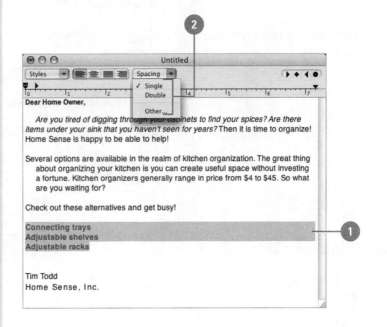

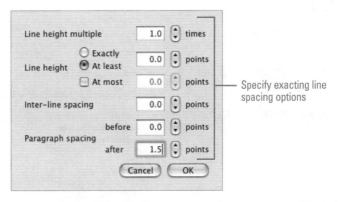

Specify exacting line spacing options

6

Applying and Creating a Style

When you want to apply multiple groupings of formatting, such as font type, size and color, use a style. A **style (New!)** is a collection of formatting settings saved within a document or favorites list that you can apply to text. TextEdit keeps track of all the styles in the current document. If you want to save a style for use in all documents, you can add it to a favorites list. TextEdit provides a few basic favorite styles. But you can add your own to create the exact look you want. If you need a quick way to apply a single instance of formatting, you can copy and paste it.

Apply a Favorite Style

1. Select the text you want to apply a style.

2. Click the Styles pop-up on the Ruler.

3. Click the style you want to apply.

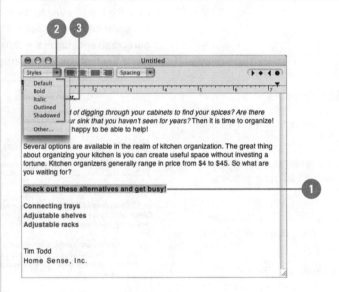

Apply a Document Style

1. Select the text whose formatting you want to save as a style.

2. Click the Format menu, point to Font, and then click Styles.

3. If necessary, click the Document Styles option.

4. Click the arrow buttons to select the style you want to apply.

5. Click Apply, and then when you're done, click Done.

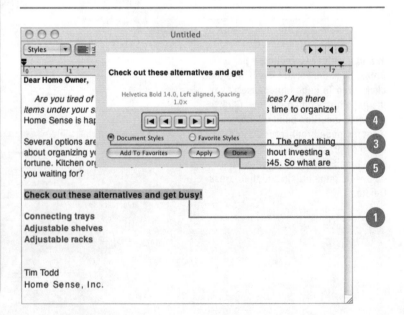

Add a Style to Favorites

1. Select the text whose formatting you want to save as a style.

2. Click the Format menu, point to Font, and then click Styles.

3. Click Add To Favorites.

4. Type a name for the style.

5. Select or clear the check boxes to include the font or ruler as part of the style.

6. Click Add.

Did You Know?

You can remove a style favorite. Click the Format menu, point to Font, click Styles, click the Favorite Styles option, click the pop-up, select the style favorite, and then click Remove From Favorites.

Copy and Paste Formatting

1. Select the text in which you want to copy the formatting.

2. Click the Format menu, point to Font, and then click Copy Style.

   TIMESAVER *Press Option+⇧⌘+Z to copy ruler.*

3. Select the text to which you want to apply a style.

4. Click the Format menu, point to Font, and then click Paste Style.

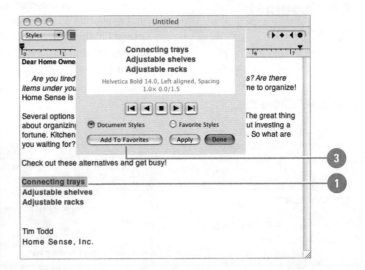

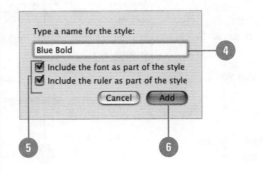

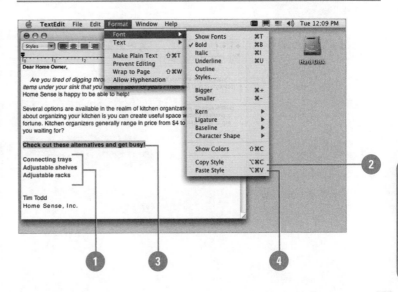

6

Inserting Special Characters

When you need to insert special characters such as ©, ™, or ® that don't appear on your keyboard, you can use a special accessory called Special Character to do the job. Special Character is available in Mac applications and displays all the characters that are available for each of the fonts on your computer.

Insert a Special Character

1. Click in the text to place the insertion point where you want to insert a special character.

2. Click the Edit menu, and then click Special Characters.

3. Click the View pop-up, and then select a character set.

4. Click the By Category tab, and then select a category. To select from your favorites, click the Favorites tab, and then select a symbol.

5. Click the special character you want to insert.

6. Click Insert.

7. To add the character to a favorites list, click Add To Favorites.

8. Click the Close button.

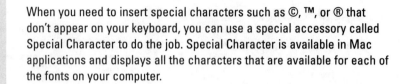

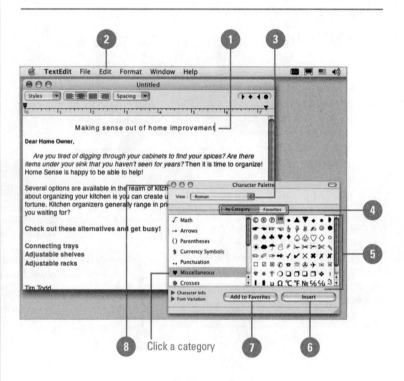

Click a category

List of favorite special characters

Adding Pictures, Movies, or Files to a Document

If you have a picture, movie, or another file, (such as another text file, spreadsheet, or PDF), you can place them within a TextEdit document. Before you can add a picture, movie, or files to a TextEdit document, the file needs to be converted to the Rich Text Format (RTF). Pictures and movies appear in the document as embedded graphics, while files appear as embedded icons. With embedding, a copy of the file becomes part of the TextEdit file. If you want to edit the embedded file, you make changes in the TextEdit file, and the original file remains intact. You can double-click the embedded graphics or icons to open and view the files.

Add a Picture, Movie, or File to a Document

1. Click the Format menu, and then click Make Rich Text.

2. Switch to the Finder, and then open the folder containing the picture, movie, or file you want to add.

3. Display the picture, movie, or file icon in the Finder and the TextEdit document on the screen where you can view them both.

4. Drag the picture, movie, or file icon from the Finder to the document window where you want to place it.

    The image is placed in your document.

5. Close the Finder window.

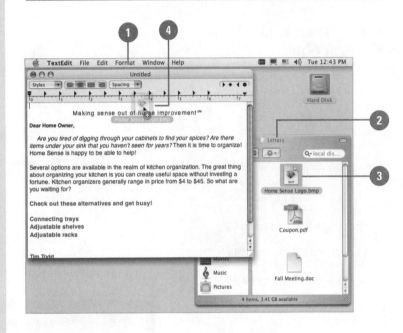

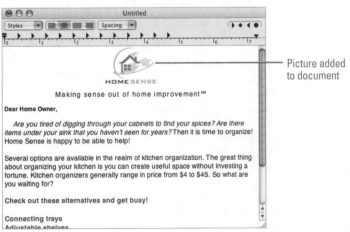

Picture added to document

6

Saving and Closing a Document

Saving your files frequently ensures that you don't lose work during an unexpected power loss. The first time you save, specify a file name and folder in the Save As dialog. The next time you save, the program saves the file with the same name in the same folder. If you want to change a file's name or location, you can use the Save As dialog again to create a copy of the original file. The Save As dialog appears in a compact view (useful for saving in the same place) and an expanded view (useful for saving in a different location or creating a new folder). Expanded view includes the Sidebar, and List and Column view (New!). To conserve your computer's resources, close any file you are not working on.

Save a Document as Rich Text or Microsoft Word

1. For plain text only, click the Format menu, and then click Make Rich Text.

2. Click the File menu, and then click Save As.

3. Type a name for the file, or use the suggested name.

4. Select the hard drive and folder in which you want to save the file.

5. To change the format of a file, click the File Format pop-up, and then click Rich Text Format (RTF) or Word Format.

6. Click Save.

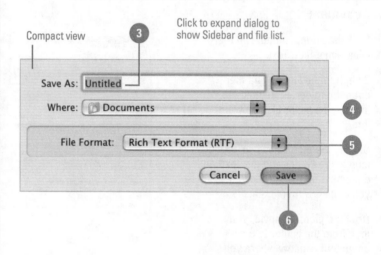

Compact view

Click to expand dialog to show Sidebar and file list.

For Your Information

Protecting Documents

If you have content in your TextEdit document that you don't want users to change, you can make the document read-only. This is useful for documents, such as "read me" files, contracts, and any other document you want users to read, but not accidentally change. To prevent others from changing your TextEdit documents, click the Format menu, and then click Prevent Editing. To allow users to make changes to a read-only document, click the Format menu, and then click Allow Editing. Another way to protect a document is to lock it. When you lock a file, users can make changes to the file, but the application prevents them from saving it. To lock a file, select the files in the Finder, click the File menu, click Get Info, select the Locked check box, and then click the Close button.

Save a Document as Plain Text

1. For plain text only, click the Format menu, and then click Make Plain Text.

2. Click the File menu, and then click Save As.

3. Type a name for the file, or use the suggested name.

4. Select the hard drive and folder in which you want to save the file.

5. Click the Plain Text Encoding pop-up, and then select an encoding format.

6. Click Save.

Did You Know?

You can revert to a previously saved document. Before you save, click the File menu, and then click Revert To Saved.

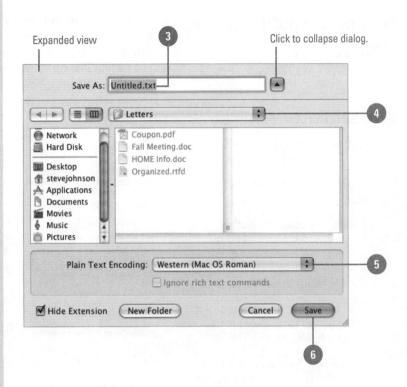

Expanded view

Click to collapse dialog.

Close a Document

1. Click the Close button.

2. If necessary, click Save to save your changes.

   TIMESAVER *When a small dot appears in the Close button, it means the document needs to be saved.*

3. Quit TextEdit.

See Also

See Chapter 7, "Printing and Faxing" on page 161 for information on printing a document.

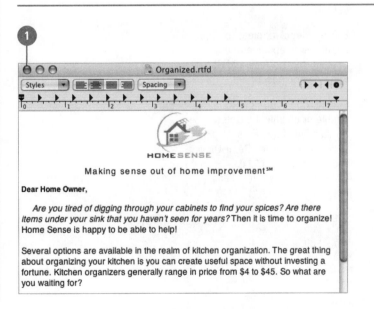

Setting TextEdit Preferences

TextEdit preferences help you configure some of the more common features of the program. You can set preferences for new documents, default fonts, rich text processing, default plain text encoding, editing, and saving. These preference areas allow you to turn features on and off as well as customize the way TextEdit works.

Set General Preferences

1. Click the TextEdit menu, and then click Preferences.

2. Select or specify the various options you want to use:

   ◆ **New Document Attributes.** Select options for document format and text wrapping, and specify the width and height you want for the document window.

   ◆ **Default Fonts.** Click Set to select the default fonts you want for rich and plain text.

   ◆ **Rich Text Processing.** Check or clear to ignore or allow rich text commands.

   ◆ **Default Plain Text Encoding.** Click the Open or Save pop-ups to select a plain text encoding default.

   ◆ **Editing.** Check or clear to enable or disable the Check Spelling As You Type and Show Ruler commands.

   ◆ **Saving.** Check or clear to enable or disable the Delete Backup File. Save Files Writable, Overwrite Read-Only Files, and Append ".txt" Extension To Plain Text Files options.

3. Click the Close button.

4. Quit TextEdit.

New Document Attributes   Default Plain Text Encoding

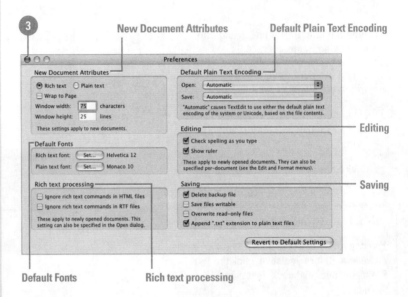

Editing

Saving

Default Fonts   Rich text processing

Printing and Faxing

7

Introduction

Let's face it, you work all day on a computer, but sooner or later, you're going to have to get your one-of-a-kind project, text document, or photograph off the computer. Computer data finds itself in the most unlikely places. For example, you could save a text document onto a CD, and then store the CD away; never to be seen again. Probably the most common place you find computer data is on paper. It might be nice to talk of a paperless society, however, most people prefer the satisfying feel of paper in their hands, as opposed to a cold computer monitor. That's where Panther steps in and makes your life easy. Not only does Panther give you all the standard ways to print to paper or fax, it also gives you hundreds of printer drives; supporting the vast majority of printers in the market. In addition, you can save paper by previewing your jobs—using Panther's print preview feature—which shows you a color-accurate on-screen version of your print job.

If you fax documents, then Panther is an operating system tailor-made expressly for your needs. Panther integrates its faxing features with a state-of-the-art printing system. Just open the Print & Fax utility, and you'll notice a Faxing tab, where you can set up your computer to receive faxes. Then, when you go to print a document from virtually any application, you'll see a Fax button in the Print dialog. In addition, if you have a large print job that you would rather print after work, or a fax that has to be sent at a specific time; Panther lets you schedule a time to print a document, or fax with the click of a button.

Understanding Printers

Although there are many different kinds of printers, there are two main categories: ink-jet and laser. An **ink-jet printer** works by spraying ionized ink on a sheet of paper. Ink-jet printers are less expensive and considerably slower than laser printers, but they still produce a good quality output. A **laser printer** utilizes a laser beam to produce an image on a drum, which is rolled through a reservoir of toner and transferred to the paper through a combination of heat and pressure. Laser printers are faster and produce a higher quality output than ink-jets, but they are also more expensive. Ink-jet and laser printers are combined with other hardware devices, such as a copier and scanner, into a multi-function device. A **multi-function device** provides common device functionality at a lower cost than purchasing each device separately. Printers are classified by two main characteristics: resolution and speed. Printer resolution refers to the sharpness and clarity of a printed page. For printers, the resolution indicates the number of dots per inch (dpi). For example, a 300-dpi printer is one that is capable of printing 300 distinct dots in a line one-inch long, or 90,000 dots per square inch. The higher the dpi, the sharper the print quality. Printer speed is measured in pages per minute (ppm). The speed of printers varies widely. In general, ink-jet printers range from about 4 to 10 ppm, while laser printers range from about 10 to 30 ppm. The speed depends on the amount of printer memory (the more the better) and the page's contents: if there is just text or the page has only one color, the ppm is in the high range, but when a page contains graphics and/or has multiple colors, the ppm rate falls to the low range.

Ink-jet printer

Laser printer

Multi-function device

Understanding Printer Drivers

Printer drivers are lines of code designed to help an operating system communicate with a specific printer. No two printer models are created equal: Some have two paper trays, while others have one; some are ink-jet, while others are laser; some are color and some black and white. Although there are generic printer drivers available, most printers have a driver program, designed specifically for that make and model. Panther installs all of the printer drivers onto your hard drive when you run the Panther installation program.

The drivers become available when you attach your printer and run the Printer Setup Utility. The good news is that with the release of Panther, the process of hooking up your printer, and being able to print, just became a lot easier.

Although Panther comes bundled with almost every conceivable printer driver; it may not have the latest driver. In addition, new printers are being released all the time. Keep the CD that came with your printer handy; it contains a driver for that particular model of printer. In addition, the Web sites for the printer companies such as *www.epson.com* or *www.hp.com*, contain the latest updates and patches for their printers. You can visit them to see if any updates are available.

Since you'll only need one or two printer drivers, you can delete the others. All those unused drivers take up over a gigabyte of space on your hard drive. Once you've installed the necessary printers, select the Library folder (located on the main hard drive), click Printer Folders, and then delete the unused drivers. If necessary, you can always reinstall them from the OS X install disks.

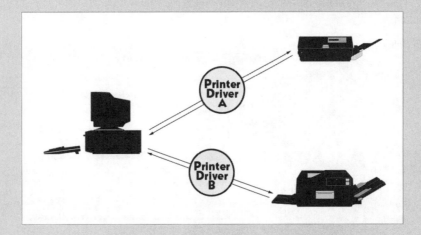

Using the Printer Setup Utility

Setting up a printer use to be a difficult and time-consuming process. There were all kinds of questions to answer, driver files to find, and after all that time, you might still have problems. With the Panther operating system, setting up a printer is easy. Adding a printer can be as simple as plugging the printer in, running the Printer Setup Utility, and clicking the Add button. The Info button on the Printer Setup Utility not only gives you the name of the selected printer, but also the ability to change the name. When you're working in an office where all the networked printers are a bunch of numbers (155.657.221) this option can be pretty helpful. You can also print to shared Windows printers over a network or share your own printer with Windows users (New!). In addition, you can use the setup utility to monitor the ink levels on your printers, perform routine maintenance, and even delete the printer.

Add a Printer

1. Open the Utilities folder, and then double-click the Printer Setup Utility icon.

2. Click the Add button to add a new printer.

3. Click the Connection pop-up to select the connection method used by the new printer, and then select a printer from the list. Select any other specific options for the new printer.

4. Click Add.

5. Click the Close button.

6. Quit Printer Setup Utility.

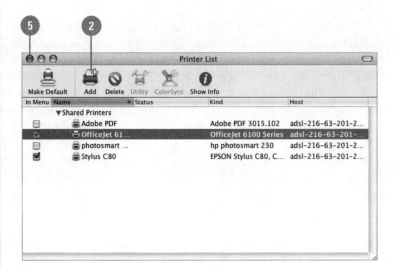

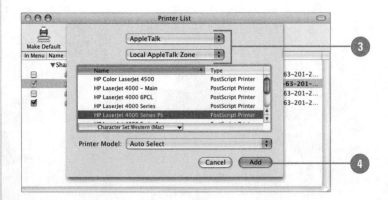

Manage a Printer

① Open the Utilities folder, and then double-click the Printer Setup Utility icon.

② Select a printer from the list.

③ Select any of the following options:

◆ **Make Default.** Click to set a printer as the default printer for all printing jobs.

◆ **Add.** Click to add a printer.

◆ **Delete.** Click to remove a printer from the active list.

◆ **Utility.** Click to perform routine maintenance on the selected printer, such as: color print test or unclogging a nozzle.

◆ **ColorSync.** Click to edit the ColorSync profile assigned to the selected printer.

◆ **Show Info.** Click to gather information on the Name, Location, Printer Model, and any installable options for the selected printer.

④ To add the printer to the list of available printers for all your applications, select the In Menu check box .

⑤ Click the Close button.

⑥ Quit Printer Setup Utility.

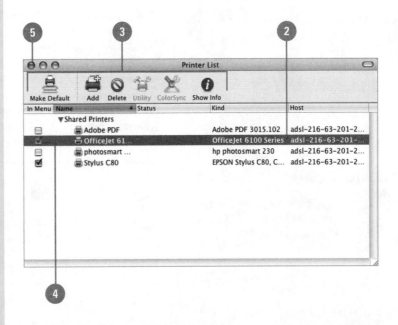

For Your Information

Customizing the Printer List

It's possible to customize the column data displayed in the Printer List dialog. Click the view window, point to Columns, and then select the column data you want displayed from the available options of: Kind, Host, Status, Location, and Jobs.

Setting Print and Fax Settings

Using your Macintosh to print and fax is an obvious extension of the normal, everyday computing process. You write and create documents, and send them to paper; you take a photograph using a digital camera and send it to a photo-quality printer; and you have a document, and you need to fax it to a co-worker or friend. The Panther operating system has several components that allow you to modify the aspects of printing and faxing; however, the initial setup is performed in the Print & Fax Utility (**New!**), located within System Preferences. It's the first step to making your Macintosh a truly awesome printing and faxing machine.

Set Print Settings

1. Click the Apple menu, click System Preferences, and then click the Print & Fax icon (or click the System Preferences icon in the Dock).

2. Click the Printing tab.

3. Click Set Up Printers to access the Printer Setup Utility.

4. If necessary, select the In Menu check box for your printer.

5. Click the Close button.

6. Click the Printer pop-up, and then select a default printer to appear first in the Print dialogs of all your applications.

7. Click the Paper Size pop-up, and then select a paper size to be used as a default in the Print dialogs of all your applications.

8. Select the Share My Printers With Other Computers check box to allow your printers to be shared across a network.

9. Click the Close button.

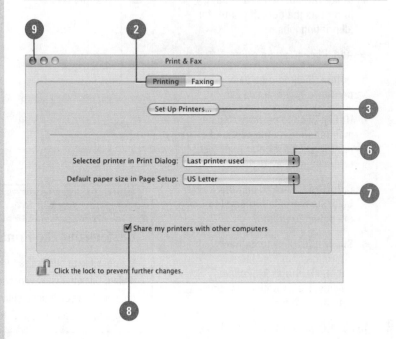

Set Fax Settings

1. Click the Apple menu, click System Preferences, and then click the Print & Fax icon.

2. Click the Faxing tab.

3. Select the Receive Faxes On This Computer check box to receive faxes.

4. Enter your fax number into the field exactly as you would dial.

   If you need to dial an additional number, such as 9 to get an outside line, enter that number before the other numbers.

5. Enter how many rings are required before the fax answers the phone.

6. Click to select the following options:

   ◆ **Save To**. Click the pop-up, and then select where to save the faxes.

   ◆ **Email To**. Click the pop-up, and then select where to email the faxes.

   ◆ **Print On Printer**. Click the pop-up, and then select a printer. Faxes automatically are printed as they are received.

7. Click the Close button.

   IMPORTANT *The faxing application on Panther does not distinguish between a fax and a voice call. Therefore, if you don't want people calling you to hear a screaming din, you'll either need a separate phone line, or a fax/voice splitter (available at most office and electronic stores).*

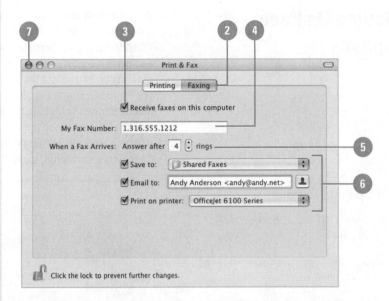

For Your Information

Scheduling Faxes

With OS X Panther, you are able to schedule faxes. Suppose you need to send a fax to Great Britain, but you would like to do it when the overseas rates are cheaper. Open the document to fax (or print for that matter), click the File menu, and then click Print. Select Scheduler from the Copies & Pages pop-up, enter the time, and then click Print or Fax. It's that easy.

Setting Up Page Options

With few exceptions, Macintosh applications give you the ability to print a document to paper. Programs such as: Microsoft Word, Corel WordPerfect; even TextEdit—Macintosh's proprietary word processing application—give you the option to print what you have committed to type. When you select the Print option (located under the File menu), you're instructing the application to use an output device (the printer) to place your words on paper. Since all printers have options, it's important to be able to set those options before printing. You might be using a specific size paper or printing orientation. For this operation, you'll use the Page Setup command, located within the File menu of most applications.

Set Up Page Options

1. Open a document, such as a text document.

2. Click the File menu, and then click Page Setup.

3. Click the Settings pop-up, and then select from the following options:

   ◆ **Page Attributes.** This option lets you select a printer, specific paper size, orientation, and print scale.

   ◆ **Custom Paper Size.** Click New to create a customized paper size by entering height, width, and margin values into the appropriate input fields.

   ◆ **Document Specific Option.** This option gives you specific options for the current application.

   ◆ **Summary.** Click Summary to see an outline of your options.

   ◆ **Save As Default.** Click this option to save your current settings as default for future printing operations.

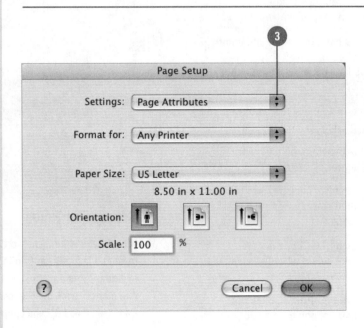

4 Click the Format For pop-up, and then select a printer from the available options.

5 Click the Paper Size pop-up, and then select a paper size from the available options.

6 Click the Orientation buttons, and then select from the following:

- ◆ Portrait
- ◆ Landscape Right
- ◆ Landscape Left

7 Enter in a printing scale percentage.

8 Click OK.

9 If necessary, save the file and close the application.

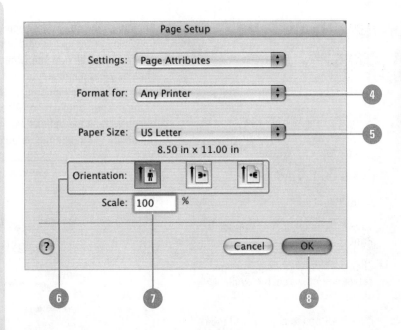

7

For Your Information

Using Page Setup

The Page Setup command changes the page properties within each application. Therefore, you can use the Page Setup command to generate individual defaults for each of your applications. To change the default settings for all applications at the same time, go to your Dock and click System Preferences, click Print & Fax, and then change the default paper size and printer in the pop-ups.

Setting Basic Print Options

All applications that allow you to send a document to a printer, give you the ability to set up specific printing parameters. Some print options are generic, such as how many pages to print, and some are more specific, such as what paper tray to use (in a multi-tray printer). Regardless of the options, they're all located in one specific location. The Print command of the opened application. When you select the Print command, a dialog opens with all the options associated with the default printer; including the ability to change the default printer, and any other printing values.

Set Basic Print Options

1. Open a document.

2. Click the File menu, and then click Print.

3. Click the Printer pop-up, and then select a printer from the available options.

4. Click the Presets pop-up, and then select a user-defined print setting.

   NOTE *Some of the following options may vary due to different applications.*

5. Click the Options pop-up, and then select from the available options:

   ◆ **Copies & Pages.** Lets you select from options such as pages to print, number of copies, and page range.

   ◆ **Layout.** When printing large documents, allows you to select how many pages per sheet, the layout direction, border options, and two-sided printing.

   ◆ **Output Options.** Check the Save As File option, select whether to save the document as a Portable Document File (PDF) or Postscript (.ps) file, and then select a name and location for the saved file.

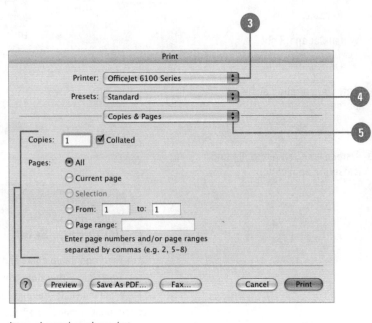

Items change based on what Options pop-up is selected.

- **Scheduler.** Lets you schedule a time for printing the document.

- **Paper Handling.** Select to print in reverse order (page 1 prints last), and whether to print all, odd, or even pages.

- **ColorSync.** Gives you access to Macintosh's ColorSync management system, and the ability to apply the new Quartz Filters to the printed document.

- **Paper Type/Quality.** Lets you select a specific paper type, the quality of the output document, and whether to print using ColorSmart III, or print in grayscale.

- **Printer Driver Information.** List the name and version release of the current printer driver.

  If you're having problems printing, use this information to determine if you have the latest drivers installed.

- **Application Specific Options.** If you're using Microsoft Word, this option lists specific options for that specific application.

- **Summary.** Shows a summary of all the printer options that have been selected.

6 Click Print.

TIMESAVER *Suppose you're printing a large job (50 pages), and you need another job (2 pages) printed right away. Just open the second job, click the File menu, and then click Print. Click the Printer pop-up, select another printer for the second job, and then click Print. Panther processes both jobs on both printers, at the same time.*

Options pop-up menu

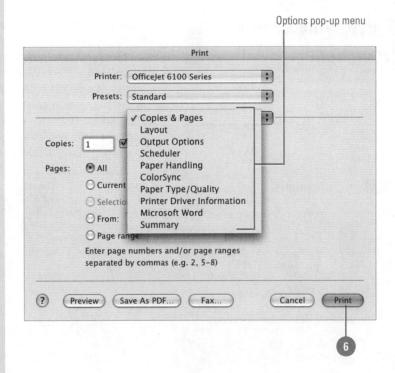

Previaging Documents

One of the most frustrating things is looking at a document on your monitor, clicking the Print command, and then deciding that what you see on the paper is not what you wanted. Unfortunately, a monitor is not a piece of paper, and the term What You See is What You Get (WYSIWYG), is a phrase that most computer users do not take very seriously. Once again, Macintosh comes to the rescue with a Preview utility that targets your default printer. If you see what you like, you can print a single copy directly from the Preview dialog, or you can close the preview, and then you can print using the standard Print option.

Preview Documents

① Open or create a document in an application.

② Click the File menu, click Print, and then click Preview.

The Preview Utility launches.

③ Select from the following options:

◆ **Drawer.** Click to expand or collapse the thumbnail page view of the images.

◆ **Back/Forward.** Click to move between pages in the document.

◆ **Page.** To move directly to a specific page within a document, enter a page number, and then press Return.

◆ **Page Up or Page Down.** Click to move up or down through the list of displayable images.

◆ **Zoom In or Zoom Out.** Click to increase or decrease the viewing size of the image.

◆ **Tool Mode.** To select a portion of the image, choose a Selection tool button, and then drag within the image.

④ Click Cancel to close or Print to print the document.

⑤ Quit Preview.

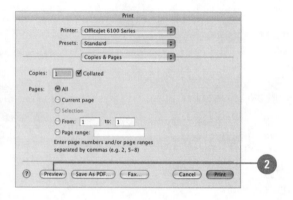

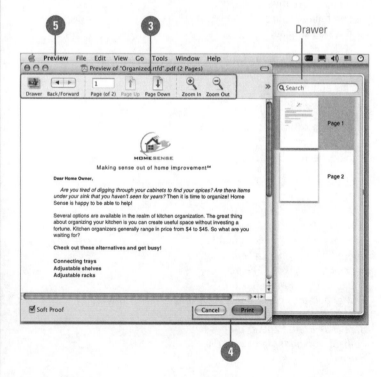

Saving Documents as PDF Documents

The PDF (Portable Document File) format is undoubtedly the most successful multi-platform format ever created by any company. Designed by Adobe, it has become the standard for transferring text and graphics documents, spreadsheets; even creating interactive forms, that can be filled out by a visitor, and then sent back to the owner for processing. The reason for the success of the PDF format is Adobe's tight control over the Adobe Acrobat application (used to create PDF's), and the Acrobat Reader application (used by visitors to read PDF's). Once a PDF document is properly saved, it can be opened by virtually anyone that has Acrobat Reader, regardless of computer or operating system. And the good news is that the Reader application is a free download, just point your browser to *http://www.acrobat.com*, and then click Download Reader to obtain the latest version of the Acrobat Reader application, tailored for your specific operating system.

Save Documents as PDF Documents

1 Open or create a document in an application.

> **IMPORTANT** *Not all applications provide the option to print out in the PDF format.*

2 Click the File menu, and then click Print.

3 Click Save As PDF.

> **IMPORTANT** *The file's name defaults to the file you opened. Make sure to change the extension to .pdf or change the file name entirely.*

4 Give the PDF document a name, and then select where the file is saved.

5 Click Save.

> The file is now a PDF and can be opened and viewed using Adobe Acrobat Reader.

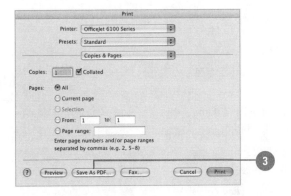

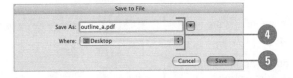

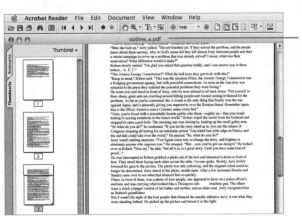

A PDF document viewed in Acrobat Reader.

Using Desktop Printers

The typical method for printing a document goes something like this: You open an application, open a document, click the File menu, and then click Print. While the majority of the time that's exactly what you want to do; especially if you need to make minor corrections to the document before printing, there is an easier way to go from document to printer: Desktop printers. Desktop printers give you the ability to create an icon of a printer, and with a drag and a drop, print a document using any connected printer (New!). Not only is this method fast, it gives you the ability to print from two or more connected printers at a time. Printer icons can be located on the desktop, inside a folder, or even placed in the Dock.

Use Desktop Printers

1. Click the Apple menu, click System Preferences, and then click the Print & Fax icon.

2. Click the Printing tab.

3. Click Set Up Printers.

4. Select a printer from the available options.

5. Click the Printers menu, and then click Create Desktop Printer.

6. Select a name and location for the printer, and then click Save.

7. Close both windows by clicking the Close button.

8. To print a document, drag a file over the desktop printer icon.

9. If the application opens, make any changes to your print options, and then click Print.

Did You Know?

You can instantly check on the status of a particular printer. Double-click on a desktop print icon, to check the status of the printer; including items waiting to print.

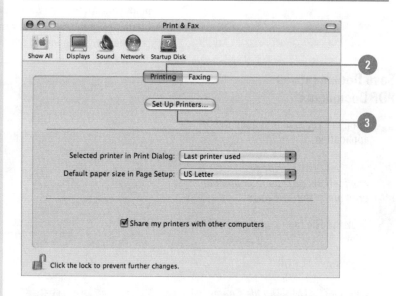

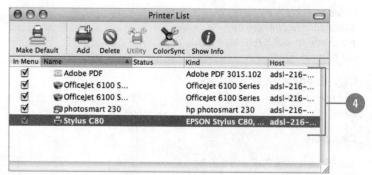

Managing Print Queues

The definition of a queue is a line. In Great Brittan the term is used to describe a line of people waiting to get into a movie or restaurant. In printing terms a **queue** is a group of documents all waiting to be printed on the same printer. Panther handles the queue like a master conductor; keeping everything in order, as it smoothly instructs the printer to print each document in turn. However, sometimes problems can occur that the Print Queue utility doesn't quite know how to handle. For example, it's possible that you want to place a job on hold while other jobs print (preferably yours), or you many want to delete a job. In fact, you can even instruct the printer to stop printing altogether.

Manage Print Queues

1. Open the Utilities folder, and then double-click the Printer Setup icon.

2. Double-click on a printer displaying a status of Printing.

3. Select a job, and then click one of the following:

   ◆ **Delete.** Deletes the job from the queue.

   ◆ **Hold.** Stops the printing of the selected job.

   ◆ **Resume.** Resumes printing of a held job.

   IMPORTANT *If the jobs in the queue are already stopped, the Stop Jobs button changes to a Start Jobs button.*

   ◆ **Stop Jobs.** Stops the printing of all the jobs in the queue.

   ◆ **Utility.** Performs routine maintenance to the printer.

4. Click the Close button.

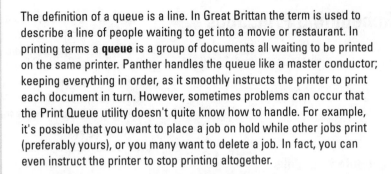

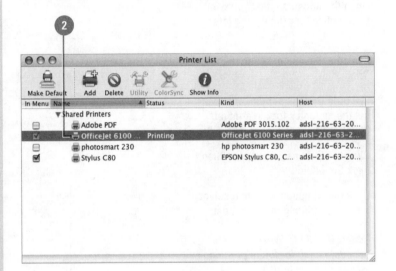

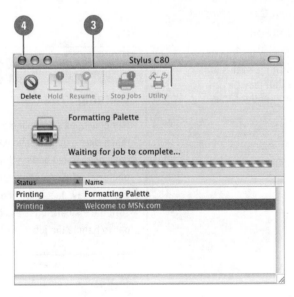

Scheduling Print Jobs

Sometimes it's just not the best time to print a document. For example, it's 10:00AM and the network printer is jammed with jobs being printed by fellow office workers, who are attempting to get their documents out before lunchtime. You know that by 12:15PM everyone is out to lunch, and the printers are free, but you don't want to lose a quarter of your lunch break just to click the Print button. The solution is to instruct the sending application to click the Print button for you, while you enjoy your much-deserved break.

Schedule Print Jobs

1. Open the document that you want to schedule for printing at a later time.

2. Click the File menu, and then click Print.

3. Click the Options pop-up, and then set the specifics for the print job (number of pages, paper, quality).

4. Click the Options pop-up, and then click Scheduler.

5. Click the At option, and then select a time for printing the document.

   IMPORTANT *When you schedule a job for future printing, you can only schedule into the future by 24 hours (23 hours and 59 minutes).*

6. Click the Priority pop-up, and then select the importance of this job, over other jobs that may be scheduled to print at the same time.

7. Click Print.

8. Quit your application.

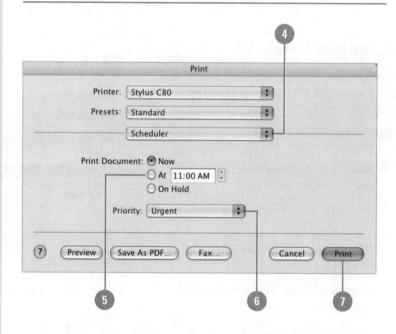

For Your Information

Running Print Jobs

Not only does scheduling a print job help you keep your lunch appointment, they can also save you a lot of time waiting for jobs to print. If you know ahead of time that you have a fifty-page report to print, you could schedule the job to print in the evening, and it'll be ready for you the next day. Just remember the printer will be running solo, so make sure the ink cartridges are okay and there's enough paper in the hopper to handle the job.

Creating a Cover Page

When you send a fax (**New!**), Panther now allows you to create a cover page. A cover page indicates to the person receiving the fax, the number of pages in the fax, who is sending the fax, the date and time the fax was sent, and a short text paragraph. Since the cover page represents how, and where the fax was sent, many companies require a cover page to be sent with every fax. In addition, the cover page acts as a protective cover over the fax, preventing others from reading sensitive material. On the other hand, some people feel the cover sheet is just a waste of a piece of paper. A good rule of thumb is use a cover page if the total fax pages equal five or higher. That way the receiver knows how many pages are coming his way. Since the decision to use a cover sheet is dependent on the document, Panther gives you the choice to add a cover sheet each time you generate a fax.

Create a Cover Page

1. Open a document that you want to fax.

2. Click the File menu, and then click Print.

3. Click Fax.

4. Select the Cover Page check box, and then type a short descriptive paragraph for the cover page.

5. Click Fax.

> **IMPORTANT** *You cannot press the Return key (to create a new paragraph) while generating the cover page text. Pressing the Return key only sends the fax prematurely. To get around this, create the cover page text in another application such as Microsoft Word, and then copy and paste it into the cover page field.*

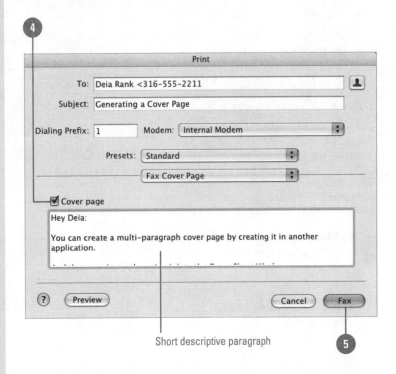

Short descriptive paragraph

Sending Fax Documents

Send Fax Documents

1. Open a document that you want to fax.

2. Click the File menu, and then click Print.

3. Click Fax.

4. Enter any prefixes into the Dialing Prefix field.

5. Click the Modem pop-up, and then select the modem that will be used to send the fax.

   IMPORTANT *If your modem does not appear in the list, click Show Fax List for a listing of all available fax output options.*

6. Click the Fax Options pop-up, and then select from the following options:

   ◆ **Fax Cover Page.** Select the Cover Page option, and then type the text to display on the Cover Page.

   ◆ **Modem.** Select between tone or pulse phones, whether to hear the dialing through your computer speakers, and if you want the modem to wait for a dial tone before beginning the fax process.

   ◆ **Copies & Pages.** Lets you select from options such as pages to print, number of copies, and page scaling.

Once you've decided whom the fax is to be sent to, and what the fax number is, the next step is to send the fax (**New!**). Sending a fax requires a knowledge of what type of modem you'll be using and what, if any, dialing prefixes are needed such as dialing 9 to get an outside line. Once you have that information, you're ready to send your document.

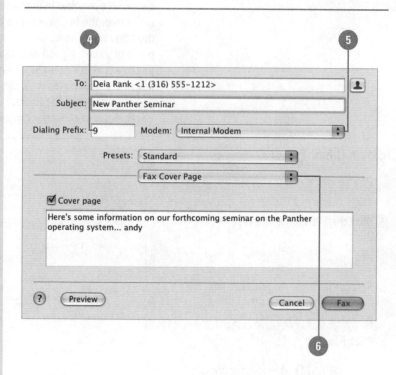

- **Layout.** When printing large documents such as spreadsheets, allows you to select how many pages per sheet, the layout direction, border options, and two-sided printing.

- **Output Options.** Saves the document as a Portable Document File (PDF) or Postscript (.ps) file.

- **Scheduler.** Lets you schedule a time for faxing the document.

- **Paper Handling.** Select to print in reverse order (page 1 prints last), whether to print all, odd, or even pages.

- **ColorSync.** Gives you access to Macintosh's powerful ColorSync management system, and the ability to apply the new Quartz Filters to the printed document.

- **Printer Features.** Select between low and high quality output.

- **Summary.** Summarizes all of the current settings.

7 Click Fax.

8 Close your document.

See Also

See "Scheduling Print Jobs" on page 176 for more information on scheduling print jobs.

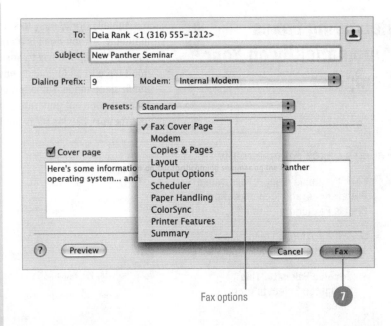

Fax options

Receiving Faxes Automatically on Your Computer

It's actually pretty easy to set up your computer to receive faxes automatically. All you need is a phone line, and Panther's Fax utility (New!). You can set up the Fax to answer after a certain number of rings, and you don't have to be logged in; however, your Macintosh needs to be on and not in sleep mode. Although your Macintosh can be set up to receive faxes, it does not generate a record of what you've received (or sent for that matter), like most fax applications.

Receive Faxes Automatically

① Click the Apple menu, click System Preferences, and then click the Print & Fax icon.

② Click the Faxing tab, and then select from the following options:

◆ **Receive Faxes On This Computer.** Select to receive faxes.

◆ **My Fax Number.** Enter your fax number into the field, exactly as you would dial the number.

◆ **When a Fax Arrives Answer After.** Enter how many rings are required before the Fax answers the phone.

◆ **Save To.** Select the check box, and then select where to save the faxes.

◆ **Email To.** Select the check box, and then select where to e-mail the faxes.

◆ **Print On Printer:** Select the check box, and then select a printer. Faxes automatically are printed as they are received.

③ Click the Close button.

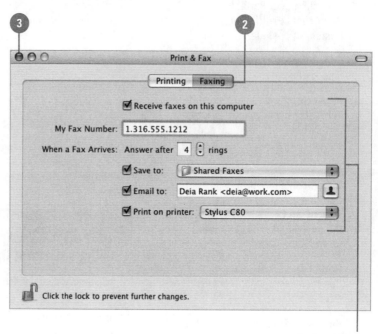

Faxing options

Turn Sleep Mode Off

1. Click the Apple menu, click System Preferences, and then click the Energy Saver icon.

2. Click the Sleep tab.

3. Drag the slider to the Never option.

4. Click the Close button.

Did You Know?

You can set up the computer and monitor to sleep at different times.
If you want your computer to stay awake, but don't want your monitor to stay on, open the Energy Saver, and then drag the Put The Monitor To Sleep to the right. Your computer stays awake, the monitor sleeps after the inactive time passes, and you won't waste power.

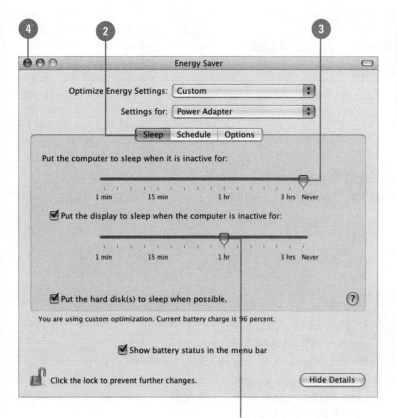

Monitor goes to sleep after one hour of inactivity.

Addressing Faxes from the Address Book

When you send a Fax, you need a document, and a fax number to send it. For example, you have a document that needs to be sent to your co-worker, and you remember that you added her fax number to her address card in the Address Book application (smart move). Do you need to open the Address Book, and write that number down, so that you have it when you send the Fax? No. Panther gives you the ability to pull that information directly from the address card with the click of a button (New!). Remember that in order for an address card to be used for faxing, it must first have a fax number entered into the card.

Address Faxes from the Address Book

1. Open a document that you want to fax.

2. Click the File menu, and then click Print.

3. Click Fax.

4. Click the Address Book button, and then select a name from your address list.

5. Click the To button to add the name and fax number to the current fax request.

6. Click the Close button.

7. Click the Subject field and type a subject for the fax.

   Continue on with your fax requirements.

   IMPORTANT *The Address Book feature does not currently work when using Microsoft Word or Excel. Point your browser to http://www.microsoft.com/mac/, and check for the latest Microsoft updates and patches.*

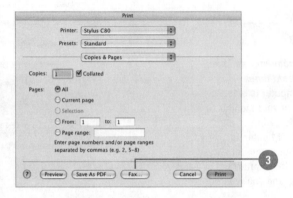

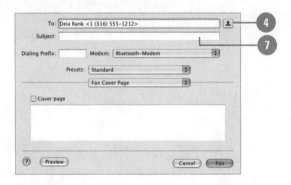

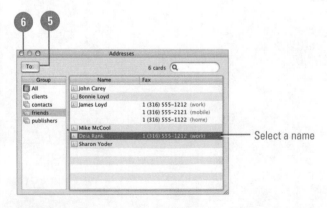

Select a name

Exploring the Internet

8

Introduction

The **Internet** is a global collection of more than 100 million computers (and growing) linked together to share information. The Internet's physical structure includes telephone lines, cables, satellites, and other telecommunications media. Using the Internet, computer users can share many types of information, including text, graphics, sounds, videos, and computer programs. The **World Wide Web** (also known as the Web or www) is a part of the Internet that consists of Web sites located on different computers around the world.

History of the Internet and the World Wide Web

The Internet has its roots in the Advanced Research Projects Agency Network (ARPANET), which the United States Department of Defense started in 1969. In 1986, the National Science Foundation formed NSFNET, which replaced ARPANET. NSFNET expanded the foundation of the U.S. portion of the Internet with high-speed, long-distance data lines. In 1991, the U.S. Congress expanded the capacity and speed of the Internet further and opened it to commercial use. The Internet is now accessible in almost every country in the world. The World Wide Web was developed in Switzerland in 1991 to make finding documents on the Internet easier. Software programs designed to access the Web, known as Web browsers, use point-and-click interfaces. The first such Web browser, Mosaic, was introduced at the University of Illinois in 1993. Since the release of Mosaic, Microsoft Internet Explorer, Netscape, and AOL have become some of the most popular Web browsers.

Connecting to the Internet

Universities and large companies are most likely connected to the Internet via high-speed wiring that transmits data very quickly. Home computer owners usually rely on a modem and the phone lines already in place. In some areas, however, several faster connection options are becoming available and affordable. There are **DSL** (Digital Subscriber Lines), wires that provide a complete digital connection; **cable modems**, which use cable television lines; and **wireless**, which doesn't use wires or phone lines. DSL and cable modems, also known as **broadband** connections, are continually turned on and connected to an Ethernet network so you don't need to establish a connection using a dial-up modem. Data travels more slowly over phone wires than over digital lines and cable modems. Wireless provides a mobile connection to the Internet using an AirPort connection anywhere there is a wireless base station, such as a router or a network hub. Whether you use a phone line, a DSL line, a cable modem, or a wireless device, Mac OS X Panther can help you establish a connection to the Internet.

Before you start the process to set up an Internet connection, you need to select an ISP (Internet Service Provider), which is a company that sets up an Internet account for you and provides Internet access. ISPs maintain servers connected directly to the Internet 24 hours a day. You pay a fee, sometimes by the hour, but more often a flat monthly rate. To connect to the Internet, you need to obtain an Internet account and connection information from your ISP or your system administrator. Each type of Internet connection requires certain connection information, including:

◆ **ISP Phone Number.** A number to create a dial-up connection.

◆ **Account Name.** A user name for the Internet account.

◆ **Password.** A security password for the Internet account.

◆ **IP Address.** An IP (Internet Protocol) address is a unique identifier of your computer on the Internet.

◆ **Subnet Mask.** A filter that helps your computer differentiate between computers on a local network and on the Internet.

◆ **Router.** A device address that sends and receives information over the Internet.

◆ **Domain Name Server (DNS).** A computer that translates a Web site name, such as *www. perspection.com*, into an IP address.

◆ **Proxy.** A computer your Macintosh uses to access the Internet.

When you have the connection information from your ISP or network administrator, you can use the Network pane (New!) in System Preferences to set up, configure, and display status for all your network connections, such as Internal Modem, Built-in Ethernet, and AirPort.

Network pane in System Preferences

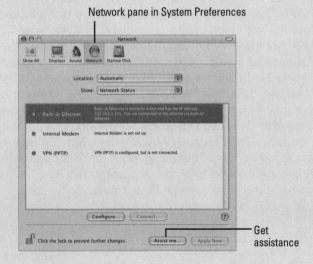

Get assistance

Getting Internet Connection Assistance

At the bottom of the Network pane is the Assist Me button. When you click the Assist Me button, it starts the Network Setup Assistant, which asks you a series of questions to help you set up your Internet Connection.

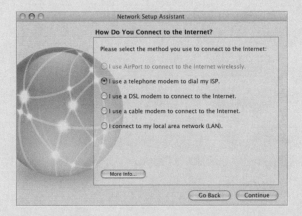

Creating Multiple Connections

If you have a mobile computer, such as a PowerBook, you can set up multiple connections for different locations. Setting up multiple connections allows you to connect to the Internet at home using a dial-up connection, at the office using an ethernet connection, or on the road using a wireless connection.

If you have a dial-up modem or AirPort card, you can use the Internet Connect application located in the Applications folder to help you quickly create an Internet connection to different configurations in your current location.

Protecting your Computer from the Internet

When you connect to the Internet, you can access Web sites and information on the Internet, but other users on the Internet can also access information on your computer. You can prevent this by activating a firewall, another security layer of protection. A **firewall** is a security system that creates a protective barrier between your computer or network and others on the Internet. The firewall monitors all communication between your computer and the Internet and prevents unsolicited inbound traffic from the Internet from entering your private computer. The firewall discards all unsolicited communication from reaching your computer unless you specifically allow it to come through. If your computer is directly connected to the Internet, you should activate a firewall. If you are sharing an Internet connection on your network to provide Internet access on multiple computers, you should activate the firewall on the computer connected to the Internet only to avoid creating network communication problems. For more information and instructions on setting up a firewall, see "Configuring an Internet Firewall," on page 407 in Chapter 17.

Sharing an Internet Connection

If you have an Internet connection and work on a network, you can share the Internet connection with other computers on your local area network. For more information and instructions on sharing an Internet connection, see "Sharing an Internet Connection," on page 406 in Chapter 17.

Setting Up a Modem Connection

If you have a dial-up modem installed on your computer, you can set up and use a modem connection to access the Internet or another computer. You only need to set up a dial-up connection once. After you set up the dial-up connection, you can use the Show Modem Status menu to easily connect and disconnect from the Internet or network, and show modem connection information. When you are connected, the Finder displays a connection icon and connects information in the menu.

Set Up a Modem Connection

1. Click the System Preferences icon in the Dock, and then click the Network icon.

2. Click the Show pop-up, and then click Internal Modem.

3. Click the PPP tab, and then specify your user name, password, and ISP phone number.

4. Click PPP Options to specify options to redial a busy connection, automatically connect when starting TCP/IP applications, and automatically disconnect if you select Log Out from the Apple menu.

5. Click the TCP/IP tab, and then specify any settings provided by your ISP, such as IP Address, Subnet Mask, Router, and DNS Servers.

6. Click the Proxies tab, and then specify any settings provided by your ISP.

7. Click the Modem tab, and then specify any settings specific to your computer's modem. Common commands include the option to turn off the speakers to avoid hearing the connection sound and the option to show modem status in the menu bar.

8. Click Apply Now.

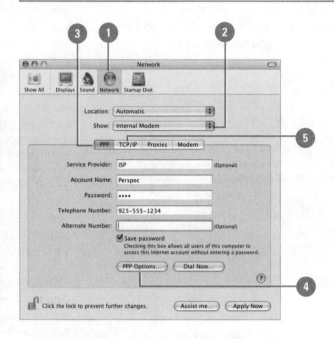

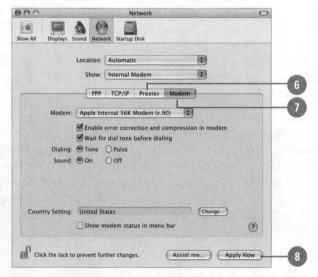

Setting Up a Built-In Ethernet Connection ▶

If you have a DSL or cable modem, you can set up and use an ethernet connection to access the Internet. In addition to connecting to the Internet, you also use ethernet to connect to a local area network (LAN). When you set up an ethernet connection using a cable modem or on a corporate network, some settings are typically configured automatically by a **BOOTP** (boot protocol) or **DHCP** (Dynamic Host Configuration Protocol). If your network supports ones of these services, you can use the Configure IPv4 pop-up in the TCP/IP area to select a protocol. Check with your ISP or network administrator to determine if this applies to you.

Set Up a Built-In Ethernet Connection

1. Click the System Preferences icon in the Dock, and then click the Network icon.

2. Click the Show pop-up, and then click Built-In Ethernet.

3. Click the TCP/IP tab, and then specify any settings provided by your ISP or network administrator, such as IP Address, Subnet Mask, Router, and DNS Servers.

   TROUBLE? *If your Internet connection is having problems, click Renew DHCP Lease to refresh your IP address, which can sometimes correct the problem.*

4. Click the PPPoE tab, select the Connect Using PPPoE check box, and then specify your account name and password.

5. Click the AppleTalk tab, and then specify settings to control whether you want to be part of a local AppleTalk network.

6. Click the Proxies tab, and then specify any settings provided by your ISP or network administrator.

7. Click the Ethernet tab, and then select a configuration (automatic or manual) and specify settings.

8. Click Apply Now.

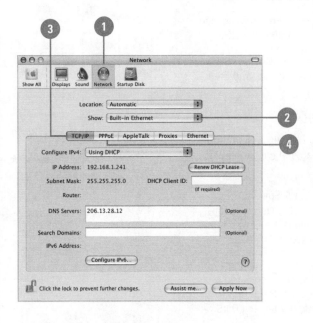

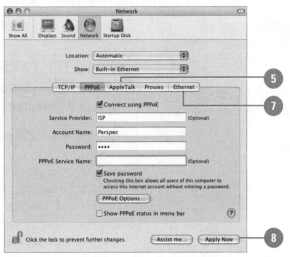

Setting Up an AirPort Connection

If you have an AirPort card on your computer and are within range of a wireless base station, such as a router or network hub, you can set up and use an AirPort connection to access the Internet. AirPort is Apple's 802.11b-based wireless networking device that enables you to connect to the Internet without using network wires or phone lines. Setting up an AirPort connection is similar to setting up an ethernet connection. AirPort networks are identified by a network name. You can join a specific network or select one of the detected AirPort networks.

Set Up an AirPort Connection

1. Click the System Preferences icon in the Dock, and then click the Network icon.

2. Click the Show pop-up, and then click AirPort.

3. Click the AirPort tab.

4. Click the By Default, Join pop-up, and click Automatic or A Specific Network.

5. If you selected A Specific Network, click the Network pop-up, and then select a network, and type the password.

6. Click the TCP/IP tab, and then specify any settings provided by your ISP, such as IP Address, Subnet Mask, Router, and DNS Servers.

7. Click the AppleTalk tab, and then specify settings to control whether you want to be part of a local AppleTalk network.

8. Click the Proxies tab, and then specify any settings provided by your ISP.

9. Click Apply Now.

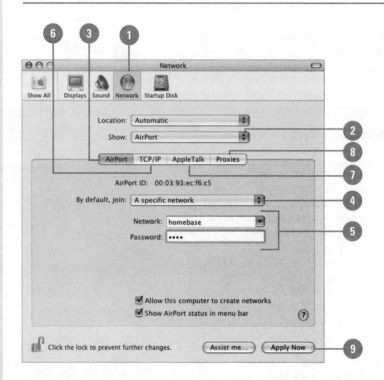

For Your Information

Create a Computer-to-Computer Network

When you select an AirPort network connection in the Network pane, you have the option to create a computer-to-computer network with other AirPort-enabled computers even if no official network is present. To create the network, click the AirPort tab, select the Allow This Computer To Create Networks and the Show AirPort Status In Menu Bar check boxes, click the AirPort status menu, click Create Network, enter a network name, an optional password, and then click OK.

Setting Up Multiple Connections

If you have a mobile computer, such as a PowerBook, you can set up multiple connections. For example, you can use a laptop to access the Internet at home using a dial-up modem, go to work and connect to a network using ethernet, or relax at a coffee shop and browse the Web using AirPort. When you have multiple connections, the Mac OS X attempts to connect to these networks in the order they appear from top to bottom in the Network pane. Each set of network connections is called a **network port configuration**. You can create different port configurations with unique priorities for different locations, which makes switching from one location to another easier. You can quickly access different locations using the Location submenu on the Apple menu.

Set Network Port Priorities and Locations

1. Click the System Preferences icon in the Dock, and then click the Network icon.

2. Click the Show pop-up, and then click Network Port Configurations.

3. Click the Location pop-up, and then select one of the following options:

   - **Automatic.** Default location.

   - **A location name.** Switches to the location name.

   - **New Location.** Creates a new location, such as "home".

   - **Edit Location.** Changes settings for a location.

4. Select or clear the check boxes with the network you want to enable or disable.

5. To change the connection order (priorities), drag the network port configurations up or down in the list.

6. To create alternative configurations for each connection method, use the New, Edit, Delete, and Duplicate buttons.

7. Click Apply Now.

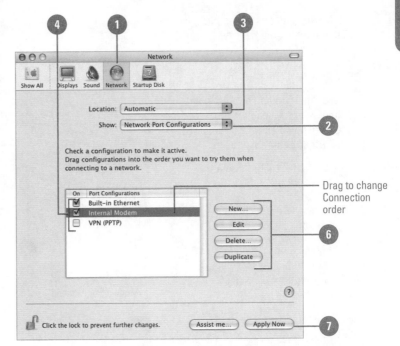

Drag to change Connection order

For Your Information

Understanding Infrared Wireless Communication

Infrared wireless communication technology allows you to transfer files between computers, typically laptops, with infrared ports even when no formal network is available. IrDA is an infrared wireless communication protocol, a set of rules, that enables computer-to-computer interaction.

Using Internet Connect

Instead of performing separate tasks to change a network port configuration in the Network Preferences pane and connect to the Internet, you can use the Internet Connect application to perform both tasks at the same time. The Internet Connect application makes it easy to quickly log into different configurations in your current location for dial-up modem, ethernet, and AirPort connections. For an AirPort connection, the Internet Connect application also displays a readout of the wireless signal strength, the base station id you are connected to, and the status of the connection.

Use Internet Connect for a Modem

1. Open the Applications folder, and then double-click the Internet Connect icon.

2. Click Internal Modem.

3. Click the Configuration pop-up, and then select a modem configuration you already created, or click Other to create one.

4. Enter the phone number for your ISP.

5. Type the Internet Account Name and Password.

6. To display the modem menu for easy connection access, select the Show Modem Status In Menu Bar check box.

7. Click Connect to start a dial-up connection.

8. Click the Close button, and then name and save the configuration.

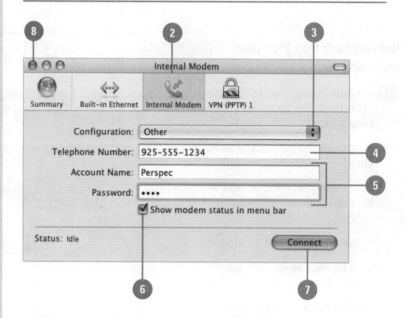

Use Internet Connect for a Built-In Ethernet

1. Open the Applications folder, and then double-click the Internet Connect icon.

2. Click Built-In Ethernet.

3. Enter the PPPoE Service Provider.

4. Type the Internet Account Name and Password.

5. To display the modem menu for easy connection access, select the Show PPPoE Status In Menu Bar check box.

6. Click Connect to start a dial-up connection.

7. Click the Close button, and then name and save the configuration.

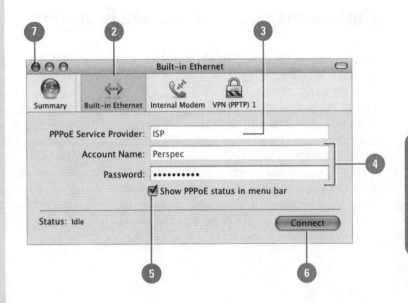

Use Internet Connect for AirPort

1. Open the Applications folder, and then double-click the Internet Connect icon.

2. Click AirPort.

3. Click Turn AirPort On or Turn AirPort Off to enable or disable the AirPort card in your computer.

4. Click the Network pop-up, and then select the wireless network that you want to connect.

5. To display the AirPort menu for easy connection access, select the Show AirPort Status In Menu Bar check box.

6. Click the Close button, and then name and save the configuration.

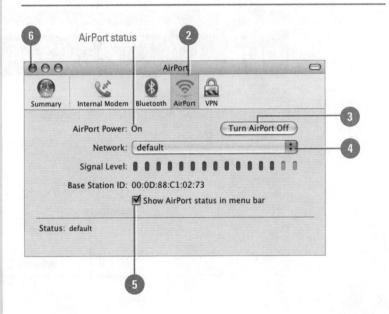

Understanding Web Sites and Browsers

A **Web site** contains Web pages linked together to make searching for information on the Internet easier. **Web pages** are documents that contain highlighted words, phrases, and graphics, called **hyperlinks** (or simply **links**) that open other Web pages when you click them. Some Web pages contain frames. A **frame** is a separate window within a Web page that lets you see more than one Web page at a time. **Web browsers** are software programs that you use to "surf the Web," or access and display Web pages. Browsers make the Web easy to navigate by providing a graphical, point-and-click environment. Safari is a new browser from Apple that is built into Mac OS X Panther. Microsoft Internet Explorer and Netscape Navigator are other popular browsers. With a Web browser, you can display Web pages from all over the world, use links to move from one Web page to another, play audio and video clips, search the Web for information, bookmark Web pages for easy access, and print text and graphics on Web pages.

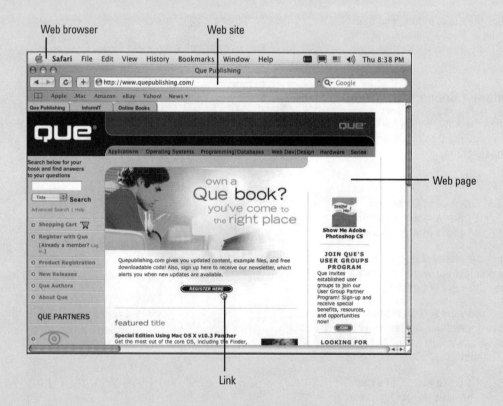

Web browser

Web site

Web page

Link

Starting Safari

Safari (**New!**) is a Web browser that you use to search the World Wide Web. You can start the Safari application using the Safari button in the Dock or the Safari icon in the Applications folder. After you start Safari, you might need to enter a user name and password when you use a dial-up modem to establish a connection to the Internet. After you establish a connection to the Internet, you are ready to explore Web pages on the Internet.

Start the Safari Application

① Display the Dock on the desktop, and then click the Safari icon.

② If necessary, click Connect to dial your ISP. You might need to type your user name and password before Safari connects to the Internet.

The Safari window opens.

Did You Know?

You can start Safari from your hard drive. Double-click your hard drive icon, double-click Applications, and then double-click the Safari icon.

Safari automatically imports bookmarks upon initial launch. The first time you start Safari, the application imports your bookmarks from Microsoft Internet Explorer, Netscape Navigator, and Mozilla.

See Also

See "Customizing the Safari Window" on page 195 for information on showing and hiding Safari window elements.

Viewing the Safari Window

Menu bar
Contains all the commands you need to access and move around Web pages, customize Safari, and get Help.

Address bar
Provides buttons to locate and move around Web pages, as well as a place to enter or display the address of the current Web page.

Bookmarks bar
Contains buttons for quick access of favorite Web sites.

Google Search bar
Provides the ability to search the Web using the Google search engine.

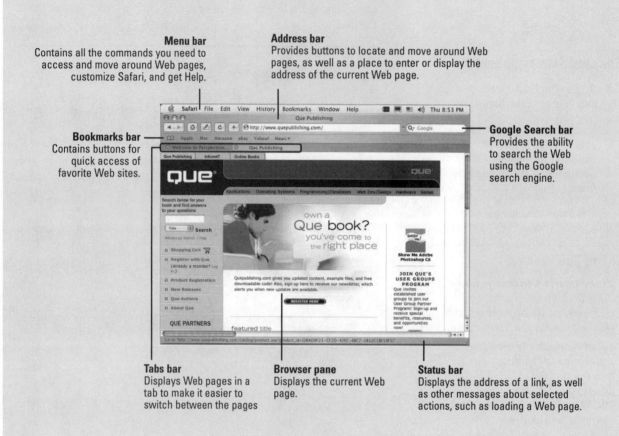

Tabs bar
Displays Web pages in a tab to make it easier to switch between the pages

Browser pane
Displays the current Web page.

Status bar
Displays the address of a link, as well as other messages about selected actions, such as loading a Web page.

Customizing the Safari Window

When you start Safari, the program window displays buttons on the toolbar, status bars, and tabs. The elements of the Safari window allow you to view, print, and search for information on the Internet. You can customize the Safari window display to conform to the way you work. The View menu allows you to turn on and off different display elements. A check mark next to an item on the View menu indicates the element appears in the Safari window, while a blank area indicates it's hidden.

Customize the Safari Window

① Click the View menu.

② Click the menu item with the element you want to show or hide in the Safari window.

- ◆ Address Bar
- ◆ Back/Forward
- ◆ Home
- ◆ AutoFill
- ◆ Text Size
- ◆ Stop/Reload
- ◆ Add Bookmark
- ◆ Google Search
- ◆ Bug
- ◆ Bookmarks Bar
- ◆ Status Bar

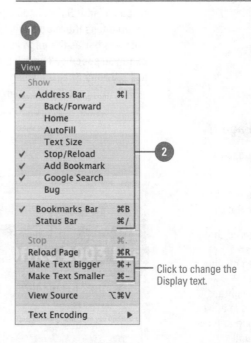

Click to change the Display text.

For Your Information

Selecting a Text Encoding

Text encoding determines how characters appear in a Web page. When a Web page doesn't specify text encoding, Safari uses the default text encoding specified in the Appearance pane of Safari preferences. Sometimes when the Safari default text encoding doesn't correspond with the desired Web page text encoding, you can see garbled text. If the text in a Web page is garbled, use the View menu to select a text encoding that corresponds to the language used in most of the Web pages you visit. This may fix the problem.

Browsing the Web

A **Web address** (also known as a **URL**, which stands for Uniform Resource Locator) is a unique place on the Internet where you can locate a Web page. With Safari, you can browse sites on the Web with ease by entering a Web address or by clicking a link. You might type an address in the Address bar to start your session. Then you might click a link on that Web page to access a new site. With Safari, you can enter Web addresses faster. When you type a Web address in the Address bar, Safari tries to find a recently visited page that matches what you've typed so far. If Safari finds a match, it fills in the rest of the address. As Safari opens the Web page, the Address box shows a blue-shaded progress bar as the page loads. The first page you open in a window or a page you specifically mark is the SnapBack page (**New!**). Each window has only one SnapBack page. Safari remembers this page so you can quickly return to it after opening other Web pages.

Open and View a Web Page

Use any of the following methods to display a Web page:

◆ In the Address box, type the Web address, and then press Return.

If you have recently entered the Web page address, Safari remembers it and tries to complete the address for you. The suggested match is highlighted. Click the correct address in a list of possibilities or continue to type until the address you want appears in the Address list.

◆ Click any link on the Web page, such as a picture or colored, underlined text. The mouse pointer changes to a hand when it is over a link.

Type a Web address

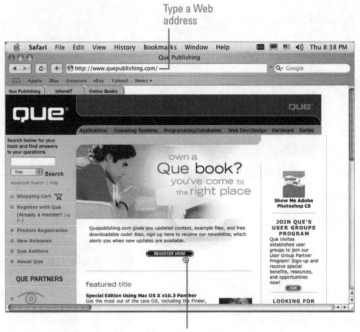

Click a link

Mark and Return to the SnapBack Page

1. Open the Web page you want to be the SnapBack page.

2. Click the History menu, and then click Mark Page For SnapBack.

3. Click a link to another Web page.

   IMPORTANT *If you type an address in the Address box, select a bookmark or select a Web page from the History menu, the Web page is marked as the SnapBack page.*

4. Click the SnapBack button (an orange circle) in the Address box.

   IMPORTANT *If you perform a Google search or click the SnapBack button in the Google search box, Safari removes the SnapBack button from the Address box.*

Did You Know?

You can open a Web page on your hard disk or network server. Click the File menu, click Open File, type the complete path and file name of the Web page, and then click Open.

You can open a Web page from a document in another application. Select the Web address, click the application menu (such as TextEdit), point to Services, and then click Open URL.

For Your Information

Understanding a Web Address

The address for a Web page is called a URL. Each Web page has a unique URL that is typically composed of four parts: the protocol (a set of rules that allow computers to exchange information), the location of the Web site, the name that maintains the Web site, and a suffix that identifies the type of site. A URL begins with a protocol, followed by a colon, two slashes, the location of the Web site, a dot, the name of the Web site, a dot, and a suffix. The Web site is the computer where the Web pages are located. At the end of the Web site name, another slash may appear, followed by one or more folder names and a file name. For example, in the address, http://*www*.perspection.com/downloads/main.htm, the protocol is *http* (HyperText Transfer Protocol), the location of the Web site is *www* (World Wide Web), the name of the Web site is *perspection*, and the suffix is *com* (a commercial organization); a folder at that site is called */downloads*; and within the folder is a file called *main.htm*.

Browsing the Web Using Tabs

When you open a Web page, it opens in the same window you are using. If you want to view more than one page at a time, you can open Web pages in separate tabs or new windows (New!). Before you can open Web pages in tabs, you need to turn on tabbed browsing in Safari Tab Preferences. You can also specify other tab options to select new tabs as they are created or always show the Tab bar. When you open a page in a tab or set the Safari Tab Preference option, the Tab bar appears (below the Bookmarks bar) with the name of the Web page along with a box you can use to close the tab. If you select a Web page from the History or Bookmarks menu, the page opens in the current tab. When you use the Back and Forward buttons in the Address bar, Safari displays Web pages previously viewed in the current tab.

Enable Tabbed Browsing

① Click the Safari menu, and then click Preferences.

② Click Tabs.

③ Select the Enable Tabbed Browsing check box.

④ To open new tabs in front of the current tab, select the Select New Tabs As They Are Created check box.

> **IMPORTANT** *When you enable tabbed browsing or Select New Tabs As They Are Created, shortcuts for opening Web pages in separate tabs and windows change. The bottom of the Tab Preferences window displays the new shortcuts. The shortcuts change revert back when you disable the options.*

⑤ Select or clear the Always Show Tab Bar check box.

⑥ Click the Close button.

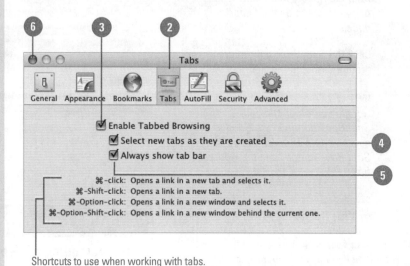

Shortcuts to use when working with tabs.

Open and View a Web Page in a Tab

◆ To open a Web page in a tab, click the File menu, click New Tab, type the Web address, and then press Return.

◆ To open a link or bookmark in a tab, hold down ⌃⌘, and then click the item.

◆ To open a bookmark collection in the Bookmarks bar in tabs, hold down the Control key, click the collection in the Bookmarks bar, and then click Open In Tabs.

◆ To open a folder of bookmarks in the Bookmarks Library in tabs, click the Bookmarks menu, click Show All Bookmarks, hold down the Control key, click the folder in the right pane, and then click Open In Tabs.

◆ To switch between Web page tabs, click the tab in the Tab bar.

◆ To close a tab, click the Close box on the tab.

TIMESAVER *Hold down the Option key and click the Close box to show the Web page and close all other tabs.*

Tab   Close box

Did You Know?

You can open a Web page in a different window. Click the File menu, click New Window, type the Web address, and then click Open. To open a Web page in a new window using a link, hold down the Control key, click a link or bookmark, and then click Open Link In New Window. To find out the address of a link, point to it, and then view the Status bar. To switch between open windows, use the Window menu.

Navigating Basics

As you browse the Web, you may want to retrace your steps and return to a Web page you've recently visited. You can move backward or forward one location at a time to show sites you've previously visited in this session. After you start to load a Web page, you can stop if the page opens too slowly or if you decide not to access it. If a Web page loads incorrectly or you want to update the information it contains, you can reload, or refresh the page. If you get lost on the Web, you can start over with a single click of the Home button.

Move Back or Forward

◆ To move back or forward one Web page at a time, click the Back button or the Forward button on the Address bar.

   TIMESAVER *To move back, press* ⌘+[*(left bracket). To move forward, press* ⌘+] *(right bracket).*

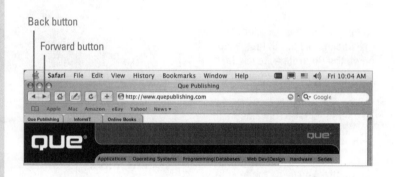

Back button

Forward button

Stop, Reload or Go Home

◆ To stop a page from loading, click the Stop button on the Address bar, or click the View menu, and then click Stop.

   TIMESAVER *Press* ⌘+. *(period).*

◆ To reload a page, click the Reload button on the Address bar, or click the View menu, and then click Reload.

   TIMESAVER *Press* ⌘+R.

◆ To go to the Home page, click the Home button on the Standard toolbar, or click the View menu, and then click Home.

   TIMESAVER *Press* ⌘+Shift+H.

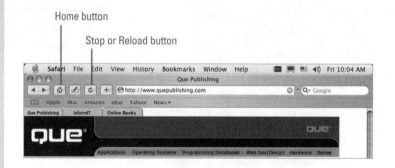

Home button

Stop or Reload button

Changing the Home Page

Your **home page** in Safari is the page that opens when you start the program. When you first install Safari, the default home page is the Apple Netscape Web site. If you want a different page to appear when you start Safari and whenever you click the Home button, you can change your home page. You can select one of the billions of Web pages available throughout the Internet.

Change the Home Page

1. Open the Web page you want to be the new home page.

2. Click the Safari menu, and then click Preferences.

3. Click General.

4. Click Set To Current Page.

5. Click the Close button.

Did You Know?

You can type a Web address for your home page. Click the Safari menu, click Preferences, click General, type a Web address in the Home Page box, and then click the Close button.

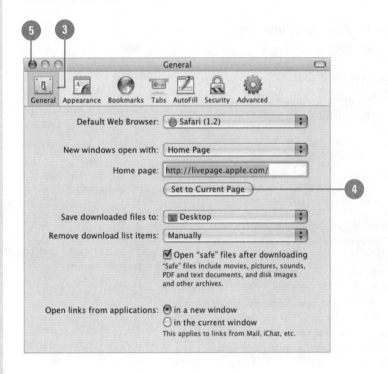

Viewing a History List

Sometimes you run across a great Web site and simply forget to add it to your Bookmarks list. With Safari there's no need to try to remember all the sites you visit. The History list keeps track of where you've been for a week organized by the date. To view the History list, click the History menu, and then point to a day. Safari deletes Web pages from the History list older than a week. If you no longer need the pages in the History list, you can clear the entire list.

Open a Web Page from the History List

1. Click the History menu.

2. If you want to open a Web page from another day, point to the date.

3. Scroll through the list, and then click the Web page.

Did You Know?

You can delete individual entries in the History. Click the Bookmarks menu, click Show All Bookmarks, click History in the Collections column, select the entry you want to remove, press Delete, and then click the Close button.

You can clear the entire History list. Click the History menu, and then click Clear History.

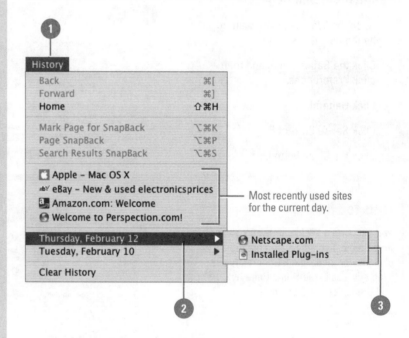

Most recently used sites for the current day.

For Your Information

Emptying the Cache

As you open Web pages, Safari saves the page content in a temporary location on your local hard disk, known as the **cache**, to make it faster to open the same pages next time. Anytime you display new content, the cache continues to increase in size, taking up valuable hard disk space. You can empty the cache at anytime to remove the local version of the Web page content and free up hard disk space. To empty the cache, click the Safari menu, click Empty Cache, and then click Empty.

Bookmarking a Web Page

Rather than memorizing URLs or keeping a handwritten list of Web pages you want to visit, you can use the Bookmarks Library (**New!**) to store and organize the addresses. When you display a Web page that you want to display again at a later time, you can add the Web page to your Bookmarks Library. After you add the Web page to the Bookmark Library, you can quickly return to the page by using the Bookmarks bar or Bookmarks menu to select it. This first time you start Safari, it automatically imports bookmarks from Internet Explorer, Netscape Navigator, and Mozilla in the Bookmarks Library. You cannot import bookmarks from other Web browsers in version 1.2 of Safari.

Add and Return to a Web Page in the Bookmarks Library

1. Open the Web site you want to add to your Bookmark list.

2. Click the Add Bookmark button in the Address bar.

   TIMESAVER *Drag the icon in the Address box to the Bookmarks bar to quickly add a bookmark.*

3. Type the name for the bookmark, or use the default name supplied.

4. Click the pop-up, and then select where you want to place the bookmark, either the Bookmarks Bar, Bookmarks Menu, or a collection of bookmarks in folders.

5. Click Add.

6. To quickly return to a bookmarked Web page, use the Bookmarks bar or Bookmarks menu.

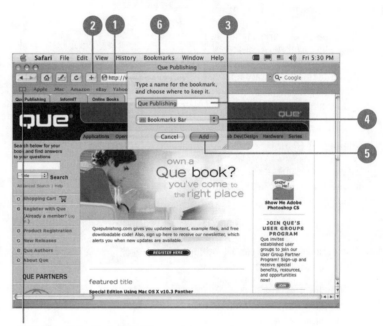

Click to go to the Bookmarks Library.

Did You Know?

You can drag a bookmark to move or delete it. Drag a bookmark to another place on the Bookmarks bar to move it, or outside the Safari window to delete it. You can also drag bookmarks and folders from the Bookmarks Library to the Bookmarks bar.

Working with Bookmarks

If your list of bookmarks grows long, you can use the Bookmarks Library to delete bookmarks you don't visit anymore or move bookmarks into folders to make them easier to find. The Bookmarks Library shows your collections of bookmarks in the left column, and the names and addresses of bookmarks and folders in the right column. You also use the Bookmarks Library to work with Web sites from cards in your Address Book and Rendezvous Web sites (New!). Safari uses Rendezvous to find any Web sites on your local network or subnet. Before you can work with the Address Book and Rendezvous, you need to enable the options in the Bookmarks pane of Safari preferences.

Create a Bookmark Folder

1. Click the Bookmarks menu, and then click Add Bookmark Folder.

   The Bookmarks Library opens, displaying a new untitled folder with the name selected.

2. Type a name for the folder, and then press Return.

3. Display the bookmarks you want to move in the folder in the right column.

4. Drag the bookmarks to the folder.

5. Click the Bookmarks Library button on the Bookmarks bar to close it.

   The folder appears on the Bookmarks bar with a triangle next to the name.

Did You Know?

You can add Rendezvous Web sites to the Bookmarks bar or menu. Click the Safari menu, click Preferences, click Bookmarks, select the Include Rendezvous check box where appropriate, and then click the Close button.

You can view a list of Rendezvous Web sites. Click the Bookmarks Library button on the Bookmarks bar, and then click Rendezvous in the Collections column.

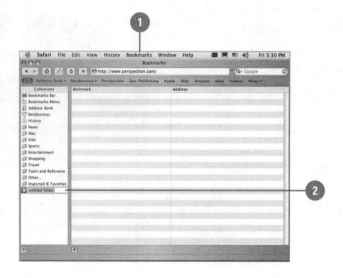

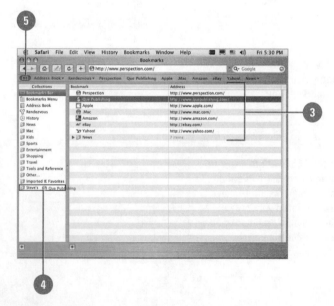

Organize Bookmarks in the Bookmarks Library

◆ **Show and hide Bookmarks Library.** Click the Bookmarks menu, and then click Show All Bookmarks or Hide All Bookmarks.

◆ **Create a collection.** Click the Add button (+) at the bottom of the Collections column.

◆ **Rename a collection.** Double-click the name, type a new name, and then press Return.

◆ **Add a folder to a collection.** Select a collection, and then click the Add button (+) at the bottom of the Bookmark column.

◆ **Rename a bookmark or folder.** Control-click the name, click Edit Name, type a new name, and then press Return.

◆ **Remove a collection, folder, or bookmark.** Select the item, and then press Delete.

◆ **Move or rearrange a collection, folder, or bookmark.** Locate the item, and then drag its icon to the location or icon where you want to place it. To copy it, hold down the Option key as you drag the icon.

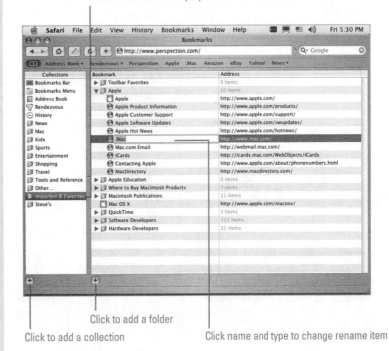

Click a collection to display folders and bookmarks

Click to add a folder

Click to add a collection

Click name and type to change rename item

Did You Know?

You can add Address Book home pages to the Bookmarks bar or menu. Click the Safari menu, click Preferences, click Bookmarks, select the Include Address Book check box where appropriate, and then click the Close button.

For Your Information

Syncing Bookmarks on Multiple Computers

Using iSync 1.1 or later and your .Mac account, you can automatically synchronize your bookmarks (**New!**) on different computers so they are the same. To get the latest version of iSync and sign up for a .Mac account, visit *www.apple.com*. When iSync discovers a change in a bookmark, Safari asks you to update your computer and the .Mac server using your .Mac account. Before you can use the service, you need to register your computer with the .Mac synchronization server. To do this, click Configure in the Bookmarks pane of Safari preferences, and then click the button to register in the iSync window; at this point you can also click Sync Now to manually synchronize bookmarks. To start synchronizing bookmarks, select the Synchronize My Bookmarks Using .Mac check box in the Bookmarks pane.

Filling Out Forms on the Web

Safari can use information in your Address Book or data you previously entered in an online form to automatically complete online forms you need to fill out in the future. **AutoFill (New!)** is a service that helps you complete online forms and log in to Web sites with a user name and password. You use the AutoFill pane of the Safari preferences to select, modify, or delete which information AutoFill uses to complete a form or log in. When you use AutoFill to automatically fill in information, Safari highlights the data in yellow so you can see the changes. If you no longer need the AutoFill service, you can keep Safari from automatically completing forms and log ins.

Set AutoFill Preferences

1. Click the Safari menu, and then click Preferences.

2. Click AutoFill.

3. Select or clear the Using Info From My Address Book Card check box to enable or disable AutoFill from information in your Address Book.

4. Select or clear the User Names And Passwords check box to enable or disable AutoFill from Web site log in information you've entered.

5. Select or clear the Other Forms check box to enable or disable AutoFill based on data from other online forms.

6. For any of the selected check boxes, click Edit to view or remove information stored by AutoFill.

7. Click the Close button.

> ### Did You Know?
>
> **You can display an alert before you send a non-secure form.** Click the Safari menu, click Preferences, click Security, select the Ask Before Sending A Non-Secure Form To A Secure Website check box, and then click the Close button.

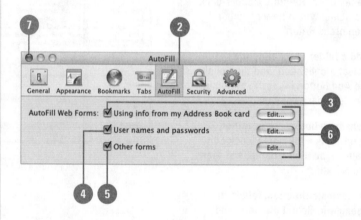

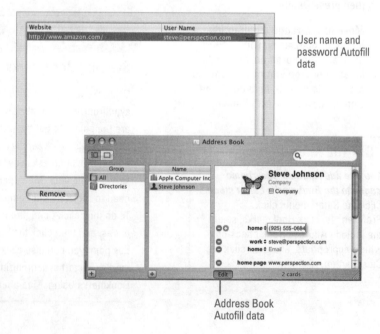

User name and password Autofill data

Address Book Autofill data

Fill Out Forms in Web Pages

1 Select the AutoFill data and set AutoFill options in the AutoFill pane of the Safari preferences window; click the Safari menu, click Preferences, and then click AutoFill.

2 Use any of the following methods to fill out forms using AutoFill:

◆ **Complete user name and password in a log in.** Display a log in screen, enter a user name and password, and then click Yes to save the log in information so you don't have to do again; click Not Now to defer saving the log in information until later; and click Never For This Website to not save log in information for this Web site.

◆ **Complete a Web form.** Open the Web page, and then click the AutoFill button in the Address bar.

◆ **Complete individual boxes in a form.** Open the Web page, select a text box, and then start typing. If AutoFill retrieves a match, it completes the text. If several items match, a list appears, where you can select the one you want to use.

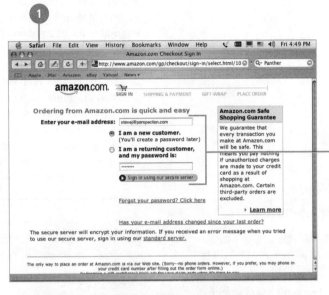

Enter user name and password

Click an AutoFill save option

For Your Information

Checking Spelling in Safari

You can't spell check the content of a Web page, but you can spell check any text you enter in a text box on a page. For example, if you type a word in a text box on a form or in the Google box in the Address bar, you can check its spelling before you complete the form or start the search. To check spelling, click in a text box, click the Edit menu, point to Spelling, and then click Check Spelling. If your computer doesn't recognize a word, a dialog opens, asking you to correct, ignore, or add the word to a dictionary. You can also check spelling as you type, like many word processing programs. When you select the Check Spelling As You Type command on the Spelling submenu located on the Edit menu, Safari displays a wavy red line under any term your computer doesn't recognize.

Searching the Web

You can find all kinds of information on the Web. The best way to find information is to use a search engine. A **search engine** is a program you access through a Web site and use to search through a collection of Internet information to find what you want. Safari comes with the Google search engine built-in to the program (New!). When performing a search, the search engine compares keywords with words that it finds on various Internet Web sites. **Keywords** are words or phrases that best describe the information you want to retrieve. If the search engine finds your keywords in the stored database, it lists links to the matched sites. When you open a link from the results, you can use the SnapBack button to quickly return to your search results. The company that manages the search engine determines what information its database stores, so search results of different search engines vary.

Search for Information

1 Click the Google Search box, type a word or phrase you want to find, and then press Return.

2 Click a link in the list of search results to open a Web page.

3 To return to the last page of Google search results, click the SnapBack button in the Google Search box.

4 To repeat a previous search, click the magnifying glass in the Google Search box, and then select the search term you want from the pop-up menu.

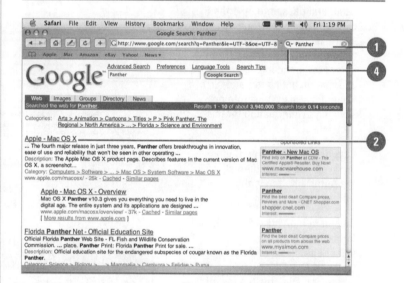

Did You Know?

You can find specific text on a Web page. Click the Edit menu, point to Find, click Find, type the text you want to find, and then click Next. The Find sub-menu also contains other Find commands: Find Again, Find Previous, and Use Selection For Find.

Printing a Web Page

Web pages are designed for viewing on a computer screen, but you can also print all or part of one. Before you print, you should preview the page to verify that it looks the way you want. When you are ready to print, Safari provides many options for printing Web pages. If the Web page consists of frames, you can print the specific frame you want to print. You can also use the Print dialog to create a PDF of a Web page or send a Web page as a fax.

Print a Web Page

① Open the Web page you want to print, click the File menu, and then click Print.

② Click the Printer pop-up, and then select from the available printer descriptions.

③ Click the Presets pop-up, and then select from the available preset options.

④ Click the Print Options pop-up, and then select from the available print options, such as Safari.

⑤ Choose the various options for the specific Print Option. When you select the Safari print option, you can print a Web page background.

⑥ Click the following options to finalize your print: Preview, Save As PDF, Fax, Cancel, or Print.

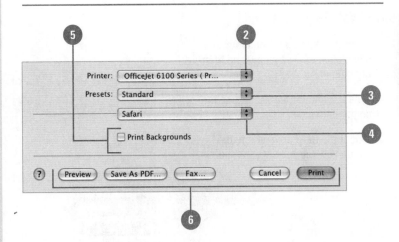

See Also

See Chapter 7, "Printing and Faxing," on page 161 for information on setting up and printing a page.

Did You Know?

You can print a frame of a Web page. Hold down the Control key, click the frame you want to print, click Print Frame, specify the options you want, and then click Print.

Saving a Web Page

You can save a Web page, and view it later from your local hard drive or use it as source for **HTML** (HyperText Markup Language) code, which instructs the browser how to display the Web page. When you save a Web page, Safari saves only the HTML text content of the current page. Other page elements, such as pictures, are not saved. Before you save a Web page you can view the HTML code to determine if you need it.

Save Web Page Text

1. Open the Web page you want to save, click the File menu, and then click Save As.

2. Type a name for the file, or use the suggested name.

3. Select the hard drive and folder in which you want to save the file.

4. Click Save.

Did You Know?

You can view the HTML code of a Web page. Open the Web page, click the View menu, and then click View Source. When you are done viewing, click the Close button.

See Also

See *"Saving and Closing a Document"* on page 158 for more information on using the Save As dialog.

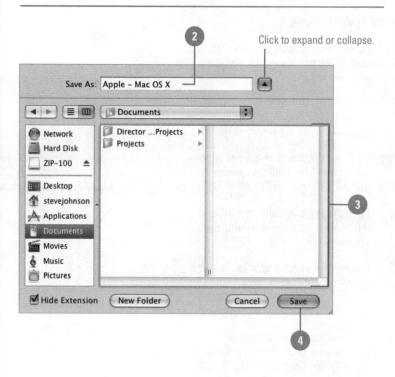

Click to expand or collapse.

Saving Pictures or Text from a Web Page

If you find information on a Web page that you want to save for future reference or share with others, you can copy and paste it to another document or save it on your computer. When you copy information from a Web page, make sure you're not violating any copyright laws.

Save a Picture from a Web Page

1. Open the Web page with the picture you want to save.

2. Control-click the picture, and then click Save Image As.

3. Type a name for the file.

4. Select the drive and folder in which you want to save the file.

5. Click Save.

Did You Know?

You can copy a picture to the clipboard. Control-click the picture, and then click Copy Image To Clipboard.

Copy Text from a Web Page

1. Open the Web page with the text you want to copy.

2. Select the text you want to copy.

   TROUBLE? *The I-beam cursor may or may not appear. You can still select the text.*

3. Control-click the selected text, and then click Copy.

4. Switch to where you want to paste the text.

5. Click the Edit menu, and then click Paste.

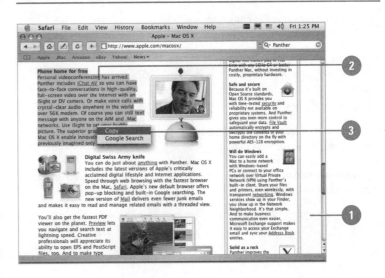

Downloading Files from the Web

There are thousands of sites on the Internet offering all sorts of files you can download to your computer, from trailers to the latest game demos. You can download files (**New!**) from any Web site by finding the file you want, and then clicking the download link. Safari automatically downloads the file to the location specified in the General pane of Safari preferences. During the downloading process, the Downloads window appears, displaying progress and status information. You can stop downloading a file, view a downloaded file in the Finder, and clear the Downloads window when it gets to full.

Download a File from a Web Page

1. Open the Web page that you want to download a file.

2. Click the Download Now link, or Control+click the link pointing to the actual file, and then click Download Linked File As.

   The Downloads window appears, displaying the estimated time to download the file, along with the estimated transfer time.

   TROUBLE? *If the Downloads window doesn't open, click the Window menu, and then click Downloads.*

3. When the download is complete, click the Close button.

   You may need to Quit Preview.

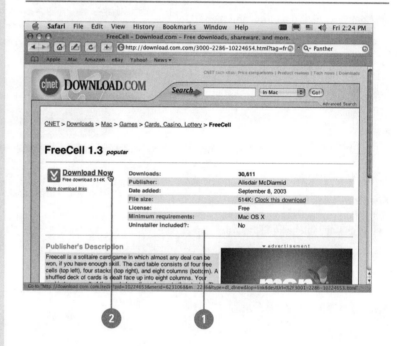

Safari opened the file

Did You Know?

You can access a site with lots of files to download. Try these sites to find plenty of files to download: *http://www.download.com* and *http://www.shareware.com*

Work with Files in the Downloads Window

1 If necessary, click the Window menu, and then click Downloads.

2 Perform any of the following operations.

◆ **Stop a downloading file.** Click the Stop icon to the right of the file name; to restart the download, click the icon again.

◆ **View a downloaded file.** Click the Magnifying Glass icon to the right of the file name.

◆ **Clear the Downloads window.** Click the Clear button. Clearing the window does not clear files that are being downloaded.

◆ **Remove a downloaded file.** Control-click the file name, and then click Remove From List.

3 Click the Close button.

See Also

See "Setting Safari Preferences" on page 214 for information on selecting the download file location and specifying when to remove downloaded items from the Downloads window.

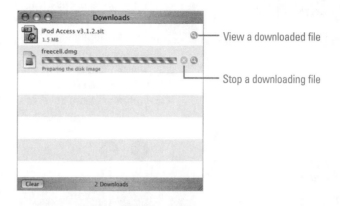

View a downloaded file

Stop a downloading file

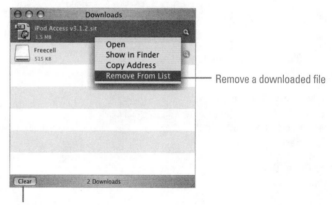

Remove a downloaded file

Clear the Downloads window

For Your Information

Downloading Disk Images and Installing Software

When you download a disk image, Safari decompresses the file and in some cases mounts a volume, and opens an installer program (if available). There are several different types of disk images. Safari works a little differently for each type. If you download a disk image in the MacBinary, BinHex, or gzip file format, Safari decompressed the file and opens an installer (if available). If you download an Internet Disk Image, Safari decompresses the file, opens an installer (if available), and moves the disk image to the Trash. If you download a disk image file, Safari decompresses the file, mounts the disk image volume, and opens an installer (if available).

Setting Safari Preferences

Safari preferences help you configure some of the more common features of the program. You can set preferences for General and Advanced options, Appearance, Bookmarks, Tabs, AutoFill, and Security. These preference areas allow you to turn features on and off as well as customize the way Safari works. General, Appearance, and Advanced preferences are covered here, while Bookmarks, Tabs, AutoFill, and Security preferences are covered throughout this chapter.

Set General Preferences

1 Click the Safari menu, and then click Preferences.

2 Click General.

3 Select or specify the various options you want to use:

- ◆ **Default Web Browser.** Select a default browser.

- ◆ **New Windows Open With.** Click the pop-up, and then click Home Page, Same Page, Empty Page, or Bookmarks.

- ◆ **Home Page.** Specify a Web address.

- ◆ **Save Downloaded Files To.** Click the pop-up, and then select Desktop or Choose Other to specify another location.

- ◆ **Remove Download List Items.** Click the pop-up, and then click Manually, When Safari Quits, or Upon Successful Download.

- ◆ **Open "Safe" Files After Downloading.** Check to automatically activate safe downloaded files, such as movies, pictures, sounds, PDF and text documents.

- ◆ **Open Links From Applications.** Select an option to open links in a new window or current tab.

4 Click the Close button.

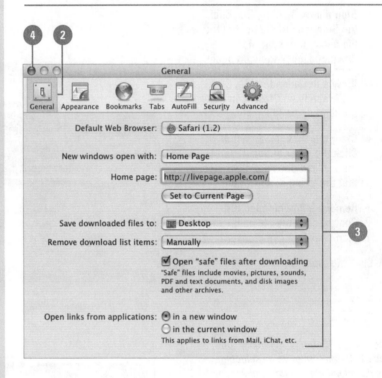

214

Set Appearance Preferences

1. Click the Safari menu, and then click Preferences.

2. Click Appearance.

3. For the Standard Font, click Select to choose a font for Web pages that don't specify one.

4. For the Fixed-Width Font, click Select to choose a fixed-width font for Web pages when you need to align text in a specific way.

5. Select or clear the Display Images When The Page Opens check box.

6. Click the Default Encoding pop-up, and then select a character encoding set, which tells your browser how to interpret and display characters in a Web page.

7. Click the Close button.

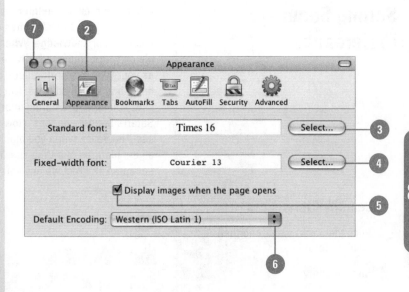

Set Advanced Preferences

1. Click the Safari menu, and then click Preferences.

2. Click Advanced.

3. Click the Style Sheet pop-up, and then click None Selected or select a style sheet, which specifies a uniform format for the appearance of Web pages.

4. Click Change Settings to modify settings for a proxy server. Setting typically required when you use an Internet firewall. See your ISP or network administrator for settings.

5. Click the Close button.

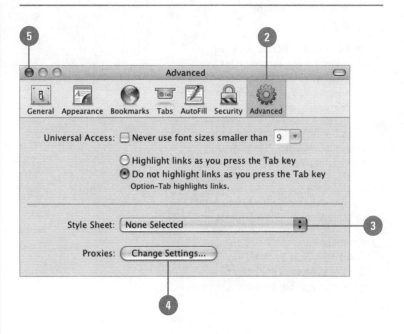

Setting Security Preferences

When you browse the Internet, you can access and gather information from Web sites, but Web sites can also gather information about you without your knowledge. When you visit a Web site, the site creates a file on your computer, known as a **cookie**, which stores information, such as your Web site preferences or personal information, including your name and e-mail address. Not all cookies are harmful; many cookies save you time re-entering information on a return visit to a Web site. Safari's Security options allow you to block or permit cookies from Web sites; however, when you block cookies, you might not be able to access all the features of a Web site. You can view the cookies that you have accepted and remove any you don't want.

Set Security Preferences

1. Click the Safari menu, and then click Preferences.

2. Click Security.

3. Select the Web Content check boxes you want to enable:

   ◆ **Enable Plug-ins.** A software module that provides additional functionality outside of HTML.

   ◆ **Enable Java.** A programming language for writing interactive Web pages.

   ◆ **Enable JavaScript.** A simple programming language for displaying simple interaction, such as image mouse rollover, or opening windows.

4. Click the Accept Cookies option you want: Always, Never, or Only From Sites You Navigate To.

5. To show the cookies on your computer and delete any you want to remove, click Show Cookies.

6. Select or clear the Ask Before Sending A Non-Secure Form To A Secure Website check box to enable or disable the option.

7. Click the Close button.

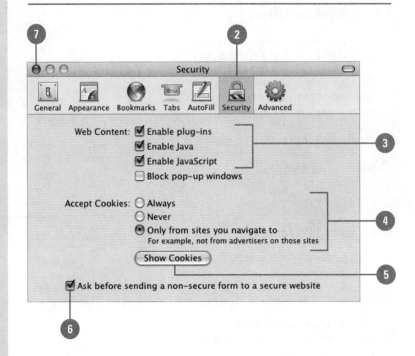

Blocking Pop-Up Windows

When you open or close a Web page, some pages display pop-up windows to advertise products and services or request login and other information. Pop-up windows can be extremely annoying. Most of the time you end up closing them. To avoid the continual borage of pop-up windows, you can block them in Safari. When you set Safari to block pop-up windows (**New!**), the program only stops pop-up windows that appear when you open or close a page, but not when you click a link.

Block Pop-Up Windows

① Click the Safari menu, and then click Preferences.

② Click Security.

③ Select the Block Pop-Up Windows check box.

TIMESAVER *Click the Safari menu, and then click Block Pop-up Windows to display a check mark on the menu.*

④ Click Block to confirm the option selection to block pop-up windows.

⑤ Click the Close button.

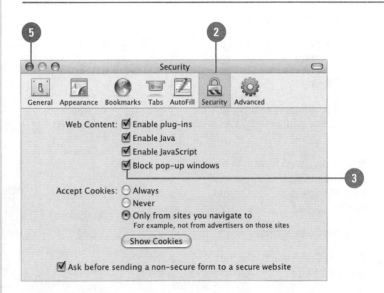

For Your Information

When Web Pages Don't Work

If you are getting error messages or having problems displaying all or part of a Web page, your security settings may be the cause of the problems. To potentially correct the problems, click the Safari menu, click Preferences, click Security, select the check boxes to use plug-ins, Java, and JavaScript, clear the Block Pop-Up Windows check box, and then click the Close button. A **Plug-in** is a software module developed by a third-party for use with Safari to provide additional functionality outside of HTML. Safari works with common plug-ins including Java, QuickTime, Shockwave Flash, and Shockwave for Director. To view which plug-ins recognized by Safari are installed on your computer, click the Help menu, and then click Installed Plug-Ins. If you continue to have problems, click the Apple menu, and then click Report Bugs to report the problem to Apple Computer.

Selecting a Default Browser

Mac OS X Panther comes with Safari as the default Web browser. If you prefer to use another browser, you can remove Safari from your computer, install another browser, such as Microsoft Internet Explorer or Netscape, and set it as your default Web browser program. When you click links in other applications, such as Mail messages, or double-click a Web Internet Location file icon, your default browser launches and opens the Web page in a new window or tab in the current window.

Select a Default Browser

1. Click the Safari menu, and then click Preferences.

2. Click General.

3. Click the Default Web Browser pop-up, and then select a Web browser.

4. In the Open Links From Applications area, click the In A New Window or In The Current Window option.

5. Click the Close button.

6. Click the Safari menu, and then click Quit Safari.

See Also

See "Downloading and Installing Software" on page 414 for information on adding or removing applications.

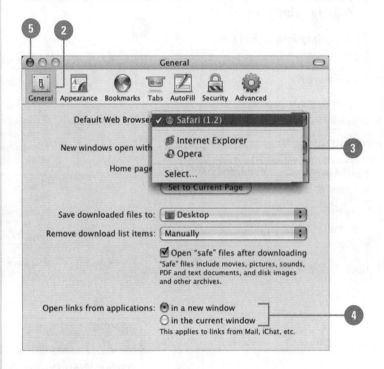

For Your Information

Reset Safari Settings

If you use a shared or public computer, you might want to reset Safari (New!) to prevent other people from seeing what you have been doing. When you reset Safari, the Web browser program clears the history list, Google search entries, and the Downloads window; removes all cookies saves by Safari and other related applications, such as Sherlock, and any saved AutoFill data, such as user names and passwords; and empties the cache. To reset Safari, click the Safari menu, and then click Reset.

Using Sherlock for Internet Searches

Introduction

Macintosh's Sherlock application is a slick way for you to create customized collections of Web services using individual channels that organize the information, which makes it easy to understand. For example, you can get organized information for movies that you like, as well as a listing of your favorite restaurants; even track your stock portfolio, all from one application.

Sherlock takes the confusion out of surfing the Internet, by letting you quickly decide what information you want, and how it's displayed—all without pop-up windows and annoying advertisements. You can quickly wade through the information to find exactly what you're interested in, and Sherlock changes the window display as you move through the preset and user-defined channels. If you want more channels, you can use the Internet channel to search for more channels.

Sherlock also allows you to search for standard Web pages by using the Internet channel and typing search words, just like any search engine. The difference between searching for Web content using Sherlock over a standard Web search engine, is that Sherlock searches at least six search engines simultaneously (listed at the bottom of the Sherlock window). That gives you the power to locate the information you're after in a minimum amount of time.

What You'll Do

Understand Collections and Channels

Use the Internet Channel

Use the Pictures Channel

Use Third-Party Channels

Use the Stocks Channel

Use the Movies Channel

Use the Phone Book Channel

Use the eBay Channel

Use the Flights Channel

Use the AppleCare Channel

Use the Dictionary Channel

Use the Translation Channel

Customize Sherlock

Understanding Collections and Channels

Sherlock is like using a Web browser to gather information over the Internet such as: stocks, flight information, movies, phone numbers, and much more. Sherlock uses a system of collections and channels to organize your Internet contacts, almost like a sophisticated bookmark system. **Collections** (New!) represent group names for specific areas of interest. For example, you could have a collection representing Web sites that offer help on Panther, or a collection of your favorite cooking sites. **Channels** are the actual sites assigned to the collections. By navigating through the channels you can quickly locate the exact information that you need. To use Sherlock you'll need a connection to the Internet, a desire to explore, and that's it.

Due to the differences between Panther, and earlier versions of the operating system, you cannot use channels and plug-ins from earlier versions of Sherlock with Sherlock 3. The Sherlock application is located in the Dock, or you can find it in the Applications folder. Once the program is opened, you can select from the preset collections on the toolbar or through the Collections column, and then select from the available channels. Clicking on a channel opens the specific choice within the Sherlock window. At that point, it's almost like browsing a very organized Web page: You can click on links, open pages within a browser window, even upload images and documents to your computer. It's a one stop, one shop, ultimate Web surfing application.

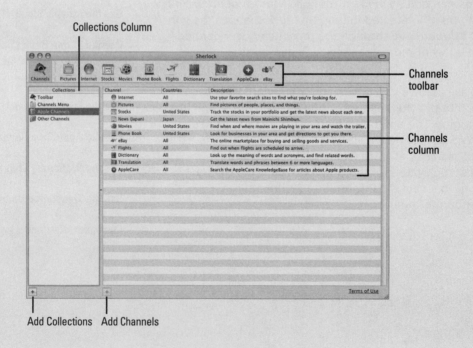

Collections Column

Channels toolbar

Channels column

Add Collections   Add Channels

Using the Internet Channel

The Sherlock Internet channel is your gateway to performing searches on a collection of Web sites, all strung together by a billion miles of wires, cables, fiber optics, and satellites, that we affectionately call the World Wide Web. Not all sites are Sherlock friendly and therefore, not all the information that we want is available for display within the Sherlock window. When you use the Internet channel, you type the search criteria for the information you're looking for, and Sherlock displays a listing of all sites listed by relevance to your search criteria. Therefore, the better you describe what you're looking for, the faster Sherlock can sort through the maze of possible Web sites, and give you the results you're after.

Use the Internet Channel

1 Open the Applications folder, and then double-click the Sherlock icon.

2 Click the Internet button.

3 Type the words or phrase you want to use to search the Internet into the Topic Or Description field.

4 Click the Search button (magnifying glass) or press Return.

5 Web sites are displayed (by default) in order or relevance.

6 Click on a Web site to display the first paragraph of text on the site.

7 Use the Scroll bar to move up and down through the list.

8 Double-click on any displayed site, to launch the Web site in your browser application (default Safari).

9 Quit Sherlock.

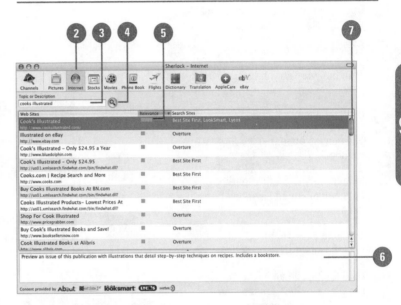

9

Using the Pictures Channel

It's been said that a picture is worth a thousand words. Pictures convey so much information. For example, the imprint of Neil Armstrong's boot print on the moon is more than just a dusty footprint, especially for those old enough to remember the event. And photographs mean different things to different people. A photograph of Paris might just be another boring travel image to one person, while to another it invokes memories of a exotic vacation, and desires to return to the City of Lights. We're constantly searching for that one perfect image that says exactly what we want, and Sherlock gives us an easy way to find it.

Use the Pictures Channel

1. Open the Applications folder, and then double-click the Sherlock icon.

2. Click the Pictures button.

3. Type the words or phrase you want to use to search the Internet.

4. Click the Search button.

5. The images appear in the Sherlock window.

6. If necessary, click the Search button again to add more pictures to the list.

7. Continue clicking the Search button until the images are loaded.

8. Double-click on an image, to open the Web site that contains the original photo, clipart, or graphic.

9. Follow the site instructions for using the image.

   IMPORTANT *When you download an image from the Internet, you typically have to pay a fee for the use of the photo. Failure to do so constitutes a copyright infringement. Most stock photo companies are using watermark technology to track unauthorized use of their images.*

10. Quit Sherlock.

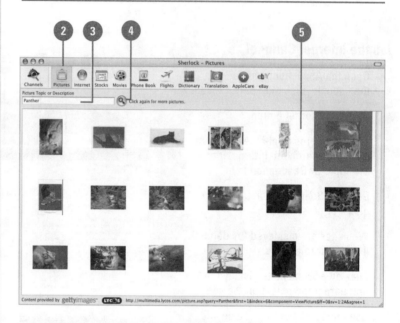

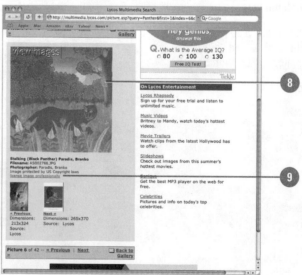

Using Third-Party Channels

Third-party channels (**New!**) are additional Sherlock friendly Web sites. Sherlock friendly means a Web site has designed an interface that is compatible with the Sherlock window. It also means that you can view the site without actually opening your Web browser application. Each day more and more sites are creating Sherlock friendly versions of their sites, which mean there are more and more sites available. Panther comes shipped with a dozen or more third-party channels, and gives you the ability to add more as they become available.

Use Third-Party Channels

1. Open the Applications folder, and then double-click the Sherlock icon.

2. Click Other Channels, and then select from the available third-party channels.

   IMPORTANT *When you access the third-party channels for the first time, a warning disclaimer from Apple appears. You'll need to click Cancel or Proceed before the channels are downloaded.*

3. Click the Content Provided By link to gain access to additional Sherlock friendly sites.

4. Click on a site to load it into the Sherlock window, and then click Cancel or Proceed to add it to the third-party channel.

5. Click the Channel menu, and then click Add Channel.

6. Select a location for the new channel.

7. Click Add.

8. To remove the channel from the list, select a channel, and then press Delete.

9. Click the User Submissions link to obtain more information on third-party channels and current channel development at Apple.

10. Quit Sherlock.

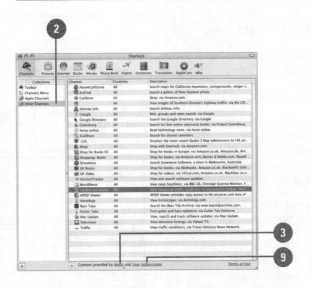

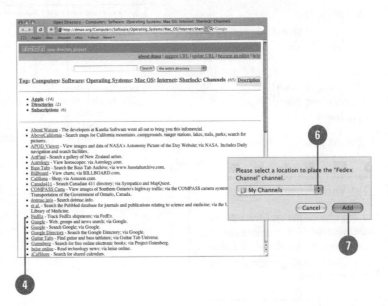

Using the Stocks Channel

With the Stocks channel, you can view any number of stocks in your portfolio, and track their ups and downs using easy-to-read graphs. While having this information does not make the roller-coaster ride of trading on the Stock Exchange any better, it does give you an easy way to see how various stocks are performing, and helps even the novice trader, make decisions as whether to buy more, or run quickly away. If you've ever been interested in watching the stock market, or if you're an experienced trader, the Stocks channel is the place to be, for the up-to-date information you need to make intelligent decisions.

Use the Stocks Channel

1. Open the Applications folder, and then double-click the Sherlock icon.

2. Click the Stocks button.

3. Add stocks to the list by typing the ticker symbol (an abbreviation of the company), or the company name, into the Company Name Or Ticker Symbol field.

4. Click the Search button or press Return to add the stock.

5. To remove a stock from the Stock window, click on the stock, and then press Delete.

   IMPORTANT *There is no undo for deletion of a stock; nor is there an "Are You Sure" message.*

6. To change the width of the columns, click on the edge of the column and drag to increase or decrease.

7. Quit Sherlock.

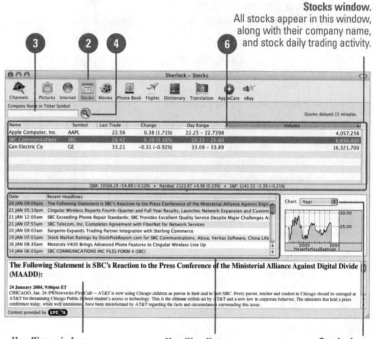

Stocks window. All stocks appear in this window, along with their company name, and stock daily trading activity.

Headline window. Click on a headline in the Headlines list, and then read the headline.

Headline list. Lists all the headlines, gleaned over the Internet, relevant to that particular stock.

Stock chart. Displays a year-to-date, week, or intra-day chart of the ups and downs of the selected stock.

> ### Did You Know?
>
> **You can change the sort order of the stock window.** Click on the headings to view your stocks, sorted by: Name, Symbol, Last Trade, Change, Day Range, or Volume.

Using the Movies Channel

If you like to go to movies, this channel is almost worth the entire Sherlock application, because before going to the movies there are questions to be asked. What movie do you want to see? Where is it playing? Is it really as good as the reviewers say? The Movies channel take guesswork out of movie selection, and helps you pick a winner every time… well, almost every time. You can even add the movie theather to your Address Book (**New!**). So fire up the popcorn machine, pull out the boxes of candy; it's time for Sherlock to take us to the movies.

Use the Movies Channel

1. Open the Applications folder, and then double-click the Sherlock icon.

2. Click the Movies button.

3. Type an address or zip code into the Find Near field, and then press Return.

4. Click the Movies or Theaters buttons to sort the list by movies or theaters.

5. Click the Showtime pop-up to list times for today, or up to 5 days in the future.

6. Click a movie in the movie window, to display a listing of theaters.

7. Click a theater to list the available show times.

8. Click the movie link to access more information.

9. Read a short description of the movie in the Info window.

10. View a trailer of the movie (if available), in the Trailer window.

11. Click the Add button to add this theater to your Address Book.

12. Click the Map button to get detailed driving directions.

13. Quit Sherlock.

Available showtimes

Rating and run times for the movie

Using the Phone Book Channel

Sherlock's Phone Book channel (New!) is a slick way to get the phone number of a business or lost acquaintance. As with all of Sherlock's channels, you'll need an Internet connection. Other than that, Sherlock requires as much specific information as you have on the business or person you're trying to locate. And you won't just get a simple phone number, Sherlock provides you with the address, driving directions (if available); even a map, to help you in your quest.

Use the Phone Book Channel

1. Open the Applications folder, and then double-click the Sherlock icon.

2. Click the Phone Book button.

3. Click the Business or People button, to search for a specific business or individual.

4. Click the Business Name Or Category pop-up to select a lookup.

5. Type the city name, state, or zip code to perform the search.

6. Click the Search button to generate a list of possible matches.

7. Continue clicking the Search button to add more matches to the list.

8. Click on a business (or name), to display driving directions and a map.

9. Type in a zip code, state, or address to begin the driving directions.

10. Use the Pan and Zoom buttons to manipulate the map image.

11. Click the Print button to generate a printout of the address, driving directions, and a map.

12. Quit Sherlock.

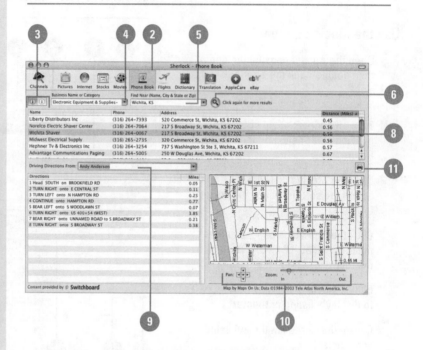

For Your Information

Searching for Location Information

When you type in your search criteria, be as specific as possible. If you're looking for a hardware store, don't just type "hardware stores" and press the Search button. Remember to type a location into the Find Near field. In addition, if you can narrow down the search even further by using a company name, such as Ace Hardware stores, located in Wichita, Kansas. You'll find what you are looking for even faster. The key is to give Sherlock as many details as possible.

Using the eBay Channel

Use the eBay Channel

1. Open the Applications folder, and then double-click the Sherlock icon.

2. Click the eBay button.

3. Type the item you're searching for in the Item Title field.

4. Click the Category pop-up, and then select from the available options.

5. Click the Regions pop-up, and then select a region.

6. Enter a price range into the Priced Between fields (optional).

7. Click the Sort pop-up, and then select how you want the matches sorted.

8. Click the Search button or press Return to generate a list of possible matches.

9. Select an item from the list to display an image (if available), and an informational window, describing the object, and how to bid.

10. Click the Track Listing button to add the item to the tracking list.

11. Click the Track button to view the recent bidding history of all tracked items.

12. Quit Sherlock.

All you Internet shoppers out there pay attention, because eBay has created a Sherlock friendly version of their Web site, especially for you. For example, you're looking for an antique Tiffany lamp, you don't want to pay more than five-hundred dollars, and you want the seller to be within your state, so you can drive and see before you buy. No problem, all you'll need is an Internet connection, a sense of adventure, a willingness to bid against others, who may desire the same Tiffany lamp, and a checkbook—Sherlock provides the rest.

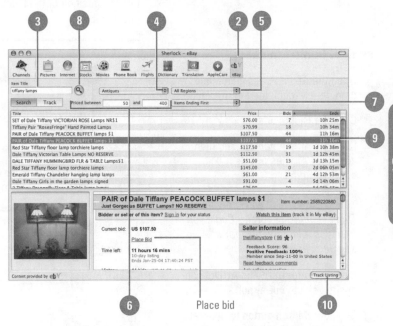

Place bid

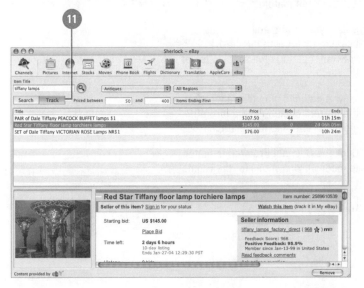

9

Using the Flights Channel

If you fly a lot, you'll like the ability to check flights directly from Sherlock's Flights channel. While checking flights online is not new, Sherlock makes the process fast and painless. For example, your sister is flying in from Florida to be with you for a week. So, you hop in your car, drive an hour to get to the airport, only to find that the flight has been delayed by two hours. You can't go home, so you cool your heels, waiting. That's a situation that would not have happened, if you had used Sherlock. Not only does Sherlock let you know when the flight is arriving, it lists all the legs of the flight, and even displays a map showing you the current position of the flight in the air. Now that's what I call real-time information.

Use the Flights Channel

1. Open the Applications folder, and then double-click the Sherlock icon.

2. Click the Flights button.

3. Click the Airline pop-up, and then select All Airlines or select a specific airline.

   TIMESAVER *If you know the Flight Number or Airport Code, you can type it into the field for a specific search.*

4. Click the Departure and Arrival pop-ups to select your airports.

5. Click the Search button to generate a list of flight matches.

6. Select your flight, and then click the Leg pop-up (new to Panther), to view information on a specific leg of the flight.

7. View a detailed map (if available) of the current position of the aircraft; including weather information.

8. Click the Channel Preference button to modify preferences for the Flights channel.

9. Quit Sherlock.

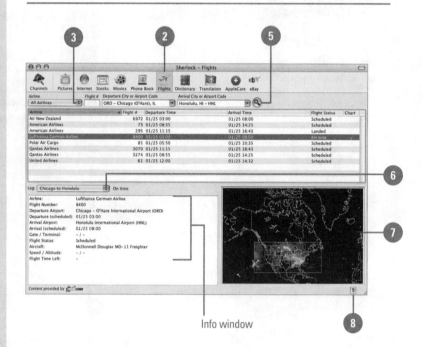

Info window

Using the AppleCare Channel

The AppleCare channel gives you direct access to the Apple site, containing Apple's Knowledge Base. The **Apple Knowledge Base** is a huge database containing tips, tricks, features, troubleshooting, and answers to questions concerning every Macintosh model that was ever made. This is the same database used by Apple support techs, when they're trying to help you solve a problem, and it's available to you through Sherlock. The AppleCare channel is not just for information. For example, you might want to download the latest software updates for Panther, so you open the AppleCare channel, type Panther updates into the search field, and then click the Search button. AppleCare lists what's available in the way of downloads, and give you the ability (through links) to download the updates.

Use the AppleCare Channel

1. Open the Applications folder, and then double-click the Sherlock icon.

2. Click the AppleCare button

3. Type the words you want to use for the search into the Topic Or Description field.

4. Click the Search button to display a list of matched topics.

5. Click on a topic to display more detailed information.

6. Click the links (if available) in the Info window to obtain more information, or to download patches and upgrades.

7. Quit Sherlock.

Did You Know?

You can make shortcuts for a channel. Activate the channel, click the Channel menu, and then select Make A Shortcut. By placing the shortcut on your desktop, you'll have instant access to that specific channel, anytime you need it.

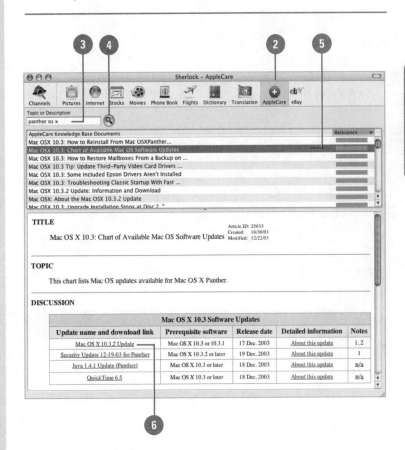

Using the Dictionary Channel

It's the last round of the big family scrabble game, and you're confronted with the word *Hematite*. You can't find your trusty dictionary, and you only have 60 seconds left. Luckily you have Sherlock, an Internet connection, and it's built-in Dictionary channel. Sherlock's Dictionary channel is a writer's dream come true (Scrabble players too). Not only does it tell you if a word exists, but if you can't spell the word, it gives you alternate (correct) spellings, and a definition of the word.

Use the Dictionary Channel

1. Open the Applications folder, and then double-click the Sherlock icon.

2. Click the Dictionary button.

3. Type the word you want to spell check or define, in the field.

4. Click the Search button to check the word against the English Dictionary.

5. If the word is not spelled correctly, check the list of alternate spellings in the Dictionary window.

6. View the definition of the word.

7. Check the Thesaurus window for a listing of alternate words with similar meaning in the English language, and view a definition of the word.

8. Click the link text to view other words related to the match word.

9. Quit Sherlock.

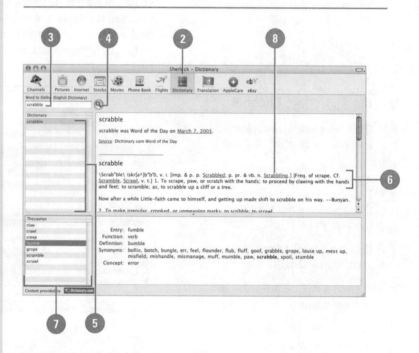

For Your Information

Using Language Tools

The Dictionary channel is an excellent tool to have available when you're writing that school paper, business letter, or that great american novel. Not only can you make sure the word is spelled correctly, but the Definition window ensures that you're using it correctly. In addition, the Thesaurus can give you other ways to say the same thing. Just remember that using big words is not the design of language. Language is used to communicate thoughts and ideas, so use the words that best describe what you're trying to say, and let the Dictionary channel help you in your quest.

Using the Translation Channel

Sherlock includes a Translation channel for all those tricky times when you need to say exactly the right words, and you need to say them in another language. Or possibly, you are corresponding with someone from another country, and you're having trouble translating the document. Whatever the situation, Sherlock gives you the ability to move seamlessly between languages.

Use the Translation Channel

1. Open the Applications folder, and then double-click the Sherlock icon.

2. Click the Translation button.

3. Type the text to translate into the Original Text window.

4. Click the Translate pop-up, and then select what language to use to translate the text.

5. Click Translate to generate the translation.

6. Quit Sherlock.

Did You Know?

You can copy and paste information into the Translation window. Open a text document, select the text, click the Edit menu, and then click Copy. Next, open the Translations channel in Sherlock, click in the Original Text window, click the Edit menu, and then click Paste. You can now translate the pasted text.

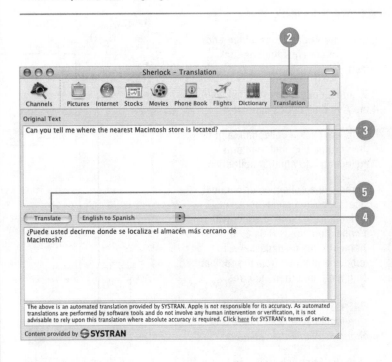

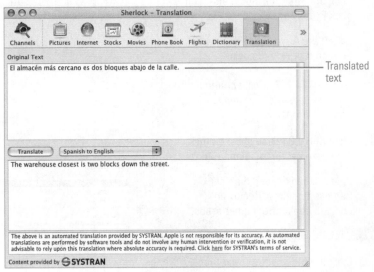

Translated text

9

Customizing Sherlock

The Sherlock program comes ready-to-use, right out of the box; however, like most applications, you have the ability to redesign some of the interface elements to suit your own personal needs. For example, you can add or remove collections, individual channels, or buttons on your toolbar (**New!**). You can also add or remove cookies from your computer.

Customize Sherlock

1 Open the Applications folder, and then double-click the Sherlock icon.

2 To add a collection to the list, click the Add Collections button (+).

3 To move, click a collection, and then drag a channel from one collection into another collection.

4 To remove a collection or channel, select a collection in the Collections list or a channel within a collection, press Delete, and then click Yes as necessary. To remove a channel from the toolbar, drag it off, and then click Yes.

IMPORTANT *When you delete a collection, you also delete any channels within the collection.*

5 Click the Sherlock menu, and then click Preferences.

6 Select the Always or Never option to accept or refuse cookies.

IMPORTANT *Some channels require the use of cookies to function properly.*

7 Click Show Cookies to list all the cookies on your computer.

8 Select a cookie, and then click Remove to delete. Removing cookies could affect other areas.

9 Click Done.

10 Click the Close button, and then Quit Sherlock.

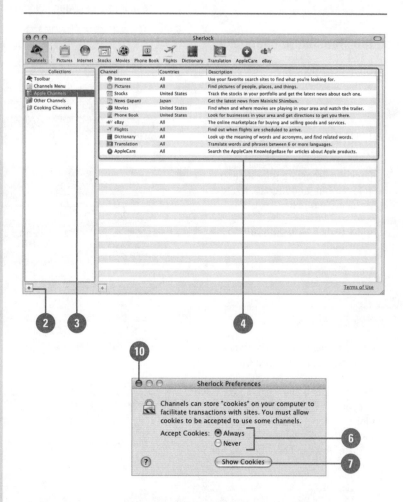

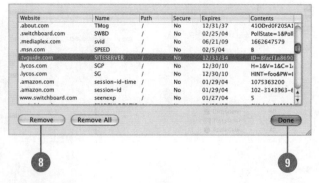

Exchanging Messages Using Mail

Introduction

If you're like many people today who are using the Internet to communicate with friends and business associates, you probably have piles of information (names, e-mail addresses, phone numbers, etc) that you need often. Unless this information is in one convenient place, and can be accessed immediately, the information becomes ineffective and you become unproductive. Apple's Mail application solves these problems by integrating management and organization tools into one simple system. Mac OS X Panther includes Mail, a powerful application for managing **electronic mail** (known as e-mail), and contact information like names, and e-mail addresses.

Using Mail with an Internet connection allows you to accomplish several tasks:

◆ Create and send e-mail messages

◆ Manage multiple e-mail accounts with different Internet service providers

◆ Use the Address Book to store and retrieve e-mail addresses

◆ Add a personal signature to your e-mail messages

◆ Attach a file to an e-mail message

◆ Print e-mail messages

Starting Mail

Whether you want to exchange e-mail with colleagues and friends or join newsgroups to trade ideas and information, Mail provides you with all the tools you need. When you install Mac OS X Panther, an icon for Mail appears in the Dock. As you receive e-mail messages with the Mail application open or hidden, the Mail icon in the Dock tells you how many new messages are in your Inbox. The first time you start Mail, you need to set up an e-mail account by answering a few step-by-step questions. If you are switching from another e-mail application to Mail, you can import your mailboxes and e-mail messages into Mail by answering a few questions. You can set Mail as your default e-mail application so that whenever you click an e-mail link on a Web page or select the mail command in your Web browser, Mail opens.

Start Mail

1. Display the Dock on the desktop, and then click the Mail icon.

   If you have a .Mac account, Mail automatically creates an e-mail account using your .Mac information.

2. When you start Mail for the first time, the application asks you:

   ◆ If you want to import mailboxes from another e-mail client. If so, click Yes, and then follow the on-screen instructions (see details on the next page). Otherwise, click No.

   ◆ If you want to view new features in this version of Mail. If so, click Yes to view a list. Otherwise, click No.

   ◆ If you don't have an e-mail account, follow the step-by-step instructions to set up your account.

See Also

See "Setting Up an Account" on page 236 for information on creating an e-mail account.

Dock

Number of new messages

Import Mailboxes and E-Mail

1. Click the File menu, and then click Import Mailboxes.

2. Click an option to select the importing application (use Other for Windows or UNIX), and then click the Next arrow button.

3. Follow the on-screen instructions; the steps to import mailboxes and e-mail vary between applications.

   ◆ **Import from Mac OS X Mail.** Mailboxes are located in Library/Mail/Mailboxes in your home folder.

   ◆ **Import from Windows or UNIX.** Use Standard mbox, except for Eudora or Netscape, which use their own. Microsoft Outlook and Outlook Express for the PC are not supported.

   ◆ Some options require that you have the importing application, such as Entourage, Outlook Express or Claris Emailer, open.

   The imported mail appears in the new Import mailbox.

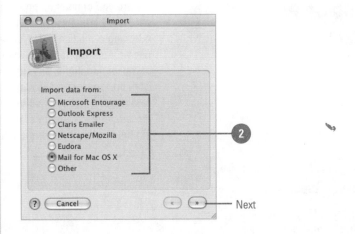
Next

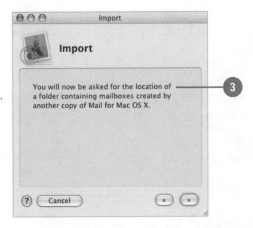

Set Options to Start Mail from Your Web Browser

1. Click the Mail menu, and then click Preferences.

2. Click General.

3. Click the Default Email Reader pop-up, and then click Mail.

4. Click the Close button.

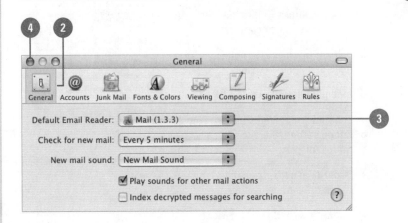

Setting Up an Account

Before you can set up an e-mail account, you need your account name, password, e-mail server type, and the names of your incoming and outgoing e-mail servers from your ISP or network administrator. You can use an AppleScript to help you set up an e-mail account by answering a series of questions, or you can set up one by using the Accounts pane of Mail preferences. Mail allows you to send and retrieve e-mail from different types of **e-mail servers**, which are the locations where e-mail is stored before you access it. You can set up Mail to receive e-mail from multiple accounts where each one can have multiple e-mail addresses.

Set Up an E-Mail Account by Answering Questions

1. Start Mail for the first time, and the series of questions begins.

   Or click the Scripts (S) menu, and then click Create New Mail Account.

2. Click an account type, and then click OK.

3. Type the information requested and then click OK, or click Yes or No to the question. Common information requested includes the following:

   ◆ **Account name.** This appears in the Mailbox list.

   ◆ **E-mail account user name and password.** This identifies you to the mail server.

   ◆ **E-mail address.** This is the From address in outgoing e-mail.

   ◆ **Full name.** This is the name used in outgoing e-mail.

   ◆ **Incoming e-mail server.** POP or IMAP.

   ◆ **Cache setting.** Store mail locally for fast display.

   ◆ **Security access.** Typically, password authentication.

   ◆ **Outgoing e-mail server.** SMTP.

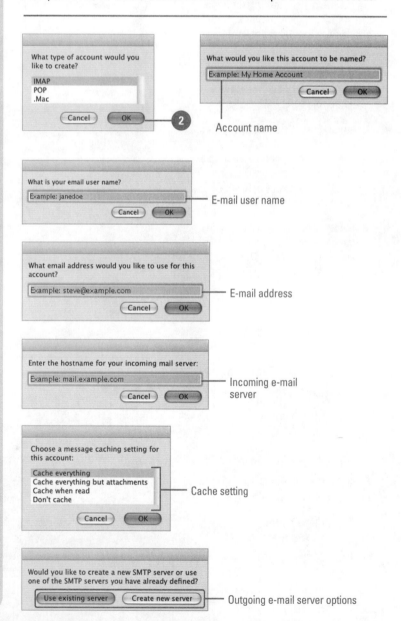

Add E-Mail Accounts

1. Click the Mail menu, and then click Preferences.

2. Click Accounts.

3. Click the Add button (+).

4. Click the Account Information tab.

5. Click the Account Type pop-up, and then select an account type: POP, IMAP, .Mac, or Exchange (New!).

   .Mac is an IMAP mail server type, while Microsoft Exchange is a POP or IMAP mail server type.

6. Specify the e-mail account information provided by your ISP:

   ◆ **Description.** The account name (appears in mailbox list).

   ◆ **E-mail Address.** The From address in outgoing e-mail. You can type multiple addresses, each separated by a comma.

   ◆ **Full Name.** The name used in outgoing e-mail.

   ◆ **Incoming Mail Server.** The POP or IMAP name.

   ◆ **User Name.** The name that identifies you to the mail server.

   ◆ **Password.** The method that provides secure access to the mail server. If you prefer to type a password every time you check mail, leave this field empty.

7. Click the Outgoing Mail Server (SMTP) pop-up, select an existing SMTP, Add Server and enter SMTP settings, or Edit Server List to change SMTP server settings.

8. Click the Close button, and then click Save.

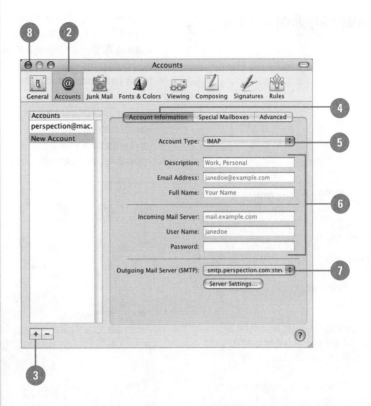

10

Frequently Asked Questions

How Do I Select an E-Mail Server?

Mail supports two types of incoming e-mail servers: **POP** (Post Office Protocol) and **IMAP** (Internet Message Access Protocol). A **protocol** is a set of rules that control the transmission of content, format, sequencing, and error management for information over the Internet or network much like rules of the road govern the way you drive. POP servers allow you to access e-mail messages from a single Inbox folder (requires you to log in and download messages), while IMAP servers allow you to access e-mail messages from multiple folder locations or different computers (messages stay on server). An example of an incoming e-mail server is *mail.server.com*. When you use POP or IMAP e-mail servers, you also need to provide an outgoing e-mail server. **SMTP** (Simple Mail Transfer Protocol) is used to send messages between e-mail servers. An example is *smtp.server.com*.

Managing Accounts

You can set up Mail to receive e-mail from multiple e-mail accounts and from different computers. As you work with multiple accounts, you can use the Accounts pane in Mail preferences to change the order, rename, or delete accounts. Account order indicates the mailbox list order and helps determine which account (if not specified) Mail uses to send an e-mail message. If an account changes, or you no longer need it, you can rename or delete it. If you're using an IMAP or a .Mac account, mail stays on the mail server so you can access it from any computer. If you're using a POP account, mail downloads to your computer unless you select an Accounts pane option to keep a copy on the mail server.

Manage E-Mail Accounts

1. Click the Mail menu, and then click Preferences.

2. Click Accounts.

3. Select the account you want to manage.

4. To change the order in which accounts are listed in the Mailbox list, drag the account names.

   TIMESAVER *Drag accounts in the Mailbox list to change the order.*

5. To delete an e-mail account, click the account name, click the Delete button (-), and then click OK.

6. To rename an e-mail account, click the Account Information tab, and then change the name in the Description field.

7. Click the Close button, and then click Save.

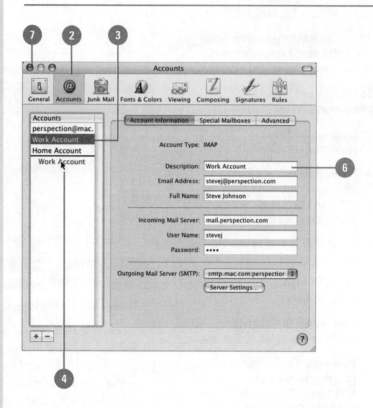

Set Advanced Account Options

1. Click the Mail menu, and then click Preferences.

2. Click Accounts.

3. Click the Advanced tab.

   ◆ **Enable This Account.** Check or clear to turn this account on or off.

   ◆ **Include When Automatically Checking For New Mail.** Check or clear to check or exclude this account from automatic mail checking.

   ◆ **Keep Copies Of Messages For Offline Viewing (IMAP only).** Click the pop-up to download e-mail to your computer for offline viewing.

   ◆ **Automatically Synchronize Changed Mailboxes (IMAP only).** Check to keep e-mail on your computer the same as the mail server.

   ◆ **Remove Copy From Server After Retrieving A Message (POP only).** Check to check e-mail from different computers, and then specify a removal duration.

   ◆ **Prompt Me To Skip Messages Over __ KB (POP only).** Check to skip retrieval of large e-mail.

   ◆ **Use SSL.** If your mail provider supports Secure Sockets Layer (SSL), check for increased security.

   ◆ **Authentication.** Click the pop-up to specify a security access method. Typically, Password.

4. Click the Close button, and then click Save.

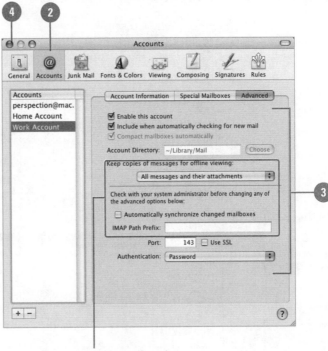

IMAP specific options

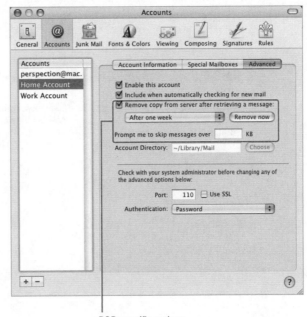

POP specific options

10

Viewing the Mail Window

Menu bar
The Menu bar gives you access to all Mail commands.

Mail Toolbar
The Mail Toolbar contains buttons for the most commonly used commands you need to work with mail messages.

Status bar
The Status bar displays information about current tasks.

Search field
The Search field allows you to find e-mail messages.

Mailbox list
The Mailbox list contains all the folders in which Mail stores e-mail messages.

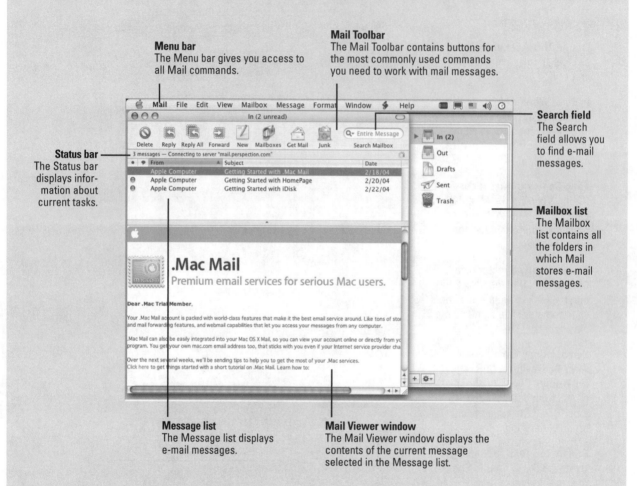

Message list
The Message list displays e-mail messages.

Mail Viewer window
The Mail Viewer window displays the contents of the current message selected in the Message list.

Composing and Sending an E-Mail

E-mail is becoming the primary form of written communication for many people. E-mail messages follow a standard memo format, with fields for the sender, recipient, date, and subject of the message. To send an e-mail message, you need to type the recipients e-mail address, type a subject, then type the message itself. You can send the same message to more than one individual, to a contact group, or to a combination of individuals and groups. If you type multiple addresses, you must separate the addresses with a comma (,). If you have multiple accounts, you can select which account you want to use to send the e-mail message.

Compose and Send an E-Mail

1. Click the New button on the Mail toolbar.

2. Type the e-mail addresses or names of each recipient or groups.

3. Type the e-mail addresses or names for those recipients or groups who should receive a carbon copy of the message.

4. Type a subject that indicates the purpose of the message.

5. To send a blind copy (address not included in recipients' list) of your message, type the e-mail addresses, names, or groups.

   IMPORTANT *Click the View menu, and then click Bcc Header to display the Bcc field (New!).*

6. Type the content of your message.

7. If a red dotted line appears under a word, Control-click the misspelled word, and then click the correct spelling.

8. If you have multiple accounts, click the Account pop-up, and then select an account.

9. Click the Send button on the toolbar.

   Messages wait in the Outbox until they are sent out, and then copies appear in the Sent mailbox.

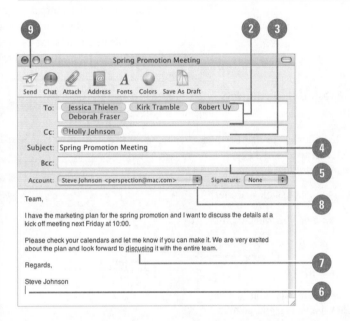

For Your Information

Checking the Spelling in E-Mail

Before you send an e-mail message, you should spell check the text to make sure your content is accurate. To start the spell check, click the Edit menu, point to Spelling, and then click Spelling. To have Mail spell check all of your e-mail messages as you type, click the Mail menu, click Preferences, click Composing, select the Check Spelling As I Type check box, and then click the Close button. You can also click Check Spelling As You Type on the Spelling submenu to enable or disable the option. If a word appears with a dotted red line under it, you can Control-click the word, and then click the correct spelling, or other options, such as Ignore Spelling or Learn Spelling.

10

Addressing an E-Mail

Mail gives you several ways to address an e-mail. You can type the address manually by typing it in the To or Cc field, or you can select or drag an address from your Address Book (**New!**). When you begin to type an e-mail address, Mail looks up the name and address in your Address Book, followed by your Previous Recipients list, and then followed by names in the LDAP database (typically for corporate use if specified in the Composing pane of Mail preferences). If Mail finds a match, it automatically completes the recipients name. If you type multiple addresses, you must separate the addresses with a comma (,). You can make addressing easier to view by using Smart Addresses, which displays the recipient name only without the e-mail address for those in your Address Book and Previous Recipients list. You can display the Previous Recipients list to remove addresses you misspelled or don't need anymore, or add addresses to your Address Book.

Select Names Using Address Complete

1. In the New Message window, type the first few letters of a name, address, or group.

   Mail suggests possible matches.

2. Click the name you want to enter.

Did You Know?

You can use Smart Addresses to show names. Click the View menu, point to Addresses, and then click Use Smart Addresses. Any names not found in your Address Book or Previous Recipients list still appear in full. Click the View menu, point to Addresses, and then click Show Name And Address to display all names in full.

See Also

See "Creating an Address Book" on page 112 for information on creating a group of recipients.

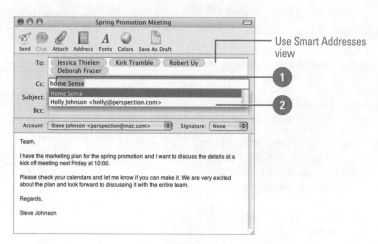

Use Smart Addresses view

Indicates recipient is available for an instant chat

Show Name And Address view

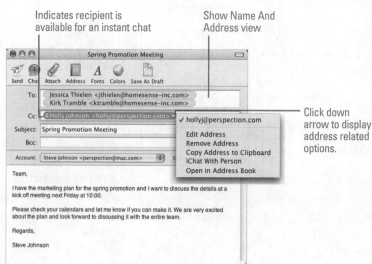

Click down arrow to display address related options.

Select Names from the Address Book

1. In the New Message window, click the Address button on the Message toolbar.

2. Click the name of a recipient or group.

3. Click the To button or the Cc button.

4. Click the Close button.

   TIMESAVER *You can drag addresses between the To, Cc, or Bcc fields in the message window.*

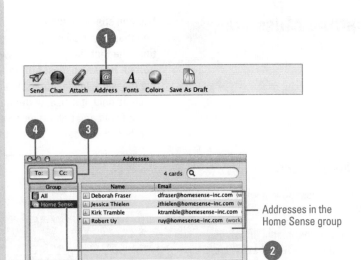

Addresses in the Home Sense group

Work with the Previous Recipients List

1. Click the Window menu, and then click Previous Recipients.

2. Select an address.

3. To remove the address, click Remove From List.

4. To add the address to the Address Book, click the Add To Address Book.

5. Click the Close button.

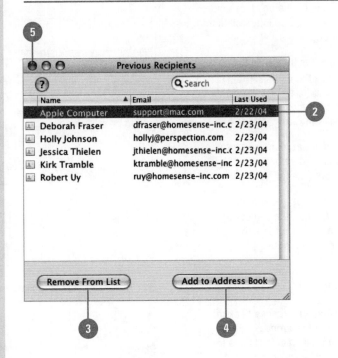

Did You Know?

You can set addressing preferences.
Click the Mail menu, click Preferences, click the Composing button, select or clear the following check boxes: Automatically Complete Addresses, When Sending To A Group, Show All Member Address, and Mark Addresses Not In This Domain, and then type a domain name such as *apple.com* to mark it as safe when using LDAP.

10

Formatting Message Text

You can specify a file format for message text. The Plain Text format is one that all e-mail programs recognize, but it doesn't support text formatting. The Rich Text format allows text formatting, but it's not always supported. However, most programs that don't recognize Rich Text, convert the message to plain text. When you use Rich Text, you can use tools, such as bold, italicize, underline, and color text, on the Format menu and in the Fonts and Color dialogs to help draw the reader's attention to key words and emphasize the meaning of your message.

Format the Message Text

1. Open the message you want to format.

2. Click the Format menu, and then click Make Rich Text, if available.

3. Select the text you want to format.

4. Click the Colors button on the toolbar, use the dialog color wheel to select a color, and then click the Close button.

5. Click the Fonts button on the toolbar, use the dialog settings (font type, size, style, and effects) to format the message text, and then click the Close button.

6. Click the Format menu, point to Style, and then select a font style, such as bold, italics, or underline.

7. Click the Format menu, point to Alignment, and then select an alignment: Align Left, Center, Justify, or Align Right.

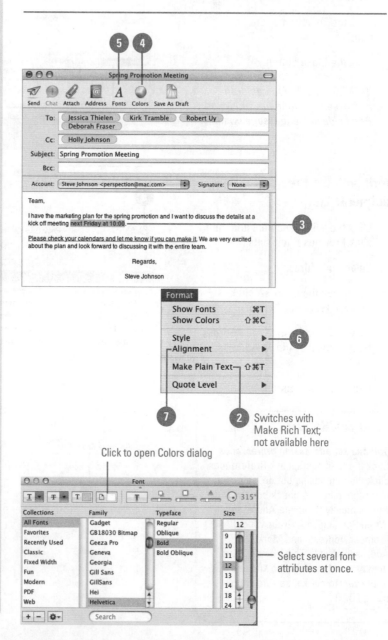

Switches with Make Rich Text; not available here

Click to open Colors dialog

Select several font attributes at once.

Did You Know?

You can set font preferences. Click the Mail menu, click Preferences, click Fonts & Colors, select default fonts for the message list, message text (Rich Text), and plain text, and then click the Close button.

Adding an E-Mail Signature

If you type the same information at the end of the each e-mail message, such as Best Regards and your name, then you can automate that task by creating a signature. You can add one signature to all messages or create several and select one when you compose a message. You can customize your signature with a variety of formatting styles, such as font type, size, and color, and you can even include a picture or attach your virtual business card, known as a **vCard**, from your Address Book.

Create a Signature

1. Click the Mail menu, and then click Preferences.

2. Click Signatures.

3. Click Add Signature.

4. Type a Description.

5. Type the signature text.

6. For a Rich Text signature, use the Format menu to change the text font, color, style, or alignment.

7. If you want, drag a picture or vCard, and then click OK.

8. Click the Automatically Insert Signature pop-up, and then select a signature, None, or an option.

9. Select or clear the Show Signature Menu On Compose Window check box.

10. Select or clear the Place Signature Above Quoted Text check box to place the signature above or below the quoted text.

11. Click the Close button.

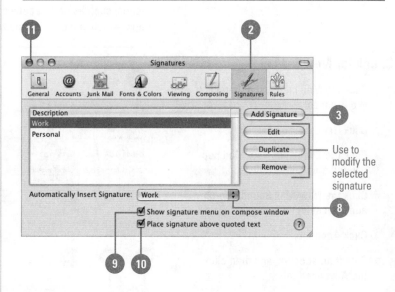

Use to modify the selected signature

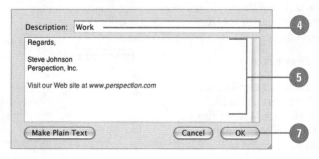

10

Did You Know?

You can add your signature to e-mail quickly. In an e-mail message, click where you want the signature, click the Signature pop-up, and then click a signature.

Receiving and Reading E-Mail

You can receive e-mail anytime day or night—even when your computer is turned off. You can retrieve your e-mail manually or set Mail to do so automatically by setting options in Mail preferences. When you start Mail, the application checks for new e-mail. It continues to check periodically while the application is open. New messages appear in the Inbox along with any messages you haven't stored elsewhere or deleted. A blue dot appears next to unread messages in the Mail Viewer window. The Message list displays the subject line of a message and other information, such as date received, senders name, attachments, and priority flags, which you can customize to display the information you need.

Check for New E-Mail

1. Click the Mail menu, and then click Preferences.

2. Click General.

3. Click the Check For New Mail pop-up, and then select a duration.

4. Click the New Mail Sound pop-up, and then select a sound.

5. Click Accounts.

6. Select an account, and then click the Advanced tab.

7. Select the Include When Automatically Checking For New Mail check box.

8. Click the Close button.

9. To check for mail manually, click the Get Mail button on the Mail toolbar, or click the Mailbox menu, point to Get New Mail, and then click In All Accounts or an account name.

Did You Know?

You can add a sender to the Address Book. Select the message in the Message list, click the Message menu, and then click Add Sender To Address Book.

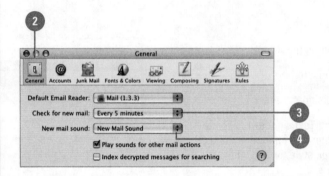

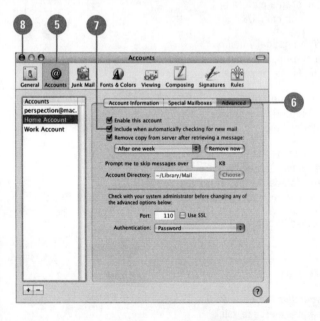

Open and Read an E-Mail

1. Click the Inbox icon in the Mailbox list to view new messages.

2. Click an e-mail message to read it in the Mail Viewer window.

3. Double-click an e-mail message to open it in its own window.

Did You Know?

You can have message text read aloud. Select the text you want to have read, click the Edit menu, point to Speech, and then click Start Speaking or Stop Speaking.

Change the Message List View

1. Click the View menu, and then point to Columns.

2. Select a column to display:

   ◆ **Attachments.** Displays a paper clip for attachments.

   ◆ **Buddy Availability.** Displays buddy status information.

   ◆ **Date Received.** Displays date received.

   ◆ **Date Sent.** Displays date sent.

   ◆ **Flags.** Displays a priority flag.

   ◆ **From.** Displays sender name.

   ◆ **Mailbox.** Displays name/account.

   ◆ **Number.** Displays sequential numbers next to the messages.

   ◆ **Size.** Displays size of a message or mailbox.

   ◆ **To.** Displays recipient name.

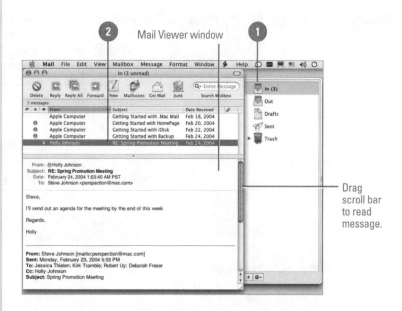

Mail Viewer window

Drag scroll bar to read message.

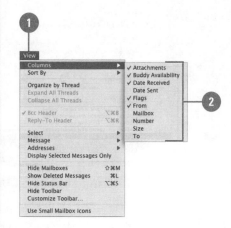

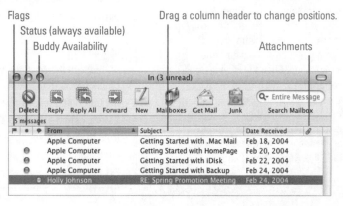

Flags

Status (always available)

Buddy Availability

Drag a column header to change positions.

Attachments

10

Responding to E-Mail

You can respond to a message in three ways: reply to it, which creates a new message addressed to the sender(s) and other recipients; forward it, which creates a new message you can send to someone else; or redirect it, which creates a new message from the original sender you can send to someone else (useful when you receive a message by mistake). When you reply or forward a message, the original message appears in the message response. You can reply to the sender only, or to all the people who received the original message.

Reply to an E-Mail

1. Select the e-mail message you want to reply to.

2. If you want, select a portion of the text to include as quoted text.

3. Click the Reply button to respond to the sender only, or click the Reply All button to respond to the sender and all recipients listed in the e-mail.

4. Add or delete names from the To or the Cc field.

5. Type your message.

6. Click the Send button on the Message toolbar.

   A curved arrow appears in the Status column next to messages you reply to.

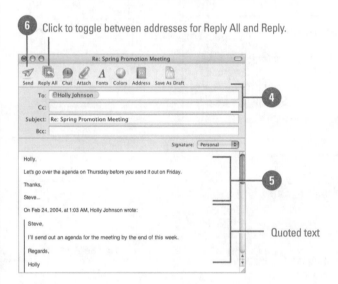

6 Click to toggle between addresses for Reply All and Reply.

Quoted text

Did You Know?

You can reply with an instant message. If you're logged into iChat, Mail displays a green dot indicator next to messages from buddies who are online, or a yellow dot indicator when the person is idle. Click the Mail menu, click Preferences, click the Viewing button, select the Show Online Buddy Status check box, and then click the Close button. Select a message in the Message list, click the Message menu, and then click Reply With iChat.

For Your Information

Quoting Text in E-Mail

When you reply to an e-mail message, you can include all or part of the original message, known as **quoted text**. The original message appears with a single quote bar to the left of the text. If the original message contained quoted text, you see an additional quote bar. To use quoted text, click the Mail menu, click Preferences, click the Composing button, select the Quote The Text Of The Original Message check box, and then click the Include Selected Text If Any, Otherwise Include All option. To change the color of quoted text, click Fonts & Colors, select the Color Quoted Text check box, and then select colors from the pop-up for Levels One, Two, and Three. When you're done, click the Close button. You can use the Quote Level submenu on the Format menu to change the number of quote bars.

Redirect an E-Mail

1. Select the e-mail message you want to redirect.

2. Click the Message menu, and then click Redirect.

3. Type or select names in the To or the Cc field.

4. Click the Send button on the Message toolbar.

   A segment arrow appears in the Status column next to messages you redirect.

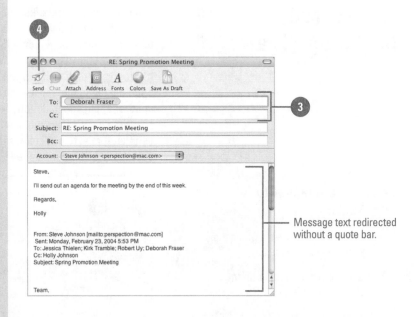

Message text redirected without a quote bar.

Forward an E-Mail

1. Select the message(s) or open a message you want to forward.

2. Click the Forward button on the toolbar.

3. Type or select names in the To or the Cc field.

4. Type your message.

5. Click the Send button on the Message toolbar.

Did You Know?

Attachments aren't sent on replies. When you reply to a message that has an attachment, the attachment isn't returned to the original sender. You can forward the message to the original sender if you need to send the attachment back.

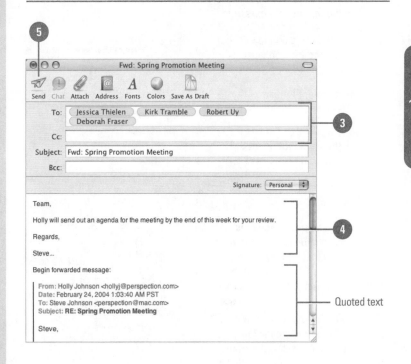

Quoted text

10

Sending and Retrieving a File

You can easily share a file, such as a picture, document, vCard (virtual business card from your Address Book), sound, or movie by attaching it to an e-mail message. Some ISPs have trouble sending attachments between 2 and 10 megabytes MB, so it's a good idea to check with your ISP for limits on file size. Upon receiving the e-mail, the recipient can open the file in the application that created it, or save it on a disk for use in other applications directly from the Mail Viewer window (New!). The Message list displays the number and size of the attachments. If you send an e-mail to a Windows user, the attachment is automatically compressed in a standard zipped (gzip) format so it can be read (New!).

Send a File Attached to an E-Mail

1. Compose a new message or reply to an existing message.

2. Click the Attach button on the Message toolbar.

   TIMESAVER *Use Expose' to hide all open windows, and then drag the file into the message.*

3. Select the drive and folder that contains the file you want to attach.

4. Click to select the file.

5. Click Choose File.

6. Click the Send button on the Message toolbar.

Did You Know?

You should compress large files before you send them. Select the file or files you want to compress in the Finder, click the File menu, and then click Archive. Rename the compressed file with a *.zip* extension as necessary.

You can send a Web link in an e-mail message. Type or paste the full URL, including "http://" in the body of the message. Your recipients can click the link to go directly to the Web page.

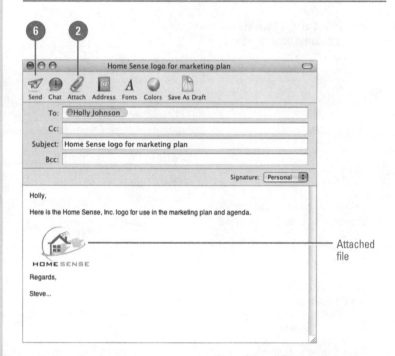

Attached file

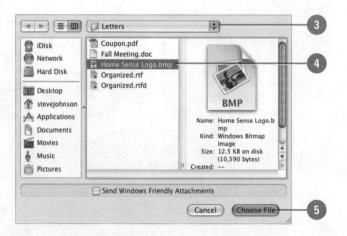

Open a File in an E-Mail

1. Select the message with the attached file.

2. Click the triangle if necessary to display the attached files.

3. Control+click the attached file icon.

4. Click Open Attachment, or point to Open With, and then select an application.

Did You Know?

You can remove attachments from an e-mail. Select the e-mail, click the Message menu, and then click Remove Attachments.

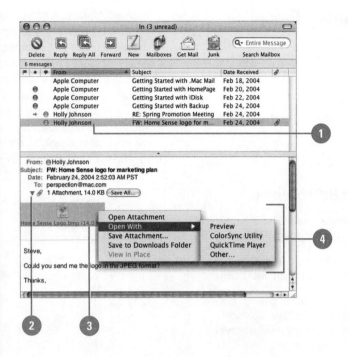

Save Files in an E-Mail

1. Select the message with the attached file.

2. Use one of the following methods:

   ◆ **Save All.** Click the File menu, and then click Save Attachment, or click Save All.

   ◆ **Save Individual.** Click the triangle in the header of the message to see the icons of each attached file. Control+ click an icon, and then click Save Attachment.

   TIMESAVER *Click Save To Downloads Folder on the shortcut menu to bypass Steps 3 and 4.*

3. Select the drive and folder where you want to save the files.

4. Click Save.

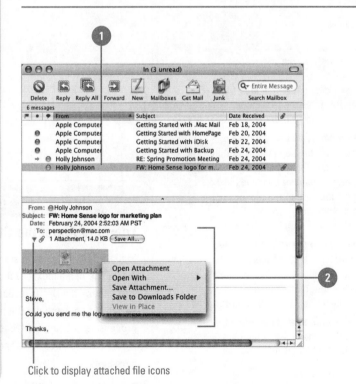

Click to display attached file icons

Managing E-Mail

A common problem with using e-mail is an overcrowded Inbox. To keep your Inbox organized, you should move messages you want to save to other mailboxes and subfolders (a mailbox inside another mailbox), delete messages you no longer want, and create new mailboxes as you need them. A mailbox can store messages on your computer, within a specific account, or within an existing mailbox. When a mailbox contains both messages and other mailboxes, the mailbox icon appears in blue. You can also organize your e-mail by **message threads** (New!), which is the chain of replies in an e-mail conversation. You can group threads together or highlight them by color to make them easier to see.

Create a New Mailbox

1 To create a subfolder in a mailbox, select the existing mailbox.

2 Click the Create A Mailbox button at the bottom of the Mailbox list.

3 Click the Location pop-up, and then select On My Mac (local computer) or an IMAP account (online mail server).

4 Type a name for the new mailbox.

5 Click OK.

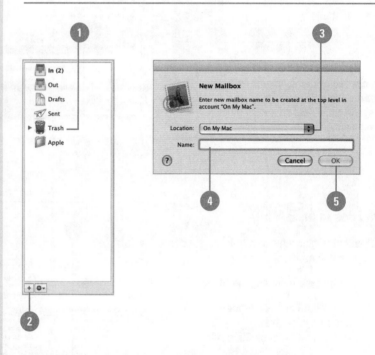

Did You Know?

You can quickly show and hide the Mailbox list. Click the Mailboxes button on the Mail toolbar.

You can rename, move, or delete a mailbox. To rename a mailbox, double-click the name, change it, and then press Return. To move a mailbox, drag it to a new location in the Mailbox list. To delete a mailbox, Control+click it, click Delete, and then click Delete.

You can change the side the Mailbox list appears. Click the Mailboxes button to close it, move the Mail window so there's enough room on the side, and then click the Mailboxes button.

You can change size of mailbox icons. Click the View menu, and then click Use Small Mailbox Icons.

For Your Information

Learning About the Standard Mailboxes

Mail comes with several standard mailboxes: In, Out, Drafts, Sent, and Trash. The In mailbox, or **Inbox**, stores messages you have received from others; the Drafts mailbox stores messages you have written and saved, but not sent; the Out mailbox, or **Outbox**, stores messages in the processing of being sent; and the Sent mailbox stores copies of messages you have sent. The Trash mailbox stores all your deleted messages.

Organize E-Mail in Mailboxes

1. Select the e-mail message you want to move. If necessary, press and hold down ⌘, and click to select multiple e-mail messages.

2. Drag the e-mail message(s) to the new folder.

Did You Know?

You can sort messages quickly. To sort messages by sender, subject, date, priority or flag, click a header in the Message list.

You can customize columns in the Message list. Drag a column header to a new location.

Organize E-Mail by Threads

1. Open the mailbox with the e-mail you want to view as threads.

2. Click the View menu, and then click Organize By Thread.

3. To see all the messages in all threads, click the triangle next to the thread.

4. To collapse a single thread, click the triangle next to the thread.

5. To ungroup, click the View menu, and then click Organize By Thread.

Did You Know?

You can change the use of a mailbox for an IMAP account. Select a mailbox, click the Mailbox menu, point to Use This Mailbox For, and then click Drafts, Sent, Trash, or Junk.

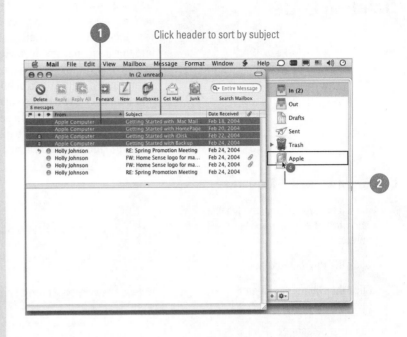

Click header to sort by subject

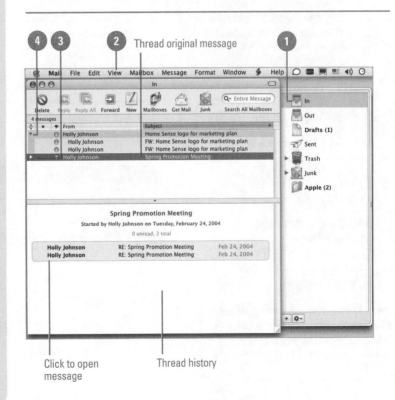

Thread original message

Click to open message

Thread history

10

Deleting E-Mail

Deleting unwanted messages makes it easier to see the new messages you receive and to keep track of messages to which you have already responded. When you delete an e-mail message, Mail simply moves it into the Trash mailbox. If you want to recover a deleted message, you just have to retrieve it from the Trash mailbox. To get rid of a message permanently, you need to open the Trash mailbox, select the message, and then click Delete. Mail automatically places e-mail messages in the Sent mailbox every time you send them. You'll want to periodically open the Sent mailbox and delete messages so your mail account doesn't get too large. You can also set account options to help you delete messages.

Delete Unwanted E-Mail

1. Click a mailbox icon in the Mailbox list with the e-mail you want to delete.

2. Click the unwanted e-mail.

3. Click the Delete button on the toolbar.

4. To erase messages in the Trash mailbox, click the Mailbox menu, point to Erase Deleted Messages, click In All Accounts or a specific account, and then click OK.

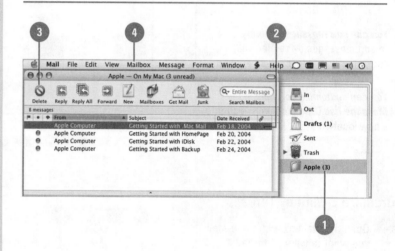

Recover E-Mail from the Trash

1. Click the Trash mailbox in the Mailbox list.

2. Select the e-mail message you want to retrieve.

3. Drag the e-mail message to another folder.

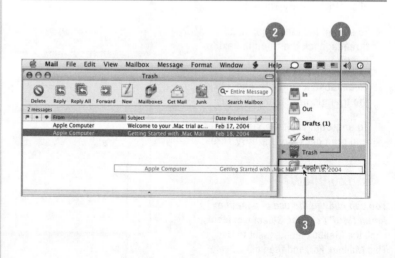

Did You Know?

You can check the size of a mailbox. Click the View menu, point to Columns, and then click Size. Mailbox size appears in the Status bar.

Change E-Mail Delete Options

1. Click the Mail menu, and then click Preferences.

2. Click Accounts.

3. Select an account.

4. Click the Special Mailboxes tab.

5. Select any of the following:

   ◆ **Move Deleted Messages To The Trash Mailbox.** Check to move deleted messages to the Trash.

   ◆ **Store Deleted Messages On The Server.** Check to keep deleted messages on the mail server for an IMAP account.

   ◆ **Permanently Erase Deleted Messages When.** Click the pop-up, and then select based on the duration you want.

6. Click the Close button, and then click Save.

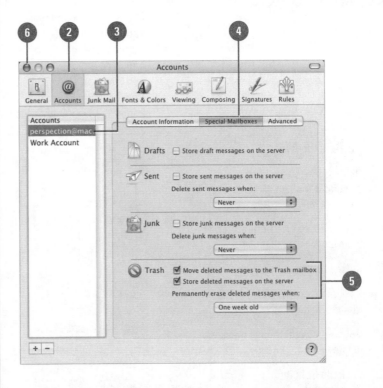

Did You Know?

You can save sent messages on the mail server. Click the Mail menu, click Preferences, click Accounts, click the Special Mailboxes tab, select the Store Sent Messages On The Server check box, and then click the Close button.

You can print e-mail messages. Select the message(s) you want to print, click the File menu, click Print, and then click Print. If you select multiple messages, the e-mails are combined into a single document in the order you selected them in the Message list.

For Your Information

Backing Up E-Mail in an IMAP Account

The information in your e-mail messages is important, so making a backup of a mailbox is a good way to protect it. You can drag a mailbox from an IMAP account to On My Mac to copy it on your computer. Likewise, you can drag a mailbox from On My Mac to an IMAP account to copy it to your mail server online. To create a copy of a mailbox, drag the mailbox from the Mailbox list to your desktop.

In the Finder, you can also backup mailboxes and addresses by copying all files located in the Home/Library/Mail folder and by copying the folder "AddressBook" located in the Home/Library/Application Support folder. To restore your mail backup, use the Import Mailboxes command on the File menu.

10

Saving E-Mail

If you have not finished composing a message, you can save it in the Drafts mailbox and work on it later. If you quit Mail with an open message, Mail automatically saves it as a draft. If you want to use the text from a message in a word processing application, such as TextEdit, you can save a message as a separate file in the Rich Text or Plain Text format. You can also save one or more messages in the Raw Message Source (mbox) format, which is a standard mail message format; you can import mbox into other mail applications, including Mail.

Save a Draft E-Mail

1. Open a new or a reply to an existing e-mail message, and then type a message.

2. Click the Save As Draft button on the Message toolbar.

3. Close the e-mail message.

4. Click the Drafts mailbox in the Mailbox list.

5. Double-click the e-mail message to view and change it.

6. Click the Send button.

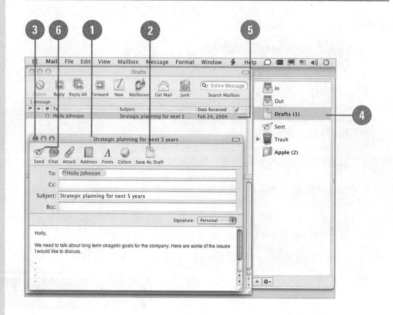

Save an E-Mail as a File

1. Open a new or a reply to an existing e-mail message, and then type a message.

2. Click the File menu, and then click Save As.

3. Select the hard drive and folder where you want to save the file.

4. Type a name for the file.

5. Click the Format pop-up, and then select a format.

6. Click Save.

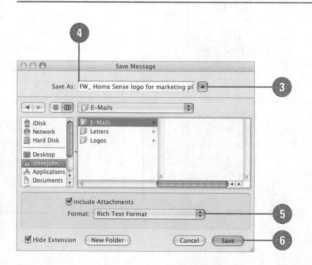

Searching E-Mail for Text

If you're looking for an e-mail message with specific information, you can use the Mail search field in the upper-right corner of the Mail toolbar to search for text in an open message, in all messages in a mailbox, in all messages for a specific account, or in all mailboxes. If you search in the From, To, or Subject fields, Mail finds messages that contain the entire search phrase as typed. If you search in mailboxes or the entire message, Mail only finds messages containing the same beginning letters you typed. To refine your search, use the words "and," "or," "not," and parentheses in the Search field. The results appear in the Message list with rankings indicating the best matches.

Search E-Mail for Text

1 To search in selected mailboxes, select the mailboxes or accounts.

2 Click in the Search box, and then type the text you want to find.

TIMESAVER *Press* ⌘+*Option+F to quickly place the insertion point in the Search field.*

As you type, Mail starts the search and displays the results.

3 Click the Search box pop-up, and then select Entire Message, From, To, or Subject for the selected mailbox or for all mailboxes.

4 Click the Search box button to end the search, and then type to start a new one, or click a mailbox or message.

Did You Know?

You can find text in an open e-mail.
Open the e-mail message, click the Edit menu, point to Find, click Find, type the text you want to find, and then click Next. If you select some text, you can also use the Jump To Selection or Use Selection For Find commands on the Find submenu.

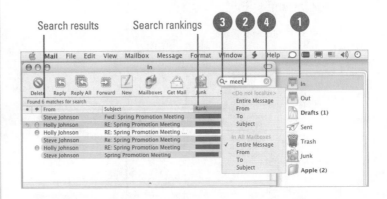

Search results   Search rankings

Search Techniques

Technique	Example
Use descriptive words	Home improvement
Place phrases in quotes	"Home Sense"
Use AND to find results containing all words	"meeting and promotion"
Use OR to find results containing at least one word	"meeting or promotion"
Use NOT to find the first one but not the second one	"meeting not promotion"
Use ( ) to find results containing combinations	"meeting and (promotion or spring)"

Diverting Incoming E-Mail to Mailboxes

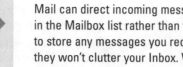

Mail can direct incoming messages that meet criteria to other mailboxes in the Mailbox list rather than to your Inbox. You can set message rules to store any messages you receive from a friend in a different folder so they won't clutter your Inbox. When you are ready to read the messages, you simply open the mailbox and access the messages just as you would messages in the Inbox. You can also set rules to automatically reply to incoming messages, which is useful when you are out of the office, or forward incoming messages with additional message text. You can also color-code the messages that you send to or receive from particular people for quick and easy recognition.

Set Rules for Incoming E-Mail

① Click the Mail menu, and the click Preferences.

② Click Rules.

③ Click Add Rule.

④ Type a name for this rule.

⑤ Click the pop-up, and then click Any or All to set initial criteria.

⑥ Use the pop-ups and fields, to specify the criteria for the rule to apply to a message.

⑦ Click the Add button (+) or Subtract button (-) to add or remove criteria.

⑧ Under the Perform The Following Actions area, use the pop-ups and fields to specify the actions you want to be take if the criteria is met.

⑨ Click the Add button (+) or Subtract button (-) to add or remove actions.

⑩ Click OK.

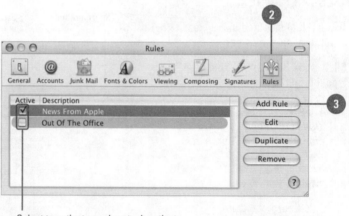

Select to activate or clear to deactivate.

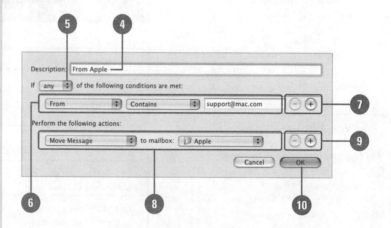

11 To edit, duplicate, or remove a rule, select a rule, and then click Edit, Duplicate, or Remove.

12 Click the Close button.

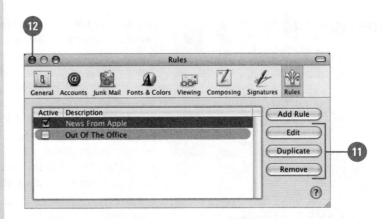

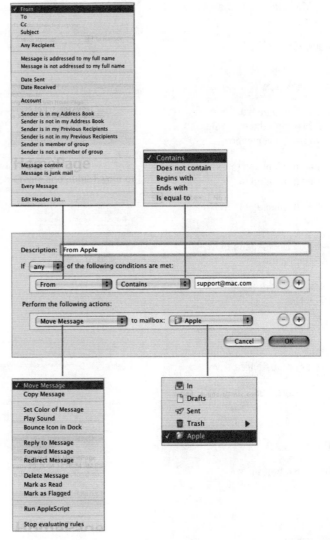

Blocking and Bouncing E-Mail

You can have Mail handle junk e-mail for you. You can specify what should be considered junk e-mail and how Mail should handle that e-mail. You can ensure that e-mail which might seem to be junk e-mail, but is actually from a person or site that you are interested in, gets to you. You can mark messages as junk mail to help train Mail (set rules) to more effectively distinguish between junk and non junk (New!). If you receive annoying mass mailings, you can **bounce** (New!), or reject, the message back to the sender (as long as their return address is valid, which isn't usually the case with spam) and the message appears to the sender as if your address is invalid and the message could not be delivered. Mail also moves the message to the Trash.

Change Junk E-Mail Options

1. Click the Mail menu, and then click Preferences.

2. Click Junk Mail.

3. Select the Enable Junk Mail Filtering check box.

4. Click the option to leave it in my Inbox and change the text color or move it to the Junk mailbox.

5. Select the check boxes to exempt e-mail from junk filtering:

    ◆ Sender Of Message Is In My Address Book

    ◆ Sender Of Message Is In My Previous Recipients

    ◆ Message Is Addressed Using My Full Name

6. Click Advanced.

    The default junk mail rule appears, which you can customize.

7. Use the pop-ups, fields, and buttons to specify the criteria for the junk rule to apply to messages.

8. Click OK.

9. Click the Close button.

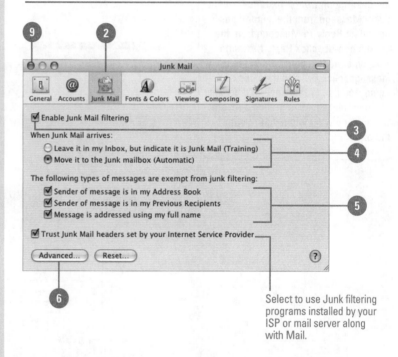

Select to use Junk filtering programs installed by your ISP or mail server along with Mail.

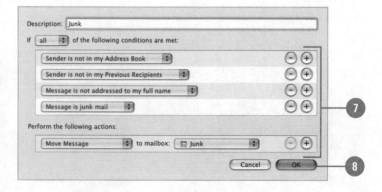

Mark E-Mail as Junk or Not Junk

1 Select the e-mail you want to mark as junk or not as junk.

2 Click the Junk button or Not Junk button on the Mail toolbar.

The button toggles between Junk and Not Junk.

3 To erase messages in the Junk mailbox, click the Mailbox menu, click Erase Junk Mail, and then click Yes.

Did You Know?

You can reset junk mail rules to the default. Click the Mail menu, click Preferences, click the Junk button, click Reset, click Yes, and then click the Close button.

Message currently marked as Junk mail   Junk mailbox

Bounce an E-Mail

1 Select the unwanted e-mail message you want to bounce.

2 Click the Message menu, and then click Bounce.

3 Click OK.

The message is bounced back to the sender and moved to the Trash mailbox.

Did You Know?

You can resend a message. Select the message in the Sent mailbox, click the Message menu, click Send Again, add or change recipients, and then click the Send button.

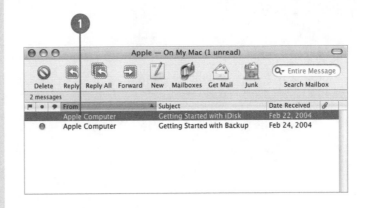

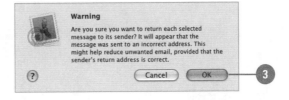

10

Exploring .Mac Services

Introduction

Apple's .Mac services are not new to the Macintosh, but as technology advances and bandwidths expand, the number of services offered gets better and better. The genesis of .Mac services was born from the fact that Apple controls both ends of the connection (they own the Apple Web site, and they make the computers). The developers at Apple decided to come up with some really great proprietary services, and then make them available to Macintosh users.

For example, Macintosh users should be able to communicate easily with other Macintosh users, so iChat was invented. In addition, Macintosh users should be able to have a virtual hard drive (iDisk) to store their stuff, and they should be able to open it and use that stuff on any other computer; even a Windows machine. And that's not all, faithful Mac users should have sophisticated e-mail services, video conferencing abilities, and the ability to build and maintain a Web site; plus you should have access to programs to backup your important documents. In truth, there are dozens of .Mac features, and more being added all the time.

You can join the .Mac community for free, and receive some limited features; however, if you want to utilize the full power of a .Mac subscription you'll pay over one hundred dollars a year. While that may seem like a substantial chunk of change, the benefits of the services are great and if you do the math, it breaks down to about eight dollars a month.

What You'll Do

Join the .Mac Community

Access Your .Mac Account

Set Up .Mac Mail

Manage .Mac Mail

Send an iCards Message

Create a .Mac Address Book

Sync a .Mac Address Book

Work with .Mac Bookmarks

Create Web Pages with HomePage

Edit Web Pages with HomePage

Back Up Your Files Using .Mac

Manage Files with iDisk

Protect Files with Virex

Get Online Support

Joining the .Mac Community

When you join the .Mac community, you're immediately connected with thousands of other happy Macintosh users. Not only does a subscription to .Mac give you access to all kinds of cool stuff, it also gives you access to stable e-mail, communications software, and a Help system geared specifically to the Macintosh operating system. Joining the .Mac community is quick and simple; however, there are system requirements you should check before you begin the process. If you meet all of the requirements, you'll need a credit card to complete the online purchase.

Join the .Mac Community

1. Open your browser, and then point to *http://www.apple.com*.

   IMPORTANT *Before you continue, make sure your computer meets the following systems requirements: Mac OS X v10.2.5 or later, 128MB of SDRAM (256MB recommended for iPhoto), Internal Apple CD-RW drive, Combo drive or SuperDrive (to back up files to CD or DVD), An active Internet connection, Safari, Netscape 7 or later, or Microsoft Internet Explorer 5 or later.*

2. Click the .Mac tab located on the Macintosh navigation bar.

3. Click the Ready To Join? link.

4. Fill out the 3 registration information screens.

5. Click Submit, and then follow any additional online instructions.

Did You Know?

You can check for special deals on the .Mac page. The people at Apple, in order to increase membership, occasionally offer specials, reduced rates and software discounts, to entice people to join. When you enter the .Mac page, check around and see if they're offering any specials.

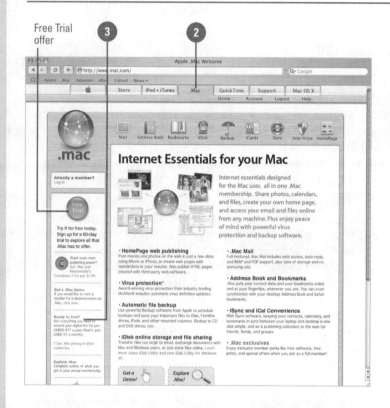

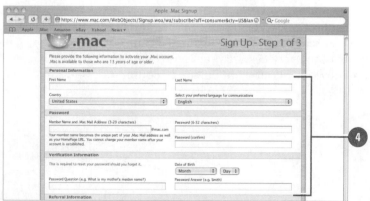

Accessing Your .Mac Account

Once you've filled out all the information on the 3-screen registration form, and then clicked Submit, you now have instant access to the full power of the Apple .Mac community and the Web. The good news is that you can access your account from any computer, anywhere, at any time of the day or night. You might say that the .Mac community never sleeps. Your .Mac account is not measured by time spent online. Once you pay your subscription fee, you can use the account as often as you want. The process of signing on is simple and painless; in fact, you could create a bookmark for the Macintosh in your browser, and automate the entire process.

Access Your .Mac Account

1. Open your browser (Safari, Netscape, Explorer).

2. Point to *http://www.mac.com*.

3. Click the Login link.

4. Type your .Mac member name and password.

5. Click Enter.

6. A message appears asking you if you'd like to save your password. Click an option:

    ◆ Never For This Website

    ◆ Not Now

    ◆ Yes

You are now signed in and ready to begin.

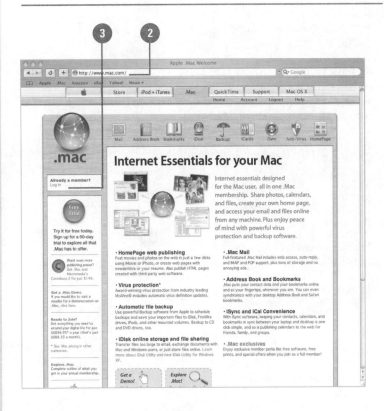

11

Setting Up .Mac Mail

Once you're registered as a user, all of the advantages of the .Mac site become instantly available; including the ability to read and send e-mail from you new mail account. The .Mac Mail service gives you a way to keep in touch with friends, family, and clients at home, or wherever you travel. And you don't even have to have your own computer. You can access, read, and save your e-mail using any computer, anywhere, through the *www.mac.com* Web site. To begin receiving and sending e-mail messages, you'll first have to set up your Macintosh.

Set Up .Mac Mail

1 Click the Apple menu, click System Preferences, and then click the .Mac icon.

IMPORTANT *If you haven't registered on the .Mac site, you'll see the Internet icon. Once registered, it's renamed the .Mac icon.*

2 Click .Mac tab.

3 Type your .Mac member name and password.

4 Click the Close button.

5 Point your browser to *http://www.mac.com.*

6 If necessary, click the .Mac tab.

7 Click the Mail link, verify your password, and then click Enter.

8 Click Preferences.

9 On the .Mac menu bar, click Account, and then select Add or Create Account.

10 Click the Account Type pop-up, and then select .Mac.

11 Type your .Mac member name and password.

12 Click Submit.

Your .Mac account and computer are now ready to send and receive messages.

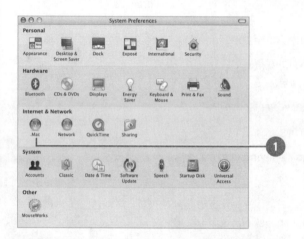

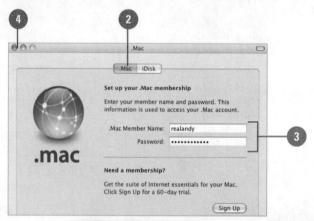

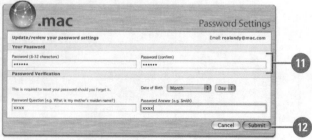

Managing .Mac Mail

Once you've set up your System Preferences, you are now ready to receive and send e-mail to other .Mac members, or to anyone with an Internet e-mail address. Since .Mac Mail is essentially run through your browser application, you'll want to own a reliable browser. When you installed the Panther operating system, it came bundled with the Safari browser.

Manage .Mac Mail

1. Open your browser, sign on to your .Mac account, and then click the Mail link.

2. Click Get Mail to check for e-mail.

3. Click on an e-mail in your Inbox to open and read it.

4. If necessary, respond to an e-mail.

5. Click the Back button on your browser to return to the main .Mac Mail screen or click the Inbox link.

6. Click Compose to write an e-mail, and then click Send.

7. Click Preferences.

8. Select from the following options, and then click Save (located in the lower right-hand corner of the window.

   ◆ Composing

   ◆ Viewing

   ◆ Account

   ◆ Check Other POP Mail

   ◆ Leave Messages On Server

9. Click Mail to return to the main .Mac Mail menu.

10. Click Logout to return to the .Mac Home page.

Save in a folder   Shows folders

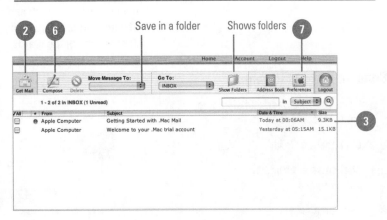

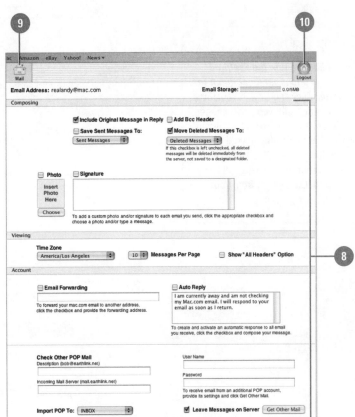

11

Sending an iCards Message

The iCards service is an exclusive .Mac area designed to let you send personalized electronic postcards to your .Mac friends, or anyone that has an e-mail account anywhere in the world. You can select from an abundance of cards, all organized into logical categories such as: Holidays, At The Office, and Just Because to name a few. New categories are being added all the time, in fact, if you're a budding photographer, you can even submit your images. The designers of the iCards service have a contest, and once a month they select a winner from the submitted artists. If you win, your images are displayed in the Featured Artist section of the iCards page.

Send an iCards Message

1 Open your browser, and sign onto your .Mac account.

2 Click the iCards link.

3 Click to select from the available categories.

4 Click on a card.

Did You Know?

You don't have to win the Featured Artist spot to add a personal touch to your iCards. Click the Create Your Own button, and then add your own images to an iCards, and create those special, one-of-a-kind messages to your friends or loved ones. You could even go on a vacation and create your own personalized iCards right from your hotel room.

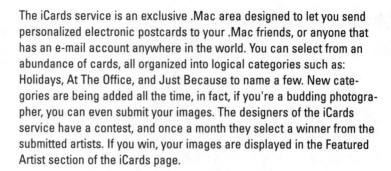

⑤ Type your message into the text field.

⑥ Select a font from the available options.

⑦ Click Continue.

⑧ Type your name and .Mac E-mail address (defaults to .Mac account).

⑨ Type the recipients e-mail address.

⑩ To send the card to more than one person, click Add Recipient.

⑪ To remove someone from the list, click Remove Recipient

⑫ Select or clear the check box to send a copy to yourself or to hide the distribution list (the recipient does not see the address of the other people receiving the card).

⑬ Click Send Your Card.

A Thank You note appears, informing you that your card has been sent.

⑭ Select an option:

◆ Return To Categories

◆ Send Same iCard

⑮ Click Home to return to the .Mac home page.

TIMESAVER *Since you're essentially running the iCard interface through your default browser, if you setup the auto-fill options, such as name and e-mail address, it saves you time when filling out the sending information on an iCard. Check the Preferences for your browser, and then activate the auto-fill fields. Click the Safari menu, click Preferences, and then click the AutoFill option, to active this time-saving feature.*

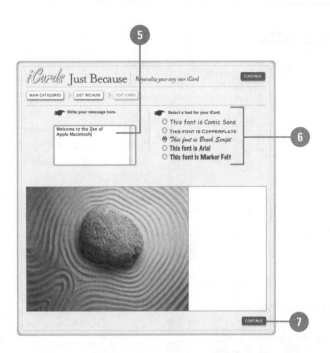

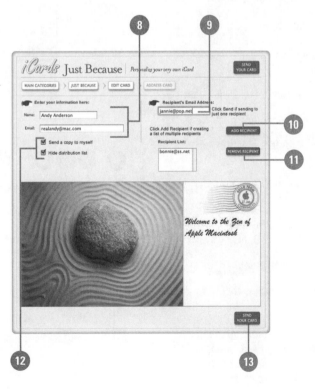

11

Creating a .Mac Address Book

Your .Mac Address Book lets you store personal and business information on all your friends, relatives, and contacts, in one safe place. In truth, you might actually have two or three other places where this same information is stored, maybe Safari, the Address Book application that comes bundled with the Panther operating system, or even your iPod. The .Mac address book is used by to maintain your mailing lists and e-mail contacts. However, before you despair of having to type in all those contacts again, Macintosh gives you a way to Sync all of the contacts and keep them up-to-date, no matter what application performed the changes.

Create a .Mac Address Book

1. Open your browser and sign on to your .Mac account.

2. Click the Address Book link.

    IMPORTANT *For security reasons, the first time you enter the Address Book application, you'll be asked to reenter your password.*

3. You'll see one contact, your .Mac account name, click the contact name to open the contact information.

4. To modify the contact info, click Edit.

5. To create a new contact, click New.

6. To remove a contact from the list, click Delete.

7. To generate an e-mail for the selected contact, click Compose.

8. To return to the Address Book main page, click Address Book.

9. Click Save to save your changes.

10. Click Logout to return to the .Mac Home page.

    IMPORTANT *Before you begin creating or recreating all of your contacts, you'll want to read the next section on Syncing a .Mac Address book.*

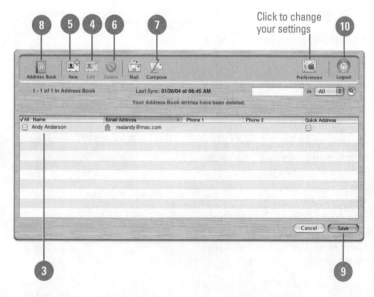

Click to change your settings

Syncing a .Mac Address Book

When you're working with the .Mac Address Book there is an excellent chance that you've already typed all your contacts in the Address Book application. Why would you ever want to type those names in a second time… and what about changes? What if one of your friends changes his or her address: Do you have to make that change in the .Mac Address Book, the Address Book application, and so on? Not really. All you have to do is set up the iSync utility, and it does all the work of keeping your various contact lists up-to-date (New!).

Sync a .Mac Address Book

1 Open the Applications folder, and then double-click iSync.

2 Click the .Mac button.

> **NOTE** *The first time you use iSync, your options differ.*

3 Select the Turn On .Mac Synchronization check box.

4 Select or clear the Automatically Synchronize Every Hour check box.

5 Select your sync options.

6 Click the Close button.

7 Open your browser, and sign onto your .Mac account.

8 Click the Address Book link, and then click Preferences.

9 Select the Turn On .Mac Address Book Synchronization check box.

10 Click Save.

11 Reopen the iSync application, and then click the Sync Now button to perform a sync between the selected applications.

12 Click the Close button on the iSync application.

Your .Mac Address Book is now synced.

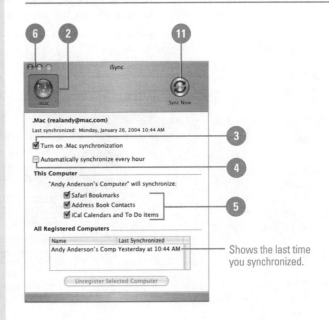

Shows the last time you synchronized.

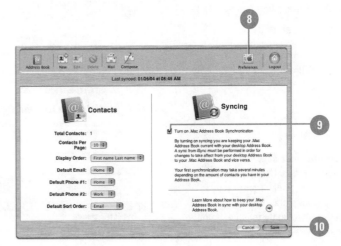

Working with .Mac Bookmarks

Bookmarks are just another place to store the addresses of all the fantastic Web sites that you are constantly going back to, time and time again. As the years roll by, you've probably generated quite a collection of bookmarks, and you need access to them. Since these great bookmarks are located within your browser, why would you need them in two places? What if you're on the road, you don't have your computer, and you need information on that great restaurant... but you don't remember their Web site? All you have to do is sign into your .Mac account (on any computer), and access your bookmarks. With the amount of traveling some people do, that can turn out to be a lifesaver.

Access .Mac Bookmarks

1. Open your browser and sign on to your .Mac account.

2. Click the Bookmarks link.

    A welcome screen appears.

    IMPORTANT *If you've previously activated synchronization within your Address Book, your Safari bookmarks will be synchronized.*

3. Click Open Bookmarks.

    The Bookmarks dialog appears with a list of folders such as News, Kids, Sports, Shopping, Travel, and any other folders you have added.

4. Click on a folder, and then a bookmark to access the site.

5. When you're done, close any open windows.

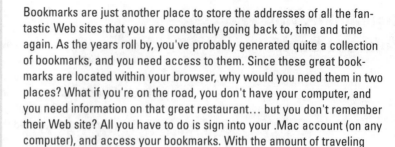

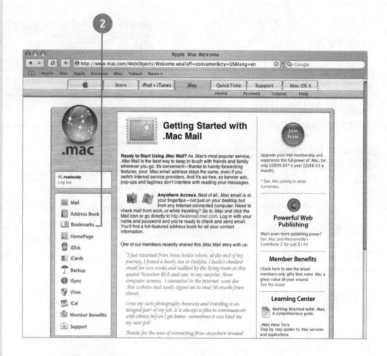

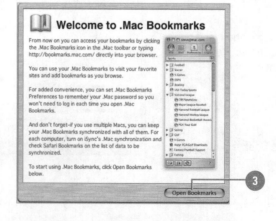

Did You Know?

You can restore your bookmarks if your system crashes. Using .Mac Bookmarks are not only a great way to access your bookmarks from any computer, they're also handy to have, if you experience a system crash.

Add a Folder or Bookmark

1. Open your browser and sign on to your .Mac account.

2. Click the Bookmarks link.

3. Click Open Bookmarks.

   The Bookmarks dialog appears.

4. Click on the Add Folder button.

5. Type the Folder Name, select a location, and then click Add.

6. Click on the Add Bookmark button.

7. Type the Bookmark Name, and then type the Bookmark URL (be sure to include www.)

8. Click the Add Bookmark To pop-up, select a folder, and then click Add.

9. Click Logout to return to the .Mac Home page.

Brings you back to .Mac Home page.

Change Bookmark Settings

1. Open your browser and sign on to your .Mac account.

2. Click the Bookmarks link.

3. Click Open Bookmarks.

4. Click Preferences, and then select between the following options:

   ◆ Always Open Pages In A New Browser Window or In The Same Browser Window.

   ◆ Select or clear the Save My Password check box.

   ◆ Select or clear the Synchronization check box.

5. Click Save.

6. Click Logout to return to the .Mac Home page.

11

Creating Web Pages with HomePage

Most of us would like to have our own customized Web site; however, many lack the experience to build the site, or don't know a Web designer who would do a good job for the least amount of money and maintenance. If you want to create a Web site that shows off pictures of your family, or you want to create an online resume, there's no need to hold back any longer, because having a .Mac account gives you the ability to create a Web site. By following step-by-step instructions using an application called HomePage. As a matter of fact, if you're a Web designer, you can create the site using programs such as Macromedia Dreamweaver, or Adobe GoLive, and upload the site. Your .Mac account lets you create a Web site, based on your level of experience, and helps you tailor the site to your specific needs.

Create Web Pages with HomePage

1 Open your browser and sign on to your .Mac account.

2 Click the HomePage link.

3 Select from the various themes.

4 Follow the step-by-step instructions (if you're creating a Pushpin Album, you'll be prompted as to the location of the images.)

5 Click Choose.

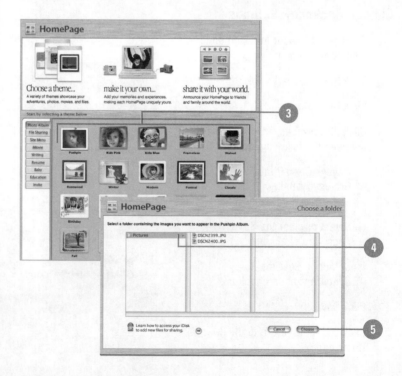

Did You Know?

Web Design help is always available. If you need more help on designing Web pages with HomePage, click the Help button. Apple provides a wealth of information to help guide you though the intricacies of Web design.

You can access HomePage in iPhoto. In iPhoto, click the Organize tab, and then click the HomePage button. Make the necessary additions.

6 Click Edit.

7 Click on the Title field, and then type a title for your Web page.

8 Click on the block of text field, and then type information about your Web page.

9 Click on the text under the image, and then type a note.

10 Click Publish to instantly broadcast your Web site to the world.

> **IMPORTANT** *When you create a Web site that requires assets such as images or text documents, the assets need to be stored within your iDisk.*

11 Click the Close button.

See Also

See "Managing Files with iDisk" on page 280 for more information on working with iDisk.

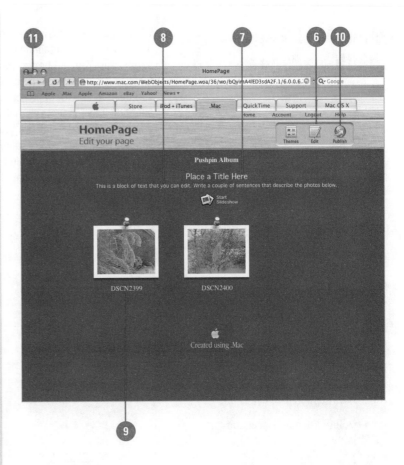

11

Editing Web Pages with HomePage

Web sites don't remain the same, they're fluid. For example, you've created a Web site containing pictures of your family, and your daughter just had a baby. You had better get that picture of the new addition to the family out there double-quick. Possibly you created a resume page, and you need to add (or subtract) some of the information. Regardless of the situation, once you create a Web site, as sure as the sun rises, you'll want to change it. Editing a Web site is actually easier than creating the site. All you have to do is select a page, make changes, and then click Publish. And, if making too many changes to your Web site has you spinning in circles, simply delete all of the pages in the old Web site, and .Mac lets you start all over.

Edit Web Pages

① Open your browser and sign on to your .Mac account.

② Click the HomePage link.

③ Select a page from the Pages window.

④ Select from the following options:

◆ **Add.** Adds a page for you to insert additional images on.

◆ **Delete.** Deletes a selected page.

◆ **Edit.** Allows you to Edit a selected page.

> ### Did You Know?
>
> **You can have more than one Web site.** Create additional Web sites (like folders in a file cabinet), and then link them together to create a complex site that's easy to organize and change.

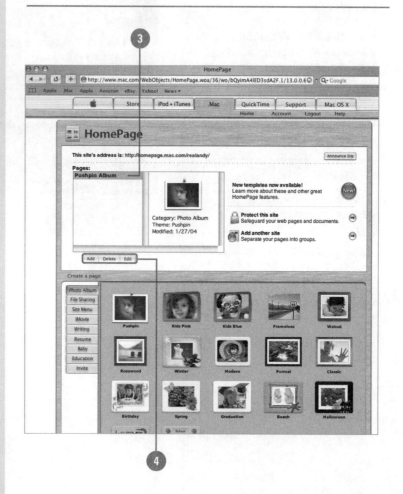

⑤ Make any text changes to the page.

⑥ To show a counter on the page to count the number of hits to your site, select the Show check box.

⑦ To show a Send Me A Message link on the page, select the Show check box.

⑧ To change a layout, click the 2 Columns or 3 Columns option.

⑨ To change the theme, click Themes.

⑩ To preview your changes, click Preview.

⑪ Click Publish to record the changes.

⑫ Click Logout to return to the .Mac Home page.

Did You Know?

You can change text settings such as Font or Speech in a text field. Control-click in a text field, and then select from the options available.

HomePage keeps track of as many pages as you need to create your personal Web space. Every time you return to the HomePage main screen, a list of all your pages appears in the window, and if you create additional pages, they'll appear in the same place.

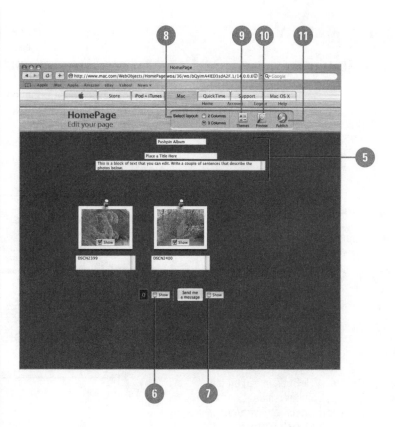

Backing Up Your Files Using .Mac ▶

Backing up your files is one of those things that most of us talk about, but seldom do on a regular basis. However, if you've ever experienced a catastrophic failure of your hard drive, a current backup can mean the difference between a simple restoration process, or the permanent loss of all your precious information. In addition, backups are not enough; they should be "off site" backups. In other words, your backup disks should not be in the same location as your computer (what if there were a fire). The good news is that owning a .Mac account makes backing up and restoring files easy (they supply you with the software), and you can create off-site backups using a CD/DVD or your iDisk.

Download and Install Backup

1. Open your browser and sign on to your .Mac account.

2. Click the Backup link.

3. Click Download Backup 2.

4. Click the Backup 2 link to download the latest version of the Backup software.

5. Double-click Backup.pkg on the Backup 2 Finder window, and then follow the onscreen instructions for installing the software.

6. If requested, type the Administrator name and password.

7. When you're done, close any open windows.

Did You Know?

The backup application is linked to the .Mac site. If you cancel your .Mac account, or if you're on the 60-day free trial subscription, the backup software ceases to function the day the cancellation becomes effective.

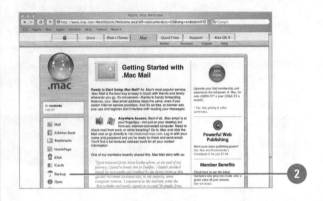

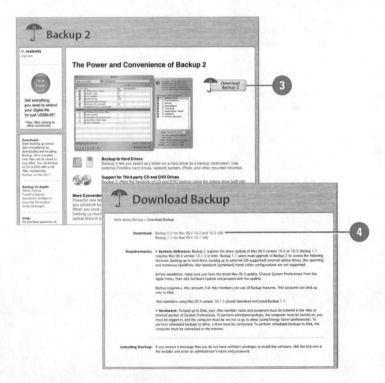

Back Up Your Files

1. Open the Applications folder, and then double-click the Backup icon.

2. Click the Backup/Restore pop-up, and then select a backup option:

   ◆ Back Up To iDisk

   ◆ Back Up To CD/DVD

   ◆ Back Up To Drive

   ◆ Restore From iDisk

   ◆ Restore From CD/DVD

   ◆ Restore From Drive

3. Check the items you wish to backup.

4. Click the Add button (+) to include additional files and folders to the backup list.

5. Click Backup Now to begin the backup process.

6. Click the Close button.

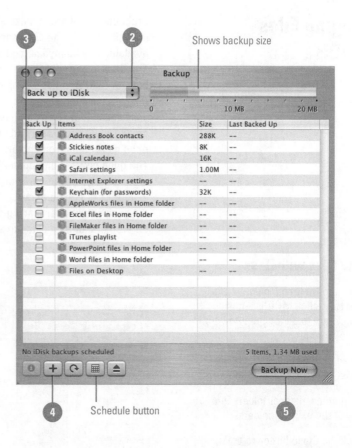

Shows backup size

Schedule button

Did You Know?

You can plan a future backup for a more convenient time. Click the Schedule button on the Backup dialog to schedule a backup that works for you and your computer.

For Your Information

Using Your iDisk for Backups

If you're looking for an off-site location to store your backups, look no further than your .Mac account. One of the options under the Backup/Restore pop-up is Back Up To iDisk. What could be more convenient? Just sign onto your .Mac account (make sure to keep up your subscription to .Mac services), click the Backup link, and then follow the instructions for Back Up Your Files on this page. Remember to select the Back Up To iDisk on the pop-up. One thing that could make it more convenient is to schedule your back up by clicking the Schedule button.

11

Managing Files with iDisk

Probably one of the coolest, and most-used features of a .Mac account is iDisk (**New!**). The iDisk service is like having a 100MB hard drive available to you anytime and anywhere you can plug into the Internet. The iDisk is perfect for performing off-site backups, or for storing large files for later use. For example, you could place large files in your iDisk (files that are too big to e-mail), and then download them when you get to your destination. Or if you have a high-speed Internet connection, you could simply use it as a secondary storage device. In addition, if you need more room, you can always upgrade and purchase more space. The good news is that once iDisk is open, you can treat it just like any other storage device on your computer. In fact, the Public folder located in your iDisk can be accessed by anyone owning a .Mac account. This is the perfect place for placing a document that needs to be distributed to co-workers, or as a place to store photos for other .Mac users to see.

Manage Files with iDisk

1 Click the Go menu, point to iDisk, and then click My iDisk (it is not necessary to be logged into your iMac account.)

2 If necessary, double-click on a folder to display its contents.

3 Drag items, files, or folders into any of the existing folders.

4 Click the Close button to collapse the iDisk window (an iDisk icon remains on your desktop).

5 If necessary, Control-click on the iDisk desktop icon, and then select Eject to remove the icon from the desktop.

Did You Know?

You can't add folders to the iDisk window. If you try to drag a folder from your hard drive directly into the iDisk window, you'll be told that you don't have sufficient privileges; however, if you drop the folder inside of one of the pre-existing folders, the operation is successful.

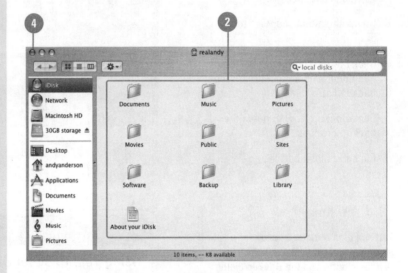

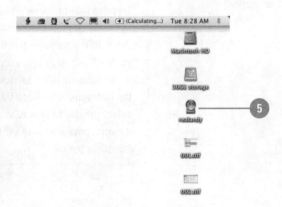

Protecting Files with Virex

One of the blessings of owning a Macintosh is that you hardly hear of any nasty viruses being sent our way. There are two reasons for this: Macintosh represents a smaller portion of the computing pie (attracting less serious hacker attention), and the Unix language (around which the Macintosh OS is modeled) is more difficult to hack. Since the release of OS X, not a single serious Macintosh virus has emerged... not a single one. Caution is advised, especially when you're working with Excel or Word macros that can hold viruses that could damage your Macintosh. The good news is that .Mac users have access to the Virex and McAfee virus protection applications, and they're only a click away.

Protect Files with Virex

1. Open your browser and sign on to your .Mac account.

2. Click the Virex link.

3. Click to download and install Virex, McAfee, or both.

4. Follow the onscreen instructions to load and activate the software.

5. When you're done, close any open windows.

> **IMPORTANT** *Both the Virex and McAfee applications are linked to your .Mac account; they only function as long as you maintain your subscription. And, since hackers create new viruses, it's important to check your .Mac account often to access the Virex and McAfee sites, and look for updates and virus warnings.*

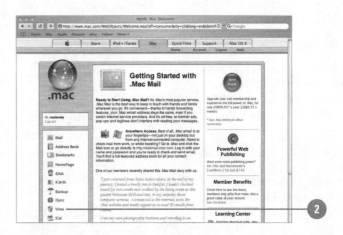

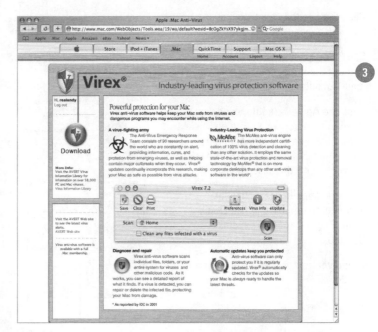

Getting Online Support

Having difficulty running your virus software? When you perform a backup, should you include application files? And what about the problems you're having loading and playing your favorite Mac game? Don't worry, help is on the way in the form of the .Mac community of users, as well as, the full support of the Apple Exchange. Apple's support system is constantly being updated to reflect the state of the current Macintosh software and hardware. If you have a question, and you need an answer, the .Mac online support system is the place to be.

Get Online Support

1. Open your browser and sign on to your .Mac account.

2. Click the Support link.

3. Click the Discussion Boards link to access a community of fellow users, and Macintosh gurus all ready and willing to answer your questions.

4. Click the FAQs (Frequently Asked Questions) link to gain access to some of the more common problems facing Mac users, and (hopefully) the answers to your problem.

5. Click the Feedback link, to ask a specific question to Apple.

6. Click the Tips and Tricks links to find out the latest tips and tricks; most submitted by users (like you).

7. Click the AppleCare Knowledge Base to gain access to Apple's huge database of information on every model of Macintosh that has ever rolled off the assembly line.

8. Click the specific Help links for information on: .Mac, iDisk, Email, HomePage, iCards, Virex, and Backup.

9. When you're done, close any open windows.

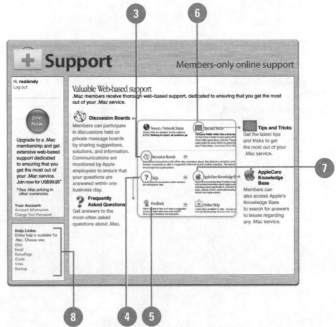

Conducting Live Chats and Video Conferences

12

Introduction

Mac OS X makes communicating with other computers over the Internet easier than ever with iChat AV. You can talk to others over the Internet (like you do on a telephone), use full screen video to see and be seen by others while you converse, share programs and files, and collaborate on documents.

You can use iChat AV to exchange instant messages with a designated list of buddies over the Internet. An **instant message** is an online typewritten conversation in real-time between two or more buddies. Unlike an e-mail message, instant messages require both parties to be online, and the communication is instantaneous.

iChat AV makes setup effortless. The first time you launch iChat AV, a setup screen appears to walk you step-by-step through the process. During the setup process, you need to create or provide a screen name, which is your instant messaging address. If you already have an AOL Instant Messenger (AIM) screen name, you can use it with iChat AV. Otherwise, you can setup a .Mac account to get a screen name. To use the AV features of iChat, you need to have a microphone (for audio only) or FireWire compatible video camera (for audio and video) installed on your computer and a fast Internet connection. iChat AV 2.0 allows you to communicate with Mac AIM users, while iChat AV 2.1 allows you to talk with both Mac and PC users. iChat 2.1 supports video conferencing with AOL Instant Messenger 5.5 or later (New!). Now you can talk to millions more people online.

In addition to using iChat AV over the Internet, you can also use it on your local network—known as **rendezvous messaging**—at the office, school, or home. iChat AV automatically locates other local users who are logged in, and lets you send messages or files to each other.

Creating an Instant Message Account

The first time you launch iChat AV, a setup screen opens to walk you step-by-step through the process. To complete the process, you need to provide or create a screen name (your instant messaging address) to send and receive instant messages with iChat AV. If you already have a .Mac account or an AOL Instant Messenger (AIM) screen name, you can use it with iChat AV. For example, a .Mac screen name is your e-mail address, such as *perspection@mac.com*, or an AIM screen name is a handle, such as *perspection*. If you don't have a screen name, you can sign up for a .Mac account at Apple's .Mac Web site during the setup process to get one. You can't use screen names from other instant messaging system, such as MSN or Yahoo, with iChat AV. If you are using iChat AV over a local network for rendezvous messaging, you don't need a screen name.

Create an Instant Message Account the First Time

1. If necessary, install a microphone or compatible video camera according to product instructions.

2. Start iChat for the first time; display the Dock on the desktop, and then click the iChat icon.

3. Read the Welcome screen, and then click Continue.

4. Type your first and last name.

5. Click the Account Type pop-up, and then select an account.

   TROUBLE? *If you don't have an account, click Get An iChat Account.*

6. Type your Account Name and Password, and then click Continue.

7. Click a rendezvous option to enable or disable iChat messaging in your local network, and then click Continue.

8. Select options to setup audio and video for iChat, and then click Continue.

9. Click Done.

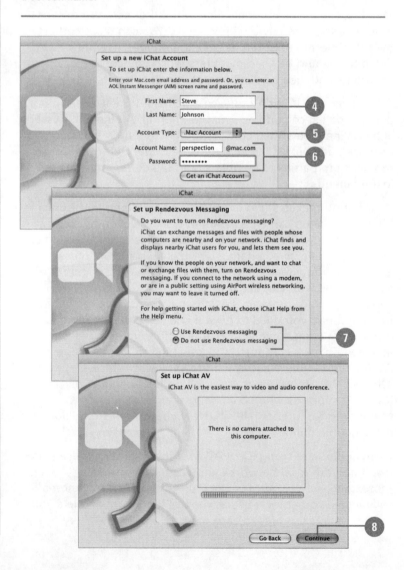

Switch Between Accounts

1. Click the iChat menu, and then click Preferences.

2. Click Accounts.

   IMPORTANT *If multiple people use a computer with separate accounts, they automatically use their own screen names.*

3. Click the AIM Screen Name pop-up, and then select one of the following options:

   ◆ **Screen name.** Click a name.

   ◆ **Use My .Mac Account.** Click to use the currently logged in account.

   ◆ **Create A New .Mac Account.** Follow the online instructions to create a new account.

   ◆ **Clear Menu.** Removes all accounts except the one currently logged in.

4. Type your screen name (if necessary) and password.

   Your password is added to your keychain, so you don't have to type it every time you log in.

5. Click the Close button.

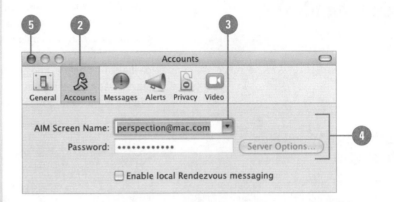

Did You Know?

You can get the latest version of iChat online. Visit the Apple Web site at *www.apple.com* to get iChat AV 2.1 or later.

You can get or change your password and account information. Visit the AOL Instant Messenger Web site at *www.aim.com*, or visit the iMac Web site at *www.mac.com*.

For Your Information

Installing and Selecting AV Hardware

Before you can start or join a video chat, you need to connect and install a microphone, a FireWire based video camera, such as iSight by Apple, built-in USB, and a broadband Internet connection, such as cable or DSL, to your Macintosh computer. If you have a Digital Video (DV) camcorder with a FireWire cable, you can also use it with iChat. You can use iChat video conferencing on Macintosh G3 computers with a 600 MHz or faster processor and Macintosh G4 computers or later; or you can use iChat audio only on a Macintosh with a G3 processor, built-in USB, a microphone, and at least a 56K modem connection. Once you attach and install (if necessary) your audio and video equipment, you can set options in the Video pane of iChat Preferences. If you are using a camera with a built-in microphone, iChat AV automatically uses the camera microphone unless you change it to another one you have attached to your computer.

12

Starting iChat AV

iChat AV is an instant messaging program that allows you to exchange instant messages with a designated list of buddies over the Internet. An **instant message** is an online typewritten conversation in real time between two or more buddies. Instant messages require both parties to be online, and the communication is instantaneous. After you start iChat AV, you sign in to let others online know you are connected. When you're done, you sign out.

Start iChat AV and Sign In and Out

1. Display the Dock on the desktop, and then click the iChat icon.

   A Buddy List window opens, displaying a "Connecting" message. Upon completion, the Buddy List expands to list your buddies and their online status.

2. If you're not automatically signed in, click the iChat menu, and then click Log In To AIM.

3. To sign out, click the iChat menu, and then click Log Out Of AIM.

Did You Know?

You can stop signing in automatically.
Click the iChat menu, click Preferences, click General, clear the When iChat Opens, Automatically Log In check box, and then click the Close button.

Your buddies might need to upgrade their AIM software. If your buddies are using older versions of the AOL Instant Messaging software, they might need to get a newer version to send messages to your .Mac screen name.

You can get help specific to iChat. Click the Help menu, and then click iChat Help. The application help system works just like Mac help.

Dock

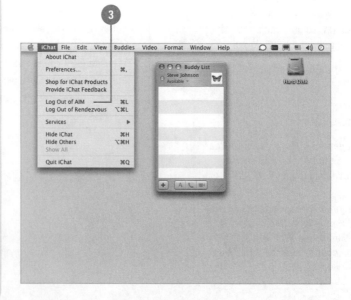

Viewing iChat AV

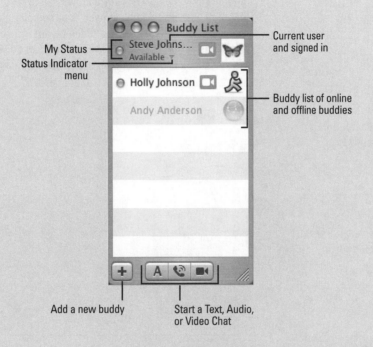

My Status

Status Indicator menu

Current user and signed in

Buddy list of online and offline buddies

Add a new buddy

Start a Text, Audio, or Video Chat

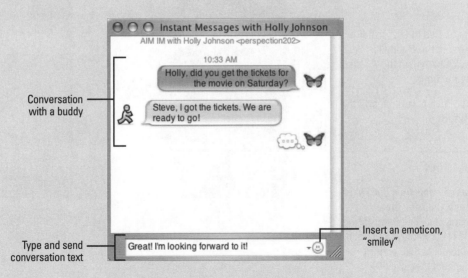

Conversation with a buddy

Type and send conversation text

Insert an emoticon, "smiley"

Changing My Status

When you sign in with iChat AV, the program notifies buddies currently online from your Buddy list that you are available to chat. While you're signed in, you might need to leave your computer for a meeting or lunch. Instead of signing out, you can change your online status to let your buddies know that you're busy, away from your desk, on the phone, or out to lunch. When your away, your buddies see that you're idle, including the length of time since you last used your computer, and any message you receive is waiting for you. If you don't want your buddies to see or send messages to you, you can go offline. You can quickly customize your status messages to suit your own needs and circumstances.

Change My Status

1. Click the Status Indicator below your name in the Buddy List.

2. Click a status type.

Did You Know?

You can set different status for AIM and Rendezvous. As long as one of them is set to offline.

Create a Custom Status Message

1. Click the Status Indicator below your name in the Buddy List, and then click Custom, in the Available or Away sections.

2. Type a custom message, and then press Return.

Did You Know?

You can change items from the Status Indicator menu. Click the Status Indicator menu, click Edit Status Menu, click the Add (+) or Remove (-) buttons, double-click items to edit, or drag items to order, and then click OK.

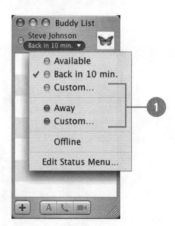

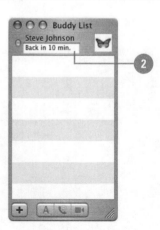

Using the iChat Status Menu

If you turn on the iChat Status menu, you can still receive instant messages, view online buddies, and change your status when you quit the iChat program. The iChat Status menu appears as a chat balloon icon on the right side of the menu bar for all applications. When the ballon icon is empty, you're online; when there is a line in the middle, you're away or offline. If you don't see the Status menu, you need to turn it on in the General pane of iChat Preferences. When the Status menu is turned off and you quit iChat, you're logged out of AIM and rendezvous messaging.

Turn On the iChat Status Menu

① Click the iChat menu, and then click Preferences.

② Click General.

③ Select the Show Status In Menu Bar check box.

④ Click the Close button.

Did You Know?

You can leave Status menu on and still log out when you quit. Click the iChat menu, click Preferences, click General, select the When I Quit iChat, Set My Status To Offline check box, and then click the Close button.

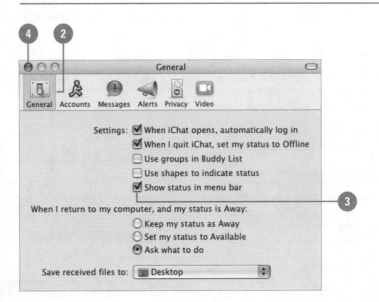

Use the iChat Status Menu

① Click the iChat Status menu, and then select an available option:

◆ **A status.** Click Available, Away, or Offline; you can also select custom available or away messages.

◆ **A buddy.** Click the name of an online buddy.

◆ **Buddy List.** Click to display your Buddy List.

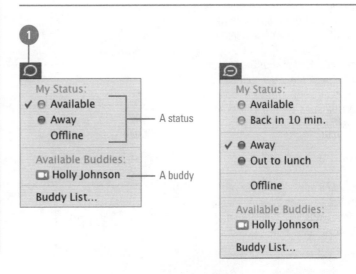

12

Adding a Buddy

Before you can send instant messages to other people, they need to be in your Buddy list. Your Buddy list shows you who's currently online and offline, their audio and video capabilities, and if they are available for chatting. You can add a person who has a screen name from a .Mac account or AIM to your Buddy list. You can add as many buddies as you like to your Buddies list. You can add them from your Address Book or type new ones. When you add a new person to your Buddy list, a new card is added to your Address Book. Your Buddy list is stored on an instant message server, so you can log in to your account from any computer and see if your buddies are online.

Add a Buddy

1. If necessary, click the Window menu, and then click Buddy List to display the Buddy List window.

2. Click the Add New Buddy button (+) in the Buddy List window.

3. Use one of the following methods:

   ◆ **Select from Address Book.** Select a name from your Address Book, and then click Select Buddy.

   ◆ **Create New.** Click New Person, select an account, type the screen name for the person, and then click Add.

   TIMESAVER *If your buddy uses more than one screen name, you can type more than one by separating each with a comma.*

   TROUBLE? *If your Buddy list is empty, click the View menu, and then click Show Offline Buddies to show all buddies, regardless of availability.*

Did You Know?

You can add a buddy from your rendezvous list. Click the Window menu, click Rendezvous, and then drag a buddy's name to the Buddy List.

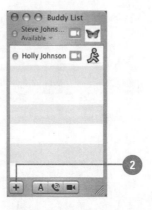

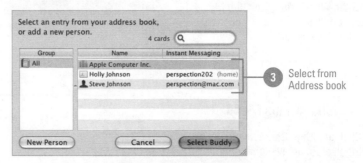

Select from Address book

Create a new person

Change the Buddy List View

1. Click the View menu.

2. Select any of the following options to show or hide:

   ◆ Show Buddy Pictures

   ◆ Show Audio Status

   ◆ Show Video Status

   ◆ Show Offline Buddies

   ◆ Show Groups

3. Select one of the following sorting methods:

   ◆ Sort By Availability

   ◆ Sort By First Name

   ◆ Sort By Last Name

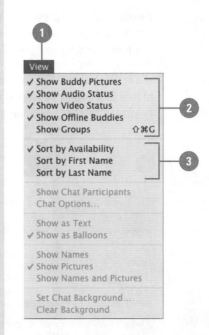

Did You Know?

You can quickly delete a buddy from your Buddy list. Click a buddy in the Buddy list, press Delete, and then click OK. People who are removed from your list can still contact you unless you block them.

You can view and edit information about a buddy. Select a buddy in the Buddy list, click the Buddies menu, and then click Get Info. The information shown is typed by your buddy.

For Your Information

Changing Buddy List Pictures

You can change the picture that appears next to your name in the Buddy List and in message windows, along with the ones that appear next to your buddies. The picture is known as the Buddy icon. The Buddy icon you select appears in the Buddy List of those in which you have a chat. To change your Buddy icon, drag an image file to your name in the Buddy List. In addition to changing your Buddy icon, you can also change your buddy's pictures. To change the picture of a buddy, select the buddy, click the Buddies menu, click Get Info, click the Show pop-up, click Address Card, clear the Always Use This Picture check box, and then select the image you want to use (double-click the picture, and then click the Choose button to select a picture file or the Take Video Snapshot button to take an online picture), and then click OK or Set. If necessary, click OK one more time to save and close. The picture has now been updated for your buddy. The picture you add to your Buddy list appear only on your computer unless you select the Always Use This Picture check box in the Get Info dialog. When you change a picture in the Buddy list, iChat also changes your Address Book.

12

Creating and Managing Buddy Groups

As your Buddy list grows, you may want to organize your buddies into groups. iChat AV makes it easy to create your own groups and use the one predefined group called Buddies that comes with iChat AV. Once you have organized your groups, you can simply drag buddies from one group to another (New!). You can use the check boxes next to the group name to hide and display buddies in a group. If a group changes, you can rename it, or if you no longer need a group, you can remove it.

Turn On the Use of Groups

1. Click the iChat menu, and then click Preferences.

2. Click General.

3. Select the Use Groups In Buddy List check box.

4. Click the Close button.

Create a Buddy Group

1. Click the All Groups pop-up, and then click Groups.

2. Click the Add button (+) in the Groups drawer.

3. Type a name, and then press Return.

4. Click to close the Groups drawer.

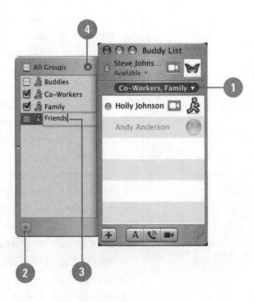

Manage Buddy Groups

1. Click the All Groups pop-up, and then click Groups.

2. Select from the following options:

   ◆ **Display all group members.** click the pop-up, and then click All Groups.

   ◆ **Display specific group members.** Select the check box next to the group name in the Groups drawer.

   ◆ **Move a buddy into a group.** Drag the buddy to a group.

   ◆ **Copy a buddy into a group.** Press and hold down the Option key while you drag the buddy to each group.

   ◆ **Delete a group.** Select a group in the Groups drawer, and then press Delete.

     You can't delete a group with buddies in multiple groups, but you can delete a group with the only buddy in it. You can't delete the last group in the list; you need to always have at least one.

   ◆ **Rename a group.** Select a group name in the Groups drawer, press Return, and then type a new name.

3. Click to close the Groups drawer.

Display all group members

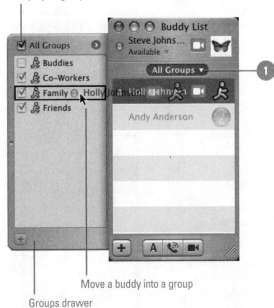

Move a buddy into a group

Groups drawer

Display specific group members

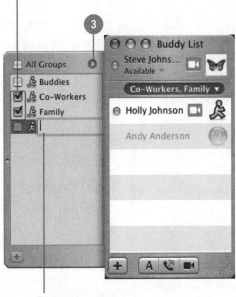

Rename a group

Sending and Receiving Instant Messages

An instant message is an online typewritten conversation in real-time between two or more buddies. As you type an instant message, you can format your messages by using fonts and color and by inserting graphical symbols called **emoticons**, or "smiley," such as a happy face, which help convey your emotions. You cannot send an instant message to more than one person, but you can invite other people to participate in an existing conversation. However, you can have instant message conversations with several different buddies at once, each in its own window.

Send and Receive Instant Messages

1. If necessary, click the Window menu, and then click Buddy List.

2. To start a chat, select a name in the Buddy list, and then click the Start A Text Chat button.

   To respond to a text chat invitation, click the invitation window, type a message, and then click Accept.

3. Type your message in the box at the bottom of the window.

   To start a new line while typing, press Shift+Return.

4. Press Return, and then wait.

5. To add another person to the chat, click the View menu, click Show Chat Participants, click the Add button (+), and then click a person from your Buddy list or Other.

6. When you're done, click the Close button to end the session.

> ### Did You Know?
>
> *You can start a new chat with one or more people.* Click the File menu, and then click New Chat With Person to start a chat with one person, enter the address of the person to invite, and then click OK. Or you can click New Chat to start a chat with multiple people.

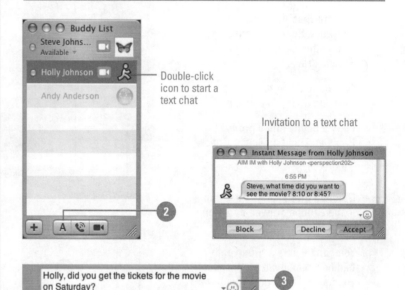

Double-click icon to start a text chat

Invitation to a text chat

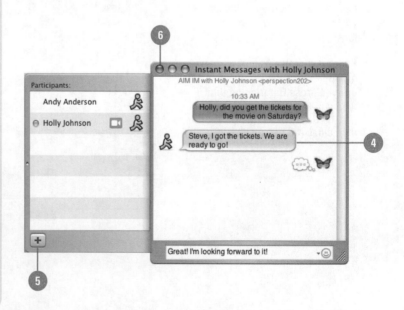

Format Message Text

① Type and then select the text you want to format.

② Click the Format menu, and then click the Show Fonts.

③ Specify the font, font style, size, color, and effect you want, and then preview the result in the sample box.

④ Click the Close button, and then send the formatted message.

Insert Emoticons

① In the Chat window, click the Emoticons button.

TIMESAVER *Type a smiley using the keyboard, such as ":-)" and iChat inserts a corresponding graphic. Point to a smiley to view its type.*

② Type your text, and then click the icon you want to insert into the conversation.

③ Press Return.

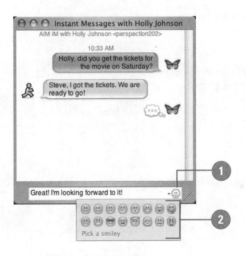

Did You Know?

You can save an instant message.
Click the File menu, click Save A Copy As, type a file name, select a location, and then click Save. To review a chat, click the File menu, click Open, select a transcript file, and then click Open.

You can save chats automatically.
Click the iChat menu, click Preferences, click Messages, select the Automatically Save Chat Transcripts check box, click Open Folder, select a folder, and then click the Close button.

Emoticon in chat

12

Blocking a Buddy

If you no longer want to receive instant messages from a specific buddy, you can block the buddy from sending you instant messages. When you block a buddy, you appear to be offline to the person, who doesn't know blocking is turned on. Blocking a buddy moves them from your Allow list to your Block list in the Privacy pane of iChat Preferences.

Block or Unblock a Buddy

1 Click the iChat menu, and then click Preferences.

2 Click Privacy.

3 Click a privacy option:

◆ **Allow Anyone.** Click to unblock everybody.

◆ **Allow People In My Buddy List.** Click to unblock buddies in my Buddy List.

◆ **Allow Specific People.** Click the option, and then click Edit List to select buddies.

◆ **Block Everyone.** Click to block everyone.

◆ **Block Specific People.** Click the option, and then click Edit List to add and remove buddies.

4 Select or clear the Block Others From Seeing That I Am Idle check box.

5 Select or clear the Block Rendezvous Users From Seeing My Email and AIM Addresses check box.

6 Click the Close button.

> ### Did You Know?
>
> **You can quickly block a buddy.** Select the buddy in the Buddy list, click the Buddies menu, click Block *buddy name*, and then click Block.

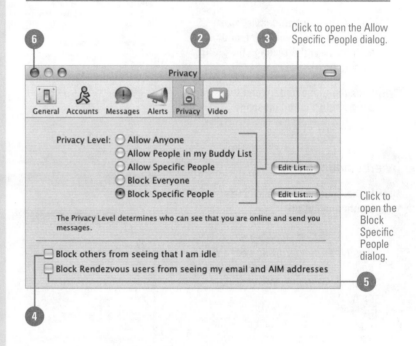

Click to open the Allow Specific People dialog.

Click to open the Block Specific People dialog.

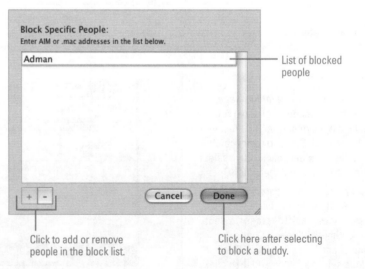

List of blocked people

Click to add or remove people in the block list.

Click here after selecting to block a buddy.

Sending a File During an Instant Message

While you are conversing in iChat AV, you can send a buddy a file or hyperlink. You can send many different types of files, including pictures, documents, and music. When you send a picture, it's displayed right beside your text in the Chat window. When you send any other type of file, a request to transfer the file is sent to your buddy. You are notified when your buddy accepts or declines your request. Before you receive files over the Internet, make sure you have virus protection software to protect your computer. You can also send a hyperlink that points to a Web site. When your buddy receives a message with a link, the person can click it to open the Web address in their Web browser.

Send a File or Hyperlink

1. Start a chat with the buddy to whom you want to send the file or hyperlink.

2. Type your message in the box at the bottom of the window.

3. Click the Edit menu, and then click one of the following:

   ◆ **Send a File.** Click Attach File, navigate to and select the file you want to send (for best results, use JPEG or GIF), and then click Open. A small icon appears to indicate the picture.

   TIMESAVER *Drag the picture file to the area where you type your message.*

   ◆ **Send a Hyperlink.** Click Add Hyperlink, type a Web address, and then click OK.

4. Type any additional text if you want, and then press Return.

   If you're sending a picture, the image appears in the chat window; if it's a file, wait for the recipient to accept or decline the file; or if it's a hyperlink, the link appears in the chat window.

5. To open a file or hyperlink, click the file or link in the chat window.

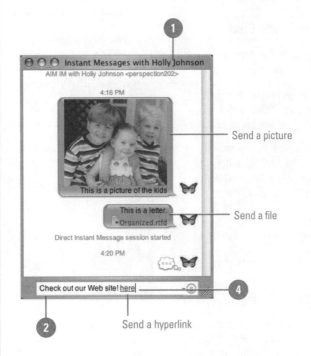

Send a picture

Send a file

Send a hyperlink

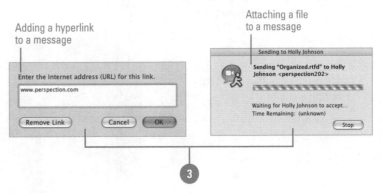

Adding a hyperlink to a message

Attaching a file to a message

12

Having a Audio and Video Chat

When used with Panther, iChat AV provides state-of-the-art computer communications features. With iChat AV, you can talk to others over the Internet as you do on a regular phone, and you can use video to see others and let others see you as you converse. Once you set up your computer hardware and software, you're ready to communicate over the Internet. You have two communication choices: audio only, or audio and video (**New!**). With audio only, you speak into a microphone and hear the other person's response over your speakers. With audio and video, you send video to others so they receive live images as well as sound. If the buddies you call don't have a video camera, they'll see you, but you won't see them. iChat AV supports only one video or audio chat at a time.

Have a Audio or Video Chat

1. If necessary, click the Window menu, and then click Buddy List.

2. To start a chat, select a name in the Buddy list, and then click the Start A Video Chat button or Start An Audio Chat button.

   To respond to an audio or video chat invitation, click the invitation window, and then click Accept.

   To decline or block a chat invitation, click Decline or Block.

3. Start talking.

4. Use video controls on the Video menu or use the following:

   ◆ **Size Video Window.** Click the double arrow button to switch between normal and full-screen modes. You can also drag the bottom right corner of the video window.

   ◆ **Pause Video.** Option+click the Microphone button. Click the button again to start it.

   ◆ **Mute Audio.** Click the Microphone button.

5. When you're done, click the Close button to end the session.

Double-click icon to start a video chat

Click to acknowledge the invitation

Click to accept or decline video chat invitation

Change Video Bandwidth Speed and Preferences

1. Click the iChat menu, and then click Preferences.

2. Click Video.

3. Click the Microphone pop-up, and then select an installed microphone.

4. Click the Bandwidth Limit pop-up, and then select a video speed option for your computer's performance and quality.

5. Select or clear the check boxes to automatically open iChat when the camera is turned on or play repeated ring sound when invited to a conference.

6. Click the Close button.

Did You Know?

You can monitor a video chat. Click the Video menu, and then click Connection Doctor. The frame rate shows the number of frames the video plays per second (fps). The Bit Rate setting show the average number of bits that one second of video data consumes in kilobits per second (kbps). The call duration shows how long the chats lasts.

You can take a picture of your video chat. ⌘+click the video chat window and drag the image (a JPEG file) out of the window to a buddy icon in your Buddy list or a location on your hard disk. You can also press ⌘+C to copy a picture of your chat and then press ⌘+V to paste it in another document.

iChat AV Performance and Quality

Option	Standard	Enhanced	High
Window Size	352x288 to Full Screen	352x288 to Full Screen	352x288 to Full Screen
Video Resolution	176x144	176x144	352x288
Frames Per Second (fps)	15	20	20/30
System Required	> 600 Mhz G3 or 350 Mhz G4	> 1Ghz G4	> dual 800 Mhz G4 and any G5
Bandwidth	100-500 Kbps	100-500 Kbps	Above 500 Kbps

12

Chatting on a Local Network

If you don't have an instant message account or server, you can still use iChat AV to chat with others on your local network. Instead of communicating with a central Internet server, each computer communicates directly with each other over network cables. iChat AV also works with a wireless connection using AirPort over a local network or the Internet. Rendezvous allows you to chat with people on your local network or wireless local community. You can't add a rendezvous user to your Buddy list. The user names are based on the log-in settings on each person's computer and are not AIM screen names. Unlike regular instant message, when you type a Rendezvous instant message, each character you type is sent immediately unless you turn off the default setting in the Messages pane of iChat Preferences.

Turn On Rendezvous Instant Messaging

1. Click the iChat menu, and then click Preferences.

2. Click Accounts.

3. Select the Enable Local Rendezvous Messaging check box.

4. Click the Close button.

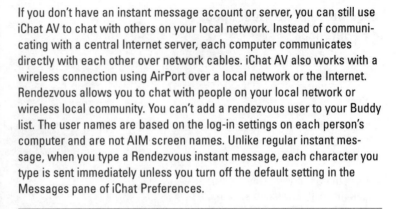

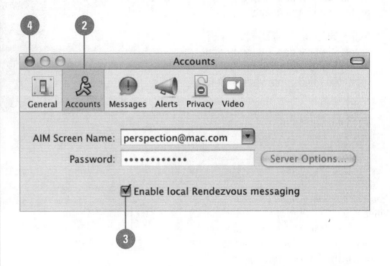

Did You Know?

You can send Rendezvous message when you're done typing. Click the iChat menu, click Preferences, click Messages, clear the Send Text As I Type (Rendezvous Only) check box, and then click the Close button.

For Your Information

Having Problems Seeing Rendezvous Users

If you're having problems seeing rendezvous users in the Rendezvous window, your network connections might be contributing to the problem. If you have firewall protect turned on, you might be unable to receive messages from other users. To use Rendezvous, you need to allow activity on port 5298. If you connect to the Internet using PPP or PPPoE, you won't be able to see other users. Check with your network administrator for information related to your network setup.

Start Rendezvous Messaging

① Click the iChat menu, and then click Log In To Rendezvous.

The Rendezvous window opens, showing iChat local network users who are available for chatting.

TROUBLE? *Click the Window menu, and then click Rendezvous to display the Rendezvous window.*

② Double-click the user to whom you want to send an instant message.

③ Type your message in the box at the bottom of the window.

④ Press Return, and then wait for a reply.

⑤ When you're done, click the Close button to end the session.

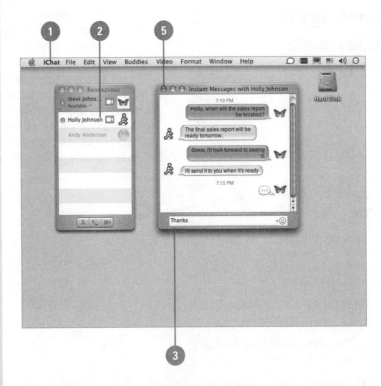

Changing the Appearance of a Chat

iChat makes it easy to customize the appearance of a chat to suit your own style and preference. You can modify the appearance of the balloons, or change a font style in a chat. The changes you make affect the format of your messages on your screen as well as messages on your buddies screen unless they have chosen to reformat incoming messages. When you reformat incoming messages, you override your chat buddy settings and display all incoming messages using your preferences. You can set your preferences and reformat settings in the Messages pane of iChat Preferences. You can also change the background of the chat window to a picture, which only appears on your computer.

Change the Appearance of a Chat

1. Click the iChat menu, and then click Preferences.

2. Click Messages.

3. Select or specify the various options you want to use:

   ◆ **My Ballon Color.** Click the pop-up, and then select a color.

   ◆ **My Font Color.** Click the pop-up, and then select a font color.

   ◆ **Set Font.** Click to select a font.

   ◆ **Reformat Incoming Messages.** Check to use your preferred settings, and then select a ballon and font color, and a font for the sender.

4. Click the Close button.

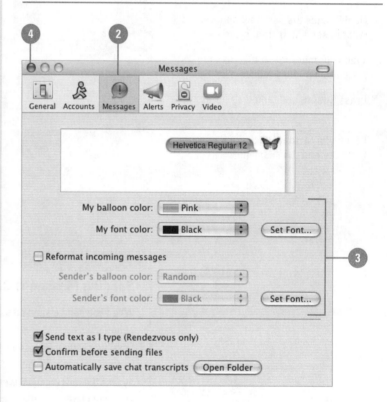

Change the Chat Window Background

1 Click the View menu, and then click Set Chat Background.

2 Navigate to the hard drive and folder from which you want to select the background file.

3 Click the image file you want to open.

4 Click Open.

Did You Know?

You can quickly remove a background from the chat window. Click the View menu, and then click Clear Background.

You can view a chat as text. Click the View menu, and then click Show As Text.

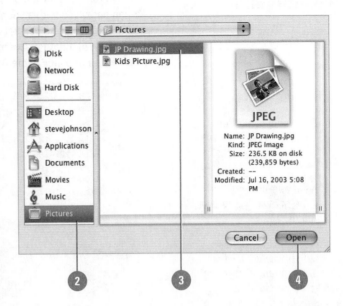

Background image in Chat window

12

Getting Notification Alerts

When certain events, such as messages arrive or buddies log in, iChat AV can notify you with a sound, spoken message, or bounce of the iChat icon in the Dock. You can set alerts that apply to every buddy in the Alerts pane of iChat Preferences, or you can set specific notification alerts for each buddy in the Actions pane of the Get Info dialog.

Set Up Notification Alerts

1. Click the iChat menu, and then click Preferences.

2. Click Alerts.

3. Click the Event pop-up, and then select the type of event you want to be notified of.

4. Select or clear the Play Sound check box. If you select it, click the pop-up, select an occurrence, and then select or clear the Repeat check box if you want the alert to occur every time.

5. Select or clear the Bounce Icon In The Dock check box. If you select the check box, select or clear the Repeat check box.

6. Select or clear the Speak Text check box. If you select it, type a message to speak, and then drag the slider to set the speech volume.

   You can enter "@" to substitute for a buddy's name. For example, if you entered "@" is online, iChat says "Steve Johnson is online."

7. Click the Close button.

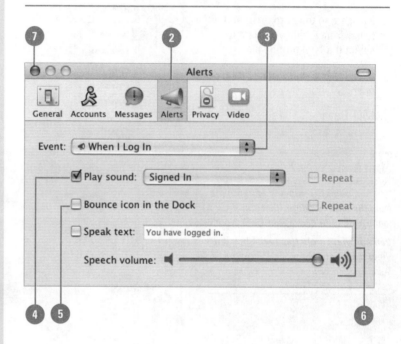

Did You Know?

You can specify different alerts for each buddy. Select a buddy in your Buddy List, click the Buddies menu, click Get Info, click the Show pop-up, click Actions, select the options you want, and then click the Close button.

Tracking and Synchronizing Information

Introduction

Computers can indeed be a blessing and a curse. On the one hand they give you instant access to mountains of information; on the other hand you're the one who has to organize and keep track of all that data. There are a lot of programs out there that claim to help you stay organized, using everything from day-planner software to relational databases. There's only one problem, you have to actually use those programs. That typically means learning new third party software, loading all your data and schedules, and then trying to keep it current, even if you move it to a different computer. The previous paragraph defined the problem; the next provides the solution.

When Apple introduced OS X, they touted it as a **digital hub**. The concept of a digital hub involves placing your daily schedules and contact data into the system one time. Then the hub would keep the data up-to-date and in sync with any other places the same data is stored. With the release of OS X, and applications such as: iSync and iCal, the folks at Apple achieved the dream of creating a true, easy-to-use digital hub. I have a graveyard of applications that promised to organize and make my life easier. However, the programs were difficult to manage, and they didn't move information easily between systems. In short, the promise was not the reality. When Panther was released, along with improved versions of its syncing and management programs, I was finally able to get control of the mountains of information that make up my daily life.

Viewing the iCal Window

iCal is the Macintosh version of a scheduling and time-management application. There are other programs out there that schedules and manages your time; however, iCal's native architecture (built by Apple), it's stability, and ability to transfer and sync information easily across multiple applications, makes it an easy choice for the busy executive, the harried designer/animator, or anyone who owns a Macintosh, and wants to keep track of what they're doing. iCal assists you by helping you automate repetitive events such as: Yoga every Friday at 8pm, the kids soccer practice, or that quarterly conference call with management. In addition, iCal notifies you of an event by using an alarm sound, pop-up note, or even e-mail. To access iCal, open the Applications folder, and then double-click on the iCal application.

Calendar selection

Calendar window

Previous, Current or Next Month mini-month view

Mini-Month view

Add New Calendar

Current Day highlighted

Show/Hide Info list

Show/Hide Mini-Month

Next Day, Week, Month view

Search field

Show/Hide To Do list

Previous Day, Week, Month view

Day, Week, Month views

Show/Hide Search results

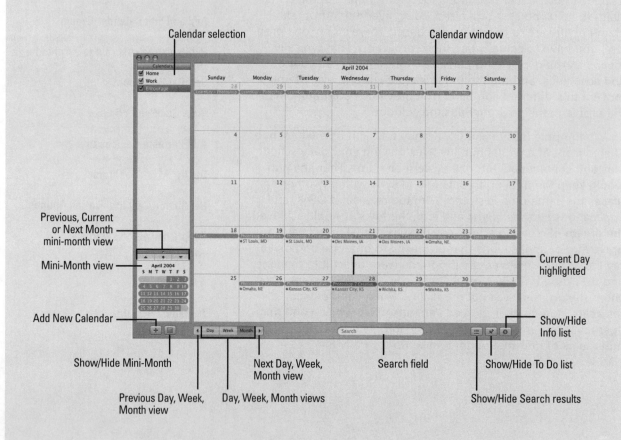

Creating a To Do List

Okay, you've created this awesome calendar that lists all of your appointments, plus things that you have to do (my wife calls this a honey do list). Not only does the iCal application let you create a To Do list, complete with every task on your list; it also helps you stay on schedule using audio or pop-up reminders. This is an easier solution than your wife tapping you on the shoulder, and asking you if you remembered to fix the screen on the back porch door.

Create a To Do List

1. Open the Applications folder, and then double-click the iCal icon.

2. Click the Pushpin button.

3. Double-click in the To Do Items window to add an event, and then press Return.

4. Click the Info button, and then add the following To Do information:

   ◆ **Completed.** Select the check box when the task is complete.

   ◆ **Priority.** Click to select a priority setting.

   ◆ **Due Date.** Select the check box, and then enter a due date.

   ◆ **Alarm.** (New!) If Due Date is checked, Alarm notifies using a Message, Message With A Sound, E-mail, or Open A File.

   ◆ **Calendar.** Click to select the calendar this list is linked to.

   ◆ **URL.** Click to add a URL address to the To Do.

   ◆ **Notes.** Click to add any notes.

5. Click the Info button again to close the drawer.

6. To modify, select an item, and then click the Info button.

7. To remove, select an item, and then press Delete.

8. Quit iCal.

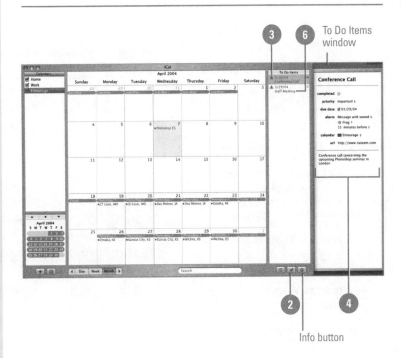

To Do Items window

Info button

Adding and Editing Calendar Events

When you first create your iCal calendar, it represents where you are with your schedule at that moment in time. Unfortunately, things change and they can change often. Therefore, iCal gives you the ability to add new events or modify existing events using the Info Drawer (New!). The beauty of iCal is that it makes calendar modifications easy, and once complete, they can be transferred to other applications and devices.

Add Calendar Events

1. Open the Applications folder, and then double-click the iCal icon.

2. Click a view button to find the date to add.

3. Double-click the day to add an event.

4. Add the following event options:

   ◆ **New Event.** Type the Event name (appears in window).

   ◆ **Location.** Type a location.

   ◆ **All day.** Check for all day event.

   ◆ **From/To.** Enter a From/To date.

   ◆ **Attendees.** Adds attendees to the event list.

   ◆ **Status.** Indicates the status of the event.

   ◆ **Repeat.** Sets this to a repeating event.

   ◆ **Alarm.** Lets you be notified before the event.

   ◆ **Calendar.** Click to select the calendar this event is linked.

   ◆ **URL.** Click to add a URL address to the event.

   ◆ **Notes.** Click to add any notes.

5. Click the Info button.

6. Click the Current Month mini-view button to go back to today's date.

7. Quit iCal.

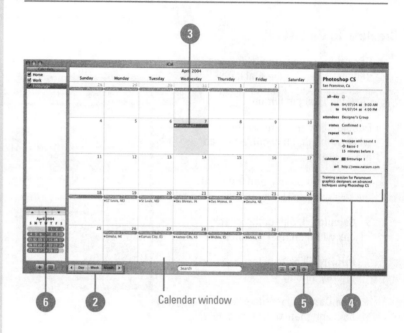

Calendar window

Edit Calendar Events

1. Open the Applications folder, and then double-click the iCal icon.

2. Click a view button to find the date to edit.

3. Click the day you want to edit.

4. Make any changes to the event, such as Location, From/To, or Notes.

   TIMESAVER *If your information of an event is only the event name, you can save time and bypass the info drawer, by double-clicking the day, and then typing the event name directly into the day window.*

5. To remove the event from the calendar, click on an existing event, and then press Delete.

6. Quit iCal.

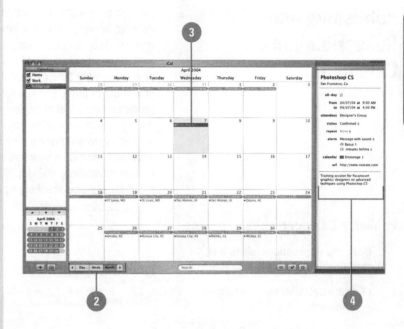

Did You Know?

You can add attendees from your Address Book. Click on the Attendees field in the info drawer, and then select Open Address Book.

Publishing and Subscribing to a Calendar

You can create a calendar that lists all of your appointments with detailed information on the who, what, when, where, and why, of the meeting. You can also create a To Do list that helps you keep track of everything from household chores to the research you need to do for next week's big funding conference. But what good is that information, if you're out of town, and you forgot to bring your trusty PowerBook? By publishing your iCal calendar, you wouldn't have a problem. If you have a .Mac account, publishing your calendar gives you access to that information anywhere there's a computer and an Internet connection. In addition, if someone else has published a calendar, you can gain access to it by subscribing (**New!**). Not only does this give you access to your calendar, but any one that requires your scheduling information.

Publish a Calendar

1. Open the Applications folder, and then double-click the iCal icon.

2. Click the Calendar menu, and then click Publish.

3. Select from the following Publish options:

   ◆ Publish Name

   ◆ Publish Changes Automatically

   ◆ Publish Subjects And Notes

   ◆ Publish Alarms

   ◆ Publish To Do Items

   ◆ Publish Calendar

4. Click Publish.

5. After publishing, a confirmation message appears saying that your iCal has been published. Click an option:

   ◆ Visit Page

   ◆ Send Mail

   ◆ OK

6. Quit iCal.

For Your Information

Using Publishing and Subscribing

After you click Publish to publish your iCal, be sure to write down the URL as it appears. This is very important if you want to view your calendar or allow someone else to subscribe to it. So, take a moment and write down that URL when the confirmation screen appears.

Subscribe to a Calendar

1. Open the Applications folder, and then double-click the iCal icon.

2. Click the Calendar menu, and then click Subscribe.

3. Select from the following Subscribe options:

   ◆ **Calendar URL.** Type the full path name to the calendar.

   ◆ **Refresh.** Check to update the calendar, and then select how often the update occurs.

   ◆ **Remove Alarms.** Check to remove any alarms.

   ◆ **Remove To Do Items.** Check to remove any To Do items.

4. Click Subscribe.

5. Quit iCal.

13

Did You Know?

You can subscribe to a friend's calendar. You'll need to get the exact URL to the calendar from the person who published the account.

You can get additional benefits from using iCal. If you want to access all kinds of iCal-shared calendars, point your browser to *www.icalshare.com*. The lists of calendars include schedules for television shows, opening and closing dates for the National Park system, and even information on sporting events.

Setting iCal Preferences

Apple's iCal application is not just a standard, one-size-fits-all calendar. As a matter of fact, you can customize the calendar interface to fit your particular needs. iCal gives you the ability to change how the calendar displays days and weeks, and months. In addition, you can instruct iCal when to delete old events and To Do items; even turn off alarms when the program is not open or turn on support for different event time zones (**New!**).

Set iCal Preferences

1. Open the Applications folder, and then double-click the iCal icon.

2. Click the Calendar menu, and then click Preferences.

3. Click the Days Per Week and Start Week On pop-ups, and then make your selection.

4. Click the Starts At and Ends At pop-ups, and then make you selection on when a day starts and ends. Click the Show pop-up, and then select how many hours to show in the view window.

5. Select or clear the Show Time In Month View check box.

6. Select how to Sort To Do Items, when to Delete Events and To Do Items, whether to Hide To Do Items if they fall outside the calendar view, and when to Hide Completed To Do Items.

7. Select or clear the check boxes to Turn On Time Zone Support and Turn Off Alarms When iCal Is Not Open.

8. Click the Close button to close the Preferences window.

   TIMESAVER *If you have a dialog or window open and you want to close it, you can press the Esc key.*

9. Quit iCal.

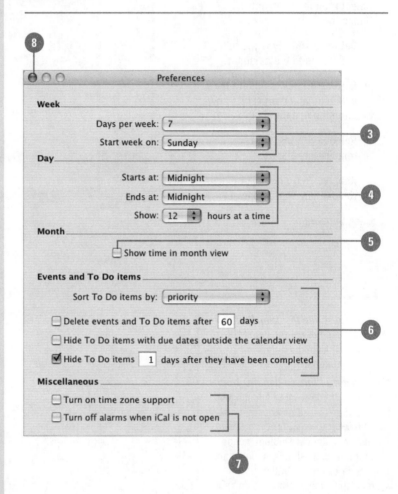

312

Viewing the iSync Window

The iSync application is a dream-come-true for all those computer users out there vainly attempting to keep their calendars and phone books synchronized (New!). Let's face it, your contacts and schedules are important. So much so, that Apple gives you several places to store this information. For example, there's the Address Book application, and then there's iCal with it's addresses. Let's not forget your calendar on your iPod, or the contacts on your PDA. Finally, there's the built in phone book on your cell phone. All that identical information, in six different places, and then one of your contacts has the audacity to change addresses. So you scramble through all your contact applications and devices; hoping against hope that you didn't miss one. It's kind of like changing all the clocks in your home to daylight savings. Did you forget the clock in your car or what about the timer on the electronic heating and air conditioning thermostat. The iSync application gives you the ability to make a change in one place (any place), and with the click of a button, change all the other places. Wish I had that kind of button for all the clocks in my home.

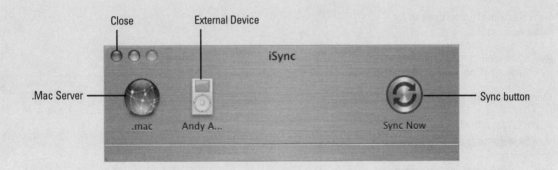

Adding Portable Devices to iSync

When you create a calendar or address/contact list; you probably want the list available on devices other than your computer. For example, you could place your contact list and calendar directly onto your iPod or iPod mini, a PDA, or even a cell phone (New!). The good news is that iSync communicates with more than applications, it talks to other devices, and changes made to your Address Book application can, with the click of a button, be transferred to any compatible device. And the list of compatible devices is growing everyday.

Add Portable Devices to iSync

1. Plug-in an iSync compatible device (such as an iPod).

2. Open the Applications folder, and then double-click the iSync icon.

3. Click the Devices menu, and then click Add Device.

4. Double click on the device to add it to the iSync application.

5. Click the Scan button to scan for more devices.

6. Add additional compatible devices by double clicking.

7. Close the Add Device window.

    IMPORTANT *To find out if your device is compatible point your browser to www.apple.com/isync/devices.html. You'll be directed to information on the iSync application, including discussion forums, and the latest device compatibility information.*

8. Quit iSync.

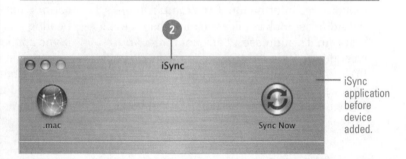

iSync application before device added.

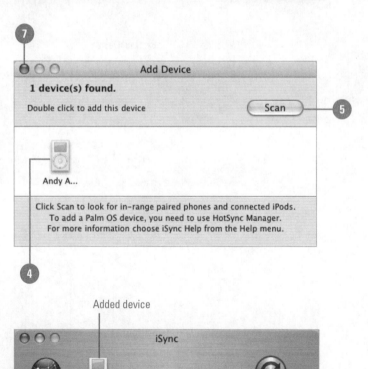

Added device

Did You Know?

You don't have to synchronize all your devices. Click on the individual devices and temporarily turn off synchronizing. Remember to turn synchronize back on for the next sync operation.

Setting Up .Mac Synchronization

If you've setup a .Mac account, then you'll want to keep your off-site information up-to-date. You'll accomplish this by using the iSync application, and using the setup options (New!) to determine exactly what you want updated. The iSync setup lets you decide exactly what you want updated, and even lets your Macintosh perform automatic updates.

Set Up .Mac Synchronization

1. Open the Applications folder, and then double-click the iSync icon.

2. Click the .Mac button.

   IMPORTANT *If you don't see the .Mac button, you'll need to set up your account.*

3. Select or clear the Turn On .Mac Synchronization or the Automatically Synchronize Ever Hour check boxes.

4. Select or clear the Safari Bookmarks, Address Book Contacts, or iCal Calendars And To Do Items check boxes.

5. Shows all computers registered for the synchronization.

6. Click Unregister Selected Computer to remove the computer from the synchronization process.

7. Click the Sync Now button to synchronize the .Mac account, and any additional devices.

8. A Data Change Alert window may appear asking you to:
   - ◆ Cancel
   - ◆ Proceed

9. Quit iSync.

See Also

See "Joining the .Mac Community" on page 264 for information on using .Mac.

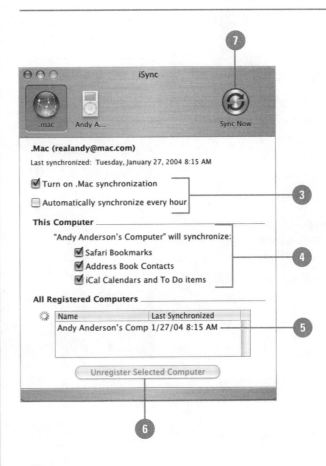

Setting Device Synchronization Options

When you add devices such as a cell phone, an iPod, or a PDA, each item has its own unique set of synchronization options. Once you've added the device, it's important to open the options, and decide exactly what you want to happen, when you click the Sync Now button. For example, you own an iPod and a PDA, you want the PDA to sync with your iCal calendar, and your contact list—but only your contacts not calendar, on the iPod. Device Synchronization options give you the control to decide exactly what does and does not sync (New!).

Set Device Synchronization Options

1. Open the Applications folder, and then double-click the iSync icon.

2. Click the button of the device that you want to modify.

3. Select from the following options:

   ◆ **Turn on Synchronization.** Activates synchronization (default: checked).

   ◆ **Automatically Synchronize.** Most devices give you the option to synchronize the device when it's first plugged in, or after a certain amount of time (default: unchecked).

   ◆ **Contacts.** Synchronizes all the contacts on the device (default: on).

   ◆ **Calendars.** Synchronizes all the calendars on the device (default: on).

4. Click the device button to collapse the Options panel.

5. Click the Sync Now button to perform the sync operation.

6. Quit iSync.

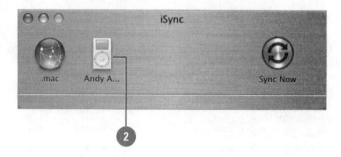

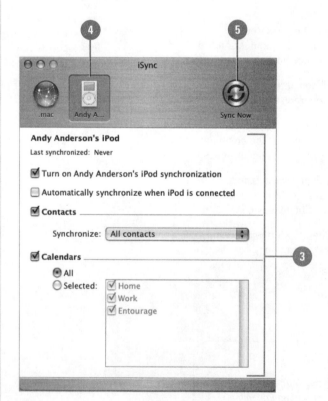

Keeping Track of Passwords with Keychain

The computer is a fantastic tool, however, the birth of the computer brought along another necessary evil, the creation of passwords. You have passwords for the Internet, FTP sites, login, and your .Mac site. Passwords, passwords, and more passwords, they multiply like rabbits. Even cars and homes have password entrance systems (called keyless entry). The solution to the problem is to create keychains.

Apple's Keychain works in the background; every time you type your login password, you're typing in the master key, and Keychain responds by filling in all the passwords blanks from that point forward. Since Keychain functions in the background, it's invisible to most users. If Keychain were not available, every time you moved around the Internet, or accessed a hard drive, or iPod, or almost any device, you would be required to type in the proper password.

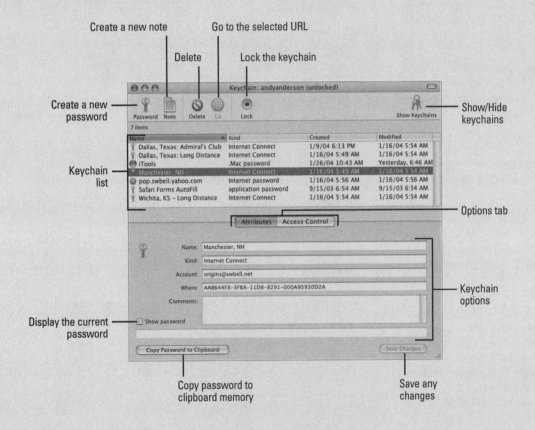

Create a new note
Go to the selected URL
Delete
Lock the keychain
Create a new password
Show/Hide keychains
Keychain list
Options tab
Display the current password
Keychain options
Copy password to clipboard memory
Save any changes

Tracking and Synchronizing Information **317**

Adding Keychains

Although the Keychain application runs in the background, and is therefore invisible to most Mac users, you have the ability to add additional keychains to the current set. To do this you'll need detailed information on the keychain that you want to add, and an application to perform the addition. In your Utilities folder is a program called Keychain Access. This program allows you to add addition keychains to the existing set. For example, you might want a keychain to manage your computer (default keychain), and another keychain to manage and secure your business documents. Since the keychain application allows you to modify existing elements within a keychain, you could easily wind up locking yourself out of devices or Web sites. Caution is advised when accessing the Keychain Access application.

Add Keychains

① Open the Applications folder, double-click Utilities, and then double-click the Keychain Access icon.

② Click the File menu, and then click New Keychain.

③ Name the keychain, and then select the file location.

④ Click Create.

⑤ Type a password for the new keychain, and then verify the password.

NOTE *Keychain passwords are case sensitive. So be sure to check that Caps Lock key if you get an error typing in your password.*

⑥ Click OK.

IMPORTANT *Keychains store all of their information as encrypted data, and the password is part of the cipher that restores the information. If you forget your password, there is nothing you can do to restore the information.*

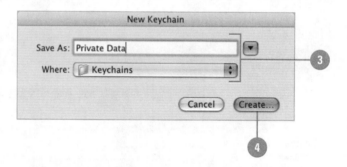

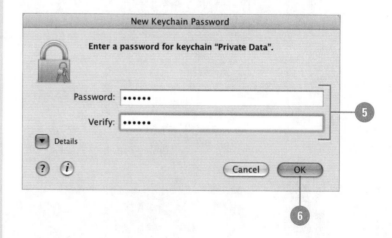

7 Click the Show/Hide Keychains button, and then select the new keychain from the list.

8 To add a new keychain password, click Password, and then type:

◆ Name, Account, Password, and then click Add.

9 To add a new note, click Note, and then type:

◆ Name, Note, and then click Add.

10 To remove the selected password or note from the list, click Delete.

A window appears asking you to confirm your Delete.

11 To open the selected site in the default browser, click Go.

12 To lock the active keychain, click Lock, and then type your password.

13 Click Save Changes when you're done.

14 Quit Keychain Access.

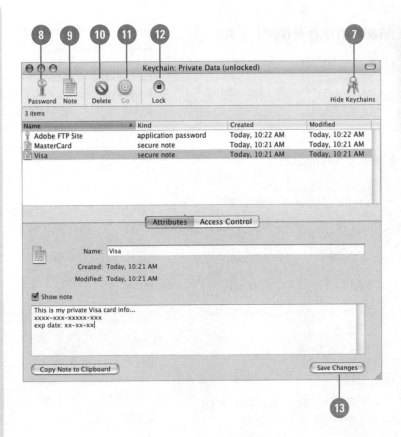

Did You Know?

You can use a keychain to keep sensitive records. Create a new keychain, give a unique password, and then type (using the Note button), all your credit card information, or the combination to your safe; whatever information you want access to but you also want it secured. Then lock the new keychain. You won't be able to access the information without the password.

Managing Keychains

The Keychain Access application gives you the ability to manage the elements within a keychain. For example, you could add an additional level of password protection, or insert a secure note. It would even be possible to delete or change the parameters of an existing element within the keychain. Since your Macintosh manages the keychain quite well in the background, it just depends on how much control you wish to exert over the Keychain already setup by your computer.

Manage Keychains

1. Open the Applications folder, double-click Utilities, and then double-click the Keychain Access icon.

2. Click the Show/Hide Keychains button, and then select the keychain you want to manage.

3. Select a keychain password from the list.

4. Click the Attributes tab.

5. Select from the following options:

   ◆ **Name.** Type a new name for the keychain item.

   ◆ **Kind.** Type a new kind such as a .Mac password or an Internet Connect.

   ◆ **Account.** Type a new account name for the keychain item.

   ◆ **Where.** Type a new location for the keychain item.

   ◆ **Comments.** Type any comments into the comments field.

6. Select or clear the Show Password check box to show the password for this keychain item.

7. Click Copy Password To Clipboard, and then select:

   ◆ Deny, Allow Once, or Always Allow.

8. Click Save Changes.

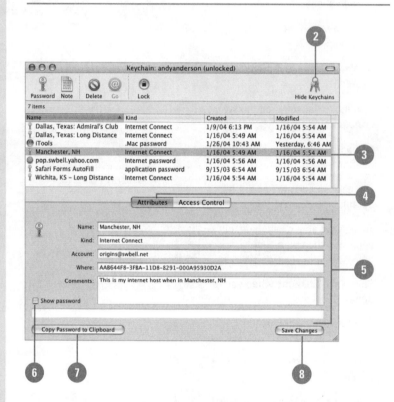

9 Click the Access Control tab.

10 Select from the following options:

◆ **Allow All Applications To Access This Item.** When selected, this item is not restricted.

◆ **Confirm Before Allowing Access.** When selected, users have to click through to get to the item.

◆ **Ask For Keychain Password.** Select or clear the check box to require users to type the keychain password.

IMPORTANT *When you click the check box to show the keychain items password, you'll first be prompted for the keychain's master password.*

11 To add specific applications, click Add, and then select the applications.

12 To remove specific applications, click the application, and then click Remove.

13 Click Save Changes to record your changes to the active keychain.

14 Quit Keychain Access.

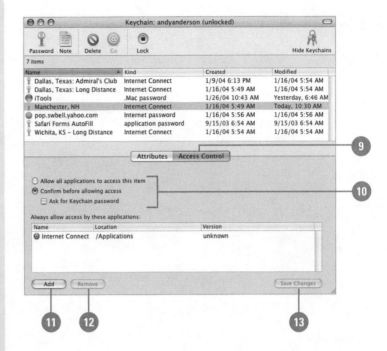

13

Working with Music and DVDs

Introduction

Macintosh computers are born number crunchers and they can perform spreadsheet calculations and balance a checkbook as fast as any computer system in the marketplace. However, Macs were born for multimedia, and even after 20 years in the business, they're still considered the best when it comes to the world of images, movies, and music. When the Panther operating system was released, it came bundled with two old friends: iTunes and iDVD.

The **iTunes** application is a software jukebox that comes with Panther, yet it's also available on Windows 2000 and Windows XP, so you can share music between Macintosh and Windows (**New!**). iTunes allows you to sort through and organize your digital music collection, convert CD's into the digital format, and even burn your favorite music onto a CD. If that's not enough, iTunes come complete with a built-in link to the iTunes music store. So if you have an Internet connection, you're one click away from a music store that contains the latest songs, as well as millions (yes, I said millions) of songs from the past. And for those of you that like to listen to the radio while you work, iTunes comes equipped with its own Internet Radio.

The **iDVD** application comes bundled on all Macintosh computers that have a SuperDrive DVD burner. Using iDVD, you can create slideshows of pictures, or become a director and create your own DVD movies, using a digital camcorder. You even have iMovie, which you'll learn more about in the next chapter, to help you edit your home movies.

Viewing the iTunes Window

When you open iTunes, you're working in an organized window that gives you access to your record collections, creates new Playlists, organizes your music, converts existing CD's into an iTunes collection, and burns selected songs onto a CD or DVD (rewritable CD, or SuperDrive DVD required). The same iTunes window that lets you listen and organize your music also lets you listen to the Internet Radio or purchase music through the iTunes Music Store. In other words, once you open the iTunes application, everything you need to enhance your music experience, including listening to audio books, is right in front of your eyes.

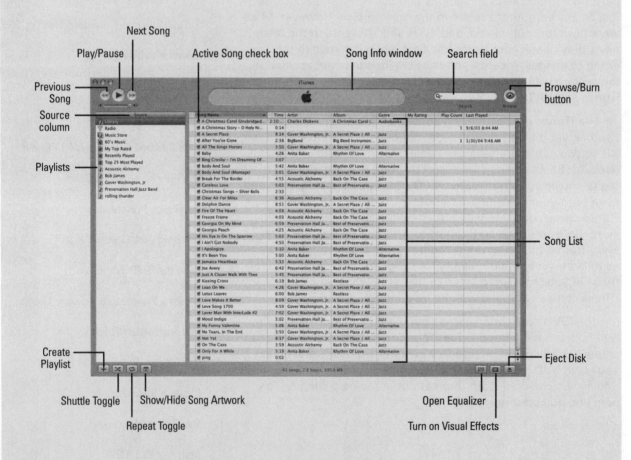

Setting Up iTunes to Automatically Play CDs

When you open the iTunes application for the first time you'll be asked a few preference questions. For example, you are asked if you want iTunes to be the application your Mac uses for playing music files from the Internet, whether you want iTunes to ask permission every time it connects to the Internet, and whether you want the program to scan your home folder for all of your music. If you select not to have iTunes automatically scan your home drive for music files, you can always drag a folder into the iTunes window. It will automatically scan the folder for any music files, and then place them within the active Playlist.

Set Up iTunes to Automatically Play CDs

① Open the Applications folder, and then double-click the iTunes icon.

② Click the Apple menu, click System Preferences, and then click the CDs & DVDs icon.

③ Click the When You Insert A Music CD pop-up, and then select Open iTunes.

④ Click the Close button to close the System Preferences window.

⑤ Quit iTunes.

Did You Know?

You can select another program to play music CDs. If you find an application better than iTunes at managing your record collection, you can always select Another Application from the CDs & DVDs pop-up menu.

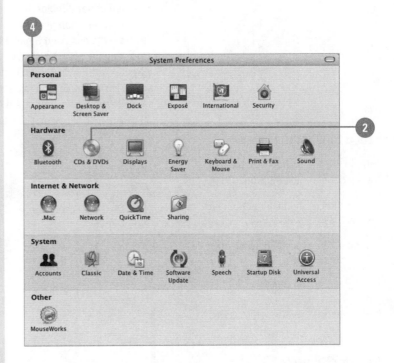

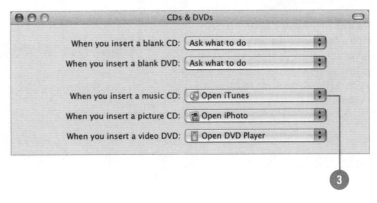

Creating Playlists

The iTunes application lets you add songs from several different sources. For example, you might have some MP3 songs on your hard drive, and you want them stored within the iTunes application, or you have a music CD that you want converted into MP3 format. Importing songs can be accomplished through the iTunes menu system, or it can be as simple as a drag and drop. Whatever method you select, you'll first want to set up a Playlist to hold and organize your songs. A **Playlist** is a folder that holds songs. For example, you could have a Playlist for all your Country & Western songs, one for your Rock & Roll; even one for audio books. When you open iTunes, you first select the Playlist you want to listen to, and then either double-click on the first song in the list, or click the Play button; iTunes then plays all the songs in that list. Playlists come in two flavors—Playlists and Smart Playlists. Playlists let you play the songs in the list again, play the songs in random order, or stop when the last song plays. Smart Playlists rebuild themselves according to the criteria you setup. For example, you might create a Smart Playlist that only plays the songs in the library you rate a 4-star or only Christmas songs.

Create a Playlist to iTunes

1. Open the Applications folder, and then double-click the iTunes icon.

2. Click the File menu, and then click New Playlist.

3. Type a name for the Playlist, and then press Return.

4. Continue to add Playlists.

5. Quit iTunes.

Did You Know?

You can drag a music folder from an open window into the Source column. iTunes automatically creates a Playlist for the songs, and the name of the Playlist is the name of the folder you dragged.

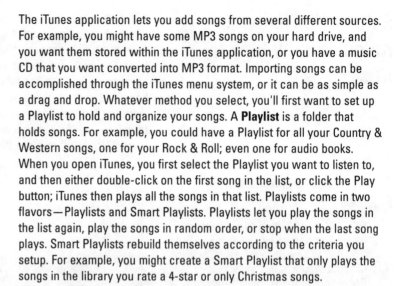

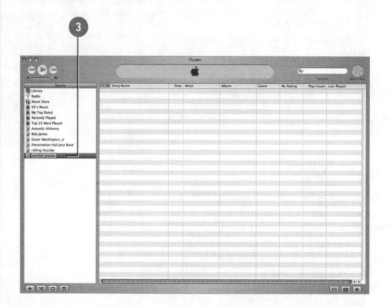

Add a Smart Playlist to iTunes

1. Open the Applications folder, and then double-click the iTunes icon.

2. Click the File menu, and then click New Smart Playlist.

3. Click the Criteria pop-up, and then select the primary selection criteria.

4. Click the Operator pop-up, and then choose a selection method.

5. Type a word or phrase to search.

6. Click the Add Criteria button (+) to add an additional search option.

7. Select the Limit To check box and pop-up to limit the number of songs, time played, or maximum size.

8. Click the Selected By pop-up, and then select how the songs are selected.

9. Select the Match Only Checked Songs check box to limit selection to songs that are checked.

10. Select the Live Updating check box to update the Smart Playlist as you add or subtract songs from the iTunes Library.

11. Click OK.

12. Name your Smart Playlist.

13. Quit iTunes.

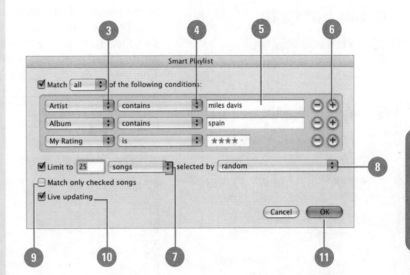

14

For Your Information

Understanding Copyright Laws

When you create Playlists you're working smart. Most iTunes users have hundreds, if not thousands of songs on their hard drives, and Playlists and Smart Playlists are the only way to help organize all those songs. A word of caution, make sure they are your songs. Piracy is a big problem in the music industry today, and it's not just what you take off the Internet. The iTunes application gives you the ability to create music tracks from most music CDs. That does not mean you can borrow all of your friend's music CDs and transfer them to your computer. Enjoy your music, but know the laws involving piracy, and copyright violation. Point your browser to: *www.dcl.edu/lawrev/97-4/muroff.htm* for a detailed account of copyright laws in the U.S.

Adding Songs to a Playlist

Whenever you add a song to the iTunes application, it stores the song in the Library, and then creates a link to the selected Playlist. As a matter of fact, Playlists simply create links to the songs in the iTunes Library. If you delete a Playlist or a song within a Playlist, it does not remove the song from the iTunes Library, only the link created in the Playlist is removed.

Add Songs to a Playlist

① Open the Applications folder, and then double-click the iTunes icon.

② Select a Playlist from the available options.

③ Add songs using the following three options:

◆ Drag songs from an open folder into the iTunes window.

◆ Click the File menu, and then click Add To Library. Locate the song or songs you want to add, and then click Open.

◆ Insert a music CD into your CD drive, and then click Import.

④ Quit iTunes.

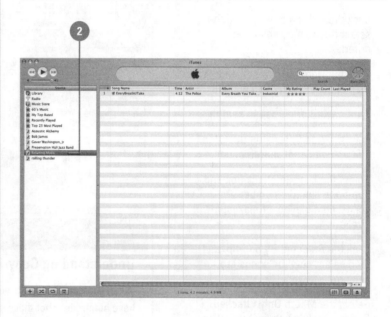

Did You Know?

You can access the names of your songs on the Internet. Insert a music CD, click the Advanced menu, and then click Get CD Track Names. The iTunes application accesses the Gracenote music title repository, and then changes the dull Track1 and Track2, with the names of the song.

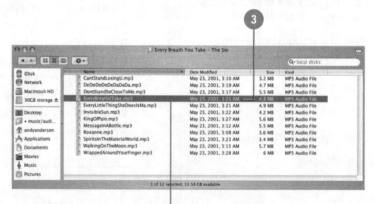

Drag songs from a folder into the iTunes window.

See Also

See "Setting Up iTunes to Automatically Play CDs" on page 325 for more information on playing CDs with iTunes.

Listening to Internet Radio

Listening to music is great, so is curling up with a cup of hot chocolate and your favorite audio book. However, sometimes you would just like to listen to a radio station. Maybe NPR (National Public Radio) is your thing, or possibly your looking for a radio station that just plays classical music. Whatever direction your tastes run, you are probably able to find it on the Internet radio, and iTunes makes the process of selecting and listening to a radio station as easy as turning on a traditional radio.

Listen to Internet Radio

1. Open the Applications folder, and then double-click the iTunes icon.

2. Click the Radio option, located in the Source column.

3. Select a group from the available options.

4. Click the expand button (triangle) to open the group.

5. Double-click on a station to begin the broadcast.

6. Use the Play/Pause button to turn the selected station on or off.

7. Use the Previous and Next buttons to move up and down through the radio station list.

8. Drag the volume slider in the upper left corner to adjust the volume.

9. Quit iTunes.

Did You Know?

You can add radio stations to the iTunes radio list. Click the Advanced menu, and then click Open Stream. Type in the station's Web address, and then click OK.

Burning CDs and Exporting to MP3 Players

While CD's are still around and popular, digital music players seem to be one of the "newer" technologies set to change how we listen to our tunes. iTunes gives us the option to use CDs and digital music players— we can burn our own customized music CDs or we can transfer the music files to any one of a number of digital music players. When you insert the CD, iTunes gives you the option of choosing the Playlist you want to use. If the playlist is too large to fit on a single CD or DVD, iTunes asks you for another disc (New!). Digital music players, more commonly known as MP3 players, hold music files using the MP3 digital format. MP3 players can be thought of as a hard drive that holds music files, and then plays them back to you through a set of speakers or a headset. When you purchase your MP3 player, it comes with software designed to move music files from your computer hard drive to the drive located on the MP3 player. Some MP3 players, when connected to your computer, appear as an external hard drive.

Burn a Music CD

① Open the Applications folder, and then double-click the iTunes icon.

② Create a Playlist with the songs that you want to burn onto the CD.

③ Insert a blank CD into your drive.

   IMPORTANT *You must have a rewritable CD drive or a SuperDrive DVD.*

④ Type a name for the music CD.

⑤ Click OK.

⑥ Click Burn Disc once to open the button, and then click a second time to perform the burning operation.

⑦ Quit iTunes.

Did You Know?

You can't burn more than 10 copies of your Playlist. If you do have a legitimate need for that 11th CD, all you need to do is change the sort order of the songs in the Playlist, and then you can burn 10 more.

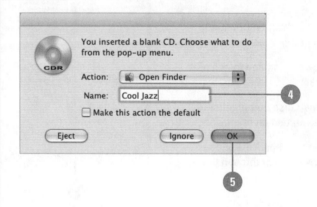

Export to MP3 Players

① Navigate to the iTunes music folder:

Main Hard Drive/Users/Your Account/Music/iTunes/iTunes Music.

② Select a folder or a list of iTunes files that you want to move.

③ Select the music file or files.

④ Drag the music files to the hard drive icon of your MP3 music player.

⑤ Control-click the MP3 player desktop icon, and then click Eject.

IMPORTANT *Not all MP3 music players allow you to drag music files between your hard drive and the player icon. When this occurs you'll have to use the transfer software that came bundled with the player. Simply load the software and follow the onscreen instructions.*

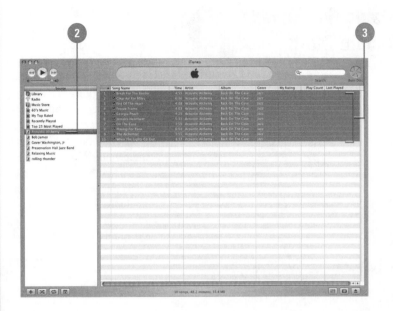

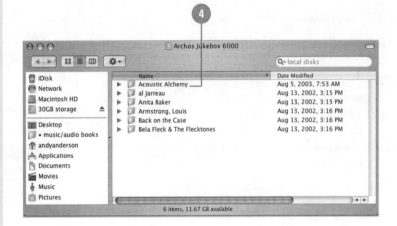

14

Using the iTunes Music Store

The iTunes music store is a dream come true for all of us that love music, but don't necessarily want to buy the whole album just to get our favorite song. The music store was born out the desire to help musicians get paid for their work (Internet piracy of music is affecting the entire music industry), and to help the end-user (you and me) get what we want. The iTunes music store was not the first to make the purchase of songs or albums easy, but they are considered the best at doing it. All you have to do to get started is open the iTunes application, click the Music Store option, and that's it (assuming you have an Internet connection). Next, setup your payment options (it's easy if you have a .Mac account), and then begin hunting for the songs you love. Once you download a song, Apple lets you copy and play that song on up to three authorized machines. When you move a song to another computer, you are prompted to type in your Apple Account number, which authorizes that computer to play that song.

Use the iTunes Music Store

1. Open the Applications folder, and then double-click the iTunes icon.

2. Click the Music Store option.

3. Click on any of the various links to access that particular title.

4. Use the Search field and type a title or artist to search, and then press Return.

Did You Know?

There are more than just songs at the Apple Music Store. The Music Store has millions of songs, but there's also audio books (**New!**) available for downloading. Just type in the name of your favorite author, and see if the books are available in audio format.

You can find audio books outside of the Apple Music Store. Point your browser to *http://www.audible.com*, for one of the largest selections of audio books in the world.

5 Double-click a song to hear a sample.

6 Click the Buy Song button, or (if available) select to purchase the entire album.

> **IMPORTANT** *If you haven't set up your payment options (credit cards), Panther prompts you to do so at this time.*

7 The song(s) or album are downloaded into iTunes.

8 Quit iTunes.

> **IMPORTANT** *If you sell or otherwise dispose of a computer that has been authorized to play your songs, before you get rid of it, make sure you click the Advanced menu, and then click Deauthorize Computer. That allows you (when you get your new Mac), to authorize it to play copies of your music files.*

Did You Know?

You can create a link to the Apple Music Store. Drag a Web page from the iTunes Music Store to a document or e-mail message (New!).

For Your Information

Using the iTunes Music Store

The iTunes Music Store is a fantastic gift from the creative minds at Apple, and one that has been copied by others. You can download any song for a buck, and there are no monthly membership fees (watch out for competitors charging usage fees), and once you've signed up and given them your credit information, all you have to do is search and select. My favorite part of iTunes is the ability to download selected songs from an album, without having to download an entire album. In addition, the Music Store gives you the ability to download entire albums, at a reduced rate over the individual songs.

14

Setting iTunes Preferences

Like any application, iTunes gives you a Preferences panel that helps you adjust the software to fit your specific needs. For example, Advanced preferences give you the option to adjust the Streaming Buffer Size to the bandwidth of your computer. If you're running at 56kbps or slower, you may want to change the buffer to Small; conversely, if you're sprinting along at DSL or cable-modem speeds, you'd select Medium or even Large. The iTunes preferences give you precise control over how the program operates on your computer.

To set your preferences, or to review the defaults that have been set in iTunes, simply open the Applications folder, and then double-click the iTunes application. Click the iTunes menu, and then click Preferences. There you'll find almost every conceivable setting that is used in iTunes. For a summary view, we've shown you each screen and what is contained on that Preference screen. After making any changes to the screens, simply click OK to change the setting or click Cancel to undo your change.

General: Controls text within the iTunes window, whether to play a CD upon insertion, whether or not to connect to the Internet.

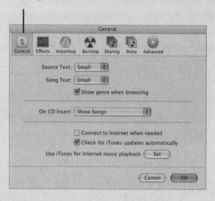

Effects: Controls audio effects Crossfade, Sound Enhancer, and Sound Check (plays all songs at the same volume).

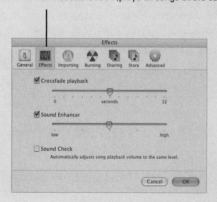

Importing: Controls settings when importing audio files.

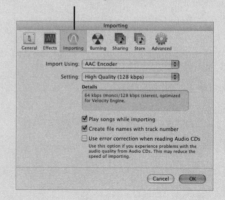

Store: Gives you options on how you purchase items in the Music Store.

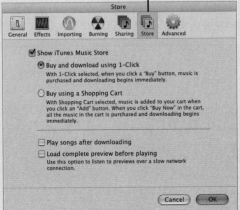

Sharing: Lets you share your music files with other users.

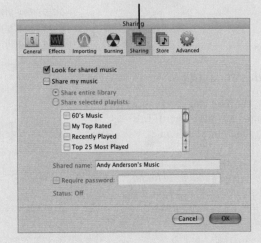

Burning: Controls the settings used when burning a CD.

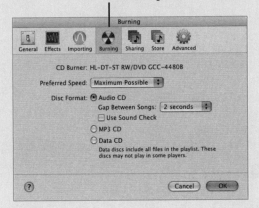

Advanced: Controls the Buffer, and helps manage and maintain the iTunes Music folder.

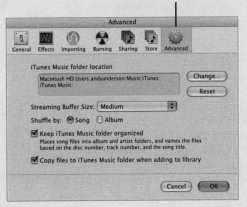

Using iPod with iTunes

There are bad MP3 players and there are good MP3 players, I would even go so far as to say there are great MP3 players… and then there's iPod. The iPod digital MP3 music player is so unique, it deserves a class all of its own. The iPod is the most successful digital music player ever created. More iPod players are sold than any other player. They're made for Macintosh and Windows machines, and it just so happens they work perfectly with the iTunes player. When you plug your iPod (FireWire) into your computer, it automatically opens the iTunes application and synchronizes playlists or voice notes that you create on your iPod (New!). It's then a simple matter of deleting songs you no longer want from the iPod, or dragging songs into your iPod.

Use iPod with iTunes

1. Plug your iPod into your computer (requires a FireWire port). This also recharges your iPod.

   IMPORTANT *The FireWire cable comes supplied with the iPod at purchase; however if you lose the cable, any standard firewire cable works.*

2. Click the iPod option located in the Source column.

3. Click the expand/collapse button (triangle) to expand the iPod listing.

4. Select a file in the iTunes window, and then press Delete to remove the song from your iPod.

5. Drag a song or Playlist from the Source column into the iPod list, to add to your iPod.

6. Click the Eject button, located at the bottom of the iTunes window, to eject the iPod.

   IMPORTANT *If you disconnect your iPod without performing an Eject, it could cause the iPod hard drive (and all your songs), to become corrupted.*

7. Quit iTunes.

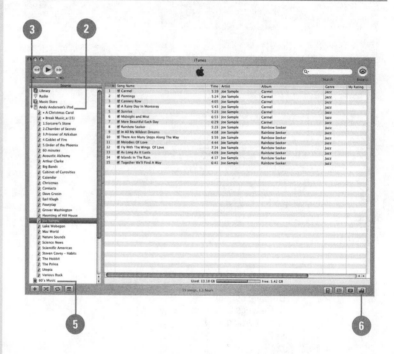

Viewing the iDVD Window

If you've ever wanted to test your skills at movie production, then the iDVD application is just what you've been waiting for all these years. There are all kinds of layout applications, such as applications for laying material out on paper (Adobe InDesign and Quark Xpress), and there are programs that layout Web pages (Adobe GoLive and Macromedia Dreamweaver). With that in mind, think of iDVD as a layout application for the creation of your Oscar-winning production.

The iDVD application that comes bundled with Macintosh computers has a SuperDrive DVD. This gives you the ability to generate slideshows, videos, or a combination of both, along with menus, buttons (just like any other DVD), and then burn it onto a blank DVD that can be viewed by anyone that owns a DVD player.

The iDVD application is powerful, but just like any other layout program, it requires material to use for the layout. For example, when you open iDVD, you need access to video files, audio files, and graphics. The iDVD application doesn't create the materials that make up the DVD; it only organizes them. And, not all DVD players are created equal. Some DVD disks do not work in all the players on the market; especially older DVD players. For information on compatibility issues between DVD writers and DVD players, point your browser to: *http://www.dvdrhelp.com*.

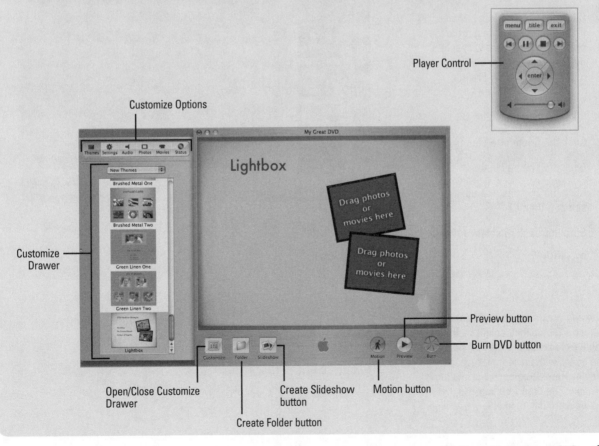

Creating a Project and Selecting a Theme

To create an iDVD movie, you'll need material in the form of video files, audio files, and graphics—whatever you need to complete your project. To save a lot of frustration and lost time, create a project folder and place all of the movie elements into that single folder. That way you know where your stuff is, and if you need to pack up and move to another computer, all you have to do is move one folder. It's a simple trick, but it can save you hours of frustration, when you need that special movie file and you can't remember where you saved it. When you open iDVD for the first time, you are prompted to Create A New Project or Open An Existing Project. This is where you work smart and save the new iDVD project file in your Project folder. Once you've opened the iDVD project, the next thing would be to choose a theme. **Themes** are the backdrops for your project, and iDVD has dozens of pre-designed themes for you to select from to match the mood of your movie.

Create a Project and Select a Theme

1. Open the Applications folder, and then double-click the iDVD icon.

2. Click the New Project button. iDVD opens up the last project created. If you want to create a new project, click the File menu, and then click New Project.

3. Name the project, select a location, and then click OK.

4. Click the Customize button.

5. Click the Themes button.

6. Click the Themes pop-up, and then select a theme.

7. Scroll through to select a theme.

8. Quit iDVD.

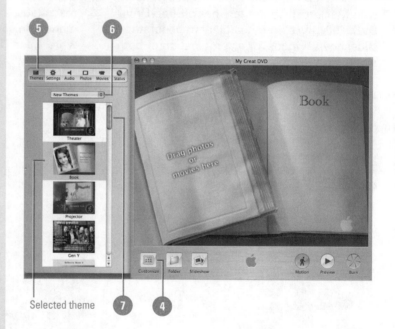

Selected theme

Did You Know?

You can create your own Themes. Select a Theme that includes a drop zone. **Drop zones** are themes that have the boxes with the words, such as Movies Here. Drag an image into the window. The drop zone remains, but the background (theme) is your image.

Adding and Modifying Titles

Each theme comes with various editable text fields. For example, if you select the Book theme, the title at the top of the page (book) is editable text. In addition to changing the actual words, iDVD gives you the ability to change the font size, font family, color, and position of the text. Or, as you develop your theme, you may find that you want to change the title. Simply select the title, and then make the desired changes to find the right style for your theme.

Add and Modify Titles

1. Open the Applications folder, and then double-click the iDVD icon.

2. Create a new or open an existing project.

3. Select the Title text, and then type the new title.

4. Click the Customize button.

5. Click the Settings button.

6. Change the Position, Font, and Color by clicking the appropriate pop-up.

7. Drag the Size slider left or right to decrease or increase the size of the font.

   IMPORTANT *It's not necessary to select the title before modifying it in the settings window. That also means that you can't select and change the title using two or more fonts. The title gets one size, color, font, and position.*

8. Quit iDVD.

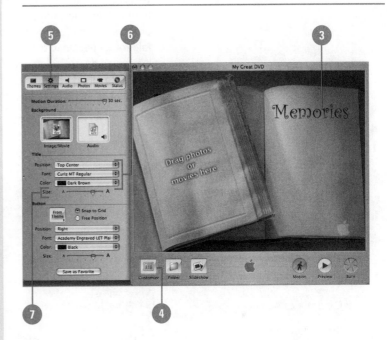

Adding Menus, Buttons, and Folders

Once you've opened iDVD and decided on the right theme, the next step is to begin adding control to the movie. Control is achieved through the introduction of buttons and menus, which the viewer can then use to control the movie when it's playing. For example, you could create a menu that contained buttons to let the viewer watch different videos or slideshows. In addition, you can create folders to separate sections of the iDVD. Think of all of this as creating an organized filing system for your movie. You can create buttons that show movies, buttons that perform a slideshow (complete with an audio track), or buttons that just display a single image. In short, a **menu** is a collection of buttons and folders, all designed to help the viewer navigate through your movie. When you create a button or folder, you're generating a new part of the movie. To access the Slideshow button contents or the new folder, double-click on the button or folder text, not the button icon.

Add Menus, Buttons, and Folders

1. Open the Applications folder, and then double-click the iDVD icon.

2. Create a new or open an existing project.

3. Click the Slideshow button.

4. Click the Customize button.

5. Click the Settings button.

6. Click the Button icon, and then select from the available button shapes.

7. Click to select between snapping the buttons to a pre-defined grid or free position (click and drag).

Did You Know?

You can change Themes in an iDVD movie. Since a folder represents a new section of the movie, double-click on the button text (this takes you to the new folder section), and then select a different theme. When you click the back arrow, the main screen still displays the original theme.

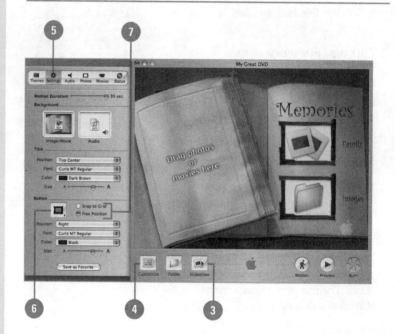

8 Change the Position, Font, and Color by clicking the appropriate pop-up.

9 Drag the Size slider left or right to decrease or increase the size of the font.

10 Click and select the text on the button, and then type in the appropriate text.

11 Click the Folder button, and then follow steps 6 through 10 to create and modify a folder button.

12 Add an image to the Slideshow or Folder button by dragging an image (or movie) from your project folder into the button/folder frame.

TIMESAVER *Think of a folder as a separate section of the iDVD movie which can contain its own buttons and folders, just like the main screen. Since a scene can only hold a maximum of six buttons, creating folders gives you a way to increase the organization of complex iDVD movies.*

13 Quit iDVD.

14

Creating a Slideshow

Creating and customizing the iDVD movie screen and populating it with buttons to access slideshows and folders is great. However, sooner or later you're going to have to add the movies, graphics, and audio files to create the final product. The iDVD application makes the process of adding files to the movie a snap. If you have a folder that contains all of your projects source files, simply open the file and begin dragging the files into the iDVD movie window. In addition, if you use iTunes and iPhoto, all you do is click a button to gain organized access to all of your files.

Create a Slideshow

1. Open the Applications folder, and then double-click the iDVD icon.

2. Create a new or open an existing project.

3. Click the Slideshow button.

4. Double-click the Slide Window button to access the file import window.

5. Select from the following importing methods:

   ◆ Click the File menu, point to Import, and then click Images.

   ◆ Open the file that contains your images, and then drag them into the slide window.

   ◆ Click the Customize button, and then click the Photos button (requires the use of iPhoto).

6. Drag the files up and down in the window to change their stacking order.

7. To remove a file from the list, click on a file, and then press Delete.

8. Select the Display check box to display left and right navigation arrows with the slides.

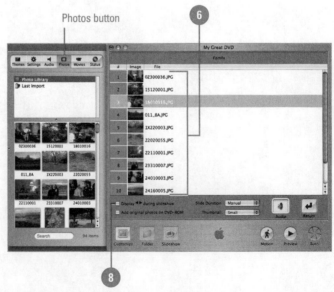

Photos button

9 Select the Add Original Photos On DVD-ROM check box to create a folder with the original images.

The user can then insert the DVD into their computer, open the folder, and then access the files.

10 Click the Slide Duration pop-up, and then select the length to display each slide.

TIMESAVER *If you're using an audio file with the images, click the Slide Duration pop-up, and then select Fit To Audio. The iDVD program times the slides to match the ending of the audio.*

11 Click the Thumbnail pop-up, and then select between small and large thumbnails (does not impact the running of the show).

12 Drag an audio file onto the Audio button to have background music play with the slides.

13 To move back to the main screen or folder, press the Return button.

14 Click the Preview button, and then click the Slideshow button to test the movie.

15 Quit iDVD.

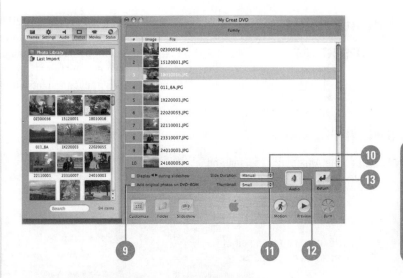

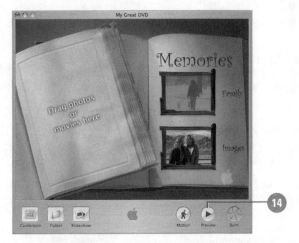

Did You Know?

You can create a narration to the slide show, and then adjust the timing to fit the slides. To add an audio file, drag the file from an open folder into the audio button.

For Your Information

Adding Movie Files

Adding movie files to iDVD is even easier than creating a slideshow. Simply drag the movie file directly into the iDVD window (not the drop zone), and the application automatically creates a button icon. Adjust and modify the button just as you would any other button. When you preview the movie, clicking on the movie button, automatically opens and plays the movie (full screen). When the movie is finished, iDVD returns you to the main screen or folder.

Setting iDVD Preferences

Like any good program, iDVD has preferences that allow you to adjust the application to fit your particular needs. When you modify the preferences, you're changing the application, not the project. Therefore, when you open a new project, the preferences reflects the last changes made. The iDVD application lets you adjust General, Slideshow, and Movies preferences.

Set iDVD Preferences

1. Open the Applications folder, and then double-click the iDVD icon.

2. Click the iDVD menu, and then click Preferences.

3. Click General, and then select from the following options:

   ◆ **Show Drop Zones.** Check to display drop zones in the movie themes.

   ◆ **Show Apple Logo Watermark.** Check to display an Apple logo watermark when the movie is playing.

   ◆ **Enable Background Encoding.** Check to let iDVD perform encoding in the background.

   ◆ **Delete Rendered Files After Closing A Project.** Check to instruct iDVD to delete its render files each time you close the project (this requires them to be rebuilt every time you reopen the project).

4. Click Slideshow, and then select from the following options:

   ◆ **Always Add Original Slideshow Photos To DVD-ROM.** Check to save the original slides to the DVD.

   ◆ **Always Scale Slides To TV Save Area.** Check to scale the slides to the safe area of a television monitor.

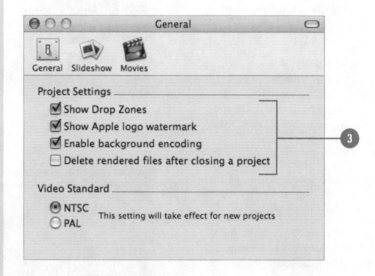

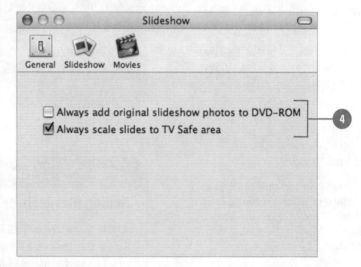

⑤ Click Movies, and then select from the following options:

◆ **Automatically Create Chapter Marker Submenu.** Click this option to automatically create chapter markers when importing a file (markers are created in the originating video-editing program).

◆ **Never Create Chapter Marker Submenu.** Click this option to turn off chapter marker generation.

◆ **Ask Each Time.** Click this option to ask each time a movie file is imported.

⑥ Click Add to add folders that you regularly use to hold movie files or click Remove to delete a selected folder.

⑦ Quit iDVD.

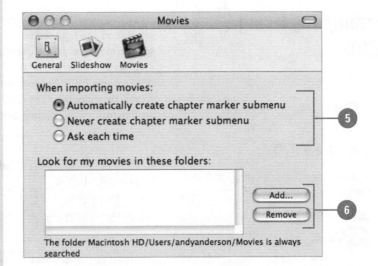

14

Burning and Using a DVD

Okay, you've worked for days on your great video masterpiece. You've created all the right themes, inserted the correct buttons; even created folders to help organize the project, and made it easy for your viewers to sit back and enjoy the show. The last step is the burning of your project onto a blank DVD. The best quality DVD's are 60 minutes or less. Going over sixty minutes forces iDVD to use additional compression to the source files and ultimately creates a lower-quality DVD.

Burn and Use a DVD

1. Open the Applications folder, and then double-click the iDVD icon.

2. Open an iDVD project.

3. Click the Project menu, and then click Project Info.

   Check marks next to each of your source files means that everything is ready for burning.

   IMPORTANT *Typically when a source file does not have a check mark, it's been moved. Creating a project folder and keeping all the source files in one place, helps eliminate the case of the missing file.*

4. Check the Project Duration at the top of the Project Info window.

5. Click OK.

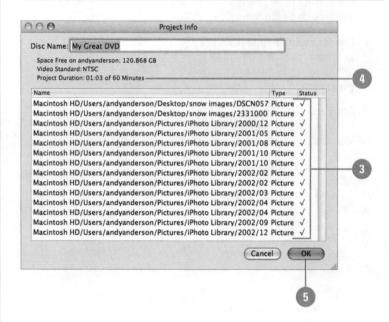

6 Click the Preview button, test the movie, and then, if necessary, make any adjustments.

7 Click the Motion button.

If the Motion button is not green, your buttons won't animate, and there won't be audio playing in the background.

8 Click the File menu, and then click Save Project.

9 Click the Burn button once to open the button, and then a second time to begin the burning process.

10 When prompted, insert a blank DVD.

11 The iDVD application automatically ejects the finished DVD.

Test the DVD at home one last time before mailing it out to your friends or family.

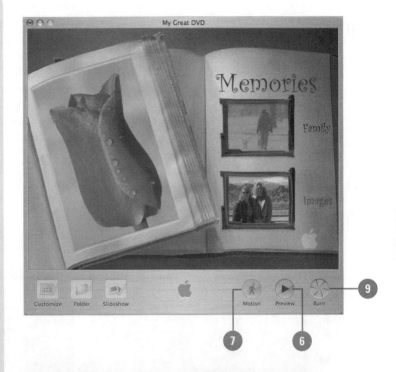

Test the movie.

Erasing a CD or DVD

If you want to reuse a CD-RW or DVD-RW disc, you need to erase it first, which you can do with Disk Utility. Before you start, there is one thing you need to know. You can't erase a standard CD or DVD that was a previously recorded CD-R aor DVD-R disc. During the process, you have the option to select Quick Erase. When you select Quick Erase setting, the contents on the CD or DVD gets overwritten when new information is placed over it. If you don't select Quick Erase setting, the contents is overwritten with zeros to completely erase the CD or DVD, which takes longer to finish.

Erase a CD or DVD

1 Open the Utilities folder, and then double-click the Disk Utility icon.

2 Select the disc in the left column you want to erase.

3 Click the Erase tab.

4 If you want, select the Quick Erase check box.

5 Click Erase.

6 Click Erase to confirm you want to erase the CD.

7 Click the Disk Utility menu, and then click Quit Disk Utility.

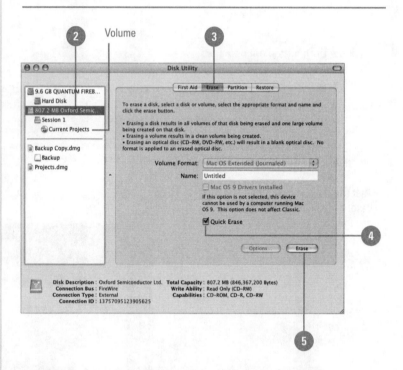

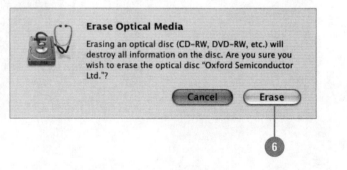

Erase Optical Media

Erasing an optical disc (CD-RW, DVD-RW, etc.) will destroy all information on the disc. Are you sure you wish to erase the optical disc "Oxford Semiconductor Ltd."?

Working with Photos and Movies

Introduction

In the previous chapter, you learned how to use the iDVD program to generate a fully functional DVD movie. However, as a layout program, iDVD requires source files. For example, you'll need some video files for your movie, possibly some still images files, and what movie wouldn't be complete without a bit of music, or narration to keep your audience interested.

Apple gives you a great program (iDVD) to generate cool DVDs and the programs to create and manipulate the files. Panther comes bundled with iMovie and iPhoto. The **iMovie** application lets you create high-quality, professional movies. Using footage from your digital camcorder (MiniDV or Digital 8 format), you can edit and combine different movie files, create transitions between scenes, even capture live video, and then add an audio track (voice or music).

The **iPhoto** application lets you organize your images into user-defined folders, edit them, and even distribute them to your friends, by placing them on a CD or DVD, or directly over the Internet. And best of all, iDVD lets you import images, movies, and audio directly from iPhoto, iMovie, and iTunes. You got to hand it to the creative minds at Apple, for giving us the ability to work with and manage multimedia, in a way that's simple, yet powerful.

What You'll Do

View the iPhoto Window

Import Images

Organize Images

Edit Photos

Create a Photo Book

Share Photos with Others Using Print or E-Mail

Understand iMovie Basics

View the iMovie Window

Create an iMovie Project

Import or Record Video and Audio

Add Media to an iMovie

Move and Trim Clips

Add Titles and Transitions

Add Effects

Export an iMovie to Camera

Export iMovies to the Web and E-Mail

Put iMovies on CD and DVD

Viewing the iPhoto Window

When you open the iPhoto application, you're treated to the ultimate in organization and simplicity. For example, you own a digital camera, and you want to move the images from the camera to your computer. Most digital cameras come with their own proprietary programs that let you hook your camera up (USB or FireWire port), and then organize and manage your files.

However, what if you own more than one digital camera? Now, you have two (or more) proprietary programs that do not communicate with each other, and each program is holding some of your digital images. That makes sorting and organizing the image files as a group nearly impossible.

Fortunately, iPhoto does away with camera-specific programs. When you plug your camera in, iPhoto recognizes the device and lets you move the image files from the camera to iPhoto. The benefits are obvious—with all your image files in one place, you can conduct searches and sorts faster; and you won't have to move from folder to folder, looking for that missing image.

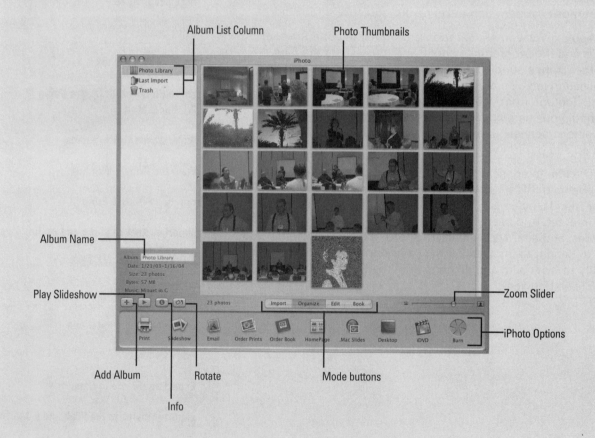

Album List Column   Photo Thumbnails

Album Name

Play Slideshow   Zoom Slider

                                                  iPhoto Options

Add Album   Rotate   Mode buttons

Info

Importing Images

It couldn't be simpler to bring your images into the iPhoto application. For example, you want to move the images from your digital still camera to iPhoto. There is one obvious assumption that must be made: The camera must have the ability to link to your computer though the USB or FireWire port (iPhoto now recognizes the FireWire port). Once you turn on and connect the camera to your computer, the iPhoto program opens automatically, and gives you the option of downloading the images from the connected device.

Import Images

1. Turn on and connect a digital camera to an available USB or FireWire port on your computer.

   Panther automatically loads iPhoto.

2. iPhoto detects if there are images to download.

3. Click Import.

4. iPhoto creates a thumbnail of each new image.

5. Select the Erase Camera Contents After Transfer check box to instruct iPhoto to erase the camera's storage device after the successful transfer of the images.

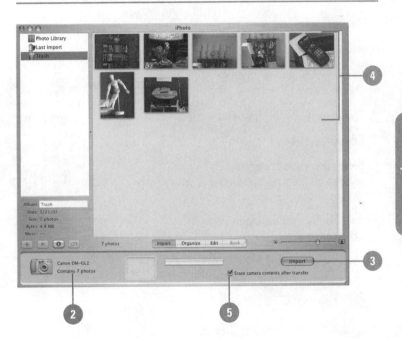

Did You Know?

You can delete images that you don't want in the iPhoto window. Select an image or images, and then click Delete. If you accidentally delete an image you wanted to keep, you can click the Edit menu, and then click Undo Move To Trash.

For Your Information

Troubleshooting iPhoto

If iPhoto does not open when you plug in your camera, first make sure the connection is good, and that your camera is turned on (it can happen to the best of us). If iPhoto still doesn't open, you need to set up the system preferences to recognize the iPhoto program. Click the Applications folder, double-click Image Capture, click the Image Capture menu, and then click Preferences. Next, click the Camera tab, click the When A Camera Is Connected pop-up, and then select iPhoto.

Organizing Images

Once you've filled up the Photo Library with images you'll want a way to organize the images. The iPhoto application makes this easy by giving you the ability to sort and organize the images into separate albums (**New!**). **Albums** are like file folders that hold a specific type of image. For example, you can create an album for images of summer, or the first big snowstorm of the season. It's totally up to you on how you proceed with organization, but it can save you literally hours of time. Imagine, you have 6,000 images, and you're looking for that one special image. You can have albums created by topic, and then search to find the image you need.

Organize Images

1. Click the Add Album button (+). to create a new album.

2. Type a name for the new album.

3. Click OK.

4. Select the Photo Library or another album, and then drag images to the new album.

5. Click on the new album, and then select an image.

6. Click the Info button.

7. In the Title field, give the image a distinctive name.

Did You Know?

The Photo Library holds all of your images. When you click the Photo Library option, you're looking at a listing of every image held in iPhoto. When you delete an image from an album, you're only removing the link; not the image. If you delete an image from the Photo Library, you're deleting the actual image file.

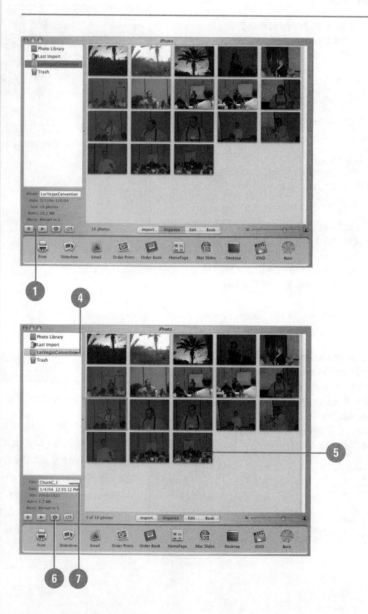

8 Click the Info button again.

9 Type in a comment concerning the image.

> **IMPORTANT** *The information you type into the Comments area of the Info window can be used for sorting and finding specific images.*

10 Click the Info button a third time to collapse the Info window.

11 To change the images display order in the window, drag an image and drop it into a new order.

12 To arrange photos in the active album, click the View menu, point to Arrange Photos, and then select from the available options:

- ◆ By Film Roll
- ◆ By Date
- ◆ By Title
- ◆ Manually

13 When you're finished, click the Close button.

Did You Know?

You can burn photos on a CD or DVD.
(**New!**) If you have a CD or DVD burner, you can create a photo CD or DVD. Organize the photos you want to use in an album, click the Burn button, insert a CD-RW disc or a blank CD-R or DVD-R disc into your drive, click the Burn button, and then click Burn in the Burn Disc window.

For Your Information

Creating a Slideshow in iPhoto

After you organize your photos in an album, you can display them in a slideshow. To play a slideshow, select an album or individual photos, and then click the Play button. Press the mouse button to stop the slideshow; press the Spacebar to pause and resume it; and use the up and down arrow keys to adjust the speed or the right and left arrow keys to manually move through the slideshow. To set slideshow options (**New!**), click the Slideshow button, specify a slide duration and whether you want a random sequence and to repeat the slideshow. If you want, select a song from your iTunes library to play during the slideshow. If you're a .Mac member, you can use the .Mac Slides button to publish a slideshow to your iDisk, where you can share it over the Internet. If you have a DVD burner, such as Apple's SuperDrive, you can use the iDVD button (**New!**) to export and create a DVD slideshow.

Editing Photos

The iPhoto application contains a few options for the editing of the images. For example, you can resize the image, perform enhancement, and retouching; even remove red eye (**New!**). Other features include the ability to convert the image to black & white, and perform adjustments to the image's brightness and contrast. It should be noted that iPhoto does not replace image-editing programs such as Adobe Photoshop; however, it does give you control over the image, and changes made are permanent. So, be careful when you adjust an image.

Edit Photos

1. Select a Photo Album, and then select an image to edit.

2. Click the Edit tab or double-click the image.

3. To rotate the image in 90-degree increments, click the Rotate button.

4. Click the Constrain pop-up, and then choose how you perform selection within the active image.

5. To crop an image, click and drag within the active image, and then click Crop.

   IMPORTANT *Cropping an object is permanent, unless you click the Edit menu, and then click Undo.*

6. To perform automated enhancement of the image, click Enhance.

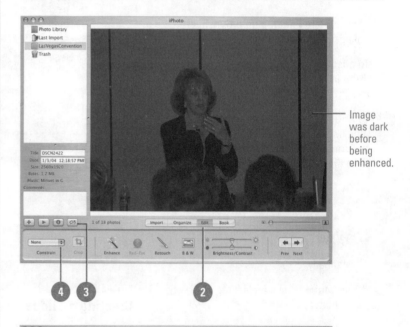

Image was dark before being enhanced.

Image has been fixed using the Enhance button.

7 To remove red eye problems with the image, select the eye of a person within the active image, and then click Red-Eye.

8 To perform specific enhancement of the image, click Retouch, and then drag the brush over the area.

9 To convert the image into black and white, click B & W.

10 Drag the Brightness/Contrast sliders left or right to increase or decrease the brightness and/or contrast values of the image.

11 Click Previous or Next to move to another image in the selected album.

12 Click the Organize tab to save your changes and return to the Photo Album.

TIMESAVER *To only view the last images imported into iPhoto, click the Last Import (icon looks like a roll of film). The iPhoto application displays the last images brought into the application.*

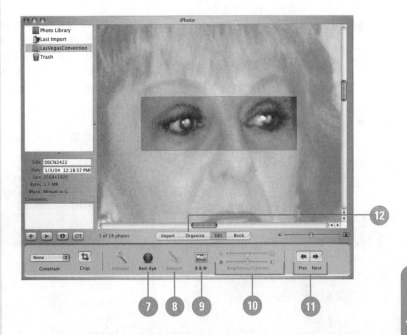

For Your Information

Editing Images

When you edit a photograph, you're changing the original image. Using the Cropping tool removes information; using the Red Eye tool remaps the color values of the eyes; and using Brightness and Contrast lightens or darkens the image. If you find that your edit has not been effective, click the Edit menu, and then click Undo. You can undo a crop, or even a conversion to B&W. But it's always best to work with a copy of the image. Remember once you change an image, and then save and close it, there's nothing you can do to return to the original. Therefore, use editing tools with caution, and always work on a copy of the original.

Creating a Photo Book

The iPhoto application gives you access to some professional features, such as the Book option. The iPhoto book option lets you create a structured order to a group of images (in an album), and then order a 9 by 11 inch hardbound book, that's printed by a bindery, and shipped back to you. The images are printed on acid-free, glossy stock paper.

Create a Photo Book

1. Select an album, or create an album for your book, and then drag the images you want printed as a book, into the new album.

2. Click the Book tab.

3. Click the Theme pop-up, and then select a theme for the book.

4. Select or clear the following options for your photo book:

   ◆ Show Guides

   ◆ Titles

   ◆ Comments

   ◆ Page Numbers

5. Click the Page Design pop-up, and then select how many images appear on each page.

   IMPORTANT *Once you decide the layout of a specific page, select the Lock Page check box.*

6. Continue selecting the page design for each of the remaining images, and then click Preview to look at the book.

7. Click Order Book, and then follow the onscreen instructions.

Did You Know?

You can order printed images on Kodak acid-free paper. Select the Order Prints button, select the images and sizes you want, place your order, and then watch the mail.

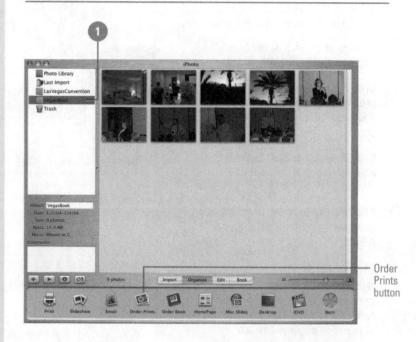

Order Prints button

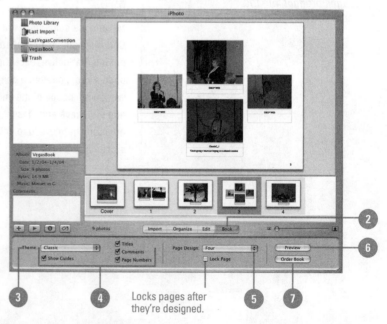

Locks pages after they're designed.

Sharing Photos with Others Using Print or E-Mail

It you've got a great photo of the new baby or that perfect sunset, and you want to share the photo or photos with all your friends, you can use iPhoto to share it with them. iPhoto lets us share photos in several ways: You can e-mail the images to your friends, you can print them using a variety of templates (New!) and send them through the mail (New!), or you can also burn a CD, or even send all your relatives a .Mac slideshow.

Print Photos

1. Select an image.

2. Click Print.

3. Select from the following Print options:

   ◆ **Printer.** Click the pop-up and select a printer.

   ◆ **Presets.** Click the pop-up and select a preset (if available).

   ◆ **Style.** Click the pop-up, select a style, and then select the options for that style.

   ◆ **Copies.** Enter how many copies.

4. Click Print.

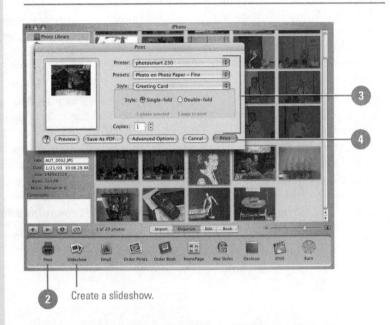

Create a slideshow.

E-Mail Photos

1. Select an image, and then click Email.

2. Click the Size pop-up, and then select the options.

3. Click Compose to compose the e-mail using Mac Email.

4. Type your e-mail, and then click Send.

5. Quit Mail.

   IMPORTANT *You can only have one .Mac slideshow, if you create another show and publish, it overwrites the old slideshow.*

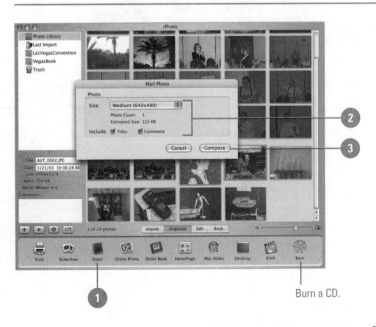

Burn a CD.

Understanding iMovie Basics

The iMovie application is simple to operate, yet powerful when it comes to creating professional movies, using footage from your digital movie camera, or any other digital multimedia files; including image stills and audio files. When you first launch iMovie you are asked whether you want to open an existing movie, or start out from scratch. The next time you open the application, it defaults to opening the last project.

To open a new or another project at this point, click the File menu, and then select New Project, Open Project, or Open Recent. Once iMovie is open, you can begin to add the multimedia elements you're going to use to create the movie. It's important to understand that creating a movie requires a lot of planning and

forethought. You need to assemble the multimedia elements that are used to create the movie.

The iMovie application controls the creative process using three elements: A Project file, a Media folder, and a Reference file. The **Project file** is created when you save the iMovie for the first time, and helps the application keep track of your files and edits. The **Media folder** is where iMovie holds all the multimedia files used in the creation of your movie. The **Reference file** is a QuickTime file of the current state of the movie; double-clicking on the Reference file shows you the movie in the QuickTime player. The iMovie application creates a folder, and then places all of these elements within that folder.

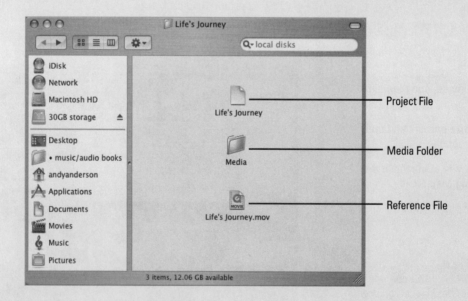

Viewing the iMovie Window

The iMovie window is your working studio. Inside this one window, you have the ability to draw together all of the elements of your movie, and then arrange them by adding titles and transitions; you can even use special effects.

For example, you could create a movie of your trip to the zoo, using a dozen movie clips, plus background music and narration. You can also add still images, create seamless fades between photos, and movies. It's all here inside the iMovie window.

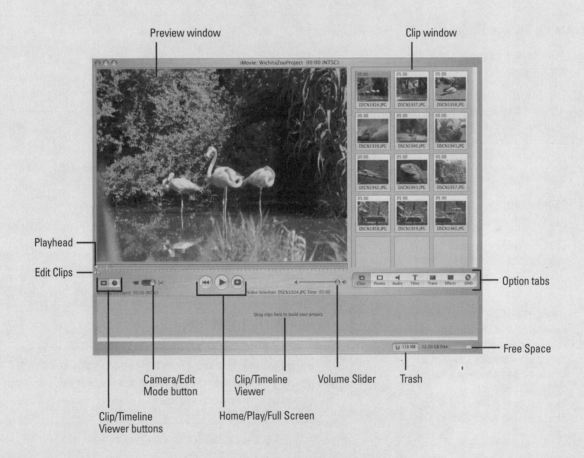

Preview window

Clip window

Playhead

Edit Clips

Option tabs

Free Space

Camera/Edit
Mode button

Clip/Timeline
Viewer

Volume Slider

Trash

Clip/Timeline
Viewer buttons

Home/Play/Full Screen

15

Creating an iMovie Project

The first step in creating a movie is to create an iMovie Project. Your project should be contained within a specified folder. For example, before opening iMovie you create a new folder, and name it: ZooProject. Then when you create your project, you can save the project file inside this folder. In addition to the project file, you should also move all the project files (audio, video, and graphics) into this folder. The Project file is created when you save the project, and is used by iMovie to keep control of all the elements used in the construction of the iMovie. You can select from two common video formats: NTSC and PAL (New!). Every time you select save, iMovie updates the project file to reflect the current working state of the movie. If you delete the Project file, you still have access to the video, audio, and image file used in the creation of the movie, but you have to begin the project all over.

Create an iMovie Project

1. Open the Applications folder, and then double-click the iMovie icon.

2. To select a movie format, click the iMovie menu, click Preferences, click the NTSC or PAL option, and then click the Close button.

3. Click the File menu, and then click New Project.

4. Give the project a distinctive name.

5. Click the Where pop-up, and then select a location for the project.

6. Click Save.

   IMPORTANT *When you record video and/or audio directly into iMovie or import multimedia files, the actual files are saved in a folder named Media, and that folder is saved in the same location as the Project folder. That's makes them easy to find and move.*

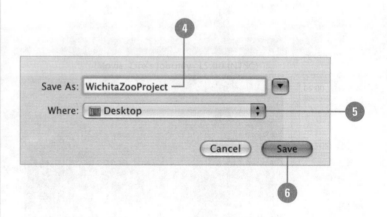

For Your Information

Navigating the Timeline

When you're working on an iMovie project in the Timeline view, you can use the left and right arrow keys to move one frame at a time. If you want to power through the timeline, press the Shift key, along with the left and right arrow keys, and you can move ten frames at a time.

Recording Video

Recording video requires access to a digital camcorder, or even devices as inexpensive as a WebCam. When you record video, remember that these are typically large files, so you'll want a lot of free hard drive space to hold the video file. Recording video is fairly simple; all you really need to do is hook your digital camera, using a USB or FireWire port, to your computer. The iMovie application basically does the rest by detecting your camera, and showing you a preview of what the camera sees. Then you simply click the Record button, and it's on with the show.

Record Video

1. Open an iMovie project.

2. Connect your digital movie camera or WebCam to your computer.

3. Click the button to Camera Mode.

4. Click Import to start the movie capture.

5. Click Import a second time to stop the movie capture.

   IMPORTANT *iMovie saves the movie clip and places it in the Movie Sorter window.*

6. Double-click the movie clip (in the Sorter window), to assign a specific name to the video file.

7. Type a Name, and then click OK.

8. Click the Clip Viewer button.

9. Drag the movie clip from the Sorter window to the Timeline.

10. Click the File menu, and then click Save Project.

Sorter window

Recording Audio

The iMovie application gives you two options when it comes time to use audio—import existing files or record directly into iMovie. When you record audio, remember that these are typically large files, so you'll want a lot of free hard drive space to hold the file. Recording audio typically means you're doing something like a voice-over narration. For example, you might have a video of a walk through the zoo, and you want to give your audience your feelings and impressions as you move through the zoo. The good news is that iMovie lets you preview the video portion of the movie as you do your narration.

Record Audio

1. Open an iMovie project.

2. Click the Timeline Viewer button.

3. Drag the Playhead to the point in the movie where you want to add the audio insert.

4. Click the Audio tab.

5. Click the Record/Stop button to start the audio insert.

   IMPORTANT *If this is a voice-over narration, the Preview window shows you the movie as you talk. And, if you want to move a clip in precise measurements, select the clip on the Timeline, and then use the left and right arrow keys to nudge the clip.*

6. Click the Record/Stop button to end the audio insert.

7. The audio file appears on the Timeline.

8. Click the File menu, and then click Save Project.

Adjust volume

Adding Media to an iMovie

Adding preexisting media to an iMovie project is obviously easier than recording it from scratch. In fact, if you use iTunes and iPhoto (**New!**) to store your images and audio, you have instant access to those files along with sound effects from Skywalker Sound (**New!**). You can add media to an iMovie through iTunes or iPhoto, by importing, or by dragging the files from a folder. When you bring an existing multimedia file into a project, iMovie saves a copy of the file inside the Media folder. In addition, if the file attributes don't match the movie, iMovie reformats the file.

Add Media to an iMovie Using iPhoto or iTunes

1. Open an iMovie project.

2. Click the Photos or Audio tabs.

3. Drag the image files or audio files from the Audio or Photo Clips window to the Timeline.

4. Click the File menu, and then click Save Project.

Did You Know?

You can drag and drop to add media to an iMovie. Open the folder that contains the multimedia files. Drag them from the folder into the open iPhoto window.

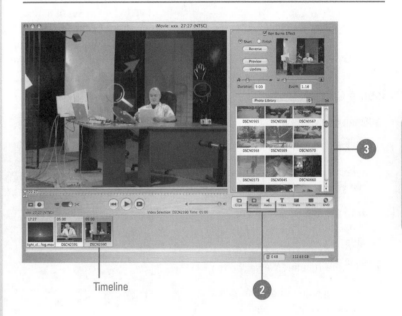

Timeline

Add Media to an iMovie Using Import

1. Open an iMovie project.

2. Click the File menu, and then click Import.

3. Locate the folder that contains the multimedia files you want to import.

4. Select a file or files.

5. Click Open to add them to the Clips window.

6. Click the File menu, and then click Save Project.

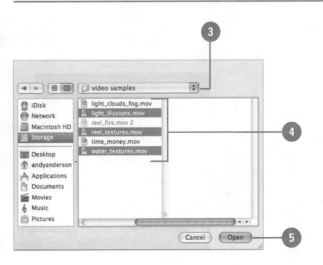

Moving and Trimming Clips

Not only does iMovie give you the ability to add audio and video clips to iMovie projects, it also lets you trim the clips. For example, you have the great video clip of your cousin catching an into-the-bleachers flyball hit by Roger Clemens; however, before you could turn off the video, your cousin turns around and gets slammed into by a guy holding a soft drink. You don't want that part in the video, and neither does your brother, so you simply use iMovie to trim out that video footage. When you place a clip onto the Timeline, its position is relative to all the other clips. You could have five different movie clips on the Timeline, and you want clip five to be the second clip. When you trim a clip, you're removing information from the beginning, end, or both sides of the clip. Trimming can be performed on any type of clip. For example, you could trim part of a video or audio file; even trim a still video that contains an effect.

Move a Clip

1. Open an iMovie project.

2. Click the Clip Viewer button.

3. Select the thumbnail of the clip that you want to move.

4. Drag the clip left or right to reinsert the clip between existing clips.

5. Click the Timeline Viewer button.

6. Drag a clip up or down, or place the clip on another track (audio clips only).

7. Click the File menu, and then click Save Project.

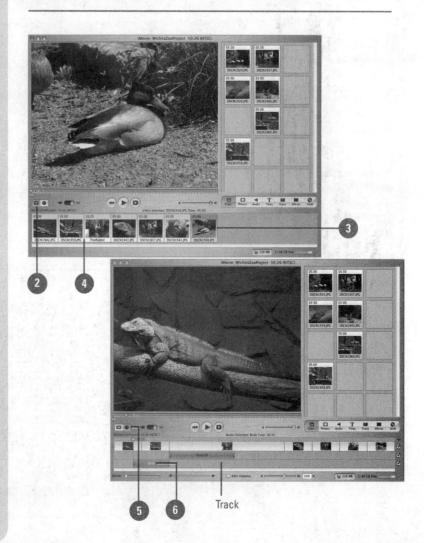

Track

Trim a Clip

1 Open an iMovie project.

2 Select the thumbnail of the clip that you want to trim.

3 Drag the clips (located under the preview window), and then position them (one or both) to represent the area of the clip that you want to keep.

4 Select the Edit menu, and then click Cut or Clear, to trim the highlighted area.

5 Select the Edit menu, and then click Crop, to trim the areas outside the highlighted area.

6 Click the File menu, and then click Save Project.

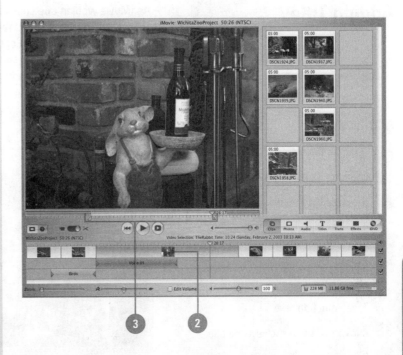

For Your Information

Trimming Clips

The ability to trim clips gives you a lot of creative power during the editing of the movie; by dragging the clips at the beginning and end of the movie, you can decide exactly what you want displayed in your final project. For a quick way to trim the end of a movie clip, move to the Timeline bar, located underneath the movie (called the Scrubber bar), and Shift-click your mouse at the point where you want the movie trimmed. The iMovie application highlights the first portion of the clip, and then trims the portion of the clip to the right of where you clicked.

Adding Titles

An iMovie wouldn't be complete without adding titles to your work of art. Titles lays over the images. You can create titles that scroll, and even use titles for credits at the end of the movie. Titles add the finishing touch to a movie. For example, you could have an opening title complete with subtitles such as: Starring, Produced by, and Directed by. At the end of the movie you could have a set of rolling credits.

Add Titles

1. Open an iMovie project.

2. Click the Timeline Viewer button.

3. Drag the Playhead where you want the title to begin.

4. Click the Titles tab.

5. Select a title style from the Titles list.

6. Type your Title text.

7. Click Preview to preview the title.

8. Drag the Speed and Pause sliders to control the speed at which the title animates and how long it remains on the clip.

9. Use the directional arrows (available for some titles), to adjust the position of the title.

10. Select the QT Margins check box to conform the title to fit a QuickTime window.

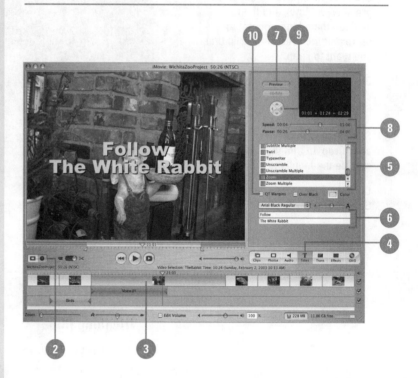

11 Select the Over Black check box to have the title play over black or select the Color box to change the color used, if Over Black is selected.

12 Click the Font pop-up, and then select a font.

13 Drag the Font Size slider left or right to decrease or increase the size of the font.

14 Click Preview again to see your changes.

15 Drag the Title from the Titles list to the Timeline.

16 Click the File menu, and then click Save Project.

Did You Know?

Titles perform various functions in an iMovie. They display the name of the movie, as well as give credit where credit is due. While most titles appear in the middle of the movie, it's sometimes interesting to select a different position, such as the very top or bottom. Adjusting the titles position forces the viewer eyes to move, and keeps things from getting too boring.

15

Adding Transitions

An iMovie wouldn't be complete without adding transitions to your work of art. **Transitions** are used to make two movie clips or images blend together. For example, you can create a transition between two clips that fade to black and then back again. Transitions help create a visual separation between two movie clips. You can also use transitions between still images in an animated slideshow. Transitions include such effects as: Fade In, Fade Out, Circle Opening, and Circle Closing. Experiment with different transitions to see which ones work the best.

Add Transitions

1. Open an iMovie project.

2. Click the Clip Viewer button.

3. Click the Trans tab.

4. Select a transition style from the Transitions list.

5. Click Preview to preview the transition.

6. Drag the Speed slider to control the speed at which the transition lasts.

7. Use the directional arrows (available for some transitions), to adjust the position of the transition.

8. Click Preview again to view the transition.

9. Drag the transition from the Transitions list to the Timeline, and then drop the transition between two clips.

10. Click the File menu, and then click Save Project.

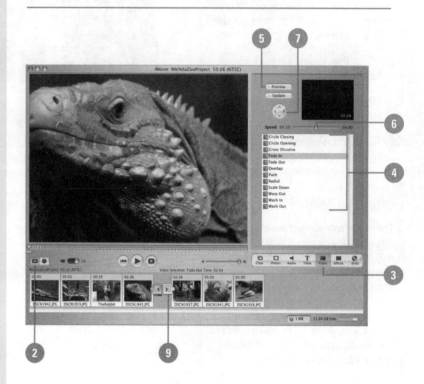

Adding Effects

An iMovie wouldn't be complete without adding effects to your work of art. **Effects (New!)** let you change the look of an image or movie clip. For example, making a clip looked aged or converting a clip from color to black and white. Effects are applied directly to a clip (still images or movies), and they change the appearance of the clip. For example, you could use the Rain effect to give a movie the appearance of rain. There's even a Fog effect to give your movies that sense of drama and mystery. It goes without saying that effects can be overused, and instead of helping support the message they actually become a distraction. Use them when needed, but use them with care.

Add Effects

1 Open an iMovie project.

2 Click the Clip Viewer button.

3 Select the clip on the Timeline in which you want to apply an effect.

4 Click the Effects tab.

5 Select an effect style from the Effects list.

6 Click Preview to preview the effect.

7 Drag the Effect In and Effect Out sliders to control the speed at which the effect enters and exits the clip.

8 Use the directional arrows (available for some transitions), to adjust the position of the transition.

9 Different effects have different options. Use the Effect options to control how the effect appears.

10 Click Preview again to view the effect.

11 Click the Apply button.

12 Click the File menu, and then click Save Project.

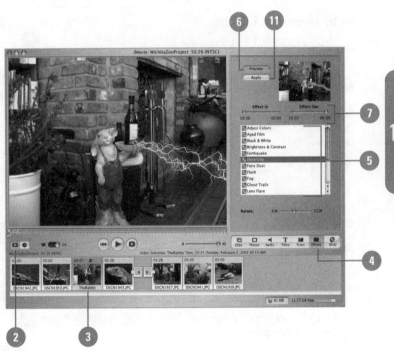

Exporting an iMovie to Camera

When you're working on an iMovie project, your goal might be to create a slideshow of still images, or a movie production complete with special effects, transitions, and titles. You could even create and store a video of your dog sleeping on the couch. Whatever your intentions, you're going to want to move it from your computer. One way to move an iMovie is to use the Export option and export the movie to an attached camera. When you export a movie, you have three options: Export To Camera, To QuickTime (New!), or To iDVD. When you export to camera, you hook your video camera to your computer, and record directly to the camera's video cartridge, or you could hook up a VHS video recorder and record back to the VHS tape.

Export an iMovie to Camera

1. Open an iMovie project.

2. Click the Full Screen Preview button, and then test the movie.

3. Attach your recording device to the computer (camera or video recorder).

4. Click the File menu, and then click Export.

5. Click the Export pop-up, and then click To Camera.

6. Select from the following To Camera options:

   ◆ **Wait *X* Seconds For Camera To Get Ready.** Enter the number of seconds you want the video to pause before starting.

   ◆ **Add *X* Seconds Of Black Before Movie.** Enter the number of seconds of black you want to appear at the beginning of the movie.

   ◆ **Add *X* Seconds Of Black To End Of Movie.** Enter the number of seconds of black you want to appear at the end of the movie.

7. Click Export.

8. Click the File menu, and then click Save Project.

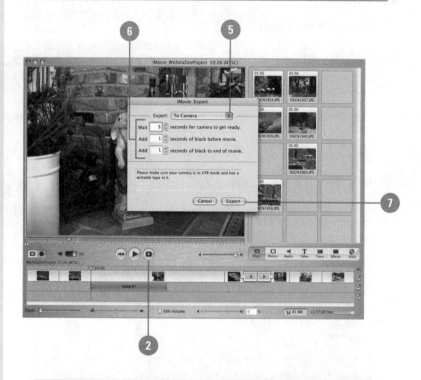

For Your Information

Video Device

If your video device is application controllable (FireWire), the iMovie application automatically turns the device on when the Export button is clicked, and off at the conclusion of the end of the movie. If your device is not controllable, you have to first turn on the recording device, click Export, and then turn it off at the end of the recording session.

Exporting iMovies to the Web and E-Mail

When you export a movie to the Internet or as an e-mail attachment, you have one major problem, speed. Since movies are typically large and the Internet is typically slow, your visitors may loose interest in waiting for your fantastic vacation movie to download, and click off long before it begins playing. The iMovie application understands that relationship of movies on the Internet, and gives you the ability to create a compressed version of your movie using predefined settings. The Web and E-mail settings typically reduces the width and height of the movie, and applies some compression to the video and audio files. The result is a smaller movie of less quality...however your movie loads quickly.

Export iMovies to the Web and E-Mail

1. Open an iMovie project.

2. Click Preview, and then test the movie.

3. Click the File menu, and then click Export.

4. Click the Export pop-up, and then select To QuickTime.

5. Click the Formats pop-up, and then select from the following options:

   - ◆ **Email.** Create and compress a movie as part of an email.

   - ◆ **Web.** Create and compress a movie for viewing on the Web.

   - ◆ **Web Streaming.** Create and compress a movie in a streaming format (begins playing before the entire movie loads).

6. Click Export.

7. Name the file, and then select a location.

8. Click OK.

   Once created, the file is now ready for the Internet.

9. Click the File menu, and then click Save Project.

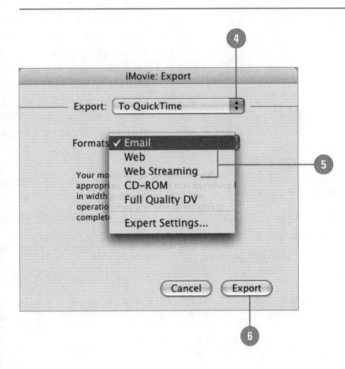

Putting iMovies on CD or DVD

When your output of an iMovie is onto a CD or DVD, you don't have to worry as much about compression settings, as when you're trying to load and play movies on the Internet. DVDs are the obvious choice for high-quality and mass storage (DVDs hold over 4GB); however, not everyone owns a DVD capable computer or player. The alternative would be to move the project to a CD. CDs don't hold as much as a DVD (typically 600 to 700 MB), but most people do own a computer with a CD player. The choice is up to you, and it requires some thought and planning on how you want the movie displayed. When you create a CD file from an iMovie project, it's not necessary to have the blank CD ready. The iMovie application creates a separate file of the movie, and then places it in a location of your choice. Then, using Panther's built-in CD burner, all you have to do is insert a blank CD, and then burn the CD. The iMovie application works seamlessly with iDVD to create interactive movies. For example, you load a "store-bought" DVD of the latest Hollywood movie into your DVD player, you see a nice menu, and have the ability to move through the movie by selecting a chapter. Not only can you easily move an iMovie into iDVD, you can first create the chapters that iDVD uses to create the interactive buttons.

Create a CD Movie

1. Open an iMovie project.

2. Click Preview, and then test the movie.

3. Click the File menu, and then click Export.

4. Click the Export pop-up, and then select To QuickTime.

5. Click the Formats pop-up, and then select CD-ROM.

6. Click Export.

7. Name the file, and then select a location.

8. Click OK.

   Once created, the file is now ready to be burned onto a CD.

9. Click the File menu, and then click Save Project.

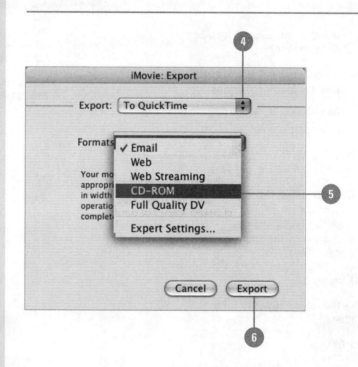

Create an iDVD Movie with Chapters

① Open an iMovie project.

② Click the iDVD tab.

③ Click the Timeline Viewer button.

④ Move the Playhead to a place where you want to insert a chapter.

⑤ Click Add Chapter.

⑥ Repeat steps 4 and 5 to add additional chapters to the movie.

⑦ Double-click the Chapter Title to change the chapter text (the chapter text is used by iDVD as the chapter buttons).

⑧ If necessary, click Remove Chapter to remove a selected chapter.

⑨ Click Create iDVD Project to move the entire iMovie (complete with interactive chapters) into iDVD.

⑩ Click the File menu, and then click Save Project.

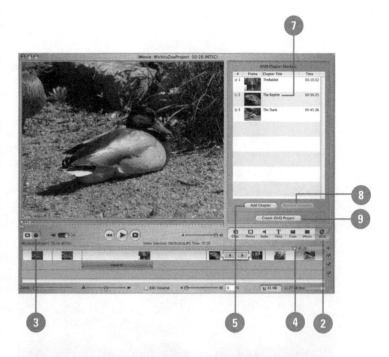

Did You Know?

You can create a DV capable movie. Click the File menu, and then click Export. Select To QuickTime from the Export pop-up, and then select Full Quality DV from the Formats pop-up. However, you'll need a program such as iDVD to complete the process of transferring the movie to a DVD.

15

Added chapters

Setting Up Accounts and Maintaining Security

Introduction

Mac OS X was designed from the ground up for sharing, and it really doesn't matter what you want to share. For example, you might want to set up a simple home-based network to share files between family members, or even hook your Macintosh into a major network using a combination of Windows, Unix, and Mac machines. In Chapter 17, Managing Files Using a Network, you'll learn how to set up a functional network using a variety of methods; however in this chapter you'll learn how to create user accounts, manage those accounts, and even protect your information from being accessed by unauthorized individuals, using Panther's new File Vault application. In addition, Panther lets multiple users log in and switch between accounts with the click of a button.

Correctly setting up user accounts is important to the security of your computer, so each account is assigned it's own name, and individual password. Take care when setting up accounts that you don't give the user more privileges (access) than needed to perform their job. Also, when setting up accounts and passwords, make sure to be accurate in your typing of passwords. Passwords are case-sensitive, and if forgotten, data can be lost forever. When setting up accounts, you can have shared files that can be available for all users on your computer or network.

Understanding User Accounts

When Macs were new, they didn't share very well; however, a lot has changed since then. OS X was designed for multi-users, and Panther has continued that tradition with the inclusion of easy user swapping and tighter file security. Think of a user account as a file drawer within a large file cabinet. A specific individual owns each file drawer, and they have access to that drawer through a unique key. That key gives them access to the contents of their drawer, and no other. Controlling the file cabinet is one person, who has a master key that gives her access to all of the file drawers; including her own. Individuals can do anything they please within their own drawer; including throwing away or adding files, but they can't access the other drawers. A User Account is a file drawer that holds all of the user's folders, files, applications; anything they select to add or subtract from their account.

The interesting thing is that on a Mac, the user account is more than just a file drawer; it's the whole user environment. Users create their own world—including desktop, fonts, and folders. For example, one user logs in and sees a background picture of her dog, while another user, logging in on the same computer, has a background of a beach in the Bahamas. In addition, users are assigned privileges that define where they can go, and what they can access. Let's say one user has access to the accounting system; including all the applications and files, and another user is locked out; all determined by the Administrator. The Administrator holds all the keys to all the accounts; they're the ones that set up the other user accounts and decide who can do what. If you're the owner of the computer, you're the Administrator. It's up to you to decide who does what on your computer.

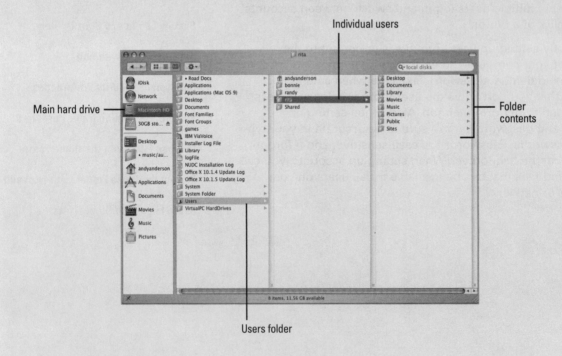

Individual users

Main hard drive

Folder contents

Users folder

Activating the Login Window

When you turn on your Macintosh for the first time, it's set up for instant access. You were asked during the initial setup to name your computer and assign a password. By default, the password protection system is not activated, so the next time you start up your Macintosh, you are granted access without having to select your account and type in your password. Before setting up User Accounts, it's a good idea to first activate password login, and then set up any additional accounts. When active, the login window appears every time you start up your computer and contains a list of all those with valid user accounts (**New!**).

Activate the Login Window

1. Click the Apple menu, and then click System Preferences.

2. Click Accounts.

3. Click Login Options.

4. Click the List Of Users or Name And Password options.

5. Select or clear the Automatically Log In As check box.

6. Select or clear the Hide The Sleep, Restart, And Shut Down Buttons to hide or show the buttons in the Login window.

7. Select the Enable Fast User Switching check box if there is more than one user.

8. Click the Close button.

> **TIMESAVER** *If your computer is in a secure location such as your home, and you don't want to deal with the hassle of logging in, just click the Accounts icon in System Preferences, and then click Login Options. Click the Automatically Log In As option, and then select who you want to log in as (you'll be prompted to type in your password). The next time you start your computer it automatically opens to the selected account.*

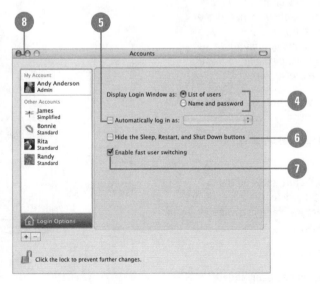

Adding a User Account

Setting up user accounts involves careful consideration as to who is this person, and what they'll be able to access and do on the computer. Panther makes the process of setting up accounts easy (New!); but don't let the ease fool you into thinking it's unsecured. Panther creates a tight wall of protection around each account. When you create a standard account, the security settings are set to their default values. Which means the account user has access to their own personal Home folder, and they are able to access applications on the hard drive. They don't have access to any other account, nor are they able to modify or delete any files or applications on the hard drive.

Add a User Account

1. Click the Apple menu, and then click System Preferences.

2. Click the Accounts icon.

3. Click the Add Account button (+).

4. Click the Password tab (default).

5. Type a name for the new account.

6. Type a Short Name for the Account (used by the server).

    IMPORTANT *The Short Name cannot contain any spaces and is case sensitive. System administrators in the corporate world typically come up with a naming convention so that all the users are set up in a consistent way. For example, Andy Anderson or Steve Johnson might be AAnd or SJoh to the server.*

7. Type and verify the password for the account.

8. Type a Hint for the password (optional).

9. Click the Picture tab, and then select a picture for the account, or drag a picture file from a window or the desktop.

10. Click the Close button.

    The Account has been added.

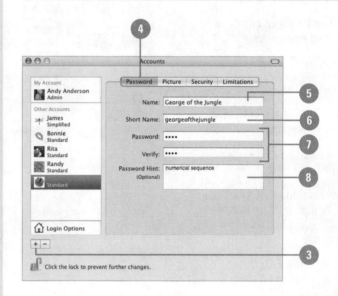

Deleting a User Account

Things change quickly in the computer world; an account for an employee that was valid a week ago is now invalid due to the employee quitting. Deleting user accounts is easy (New!), and if planned correctly does not mean that the user's data and files are deleted. You can specify to hold all of the deleted account information in a temporary holding area; where it can be accessed for as long as necessary.

Delete a User Account

① Click the Apple menu, and then click System Preferences.

② Click the Accounts icon.

③ Select an account from the available users.

④ Click the Delete Account button.

⑤ Select from the following options:

- ◆ **Delete Immediately.** Click to delete the account and all of the files within the account.

- ◆ **OK.** Click to deactivate the account and store the users' files in the Deleted User's folder.

- ◆ **Cancel.** Click to abort the operation.

⑥ Click the Close button.

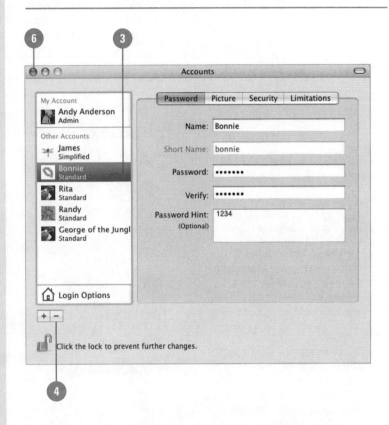

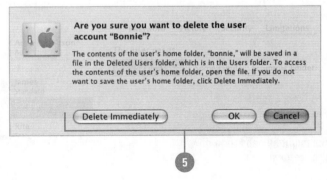

Did You Know?

You can reactivate a deleted account. Click OK instead of Delete Immediately. If you want to reactive the account, go into the Deleted User's folder (located with all the other User folders), and reactivate the account.

16

Setting Account Access Privileges

Once you have set up a user account, it's up to you to decide exactly what that particular user can and cannot have access to (**New!**). For example, you might create a user account for a graphic designer and give them access to all the design applications such as Adobe Photoshop and Illustrator; however, you don't want them messing around with the accounting programs, so you deny access to those specific applications. Once the access privileges are set for an account, they can be changed at a later date, but the Administrator is the only person authorized to change them.

Set Account Access Privileges

1. Click the Apple menu, and then click System Preferences.

2. Click the Accounts icon.

3. Select the account you want to modify.

4. Click the Limitations tab.

5. Select from the following options:

   ◆ **No Limits.** The user has the same limits as any other user. They can access files and applications on the hard drive, but they can't modify or delete them.

   ◆ **Some Limits.** Click to restrict the user's ability to perform certain functions such as Open All System Preferences, Modify The Dock, Change Password or Burn CDs or DVDs. Also, you can select what applications they can access.

   ◆ **Simple Finder.** Click to restrict the user to a stripped down version of the desktop, and only allows them access to the applications on their modified dock (selected by you). This option might be good for a new user or a guest.

6. Click the Close button.

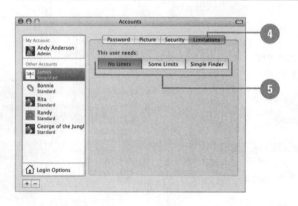

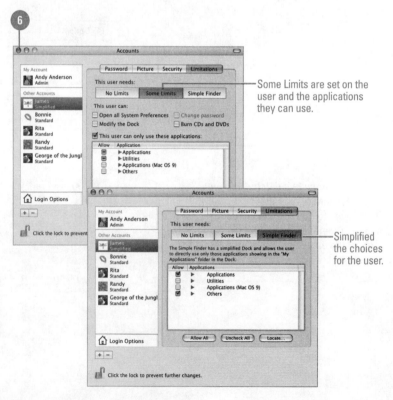

Some Limits are set on the user and the applications they can use.

Simplified the choices for the user.

Setting File Access Permissions

As the Administrator, you have one additional area where you can control what users have access to is the File Info. The **File Info** window lets you, as the Administrator, decide who has access to the files and folders on your computer. For example, you could create a folder on the hard drive and give every user account access, or you could select one file within that folder and restrict access. In fact, you can give users the ability to read a file, but not modify, or let them read and modify the file. Since handling individual files would be a bit time consuming (computers typically hold thousands of files), your Macintosh helps out by assuming users do not have access to the hard drive's files and folders (it's up to you to give them access), and you can apply general access settings to all the files and folders nested within a folder (this saves you time).

Set File Permissions

1. Open the hard drive and then select a folder, application, or file.

2. Click the File menu, and then click Get Info.

3. Click the expand button (triangle) for Ownership & Permissions.

4. Click the expand button (triangle) for Details.

5. Click the Details pop-ups, and then select what type of access you want assigned to the selected item.

    ◆ Read & Write

    ◆ Read Only

    ◆ Write Only (Drop Box)

    ◆ No Access

6. Click Apply To Enclosed Items to apply the changes to all the items within a folder.

7. Click the Close button.

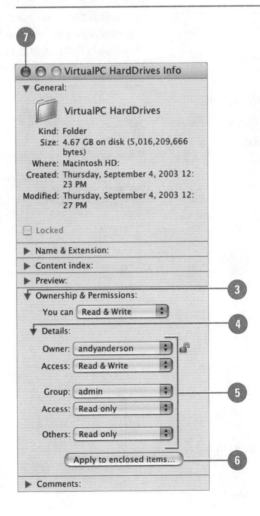

16

Specifying Log In and Start Up Items

When you first turn on your computer, it begins by access the operating system and performing a standard start up. A normal start up involves performing a system check, and then if login is activated, opening the login window and requiring you to select your account and type in your password. At that point, Panther opens your desktop and it's off to work. However, there is a way that you can alter the start up procedure, by specifying Start Up, and/or Log In items. **Start Up items** (New!) are applications or scripts that you decide to launch every time your computer is turned on. **Log In items** (New!) are specified by individual users, and launch whenever their account is accessed. For example, you might have a Start Up item (a script) that accesses the company network. In addition, you have a Log In item (a file) that launches your personal day planner, when you log in. The network script launches each time the computer is turned on, but the day planner only launches when you log in to your account. The individuals who own accounts on your computer set up log in items. In fact, log in items are one of the few things the Administrator cannot do—the user must set them up.

Work with Log In Items

1. Click the Apple menu, and then click System Preferences.

2. Click the Accounts icon.

3. Select your account (Administrator only).

4. Click the Startup Items tab.

5. Click the Add button (+) to locate a particular application or file you want opened every time you log in.

6. If necessary, click the Remove button (-) to remove an item from the startup list.

7. Select the Hide check box to open the application or file but hide it until you're ready to work.

8. Click the Close button.

> **TIMESAVER** *To see a list of all hidden applications or files, press ⌘+Tab. You'll see a list of all open applications. Continue to press ⌘, and then press Tab to move through and select any hidden application.*

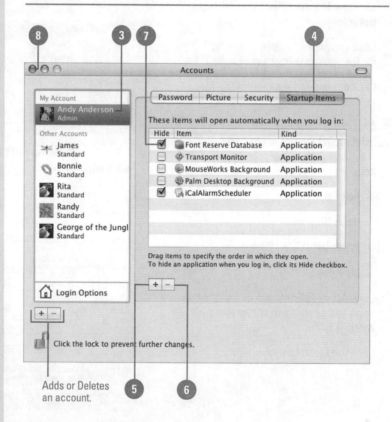

Work with Start Up Items

① Double-click the System Folder to open.

② Open the Startup Items folder.

③ Add items to the folder by dragging and dropping.

④ Remove items by dragging them out of the folder.

Did You Know?

If you don't want to drop an application into the Startup Items folder, create an alias of the application (or file), and place the alias into the folder. That way, you still have access to the original item, and if you no longer want the item in the Startup Items folder, all you have to do is move it to the trash.

See Also

See "Creating Aliases" on page 70 for information on how to create and use an alias.

StartUp Items folder

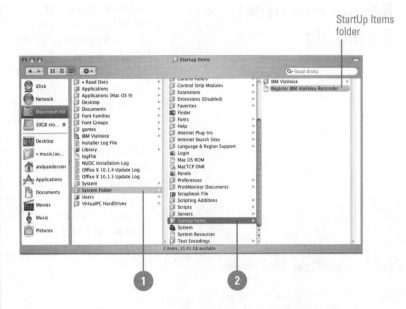

For Your Information

Creating Start Up Commands

Since Start Up items load every time your computer is running; it's a great way to perform routine maintenance and security. You could create a script that instructs the system to perform hard drive diagnostics every seven days, or you could install a security program that keeps your children off objectionable Web sites (there are several available through computer retailers). Since the items are placed within the Startup Items folder, it doesn't matter who logs into the computer; the functions load and perform as instructed.

16

Setting Fast User Switching

One of the advantages to having multiple users and owning Panther, is the ability to quickly switch between users (New!). For example, one of your users wants to quickly check her e-mail. Before Panther, you would have to close out all your files, log out, and then let her log in, but not any more. Panther allows more than one user access to your computer, and lets you switch back and forth on the fly without closing anything. Think of a large box, and each side of the box represents a user account, along with their personalized desktop, specific folders and applications. To access a new account you simply rotate the box to display another face. That's exactly how it looks when you switch users using Fast User Switching. As you watch, the screen rotates to another face on the box displaying another user, and your account is still active. When she's finished checking her e-mail, all you have to do is switch back. It's that simple, and on systems with multiple users, this one feature can save you a lot of wasted time.

Enable Fast User Switching

1. Click the Apple menu, and then click System Preferences.

2. Click the Accounts icon.

   IMPORTANT *Only the System Administrator can activate Fast User Switching.*

3. Click the Login Options button.

4. Select the Enable Fast User Switching check box.

5. Click the Close button.

See Also

See "Switching Users" on page 22 for information on switching between different users.

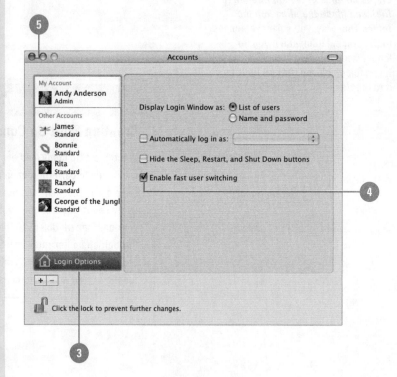

Setting System Security Preferences

The Security pane (**New!**) in System Preferences allows you to set options that prevent others from using your computer, such as requiring a password to unlock and change system preferences or wake your computer from sleep or screen saver, logging you out automatically if you're inactive for a certain amount of time (make sure you save all documents to complete logging you out), and disabling automatic login all together. The Security pane also lets you turn on or off FileVault, which protects your Home folder using encryption (secrets codes) from unauthorized users. Your files are encrypted using your login password. If you forget your login password and don't have the master password (a safety net password that lets you unlock any FileVault account), your files are lost forever.

Set System Security Preferences

1. Click the Apple menu, and then click Preferences.

2. Click the Security icon.

3. Select or clear the Require Password To Wake This Computer From Sleep Or Screen Saver check box.

4. Select or clear the check boxes related to all user accounts:

   ◆ Disable Automatic Login

   ◆ Require Password To Unlock Each Secure System Preference

   ◆ Log Out After *X* Minutes Of Inactivity

5. To set or change a master password (*something you never want to forget*), click Set or Change, type the information, and then click OK.

6. Click the Close button.

See Also

See "Protecting the Home Folder with FileVault" on page 389 for information on using FileVault.

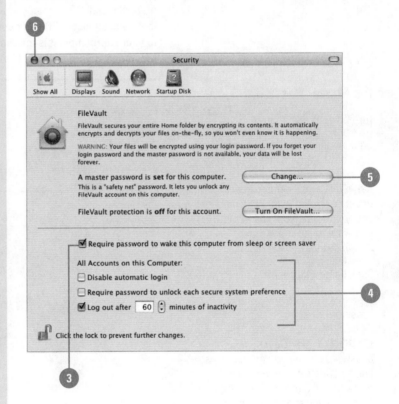

16

Restoring the Administrator Password

System Administrators are the ones that control the computer; they're the ones that set up other user accounts, and they are the ones, that tell you what you can and cannot access on that particular computer. The System Administrator knows all... sees all. However, what if the System Administrator forgets their password? Well first of all, don't tell anyone and don't worry, because you have two possible ways to get back to work. Your operating system has an Administrator password, and a Master password. If you know the master password, you have no problems whatsoever. However, if you set up a master password, turned on FileVault, and then forgot your Master password... well, not even Panther can help you out of that situation, you're data is lost forever. If you didn't set up the master password, don't despair because OS X gives you another way to reset your Administrator password—by using the original install CD. It's fairly straight forwarded, but understand others that have an install CD can perform the same operation, and gain access to your information. It is therefore recommended that you create a Master password, and use FileVault to secure your sensitive documents.

Use the Master Password

1. Turn on your computer.

2. Type anything into the password login option three times.

   IMPORTANT *After three unsuccessful attempts at typing in your password, you'll be asked if you want to reset the Administrator password.*

3. Click Reset Password.

4. Type in a new Administrator password.

   IMPORTANT *Do not make passwords common items such as your birthday, or mother's maiden name, those passwords will be the first someone tries to get into your system.*

5. Verify by typing in your Master Password.

6. Click Continue to restore the Administrator Password, and launch the operating system.

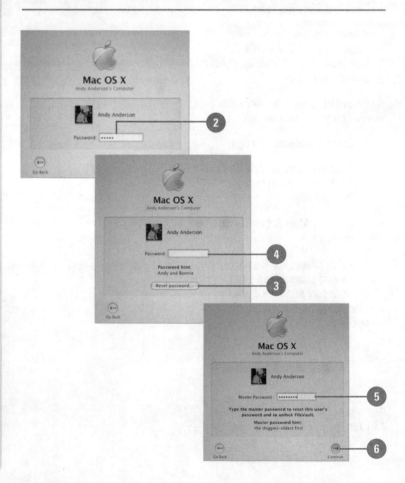

Use the OS X CD

① Insert the Mac OS X CD.

② Hold down the C key (instructs Mac to start up from the CD).

③ Click the Installer menu, and then click Reset Password.

④ Select the hard drive you want to reset.

⑤ Click the Account pop-up, and then select the name of your account.

⑥ Type and verify a new Administrator password.

⑦ Click Save, and then close the window.

⑧ Click Installer, and then restart.

Close

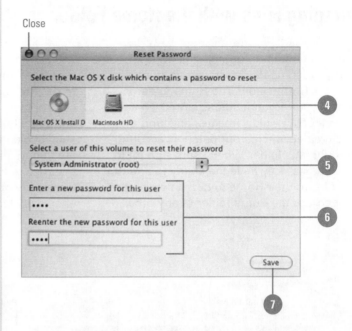

For Your Information

Using the OS X CD

The Panther OS X CD allows you to start your computer, even if the operating system on the hard drive completely fails. Sometimes it's possible to revive a crashed disk (assuming the problem is the operating system), by reinstalling the operating system over the old system, using the OS X CD. If you travel with a PowerBook, it's a good idea to burn a copy of the OS X CD and take it with you on the road. An ounce of prevention is worth a pound of cure.

16

Managing Files with the Home Folder

In a further attempt to organize, as well as secure your computer, each user account is assigned a Home folder. The **Home folder** is where all your account stuff is stored. That means all of your files, images; anything that you've created within your personal account, is stored in this folder. When users sign on to their accounts, they have the ability to add or delete files to their Home folder; however, they cannot access the Home folder of any other user, and they cannot add folders or delete files from any place else but their own Home folder. This gives you a tremendous degree of control over users, and prevents them from accidentally (or purposely) deleting or reading sensitive data. For example, users cannot create folders on the main hard drive, nor can they delete applications from the Applications folder. The other areas of the computer are effectively locked out.

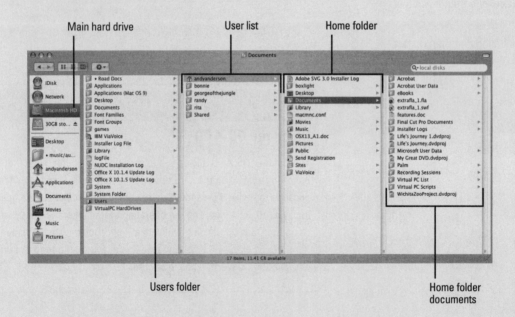

Main hard drive   User list   Home folder

Users folder   Home folder documents

Protecting the Home Folder with FileVault

Panther's FileVault feature (**New!**) finally gives you total security over your sensitive files and applications. Macintosh computers have always had security, but there were ways to get around it. That was before Panther came up with FileVault. FileVault gives you the ability to encrypt the files in your Home folder using password encryption (your log in password). It's so strong, that if you forget your password and don't know the master password, no one is able to open the files—they are lost forever. It's theorized that breaking the FileVault encryption would take a password-guessing program over 100 trillion years to figure it out. Therefore, if you decide to use FileVault, please don't forget your password. After you set FileVault, the security encryption and decryption happens on the fly, so you don't have to worry about doing anything; simply use your files normally. If someone else tries to access them, FileVault keeps them out.

Protect Your Home Folder with FileVault

1. Click the Apple menu, and then click System Preferences.

2. Click the Accounts icon.

   IMPORTANT *Encrypting the entire contents of you hard drive requires the System Administrator.*

3. Click the Security tab.

4. Click Turn On FileVault (all other uses must be logged off the computer).

5. Read the alert message if users are logged in, and then click OK.

6. Type your password, and then click OK.

7. Another alert message appears, please read it carefully, and then click Cancel or Turn On FileVault.

   Panther then goes through a creation procedure that can take 10 minutes or more to complete.

8. When the process is complete, you are brought back to the Login window.

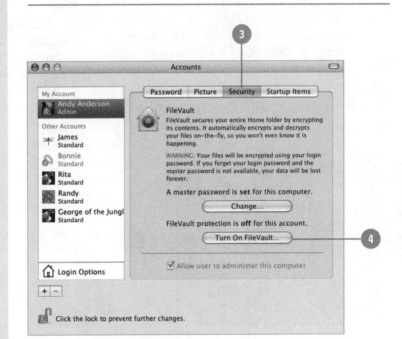

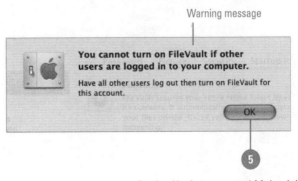

Warning message

16

Sharing Files with Other Users

When you set up a user account, that person has access to the files in his Home folder. Depending on the level of access, he can open applications, possibly read or access information on the hard drive, but he won't have access to any sensitive areas, or anyone else's Home folder. What if you want to give a file to another co-worker, but you can't drop it into their folder, and the co-worker can't access your Home folder. That's where Macintosh comes to the rescue with shared folders.

When you open your Home folder you'll see two folders named Public and Sites. The Public folder contains a nested folder named Drop Box. The **Drop Box folder** is a place where anyone can drop items for you to use. As another user, I can place things into your

Drop Box, and you can place things in my Drop Box, but I can't see what's in your Drop Box, nor can I change any items. In other words, files check in but they don't check out.

The **Sites folder** is a place where you can create a Web site, and anyone can open the Sites folder, and launch your site. You can even publish it out to the Internet or on a Local Network. As a user with an account on this system, I can launch your Web site, but I can't modify or place any items within the Sites folder.

Finally, there is a **Shared folder**, located in the Users folder. The Shared folder is the only folder (other than your own Home folder) where you have full access to the files it contains.

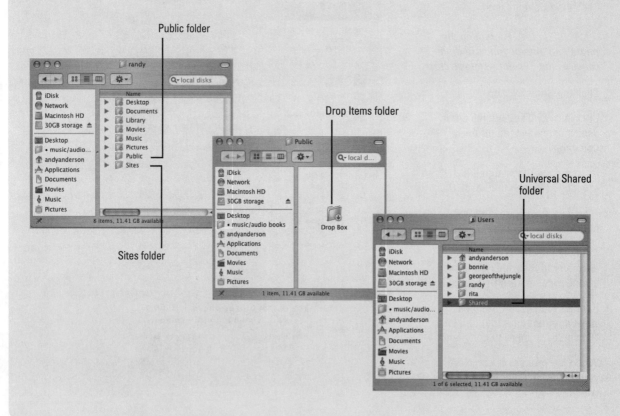

Public folder

Drop Items folder

Universal Shared folder

Sites folder

Managing Files Using a Network

Introduction

Networks are interesting systems. Not too many years ago, a network was defined as two or more computers, connected together by physical cables or telephone lines. They were slow, and they went down (crashed) as much as they were up. The word, network, could bring fear to the hearts of even the stoutest computer system managers. Today, networks are rock solid and reliable. The Web can be defined as one huge network of interconnected computers around the world.

Networks connect more than computers; they work with PDA's, cell phones, televisions, and even wristwatches. And no longer do networks require physical cables. If your computer is equipped with a wireless port, you can connect to the Internet and surf the Web or even check your e-mail, from most major airports and hotel lobbies, without plugging your computer into anything.

In addition, the speed of today's networks allows us to move massive amounts of information, and even conduct real-time video-conferences. Macintosh computers were born to network, even when networking was a difficult proposition, the minds at Apple were working hard to make it fast, easy, and secure; and with the release of Panther, the ability to set up a local network, or one that stretches around the world, is becoming easier and easier.

Using Panther's built-in systems, you can even configure a wireless network—using an AirPort or Bluetooth (wireless technologies). You can share files and information with other computers with ease and even set up protection (firewalls) to guard against unauthorized access or potential viruses. It's all made possible with a Macintosh, and the Panther operating system.

What You'll Do

Use Network Sharing Services

Set Up a Local Area Network

Set Up an AirPort Wireless Network

Set Up a Bluetooth Wireless Network

Move Items with Bluetooth

Browse the Network with the Finder

Set Up File Sharing

Connect to Another Computer for File Sharing

Connect to a Network Over the Internet

Create Privileges for Users and Groups

Connect from a Windows Computer

Share an Internet Connection

Configure an Internet Firewall

Explore Additional Utility Applications

Set Bluetooth Preferences

Using Network Sharing Services

Sharing Services are a collection of options that allow you to define what your computer shares with other computers over a network. For example, if you want to use your computer as a Web server, you would select the Personal Web Sharing Service, or by selecting the Printer Sharing Service, you can share the printers on your computer with anyone else on the network. To prevent accidental changes to your settings, click the Lock button, located in the bottom-left corner of the Sharing window. The next time you try to make changes, you'll be prompted for your Administrator's password.

Use Network Sharing Services

1. Click the Apple menu, and then click System Preferences.

2. Click the Sharing icon.

3. Click the Services tab.

4. Select from the following network services options:

   ◆ **Personal File Sharing.** Select to allow other users access to the computer's Public folders.

   ◆ **Windows Sharing.** Select to allow Windows users access to the computer's Public folders.

   ◆ **Personal Web Sharing.** Select to allow users access to the Web pages, located in the Sites folders.

   ◆ **Remote Login.** Select to allow others to login to this computer.

   ◆ **FTP Access.** Select to allow users to exchange files using FTP (File Transfer Protocol) applications.

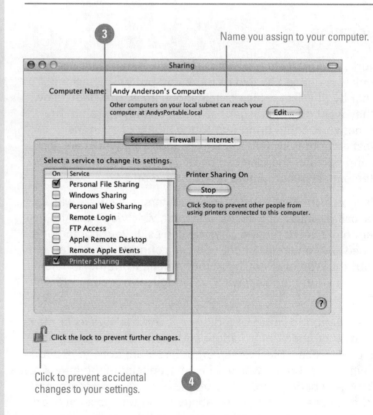

Name you assign to your computer.

Click to prevent accidental changes to your settings.

◆ **Apple Remote Desktop.** Select to allow users access to this computer through the Apple Remote Desktop application.

◆ **Remote Apple Events.** Select to allow users to send Apple Events to this computer (optional password protection).

◆ **Printer Sharing.** Select to allow other users to share this computer's printers.

⑤ Click Start/Stop to activate or disable the selected service.

The Start/Stop button toggles to Start or Stop based on what was selected.

⑥ Click the Close button.

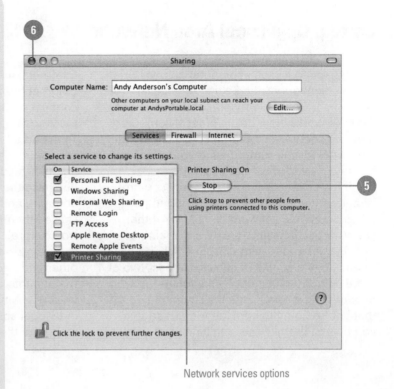

Network services options

Did You Know?

You can change your computer's local name. Click the Edit button to change the name of your local computer. The local computer name is the name that displays with all the other computer names in a network listing.

17

Setting Up a Local Area Network

Almost any Macintosh computer comes out of the box network ready. Setting up a Local Area Network or LAN, is fairly straightforward. **Local Area Networks** are a group of local computers hooked together. For example, you could create a LAN for the computers in your office or create a LAN for your home computers. Macintosh even allows you to connect with Windows computers without having to purchase additional software. In fact, all of the software you'll need to create and maintain a LAN is built into Macintosh OS X. All you have to do is buy a couple of cables, connect two or more computers together, and you're ready to network. Let's complicate the situation and say that you're going to hook up more than two computers. In that case, you'll need an Ethernet cable for each computer and an Ethernet hub. A **hub** is a device that lets you connect multiple computers together. Every Macintosh sold comes with an Ethernet port. To set up a LAN, draw out the layout for the network to determine where the computers are and the distance between each unit. Purchase the cables (make sure they're long enough), and the Ethernet hub (you can purchase Ethernet supplies at almost any electronic store). Plug one end of the Ethernet cables into each of the computers, and the other end into the hub (make sure you plug the hub into an electrical outlet). Once the network is established, you'll need to set up the individual computers for file sharing and to recognize the LAN.

Local Area Network

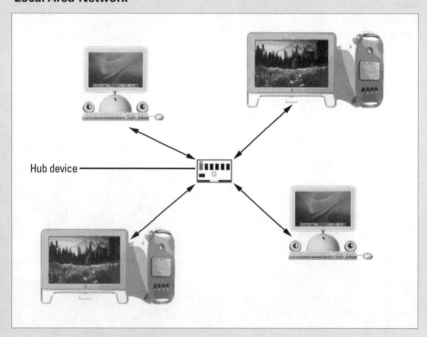

Hub device

Setting Up an AirPort Wireless Network ▶

Macintosh computers do not have to be tied down by cables. As a matter of fact, if you're the owner of a Macintosh PowerBook, you can go wireless and free yourself from connecting to anything. More and more airports, municipal properties, and even city parks are going wireless. In fact, you can have your very own wireless network in your home. To create a Macintosh wireless network, you'll need a wireless broadband router, and two or more Macintosh computers that have AirPort cards installed. If you already have an Ethernet-based LAN, you can connect an AirPort to the hub of the Ethernet. This gives you the ability to access the entire network from your wireless Macintosh.

Set Up an AirPort Wireless Network

1. Plug in the AirPort.

2. Open the Applications folder, double-click the Utilities folder, and then double-click the AirPort Setup Assistant icon.

3. Click the Set Up An AirPort Base Station option.

4. Click Continue.

5. Click the Available AirPort Networks pop-up, and then select your AirPort Base Station.

6. Click Continue.

7. Configure the AirPort settings.

8. Click Finish.

> **TROUBLE?** *If you are having problems with your AirPort settings, point your browser to www.apple.com, and then click the Support tab. There you can type **AirPort** in the Search field, and then press Return.*

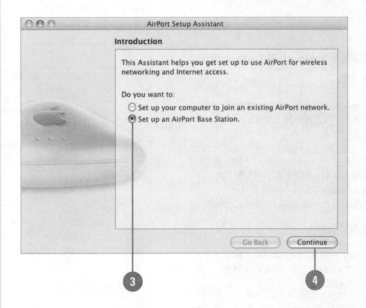

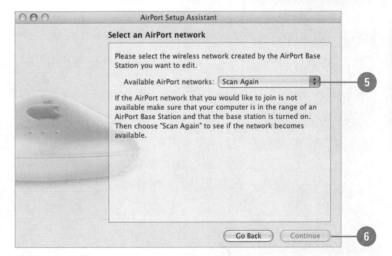

17

Setting Up a Bluetooth Wireless Network

Macintosh computers have several methods for creating networks. There are standard networks using Ethernet cables, and hubs; there are wireless networks; and then there are Bluetooth networks. **Bluetooth** (New!) technology is not so much a network, as it is a simple wireless technology that lets you transmit files and data to any other Bluetooth equipped device. For example, you could use Bluetooth to sync to your Bluetooth PDA, or even use your Address Book, and Bluetooth to automatically dial your Bluetooth cell phone. If you really want to throw away the cables, Apple even makes a Bluetooth enabled keyboard and mouse. Bluetooth uses radio signals to communicate with any other Bluetooth device, up to a maximum range of thirty feet. Think of it this way, any Bluetooth device can communicate with any other Bluetooth device, if they are both turned on and within thirty feet of each other.

Set Up a Bluetooth Wireless Network

1. Turn on the Bluetooth device and place it within 30 feet of your computer.

2. Open the Applications folder, double-click the Utilities folder, and then double-click the Bluetooth Setup Assistant icon.

3. Click Continue.

   If Bluetooth is turned off, you are instructed to turn it on before proceeding.

4. Select a Bluetooth device from the available options.

5. Click Continue.

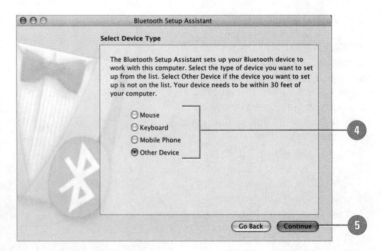

6 Select the Bluetooth device from the scan window.

7 Click Continue.

8 Enter a Passkey, and then click Continue.

9 Enter the same Passkey on your device.

10 Select from the following options:

- ◆ Set Up Another Device
- ◆ Go Back
- ◆ Quit

Did You Know?

The Bluetooth icon can be placed on your Apple menu bar. Click the Apple menu, and then click System Preferences. Click the Bluetooth icon, click Settings, and then select the Show Bluetooth Status In The Menu Bar check box.

See Also

See "Setting Bluetooth Preferences" on page 412 for information on changing Bluetooth settings, file exchange, and device options.

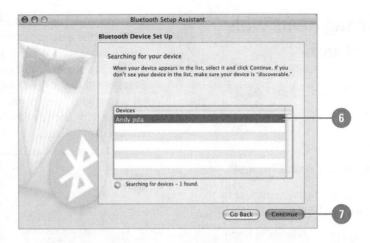

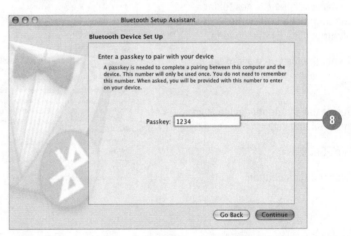

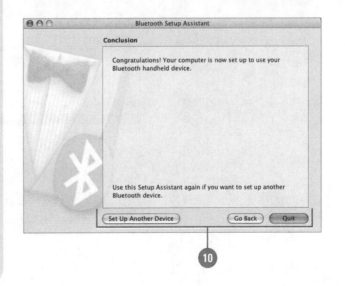

17

Moving Items with Bluetooth

Once you've set up your Bluetooth devices, it's a simple matter to transfer files to the Bluetooth device (**New!**). For example, you have a PDA device and you want to move a text file from your computer to the device. The process of moving a file from your computer to your Bluetooth device is the same; however, since each Bluetooth device is different, the process of moving a file from the device to your computer is different for each device. Consult your owner's manual for information on how to move information to your computer, from the Bluetooth device.

Move Items with Bluetooth

1. Turn on the device and place it within 30 feet of your computer.

2. Open the Applications folder, double-click the Utilities folder, and then double-click the Bluetooth File Exchange icon.

3. Select the file you want to send.

4. Click Send.

5. Select the Bluetooth device from the available list.

6. Click Send.

7. Click the Close button.

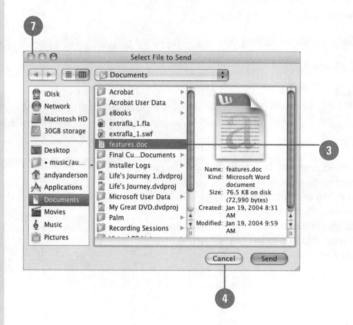

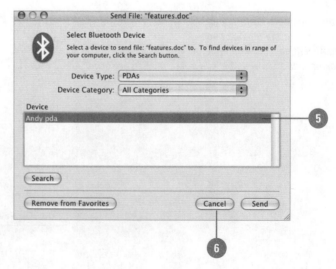

Browsing the Network with the Finder

The Finder serves as a focused network browser application (**New!**). For example, you're looking for a file with a specific name. You've used the Finder application, and checked on your machine, but can't seem to find it. The other option is that it's on your co-workers computer. The good news is that with the Finder application, not only can you search your computer; you can search any other computer on the network.

Browsing the Network with the Finder

1. Login to another computer on the network.

2. Open the Finder application.

   TIMESAVER *Click on the desktop, and then click* ⌘+F.

3. Click the Search In pop-up, and then select Specific Places.

4. Drag the Network Computer icon from the desktop into the Finder window.

5. Select the Network Computer icon's check box.

6. Type the search criteria.

7. Click Search.

See Also

See "Connecting to Another Computer for File Sharing" on page 402 for more information on using file sharing.

Did You Know?

You can also search your .Mac account. If you have a .Mac account, you can add it to your searchable items. Click the Add button, and then select the .Mac icon.

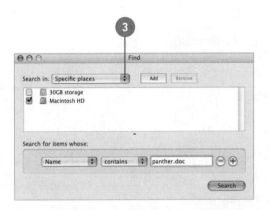

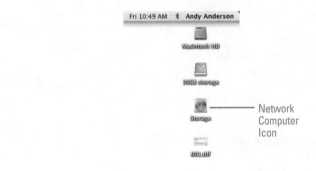

Network Computer Icon

Removes the selected device.

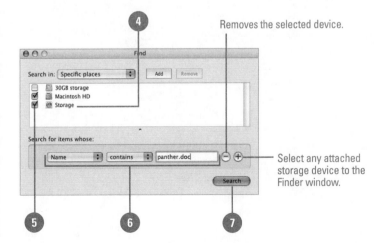

Select any attached storage device to the Finder window.

17

Setting Up File Sharing

Whenever you set up a network, regardless of the type, you'll have to configure your computer to communicate with the network. Macintosh computers are big on security, and they won't let your computer talk to any other computer unless you give the other computers permission. Permission involves setting up file sharing options, and then creating accounts with specific user names, passwords, and permissions.

Set Up File Sharing

1. Set up the accounts of the people that have access to your computer.

2. Click the Apple menu, and then click Sharing.

3. Click the Services tab.

4. Select the Personal File Sharing check box.

5. Click the Close button to return to the System Preferences main window.

   TIMESAVER *Press* ⌘+*L to quickly return to the System Preferences main window.*

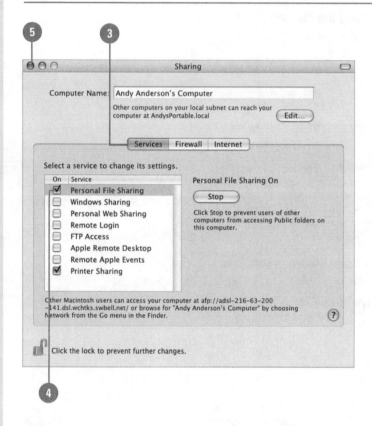

See Also

See "Setting Account Access Privileges" on page 380 for more information on giving access to your computer.

6 Click the Network icon.

7 Click the Show pop-up, and then select Built-In Ethernet.

8 Click the TCP/IP tab.

9 Click the Configure IPv4 pop-up, and then click Using DHCP.

10 Click Configure IPv6.

11 Click the Configure IPv6 pop-up, and then click Automatically.

12 Click OK.

13 Click the Close button.

Did You Know?

You can get help from Panther.
Click Assist Me, and then let Panther help you configure your system for file sharing. In most cases, if you follow these steps, your computer is ready to share files.

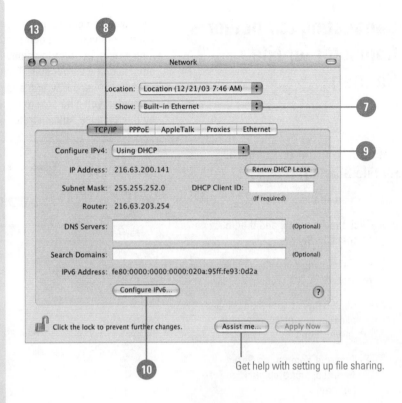

Get help with setting up file sharing.

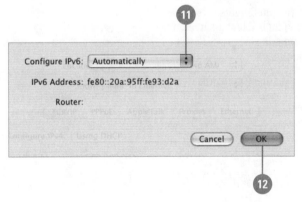

17

Connecting to Another Computer for File Sharing

Once you've connected several computers together into a network, and configured your computer for file sharing, the next step is to begin communicating. In order to communicate with another computer, you'll need access to a user account. Typically a user account defines you with a specific name, password, and permissions. Once you log into the other computer, you'll be able to access the areas (permissions) granted to you by the Systems Administrator.

Connect to Another Computer for File Sharing

1. Turn on all the computers.

2. Click the Go menu, and then click Connect To Server.

3. Connect using one of the following methods:

   ◆ Click Browse, and then double-click on one of the available server icons.

   ◆ Type the computer's Server Address, and then click Connect.

   ◆ Click the Recent Servers button, and then select a server address from the list of available options.

4. Type your Name and Password.

5. Click Connect.

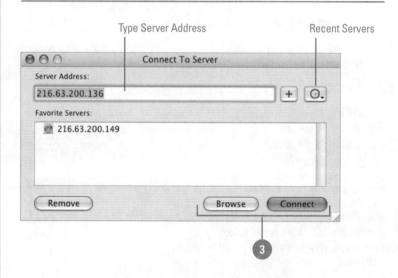

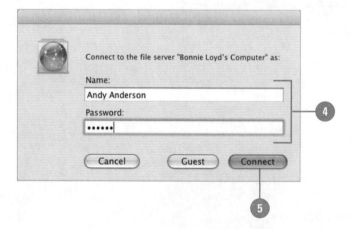

6 Select the area of the other computer you want to access.

7 Click OK.

IMPORTANT *The other computer now functions and acts as a hard drive on your computer.*

8 Drag files from your computer to the networked computer or vice versa.

9 Control-click on the Network Computer icon, and then click Eject to close the connection between the two computers.

Did You Know?

You can identify the IP (Internet Protocol) address of your computer. Click the Apple menu, and then click System Preferences. Click Network, click the Show pop-up, and then select Network Status. The current IP address is displayed next to the Built-In Ethernet option.

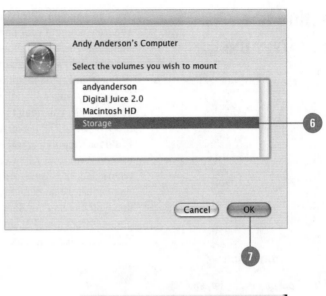

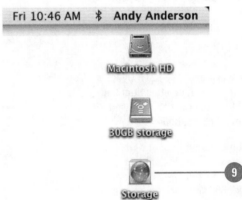

17

Connecting to a Network Over the Internet

You can create a VPN (Virtual Private Network) connection (New!) to securely connect your computer to a network over the Internet. The computer you want to connect to must support a VPN and Internet connection. Before you create a connection, you need to have the server or IP (Internet Protocol) address of the VPN computer. You use the Internet Connection application to set up a VPN connection. The first time you setup a VPN, you need to select a VPN protocol, either L2TP Over IPSec or PPTP. Use L2TP (Layer Two Tunneling Protocol) over IPSec (Internet Protocol Security), where security is a concern between your computer and pre-Windows XP, or use PPTP (Point-to-Point Tunneling Protocol) where security issues are not as much a problem, but where backward compatibility with older systems is a concern. After you set up a connection, you can use the Show VPN Status menu to easily connect and disconnect from the VPN, and show connection information.

Create a VPN Connection

1. Open the Applications folder, and then double-click the Internet Connect icon.

2. Click VPN.

3. If necessary, click the L2TP Over IPSec or PPTP option to select the type of VPN connection you want, and then click Continue.

4. Click the Configuration pop-up, and then select a modem configuration you already created, or click Edit Configuration to add, edit, or remove configurations.

5. Type the Server Address.

6. Type the Account Name and Password.

7. To display the modem menu for easy connection access, select the Show VPN Status In Menu Bar check box.

8. Click Connect to start a VPN connection.

9. When you're done, click the Close button, and then name and save the configuration.

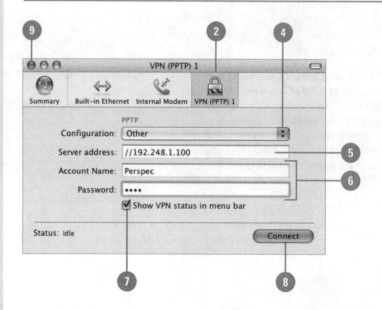

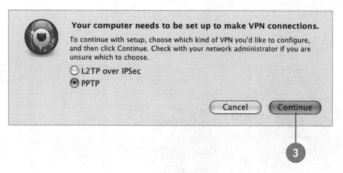

Creating Privileges for Users and Groups ▶

Once you've configured your computer to share information, you'll probably want to restrict or give access to certain files and folders. Before you set privileges for the users or groups, you must first set up the user accounts. You can decide who gets to go where and do what. There are four levels of access—Read & Write (allows user to access and change the file), Read Only (allows user to access the file, but not make changes), Write Only (Drop Box), and No Access. The levels are pretty self-explanatory; however, if you give someone Read & Write privileges, you're giving them full control over the file. For example, someone could open a text document and basically erase the contents of the letter or completely rewrite it.

Create Privileges for Users and Groups

1. Select a folder, file, or application.

2. Select the File menu, and then click Get Info.

3. Click the expand buttons (triangles) for Ownership & Permissions and Details.

4. Click the You Can pop-up, and then select from the available permission options.

   IMPORTANT *If the You Can pop-up is grayed out, the System Administrator has prevented you from changing your permissions on this item.*

5. Click the Owner and Access pop-ups to change the ownership of the file and permissions.

6. Click the Group and Access pop-ups to change the group and access permissions.

7. Click the Others pop-up to create generic permissions for all other users.

8. Click Apply To Enclosed Items to apply the modified settings to all the items within a folder.

9. Click the Close button.

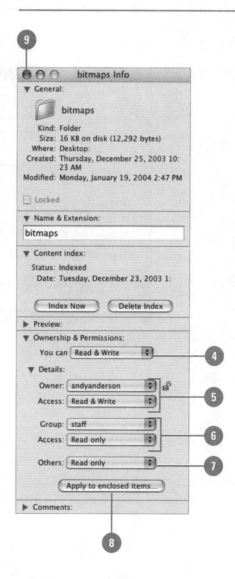

17

Connecting from a Windows Computer

After you enable Windows Sharing in the Sharing Services area of the System Preferences, Windows computers can connect to your computer. Most networks consist of multiple types of computers and operating systems. For Windows XP, My Network Places lets you view the entire network or just your part of the network to give you access to the servers, domains, and workgroups on the network. For a Windows XP computer on your immediate network, you can browse the network to access the Macintosh computer. If the Windows XP computer is outside your immediate network, you need to add a network place using the Macintosh computer address displayed in the Sharing pane when you enabled Windows Sharing.

Connect from a Windows XP Computer on a Local Network

1. Click the Start button, and then click My Network Places.

   TROUBLE? *For those using different versions of Windows, consult the online help system for specific instructions.*

2. In the Network Tasks area, click View Workgroup Computers.

3. In the Other Places area, click Microsoft Windows Network, and then click Workgroup.

4. Double-click the Mac OS X Computer icon to display the shared files, folders, and devices on the computer. If necessary, type a user name and password for the Mac account.

5. When you're done, click the Close button.

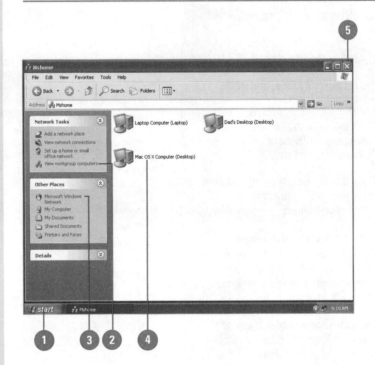

Connect from a Windows XP Computer Outside Your Network

① Click the Start button, and then click My Network Places.

② In the Network Tasks area, click Add A Network Place, and then click Next.

③ Click Choose Another Network Location, and then click Next.

④ Type the network address of your Macintosh computer. You can find the address in the Sharing pane under Services. Be sure to type it exactly as shown.

⑤ Click Next to continue.

TROUBLE? *If the addresses are not working, click View Some Examples for help.*

⑥ Type a name for the network place or use the suggested one, and then click Next.

⑦ To open the network, select the Open This Network Place When I Click Finish check box.

⑧ Click Finish.

See Also

See "Using Network Sharing Services" on page 392 for information on enabling Windows sharing and find the network address of your Macintosh computer.

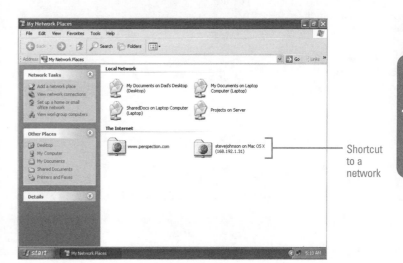

Shortcut to a network

17

Sharing an Internet Connection

If you have an always-on Internet connection, such as a cable modem or DSL, you can share that connection with all the other people in your network in two ways: purchase a router and gate everyone into the connection, or use the built-in Internet Sharing (it's free). The one requirement is that Internet Sharing must be activated on the Macintosh that's connected to the Internet.

Share an Internet Connection

1. Click the Apple menu, and then click System Preferences.

2. Click the Sharing icon.

3. Click the Internet tab.

4. Click the Share Your Connection From pop-up, and then select the method used for sharing.

5. Check Ports that other computers are using.

6. Click Start.

   IMPORTANT *If the Internet computer is shut down or in Sleep mode, the other network users won't be able to access the Internet.*

7. When you're finished, click the Close button.

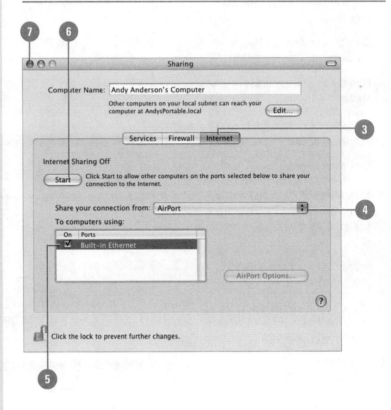

Configuring an Internet Firewall

If you're using a broadband Internet connection (always on), it's possible that a hacker could gain entrance to your system without your knowledge, and do some extensive damage or make off with your secret recipe for beef paprikash. Fortunately, Panther comes equipped with Firewall protection. A **Firewall** is a gatekeeper that in essence, stands guard over your computer; keeping it safe from all attackers. If vandals try to gain entrance to your computer, the Firewall attempts to shut them out. While no Firewall provides perfect protection from all Internet attacks, you can probably sleep soundly, knowing you probably have one of the most sophisticated protection systems on the market today.

Configure an Internet Firewall

1. Click the Apple menu, and then click System Preferences.

2. Click the Sharing icon.

3. Click the Firewall tab.

4. Check the Ports that you want to enable.

5. Click Start.

6. When you're finished, click the Close button.

Did You Know?

You can add additional access ports. Click New, and then click the Port Name pop-up to select from a list of additional ports. If your port is not listed, click Other.

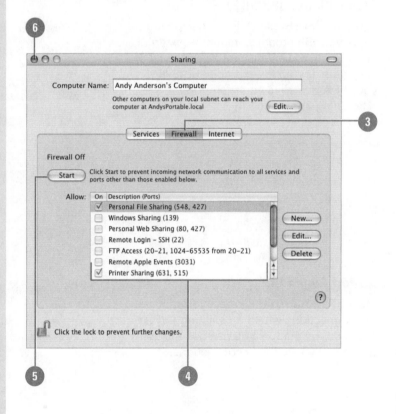

17

Exploring Additional Utility Applications

The Utilities folder, located within the Applications folder, is host to several dozen applications and utilities that help you manage the daily activities with running your Macintosh computer system, internet and wireless connections, and troubleshooting.

It's possible that you might go your entire life and never access some of the more obscure utilities located in this folder; however you should explore the available options, because some of them are useful.

Bluetooth Serial Utility

The Bluetooth Serial Utility is designed to allow your Bluetooth transmitter (external or internal), to serve as a wireless serial port, and let you, for example, HotSync your PDA device to your computer scheduling application.

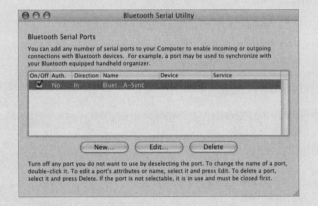

AirPort Admin Utility

The AirPort Admin Utility lets you monitor the connections within an existing AirPort network. In addition, you can use the utility to manually setup new connections.

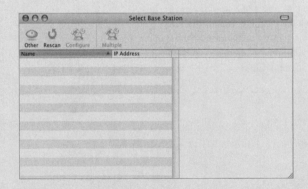

NetInfo Manager

The NetInfo Manager keeps track of all the user and group accounts currently on your computer. This is where a network manager can go to view, access, modify, and delete the various account settings.

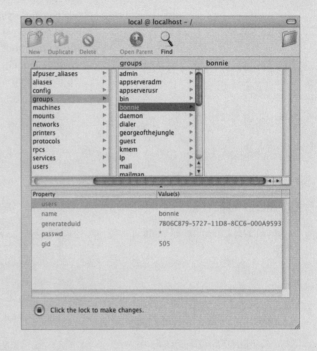

Network Utility

The Network Utility holds information on Web sites, and offers the ability to perform standard Internet services such as: NetStat, Ping, Finger, and Whois. When you're experiencing problems with your service, it's possible that a service technician (over the phone) may ask you to perform some of the above services.

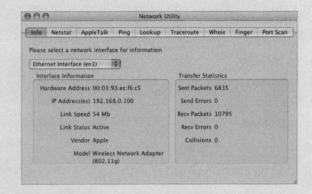

17

Setting Bluetooth Preferences

After you set up a Bluetooth wireless network on your computer, you can use System Preferences to control how to send and receive files between your computer and other Bluetooth devices (New!). You can use the Settings tab to make your Mac discoverable by other Bluetooth devices and specify whether you want to require a password. The File Exchange tab allows you to indicate what happens when someone sends you a document: accept it, refuse it, or ask what to do. Finally, the Devices tab lets you set up the use of other Bluetooth devices; use pairing to set passwords for security purposes.

Set Bluetooth Preferences

1 Click the Apple menu, and then click System Preferences.

2 Click the Bluetooth icon.

3 Click the Settings tab.

4 Select or clear the check boxes you want:

- ◆ Discoverable
- ◆ Require Authentication
- ◆ Support Non-Conforming Phones
- ◆ Allow Bluetooth Devices To Wake This Computer
- ◆ Open Bluetooth Setup Assistant At Startup When No Input Device Is Present
- ◆ Show Bluetooth Status In The Menu Bar

5 Click the File Exchange tab.

6 Select the options you want from the pop-ups:

- ◆ When Receiving Items
- ◆ When PIM Items Are Accepted
- ◆ When Other Items Are Accepted
- ◆ Folder For Accepted Items
- ◆ Allow Other Devices To Browse Files On This Computer

7 Click the Close button.

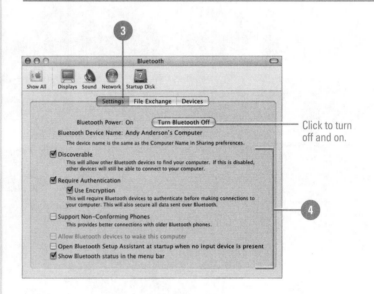

Click to turn off and on.

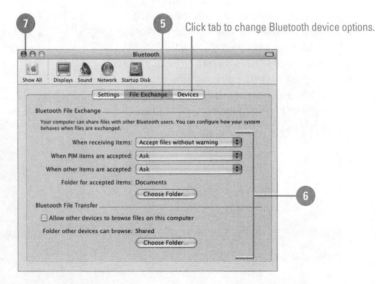

Click tab to change Bluetooth device options.

Maintaining Your Computer

Introduction

Once you've bought your Macintosh computer, installed the operating system and all your applications, it's important to be able to keep all that software up-to-date; especially the operating system software. With the consistent updates that Apple is making to the Panther operating system, Panther helps you keep all the software up-to-date with the click of a button.

In addition, loss of data can be a tragic occurrence, so Panther lets you archive or copy data from your computer to an external disk (just remember to keep your backups offsite). Panther also helps you monitor activities on your system, see who is currently using your computer, and how much processing power each program is using. This gives you the ability to fine-tune your system for maximum performance. If your system seems to be slowing down, or you're experiencing more crashes than usual (a rare occurrence on a Mac), Panther gives you the programs to optimize and repair day-to-day problems, and keep your system in tiptop shape.

Remember that maintaining your computer requires more on your part than the launching of a couple of programs. The Macintosh computer comes with several internal fans that help keep the inner workings cool; however, those fans also pull in dust. You should open your computer and vacuum out the interior about once a year, and dust the exterior surface about once a month. In addition, make sure the computer has enough room around it for air to circulate. Finally, make sure all the cables you have strung from the computer to all your peripherals are out of harms way, and in good condition. In past years, attempting to maintain your computer system was a challenge; however, today it's easy to keep things running smoothly.

Downloading and Installing Software

Let's face it, a computer without software is simply a very expensive boat anchor. On the other hand, software without a computer is useless. Once you install your software, it's important to keep up with all the updates, patches, and fixes. The Panther operating system comes bundled with literally dozens of software packages—everything from disk repair utilities to image-capture applications. In addition, hackers are causing problems and Apple stays on top of them with updates to Panther, which you can download from the Internet. After you download a software package, you can re-use the package file (.pkg) to install it on another Mac without re-downloading (**New!**).

Download and Install Software

1. Click the Apple menu, and then click Software Update.

   A screen appears with a status bar checking for software updates.

   IMPORTANT *Performing software updates requires an Internet connection.*

2. Check the software updates you want to load (if available).

3. Select an update, to read more information about that specific product.

4. Click the Install Items button.

5. Type your Administrator name and password.

6. Click OK.

   Panther begins installing the software. Follow any onscreen instructions, and then Close.

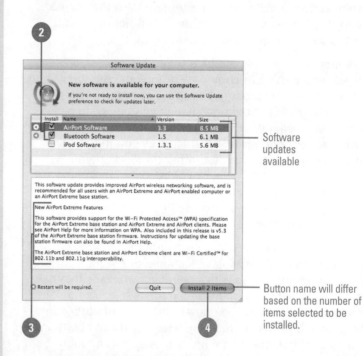

Software updates available

Button name will differ based on the number of items selected to be installed.

Did You Know?

You can uninstall software using the Trash icon. There's no uninstall program for Mac OS X. So, to uninstall an application, drag its folder from the Applications folder to the Trash icon in the Dock.

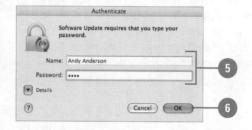

Automating Software Updates

Trying to keep up with all your software updates use to be a hassle, but not any more. Not only does Panther let you quickly download all your operating system software updates; it lets you automate the process. When you automate software updates, you select a specific time interval between checks. For example, you could instruct Panther to check for available updates every month. Panther even lets you download important updates in the background (New!), so it doesn't interrupt your workflow. With the ability not only to update your software, but also to automate the entire process, there is no longer any excuse for not having up-to-date software.

Automate Software Updates

1. Click the Apple menu, and then click System Preferences.

2. Click the Software Update icon.

3. Click the Update Software tab.

4. Select the Check For Updates check box.

5. Click the Updates pop-up, and then select how often Panther checks for updates.

6. Select the Download Important Updates In The Background check box to download updates without interrupting your workflow.

7. Click Check Now to check for any current updates.

8. To check all the updates you've currently installed, click the Installed Updates tab.

9. A list of updated files appears.

   You can scroll through the updates to view any changes to your system.

10. Click the Close button.

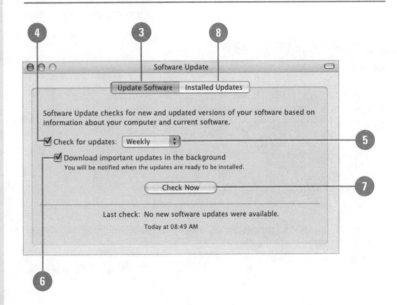

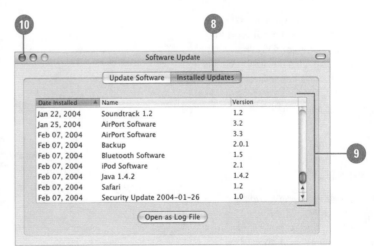

18

Opening Compressed Files

Not all compressed file formats are self-extracting. For those files you'll need a program capable of uncompressing (extracting) the files. Stuffit Expander is a universal utility that helps you open up all those pesky compressed files that other users and companies send you. The latest version (Stuffit v8), opens almost any compressed format including: .sit, .sea, .hqx, and, .bin. In addition, Stuffit can open files compressed using WinZip (Windows compression utility), and the UNIX formats: .tar, .gzip (**New!**), and .bzip. For example, you receive a WinZip file from your parents showing pictures of their trip to Hawaii or you download the latest software patch for your word-processing program, and it came the .hqz format. With Stuffit Expander, you're only seconds away from viewing those pictures and updating that word processor.

Open Compressed Files with Stuffit Expander

1. Open the Applications folder, and then double-click the Utilities folder or the Stuffit folder to locate the Stuffit Expander.

2. Select a compressed file.

3. Drag and drop the file over the Stuffit Expander icon.

4. Stuffit Expander uncompresses the file, and places it in the same location as the compressed file.

Did You Know?

The .dmg file format is self-extracting. A very popular format for OS X is the .dmg (disk image) format. When you double-click a .dmg file, it extracts the contents and creates a disk icon, which you can access and use just like any other Macintosh disk.

See Also

See "Backing Up and Restoring Compressed Files and Folders" on page 417 for information on compressing a file using Create Archive.

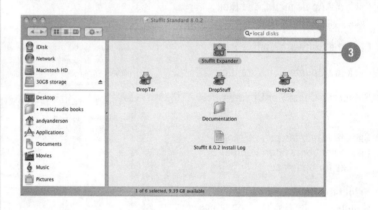

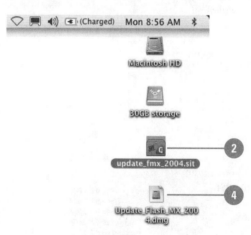

Backing Up and Restoring Compressed Files and Folders

If a computer's worth is the information it holds, then backing up your data is of extreme importance. You can create a backup of all the financial records for your company on a weekly basis, or just keep a backup of your important documents and records. If it's important to you, then back it up. Mac OS X gives you several ways to back up your data. You can use Backup, a full-featured backup utility available free for .Mac members; Disk Utility, which lets you select an entire volume to back up, or the Finder's Create Archive command (New!). The Create Archive command lets you create a highly-compressed version of one or more files or folders, and then save them onto another device, such as a rewritable CD, DVD, Zip, or JAZZ drive.

Back Up and Restore Compressed Data

1. Select a file, group of files, or a folder.

2. Click the File menu, and then click Create An Archive.

   Archive creates a zipped file with the same name as the original item.

3. To restore an archived zip, double-click it's icon.

   IMPORTANT *Remember that a back up of your data is your insurance of recovery after a disk crash or other catastrophic system failure. Always keep your backups offsite, or in a protected location, such as a fireproof safe. As tragic as a fire would be, the damage would be compounded if your backups were also destroyed.*

See Also

See "Opening Compressed Files" on page 416 for information on opening compressed files with Stuffit Expander.

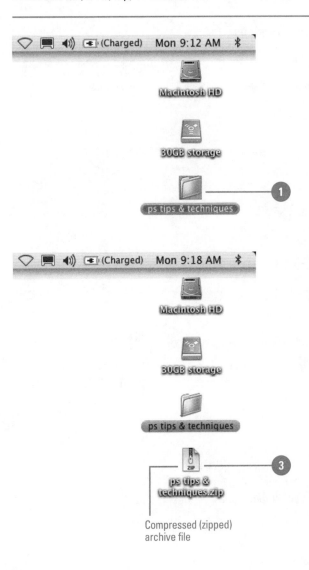

Compressed (zipped) archive file

18

Using Application Services

Application Services are a Mac OS X feature that lets you efficiently use content from one application to another application. It is based on an on-going project at Apple that would eventually give you the ability to use features between applications. For example, you could use the Services option to send selected text information in an e-mail, or use the spell-checker in MS Word to check the spelling of a document created in TextEdit. Unfortunately, it's still a work in progress, so when you select the Services option most of the choices are dimmed out. In fact, it won't work with most Carbonized versions of Mac applications. Consider it a work in progress. It does, however, work with iChat, TextEdit, Mail, and the Mac Finder.

Use Application Services

1 Open an application.

2 Click the Application menu, point to Services, and then select from the following options:

- ◆ BBEdit

- ◆ Finder

- ◆ Grab

- ◆ Import Image

- ◆ Mail

- ◆ Make New Sticky Note

- ◆ Open URL

- ◆ Script Editor

- ◆ Search With Google

- ◆ Send File To Bluetooth Device

- ◆ Speech

- ◆ Summarize

- ◆ TextEdit

3 Use the commands in the Services application you selected to insert material in your original application.

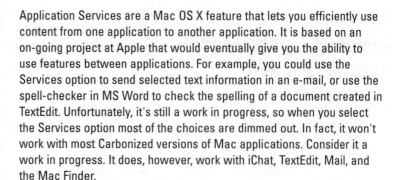

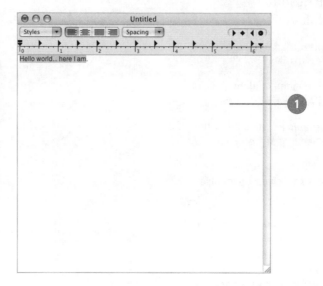

Understanding Disk File Systems

When you work on a computer, you're utilizing applications that are stored on the computer's hard drive. As you work, you're accessing and writing files back to the hard drive. For example, you open MS Word, create a document, and then save it using the name: MyLetter.doc.

Panther stores files and programs on your hard drive using a system of tracks and sectors; similar to a pie cut into equal triangular pieces. In addition, Panther divides the hard drive into logical file systems, which can help you organize your files and projects.

When you open your hard drive, you'll see that Panther has created several folders to organize your creative efforts. There's a folder for applications (both OS X and OS 9), and a folder for the System files—there's even a folder that contains all the users for the particular computer, and another for your documents.

Typically, when you load an application for the first time, you're asked to hold the application within the Applications folder. This gives Panther the ability to control the program, and even helps you when it comes time to check for updates. As you use your computer, you'll probably begin adding folders for your various projects. It's important that you create a disk file system that's well organized. Well organized file systems help you locate and retrieve files quicker and, if properly created, help you to move them from machine to machine. For example, you create a project folder for a major video project: everything that pertains to that project (video, audio, files, text, graphics), are all organized into folders within that one folder. When it come times to publish, move, or archive that information, all your files are conveniently organized in one location.

Tracks

Organized contents with folders

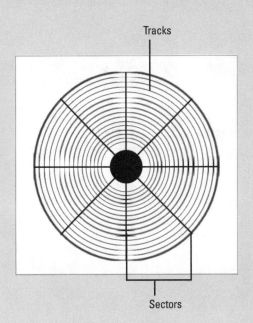

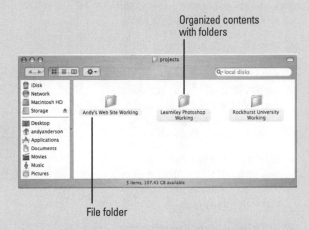

File folder

Sectors

Formatting and Copying a Disk

Computers are wonderful devices; however, it's the information they hold that makes them important. Not only is that information important on your computer, it might also be something you want to send to someone else or archive. In order to send or archive, you'll first need a disk. When you format a disk, you're actually telling the operating system to scrub the disk of all information, and prepare it for use. Make sure you backup any important data before performing the formatting operation. When using the Disk Utility to copy, Panther creates a mirror copy of the original. This differs from dragging and dropping a file onto a disk icon. When you drag and drop, Panther places the new files in whatever space is available. However, when you use Disk Utility, it places the files in exactly the same tracks and sectors as the original.

Format a Disk

1. Open the Applications folder, double-click the Utilities folder, and then double-click the Disk Utility icon.

2. Select the volume (disk) you want to format (you cannot format the startup drive).

3. Click the Erase tab.

4. Click the Volume Format pop-up, and select from the following options:

   ◆ **Mac OS Extended (Journaled).** Uses the same HFS Plus filing system as Mac OS Extended, and keeps a journal of your activities. Journaling makes for shortened startup times, and helps in the event of a crash (New!).

   ◆ **Mac OS Extended.** Formats the disk using HFS Plus filing system (helps to compress files and maximize file space).

   ◆ **UNIX File System.** Formats a disk for use on a UNIX system.

   ◆ **MS-DOS File System.** If available, formats a disk for use on a Windows (MS-DOS) system.

5. Type a Name for the formatted disk.

6. Click Erase.

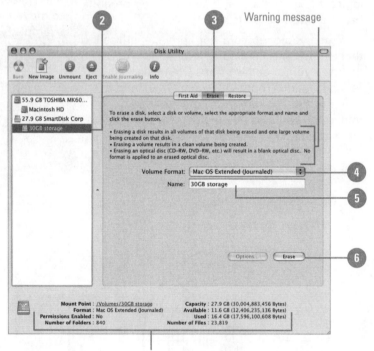

Warning message

Volume or disk statistics

Copy a Disk

1. Open the Applications folder, double-click the Utilities folder, and then double-click the Disk Utility icon.

2. Click the Restore tab.

3. Drag a disk image into the Source input box (the disk to copy).

4. Drag a disk image from the Disk Volume column into the Destination input box (the disk to copy onto).

5. Select the Erase Destination check box to instruct Panther to erase the Destination drive before performing the copy (recommended).

6. Select the Skip Checksum check box to instruct Panther not to perform a check of the Destination drive.

7. Click Restore.

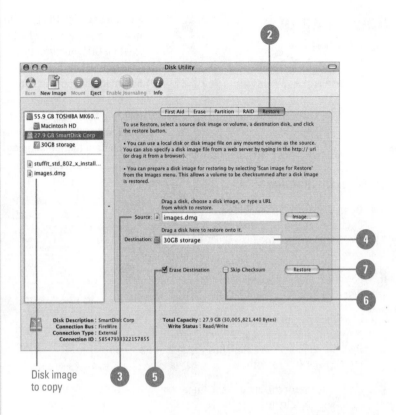

Disk image to copy

Did You Know?

You can copy information from a disk over the Internet. Type the URL of the disk you want to restore from into the Source input box.

You can create a new disk image. Select a disk or folder icon in the Disk Volume column, and then click the New Image button.

18

Recording or Duplicating a Data CD

You can use Disk Utility to quickly create a CD from data on your computer or make a copy of a CD that contains information. Before you can create a CD, you need to create a disk image (.dmg) of the contents. Once you create a disk image, you can make multiple CDs from the same disk image. If you select the Leave Disc Appendable option during the process, you can create a **multisession CD**; you burn data on a CD-R now, and then add to it later until there is no more room, just like a CD-RW. You can use the CD to transfer files from one computer to another, backup data for safekeeping, or restore the files on a disk.

Create a Disk Image

1. Open the Applications folder, double-click the Utilities folder, and then double-click the Disk Utility icon.

2. For duplicate, insert and select the disc you want in the left column.

3. Click the Images menu, point to New, and then click Image From Disk (for duplicate), or click Image From Folder (for record).

4. Type a name for the image, and then specify a save location.

5. Select an image format.

6. Click Save, and then quit Disk Utility.

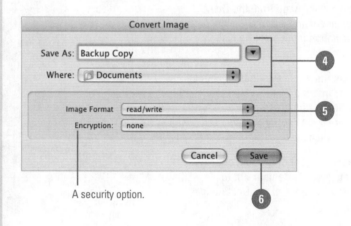

A security option.

Create a CD from an Image

1. Open the Utilities folder, and then double-click the Disk Utility icon.

2. Select the disk image or drag disk image file (.dmg) in the left column.

3. Click the Images menu, and then click Burn.

4. Insert a blank or multisession CD.

5. To burn a multisession CD, select the Leave Disc Appendable check box.

6. Click Burn or Append.

7. When it's done, quit Disk Utility.

Use Maximum Possible speed.

Click to collapse or expand dialog.

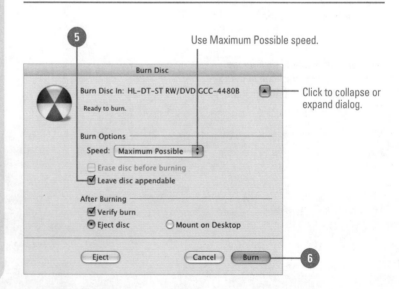

Fixing Disk Problems

It's not unusual for a hard drive to experience problems. When problems occur on the main hard drive, it can produce lock ups and slower performance. Apple helps to solve this problem by letting you perform disk repairs to any drives with the exception of the start up drive. For example, you could use disk repair to fix problems on a damaged JAZZ drive, or a secondary hard drive. Apple's Disk Utility locates and fixes problems with catalog and storage files. When information in these areas is damaged, it can cause trouble opening files and slowing down performance.

Fix Disk Problems

1. Open the Applications folder, double-click the Utilities folder, and then double-click the Disk Utility icon.

2. Click the First Aid tab.

3. Select a non-startup volume (you cannot repair the startup drive).

4. Click Repair Disk.

> **IMPORTANT** *You cannot repair the Startup volume. To perform a Repair Disk on the Startup volume, you'll have to reboot from a different disk.*

5. Repeat steps 3 and 4 until all your disks have been repaired.

> **TIMESAVER** *Applications such as Norton Utilities and Tech Tools can help to further enhance and optimize your hard drives, by performing a defrag, or by performing error checks to files not available with the Apple Disk Utility.*

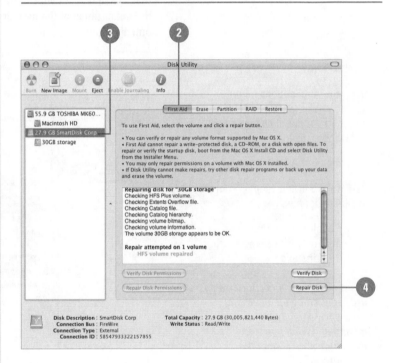

18

Optimizing a Disk

Your computer uses a storage device to hold applications and data. Typically this would be the main hard drive. Not only is the storage of that information important, but timely retrieval is also an important consideration. Every computer user wants their system to run as efficiently as possible. Faster computers should perform operations such as: opening applications, saving files, and performing normal operations faster than older computers. However, you may notice that after a while your computer doesn't seem to be operating as fast as it did previously—files that took a few seconds to open now take a minute. The problem lies in the optimization of the hard drive, and Panther gives you several ways to optimize your hard drive.

Optimize a Disk

➊ Open the Applications folder, double-click the Utilities folder, and then double-click the Disk Utility icon.

➋ Click the First Aid tab.

➌ Select the Startup volume from the available options.

➍ Click Repair Disk Permissions (available only for volumes with Mac OS X installed).

IMPORTANT *Disk Permissions are required by the operating system, and can become damaged. When they are damaged, normal operations become slower.*

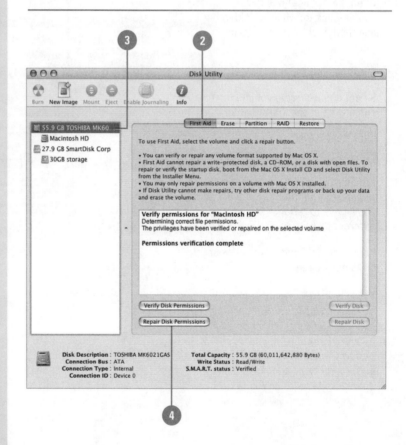

5 Select a folder or hard drive icon.

6 Click the File menu, and then click Get Info.

7 Click the expand button (triangle) for Content Index.

8 Click Index Now to create an ordered index of all the files within the item.

The Index Now button creates a physical index of all the items within the hard drive, or folder that makes search operations lightning fast.

TIMESAVER *Since the index is used in search operations, you can select certain folders that you never would need to search in, and then click the Delete Index button to remove the index file. Not only does this save disk space, but also prevents all those unwanted file names from popping up in your searches.*

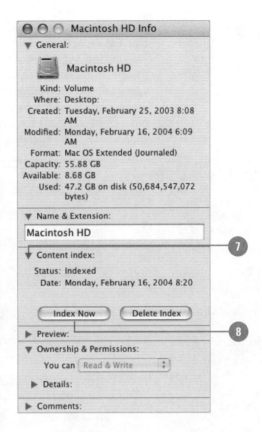

For Your Information

Optimizing Your Hard Drive

When you optimize your hard drive, you're not just increasing the drive's efficiency; you're increasing your efficiency. Benchmark tests reveal that keeping your hard drive in tiptop shape, actually makes the drive perform eight to ten percent faster. That means programs operate faster, opening and working on graphic files is faster; everything is faster. Time spent in optimizing your hard drive is time well spent.

18

Monitoring System Activities

Panther lets you view exactly how much processor power the various files and applications you have open are using, by utilizing the Activity Monitor. The Activity Monitor is a highly accurate tool that gives you up-to-date information on the various operations currently being used on your computer. It gives you the ability to view the process on a live graph, and even to halt various processes. In addition, if you own a multi-processor Mac, you'll see a separate graph for each processor to let you know how well the operating system is dividing the load.

Monitor System Activities

1. Open the Applications folder, double-click the Utilities folder, and then double-click the Disk Utility icon.

2. Select a process from the available options.

3. To view more information, click the Inspect button.

4. To save the current process list, click the Export button.

5. To force a quit of the selected process, click the Quit Process button.

6. To search for a specific process, enter a search string in the Filter field.

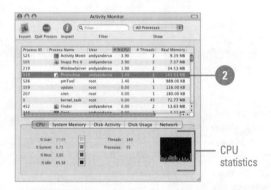

CPU statistics

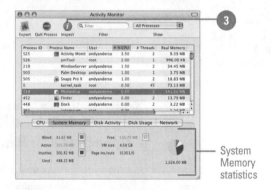

System Memory statistics

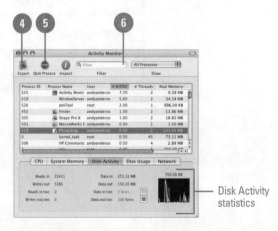

Disk Activity statistics

7 To view selected processes, click the Process pop-up.

8 Select from the following monitoring tabs:

◆ **CPU.** Select to view a graph of the process currently active.

◆ **System Memory.** Select to view the current distribution of system memory.

◆ **Disk Activity.** Select to view information on the current disk activities.

◆ **Disk Usage.** Select to view disk usage on the selected disk (click the Disk pop-up to select a disk).

◆ **Network.** Select to view the current activity across the network.

9 Click the Close button.

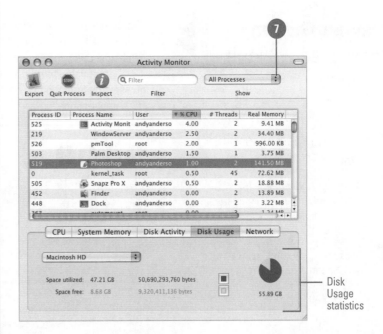

Disk Usage statistics

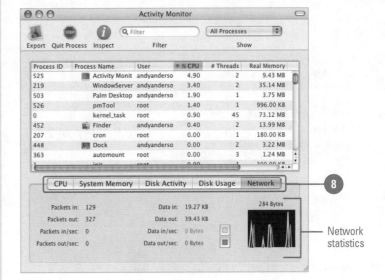

Network statistics

18

Viewing System Messages with the Console

The Console utility is a viewer that displays all the text-based messages sent between the Macintosh operating system, and all open applications. While this utility may seem a bit much for the average Macintosh user, it's of great value to programmers, or would-be programmers, because it gives you information on how the operating system communicates with OS X applications.

View System Messages with the Console

1. Open the Applications folder, double-click the Utilities folder, and then double-click the Disk Utility icon.

2. Click Logs, and then select from the available Console logs.

3. To erase the current log, click Clear.

4. To reload the active log, click Reload.

5. To add a day/date stamp to the log, click Mark.

6. To look for a specific function, type a search value into the Filter field.

7. To add or subtract buttons from the Console toolbar, click the View menu, and then click Customize Toolbar. Select the item to add or subtract.

8. To change the font used in displaying Console messages, click the Font menu, and then click Show Fonts.

9. If necessary, make any changes to the Font family and size.

10. Click the Close button.

11. Click Done.

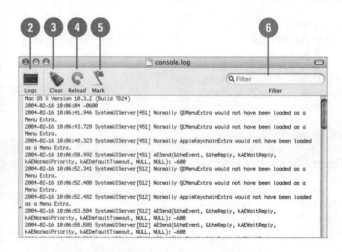

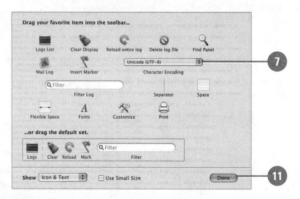

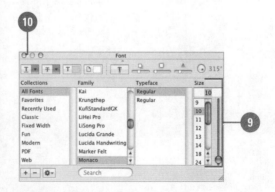

Viewing System Information with System Profiler

The System Profiler gives you an exact record of what applications you have installed on your computer; along with information on the installed hardware, system extensions, and current network. It's a great place to go, if you're curious about what you've got. For example, the System Profiler not only gives you information on your installed applications, it also tells what version (including patches) you've got, and the last time you updated it. The System Profiler also gives you detailed information on your processor; its speed, and any external devices, such as your hard drives and scanners.

View System Information with System Profiler

1. Open the Applications folder, double-click the Utilities folder, and then double-click the Disk Utility icon.

2. Select an item from the Contents column.

3. View information on the selected item in the Info window.

4. Click the View menu, and then select from Short Report, Standard Report (default), or Extended Report.

5. Click the File menu, and then click to Save Print or Export the current report.

6. Click the Close button.

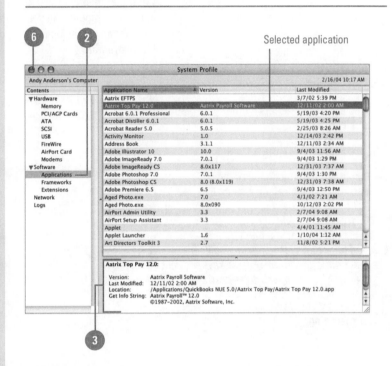

Selected application

Did You Know?

You can use System Profiler to check if you have a CD or DVD recordable drive on your computer. Launch System Profiler from the Utilities folder, click the triangle to expand the Hardware category, click the ATA (internal), USB, FireWire, or SCSI category, and then look for CD-R, DVD-R, CD-RW, or DVD-RW. Any of these means you can burn a CD or DVD. If it says simply CD or DVD, then you can't.

18

Forcing a Restart

When OS X was first unveiled to the Apple community, many users sat back and waited to see how this new operating system would fit into the Mac world, and over the years, it has won over even its harshest critics. With its ability to process information ultra fast, and its UNIX base, it has become the system of choice for the discriminating Mac user. Apple OS X is the first "true" multi-processing operating system to appear in the Mac market. When you open a program, the UNIX-based operating system runs the application within a protected area of the CPU memory. When a second program is opened, it gets its own CPU working areas. What that means to you is that a program crash no longer means restarting your computer. All you have to do is force the program to quit. In the event of a system lockup, you can even instruct the operating system to force a restart.

Force a Restart

1. Click the Apple menu, and then click Force Quit.

2. Click Finder.

3. Click Relaunch to conduct a mini restart of the operating system.

    TIMESAVER *If your system is so locked up that you can't access the Force Quit command, just hold down the* ⌘ *+Control+Power keys to force your computer to restart.*

4. Follow any onscreen instructions for restarting.

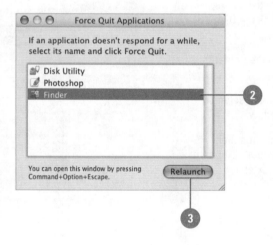

Did You Know?

When you perform a mini restart, you're just relaunching the Finder. Any other programs that were open remain open.

Managing Hardware

19

Introduction

Computer systems are composed of more than just a computer (that's why they're called systems). A computer houses a hard drive, and is connected to a keyboard, mouse, and video display. All of these hardware devices are required to operate your computer. For most users that's just the start, you'll probably have one or more printers, a scanner; maybe even a second monitor. Then of course, there are digital cameras, fax machines... you get the idea.

Computers are made up of a group of hardware devices, and like a conductor at a symphony, Panther helps you work with those devices, by making the installation, management, and removal easy. In addition, Panther can help you manage color between devices, help you install MIDI (audio) devices, and even make Internet communications easy. If the worst of the worst problems occur (a system crash), there are steps you can perform to bring your computer system back on line, and you don't even have to be a techie.

What You'll Do

Install Hardware Devices

View Hardware Settings

Change Mouse Settings

Change Keyboard Settings

Change Modem Options

Change Phone Settings

Change Monitor Display Settings

Measure Display Colors with the Digital Color Meter

Select Colors with the Color Picker

Match Colors to Devices with ColorSync

Configure Audio MIDI Devices

Prevent Hardware Problems

Remove Hardware Devices

Installing Hardware Devices

Years ago, hardware installation required all kinds of techniques and special skills. A hardware device such as a printer, could take hours to set up. There were all kinds of cabling problems, and even after it was installed, there were numerous settings to complete before you could use the device. Today, many devices are plug-and-play. You can now go out to your local computer store, pick up a FireWire hard drive, plug it in to your computer, and immediately begin using it. The same is true for many other devices, such as card readers and digital cameras. Even if the device requires the installation of a driver (printers and scanners usually do), a double-click on the install application and answering a few simple questions is typically all that's needed.

Install Hardware Devices

1. Insert the install CD into your computer (assuming the device is not plug-and-play) or navigate to the installer on your computer or network.

2. Launch the installation application.

   TROUBLE? *Some installations require the device be plugged into your computer. Make sure the device is plugged in, and if necessary, powered on.*

3. Follow the instructions for installing the device (some devices may require a reboot of the system).

4. When the installation is finished, follow the on-screen instructions to end the process.

Did You Know?

You can purchase a power strip (also known as a surge protector) to help with all those power plugs. If you install several hardware devices that require their own external power supplies, such as printers and scanners, you can invest in a power strip, and to protect against power spikes, make sure it's a surge-protected power strip.

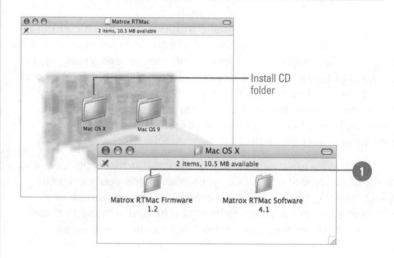

Install CD folder

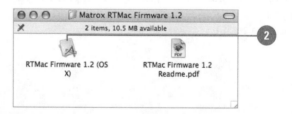

Viewing Hardware Settings

Most hardware devices have settings that control how the device operates. For example, all ink-jet printers have settings that control the type of paper used, how the inks are applied to the paper and, if your printer has more than a single paper tray, which tray is used for the current printing process. Panther uses the System Preferences panel to display all of the available hardware settings for the major components of the operating system. In addition, when you install specific hardware devices such as a third-party mouse or video-control board, you'll see an icon for controlling the device in the System Preferences.

View Hardware Settings

1. Click the Apple menu, and then click System Preferences.

   The Hardware section holds the icons to Panther's standard hardware devices.

2. Click on an icon to view or modify the hardware settings of the selected device.

3. When you're finished viewing or modifying the settings, select the following options:

   ◆ **About.** Provides information on the manufacturer of the device; including the hardware version and Web site (if any).

   ◆ **Help.** Gives you access to the Help dialog for the selected device.

   ◆ **Revert.** Puts the settings back to their previous selections.

   ◆ **Apply Now.** Applies the changes to the settings.

   ◆ **Close.** Closes the pop-up.

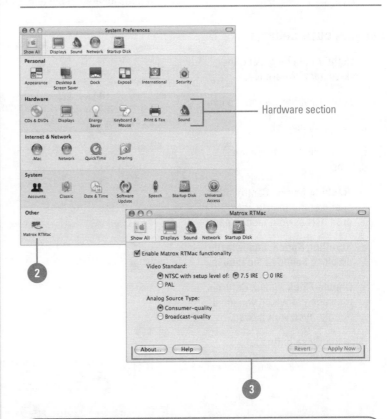

Hardware section

For Your Information

Updating Drivers

Many Mac users are purchasing the new G5 Macintosh's and are receiving the Panther operating system. Although your hardware devices may have worked without a hitch on your old G4 machine, they may not on the G5. Check out the Web site for the device that you are installing and see if you have the latest drivers. More and more hardware devices are becoming G5 compliant every day.

Changing Mouse Settings

When you use any computer, a mouse is an important part of the computing experience. Computers communicate with the user through a series of Graphical User Interfaces or a G.U.I. (pronounced Gooey). The user communicates with the computer through several devices, such as: a touch screen, a keyboard, a drawing tablet and a mouse. Using a mouse requires a bit of hand-to-eye coordination: You see something on the screen (a button perhaps), and you move the mouse pointer over the object and click. Apple understands the importance of the mouse, and gives you ways to control its movement and sensitivity through preferences located in System Preferences.

Change Mouse Settings

1. Click the Apple menu, and then click System Preferences.

2. Click the Keyboard & Mouse icon.

3. Click the Mouse tab.

4. Drag to adjust the following options:

   ◆ **Tracking Speed.** Controls the speed of the mouse as you drag across your mouse pad.

   ◆ **Scrolling Speed.** Controls the scrolling speed of the mouse.

   ◆ **Double-Click Speed.** Controls the speed at which you must double-click your mouse.

5. Click the Close button.

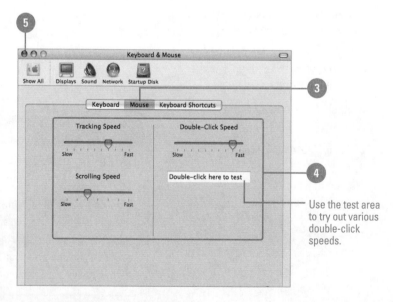

Use the test area to try out various double-click speeds.

Changing Keyboard Settings

Your keyboard is another one of those wonderful devices that help us communicate with a computer. Keyboards have what is called a **tactile feel** (the way the keys bounce back when they're pressed). Although you can't control the tactile feel of a keyboard, you can control how the keyboard's repeat functions work through System Preferences. Keyboard shortcuts allow you to quickly perform a task by pressing keys on your keyboard. You can change or disable many global keyboard shortcuts (**New!**), the same shortcuts in all applications, to avoid conflicts or customize to suit your own work preferences.

Change Keyboard Settings

1. Click the Apple menu, and then click System Preferences.

2. Click the Keyboard & Mouse icon.

3. Click the Keyboard tab.

4. Drag the Key Repeat Rate slider to adjust the speed at which a repeating key is typed.

5. Drag the Delay Until Repeat slider to adjust the length of time you have to hold down a key before it begins repeating.

6. Click the Close button.

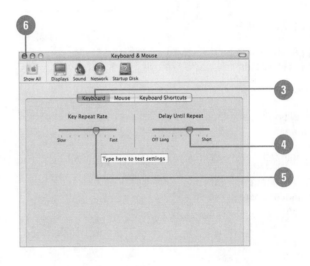

Customize Keyboard Shortcuts

1. Click the Apple menu, and then click System Preferences.

2. Click the Keyboard & Mouse icon.

3. Click the Keyboard Shortcuts tab.

4. To disable a shortcut, clear the check box next to the description.

5. To change a key combination, click the characters, hold down the new shortcut key combination you want.

6. Click the Close button, and then restart any application that uses it.

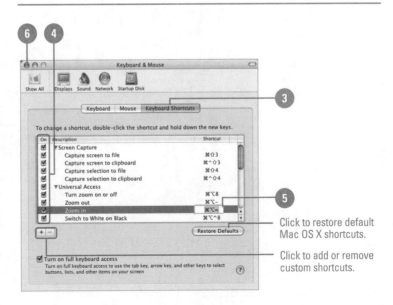

Click to restore default Mac OS X shortcuts.

Click to add or remove custom shortcuts.

Changing Modem Options

Not only are computers great devices to create text documents, generate awesome graphics and animations, they're also communication devices. Most computers come with a built-in modem that can be used to send e-mails or check the latest stock quotes by using the Web. Apple gives you the ability to modify the modem settings to fit your particular work method, and to type in information concerning your Internet service provider. Apple modems are typically built into the computer (that's why they're called internal); however, whether your modem is hidden inside your computer or attached by a cable, you'll need to run through some simple set up procedures before using it for the first time.

Change Modem Options

1. Click the Apple menu, and then click System Preferences.

2. Click the Network icon.

3. Click the Show pop-up, and then select your modem.

4. Click the Modem tab.

5. Click the Modem pop-up, and then select your modem from the available options.

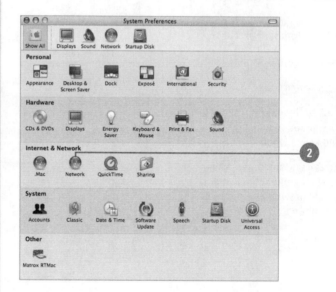

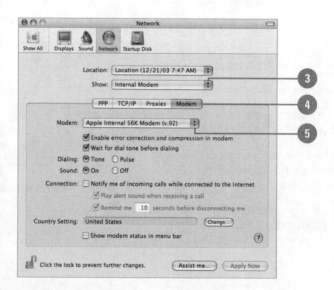

6 Select from the following modem setting options:

◆ **Enable Error Correction And Compression In Modem.** Check to activate error correction and to compress data packets during transmission (recommended).

◆ **Wait For Dial Tone Before Dialing.** Check to instruct the dialing computer to wait until it receives a dial tone.

◆ **Dialing.** Click the Tone or Pulse dialing option (most phone systems utilize tone).

◆ **Sound.** Click the On or Off option to hear dialing and connection sounds through your computer's internal (or external) speakers.

◆ **Connection.** Check to have the computer display a dialog when an incoming call is detected.

◆ **Play Alert Sound When Receiving A Call.** Check to have the computer use an audible alert for an incoming call.

◆ **Remind Me.** Check to remind, and then enter (in seconds) how long before disconnecting (due to inactivity).

◆ **Country Setting.** Click Change to modify the country settings for the modem.

◆ **Show Modem Status In Menu Bar.** Check to display the modem symbol on the Apple status bar.

7 Click Apply Now.

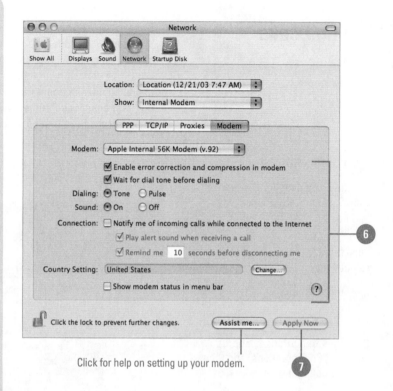

Click for help on setting up your modem.

Changing Phone Settings

Once you have your modem properly set up, it's time to begin dialing up. Your computer modem can be used to dial into the Internet, send e-mail, or even make telephone calls (Internet phone software required). Whatever you use your modem for, it requires information such as: phone number, account name, and password to complete the connection. Not only does Panther give you the ability to dial out, it lets you create several different accounts that you can switch to as needed.

Change Phone Options

1. Click the Apple menu, and then click System Preferences.

2. Click the Network icon.

3. Click the Show pop-up, and then select your modem.

4. Click the PPP tab.

5. Click Dial Now.

6. Click the Configurations pop-up, click Edit Configurations, and then select a configuration.

7. Select from the following modem options:

   ◆ **Description.** Type a short description of the account.

   ◆ **Telephone Number.** Enter the telephone number (remember to include area code, or any addition numbers, like dialing 9 for an outside line).

   ◆ **Account Name.** Type the account name (typically your e-mail address).

   ◆ **Password.** Type the password for the account.

   ◆ **Prompt For Password After Dialing.** Check to type your password in every time you dial this account.

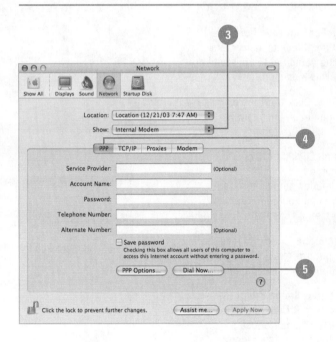

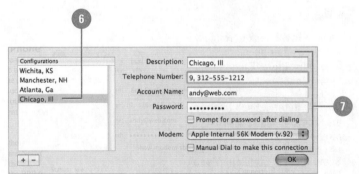

- ◆ **Modem.** Click the pop-up and select the modem.

- ◆ **Manual Dial To Make This Connection.** Check to manually dial the account (useful for pay phones where you have to type in a calling card number).

8 To add additional accounts, click the Add button (+).

9 To remove a selected account, click the Delete button (-).

10 Click OK.

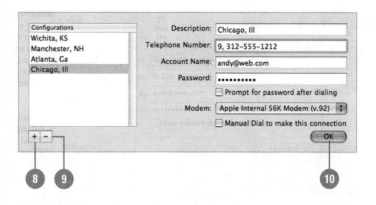

For Your Information

Moving Your Phone List

A well-developed phone list is a valuable asset. In fact, it's so valuable, you might want to use that phone list on another computer. If you would like to move your phone list to another Macintosh computer (and save yourself a lot of typing), open Internet Connect, click the File menu, and then click Export Configurations. Simply select the list items you want to export, and then click Export. You'll be instructed to name the file and select a destination, and then click Save. All you have to do is move the file to another computer, open Internet Connect, click the File menu, and then click Import Configurations.

Changing Monitor Display Settings

Your monitor is the main interface between you and your computer. A monitor displays all your programs and mouse movements. Without a monitor, you would in fact be attempting to operate your computer with your eyes closed. Apple, in a effort to give you the best possible view of it's wonderful operating system interface, gives you the ability to modify how your monitor displays data, through options located in System Preferences.

Change Monitor Display Settings

1 Click the Apple menu, and then click System Preferences.

2 Click the Displays icon.

3 Click the Display tab.

4 Select from the following options:

◆ **Resolutions.** Select a display resolution from the options.

◆ **Colors.** Click the pop-up, and then select the number of colors to display.

◆ **Refresh Rate.** Click the pop-up to set a refresh rate.

◆ **Detect Displays.** Searches for any additional displays attached to the computer.

◆ **Show Displays In Menu Bar.** (New!) Check to display the Displays icon on the Apple menu bar.

◆ **Number Of Recent Modes.** Click the pop-up, and then select how many recent modes to display.

◆ **Brightness.** Changes the bright-ness of the monitor (a PowerBook feature).

◆ **Automatically Adjust Brightness As Ambient Light Changes.** Automatically adjusts the brightness of the monitor to compensate for external lights (a PowerBook feature).

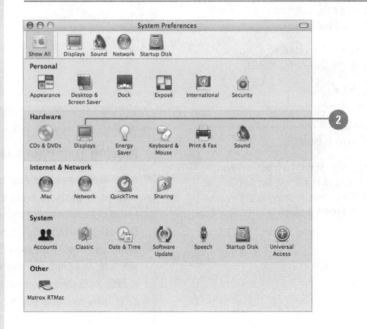

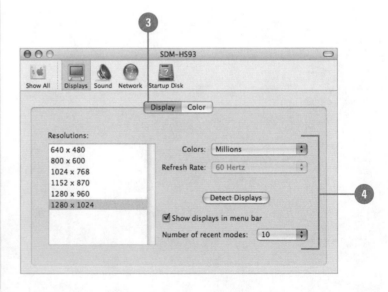

5 Click the Color tab.

6 Select from the following color options:

◆ **Display Profile.** Scroll through the list to select a color display profile for the monitor.

◆ **Show Profiles For This Display Only.** Check to display profiles for the current monitor.

◆ **Calibrate.** Click Calibrate to manually calibrate the color of the monitor.

7 Click the Close button.

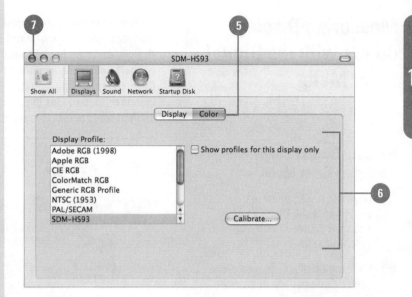

Measuring Display Colors with the Digital Color Meter

Have you ever wondered what the exact color value of an item on your monitor would be if measured using RGB (red, green, and blue) values? Or how about the hexadecimal value of a color (useful if you design Web pages)? Color is an important part of any designer's life, and the Digital Color meter lets you accurately sample colors from your monitor. Since the cursor determines the sampled color, you'll need to learn a few shortcut keys to lock, print, and save the color information.

Measure Display Colors with the Digital Color Meter

1. Open the Applications folder, double-click the Utilities folder, and then double-click the Digital Color Meter icon.

2. Click the Color pop-up, and then select a color space to measure.

3. Drag the Aperture Size slider left or right, to decrease or increase the area used for the taking of a screen shot.

4. Move the mouse over the monitor to measure the color directly underneath the cursor.

5. To hold a color into the color swatch box, press ⌘+Shift+H.

6. To lock the screen shot of the current image, press ⌘+L.

7. Click the Image menu, and then click Save As TIFF to save the current locked screen shot as a TIFF image.

8. Click the Color menu, and then click Copy Color As Text or Copy Color As Image to save the held color in clipboard memory. The color can then be copied into another program.

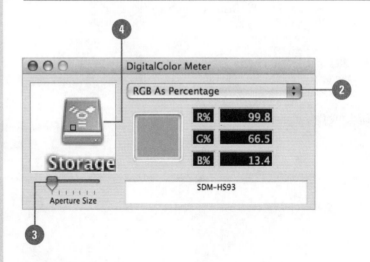

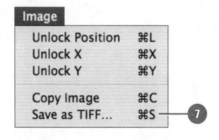

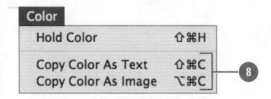

Selecting Colors with the Color Picker

The world of color on a computer is a very subjective place to live. For example, you might be using a new Macintosh Studio Display, and someone else might be using a Sony LCD monitor. What this means to you is, a color displayed on your hardware device (monitor) might look slightly different on another computer using a different monitor. In addition, it's possible that two people, owning the same monitor, may have them adjusted differently. While creating consistent color output is a difficult thing, Panther gives you a stable color picking system, which helps to stabilize colors systems. The Macintosh Color Picker is accessed through an application, such as MS Word or Photoshop, or any application that lets you select colors.

Select Colors with the Color Picker

1. Open an application, such as MS Word.

2. Select a button, such as text color, and then click More Colors.

3. Click a palette, and then select a color from the available color profiles:

   ◆ **Color Wheel.** Drag the scroll bar vertically to adjust the brightness, and then click inside the ball, to select a color.

   ◆ **Color Slider.** Select a color mixing method from the pop-up, and then drag the sliders to select a color.

   ◆ **Color Palettes.** Select a pre-designed color palette from the pop-up, and then select the color from the available list.

   ◆ **Image Palettes.** Displays a spectrum of colors. Click in the spectrum to select a color.

   ◆ **Crayons.** Select a color from the available crayons.

4. Click OK to retrieve the color or click the Close button.

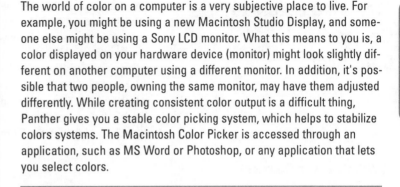

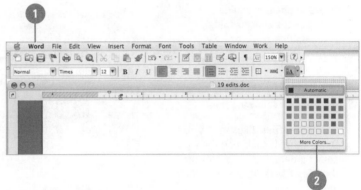

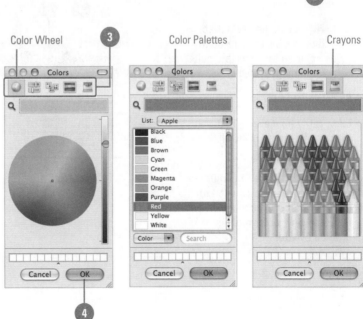

Color Wheel   Color Palettes   Crayons

Matching Colors to Devices with ColorSync

The ColorSync utility gives the designer the ability to match up colors between devices, and to check on and repair the device color profiles present on the computer. As you might have figures out by now, computer monitors are not the best at maintaining color accuracy; especially between monitor and print. The ColorSync utility strives to maintain a color standard between devices, by acting as a translator between different devices. The original scanned image, your monitor, and the output printing device are all examples of where color needs to be synced, and it is achieved though the ColorSync utility.

Match Colors to Devices with ColorSync

1. Open the Applications folder, double-click the Utilities folder, and then double-click the ColorSync Utility icon.

2. Click Preferences.

3. Select from the following tabs:

   ◆ **Default Profiles.** Click the Default Profiles tab, and then select a default color profile for the RGB, CMYK, and Gray color modes.

   ◆ **CMMs.** Click the CMMs tab, and then click the pop-up to select from the available color management systems.

4. Click Profile First Aid.

5. Click Verify (to view) or Repair (to fix) the color profiles installed on your computer.

6. Click Profiles to view a gamut grid of the color profiles installed for your computer (click the user option to view color profiles created by you).

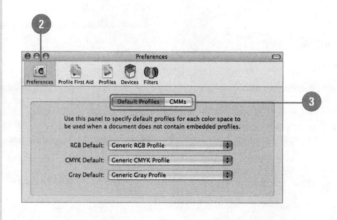

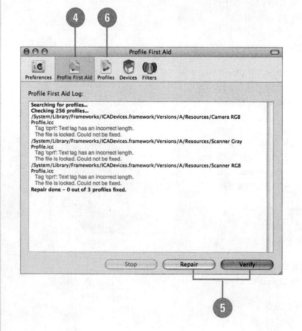

7. To select and assign color profiles to all installed devices, click Devices.

8. To view information on the currently installed filters, click Filters.

9. Click Add, Delete, and Duplicate to add a new filter, delete the selected filter, or create a duplicate of a filter.

10. Click View File With Filter to view the filter with an associated color profile.

IMPORTANT *The ColorSync Utility gives you the ability to view and change the color profiles used by different devices. This is an area where you don't want to experiment. Have a good understanding of color theory, before attempting to change any of the ColorSync settings.*

11. Click the Close button.

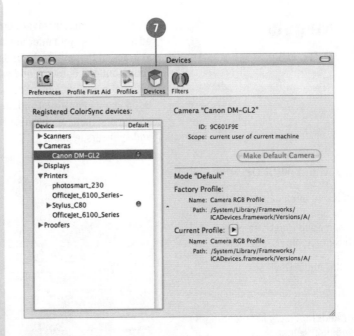

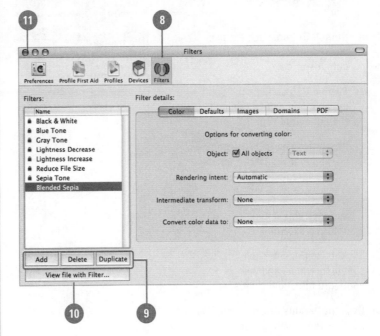

Configuring Audio MIDI Devices

Macintosh computers were born to work with music, and as the years advanced they got better and better. The Audio MIDI (Musical Instrument Digital Interface) Setup utility is designed to help you setup all your input and output sound equipment. Of course, if you don't own any external audio equipment then you'll probably never need to come here. But it you do work a lot with audio, Apple has made the process of adding and monitoring external devices, such as electronic keyboards and speakers, a snap.

Configure Audio MIDI Devices

1. Open the Applications folder, double-click the Utilities folder, and then double-click the Audio MIDI Setup icon.

2. Click the Audio Devices tab.

3. Select from the following options:

   ◆ **Default Input.** Click the pop-up, and then select a default input source.

   ◆ **Default Output.** Click the pop-up, and then select a default output source.

   ◆ **System Output.** Click the pop-up, and then select a default system output source.

   ◆ **Properties For.** Click the pop-up, and then select properties for the default audio source.

   ◆ **Clock Source.** Click the pop-up, and then select a clock (internal/external).

4. Click the various Audio Input section pop-ups, and then configure the audio input sources.

5. Click the various Audio Output section pop-ups, and then configure the audio output sources.

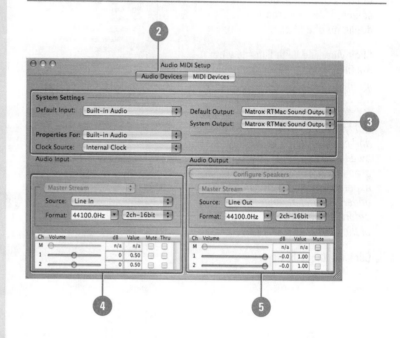

6 Click the MIDI Devices tab.

7 Select from the following options:

◆ **View Icon Size.** Drag the slider left or right to decrease or increase the size of the MIDI icons.

◆ **Configuration.** Click the pop-up, and then select from the available configuration options.

◆ **Add Device.** Click to add a MIDI device.

◆ **Remove Device.** Click to remove a MIDI device.

◆ **Show Info.** Click to show information about the selected device.

◆ **Rescan MIDI.** Click to rescan for additional MIDI devices attached to your computer.

◆ **Test Setup.** Click to test the current configuration.

8 Click the Close button.

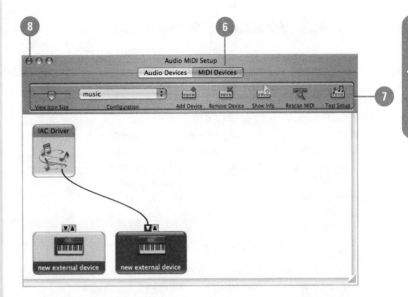

For Your Information

Customizing Icons

You can customize the icons used for additional MIDI devices. Double-click on the icon you want to change to open the Properties dialog, and then click on the image icon to open up a list of alternate images. If the additional device you're adding is a keyboard, you can use the Keyboard icon. Using icons to visually define your MIDI devices makes it easier for you to match the devices to other devices. Click the Apply button to apply the changes to the selected device.

Preventing Hardware Problems

Whenever you add hardware devices to your computer, the possibility exists that a problem will occur. Problems can fall into several categories: The device doesn't work, the device doesn't work the way you expect, or the computer refuses to boot. Apple's built-in management systems make hardware problems a rare event. However, a few careful steps on your part can help to make problems almost non-existent.

Check for hardware device compatibility

Not all hardware devices are compatible with your particular version of Macintosh. For example, you could purchase a video driver board, which works fine in a G3 or G4 model, but won't function in a G5. Make sure the user's manual lists your model of Macintosh.

Check for software compatibility

Many hardware devices require installation software to operate. Even though OS X has been in the market for a couple of years, there are still hardware devices with accompanying installation software that is not compatible with the OS X operating system. In addition, the Panther operating system changed the rules on computer architecture; therefore, make sure the software is not just OS X compatible, but is also Panther compatible.

Check the Internet

Software changes (almost on a weekly basis), when you purchase a piece of hardware, that box may have been sitting on the shelf for months. Make sure you access the device's Internet site, and determine if you have the latest version of the software. It's easy and it's free.

Plan for the future

If you haven't purchased a G5 (yet), you probably will in the future. Be advised that some of your hardware devices may not work with the G5 architecture. Many times it's the software for the device. Some hardware manufacturers can take months to develop the software necessary to operate your hardware devices on the G5, and some have no plans to upgrade at all. When you purchase new hardware, check the manufacturer's Web site, and see if they plan on supporting future Macintosh computers.

When the worst happens

Sometimes, you install a hardware device, and your Macintosh refuses to startup. Many times it's because you just installed a new hardware device. Unfortunately, when you disconnect the device your Mac still won't startup. The reason is because the software that runs the device is still installed. When this happens you can attempt a fix by performing a "Safe" boot.

First, you'll need to power down your computer. After your computer has shut off, go ahead and press the power button. After you hear the startup tone, immediately press and hold the Shift key. You'll release the Shift key when you see the gray Apple and progress indicator (looks like a spinning gear).

The Safe Mode takes awhile to boot (several minutes). That's because Safe Mode performs a system check before starting. Then, you'll use the hardware device's installation CD to remove the installed hardware. After that is done, restart your computer the normal way (without holding the Shift key).

If removing the device software does not solve the problem, your glitch may be caused by something more serious. You can attempt a reinstall of the OS X operating system, but before doing that, go online and check out the .Mac Web site and search for help on your problem. When there is no solution but to start over, or get a new device, you'll need to remove the hardware device and the software that controls it.

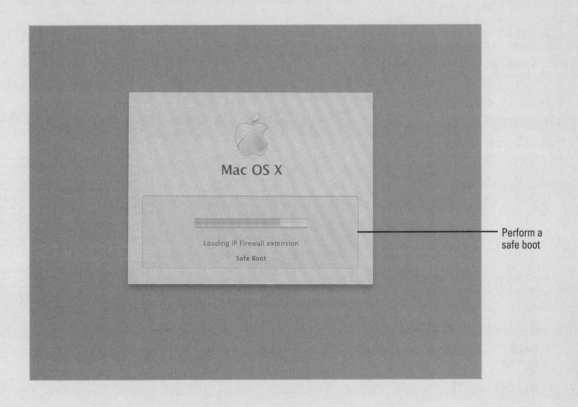

Perform a safe boot

Removing Hardware Devices

Installing hardware can be relatively easy: you insert the installation CD and follow the onscreen instructions. However, when you remove a hardware device, the software that ran the device is still on your computer. It's important to remove any software that is not longer needed for two reasons: it takes up space on your hard drive, and it could cause problems in the future with the installation of other hardware devices.

Remove Hardware Devices

1 Startup your computer.

2 Use the third-party software's original installer CD to remove the recently installed software.

   IMPORTANT *If you do not have the original CD, check the manufacturer's Web site. Most have an uninstall program that you can download for free.*

3 If you are uncertain about which software was installed last, perform the following steps:

   ◆ Open the Startup Items folder, located in the Systems folder, and temporarily remove one or more items.

   ◆ Perform a restart and see if the problem goes away.

4 If the problem still exists, perform the additional steps:

   ◆ Open the Extensions folder, located in the Systems/Library/ Extensions folder.

   ◆ View files by Date Modified.

   ◆ Temporarily move into a folder any relevant, recently modified, third-party .kext files, and then restart the computer.

   ◆ Add back the moved .kext files one at a time and restart, until the problem reoccurs.

5 Click the Close button.

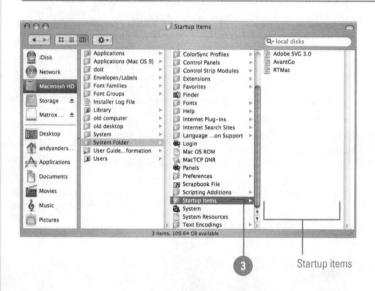

Startup items

View by Date Modified

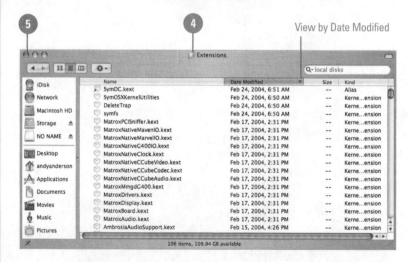

Using Basic Unix Commands

Introduction

The Macintosh OS X operating system changed the rules on reliability and user interactivity. Mac OS X uses a modular structural design built around the Darwin core operating system, a suite of application frameworks, standards-based graphics systems, and the easy-to-use Aqua user interface. **Aqua** represents the user interface for Mac OS X, it utilizes color, images, variable transparency; even animation to create an easy-to-use graphical user interface (GUI). **Frameworks** includes an assortment of application frameworks that support developers from all levels. For example, Cocoa is a set of object-oriented frameworks designed for quick application development, and Carbon is designed to provide a path for developers moving their applications from the OS 9 operating system to Mac OS X. Java allows development and execution of cross-platform Java 2 Standard Edition programs in Mac OS X.

Graphics in OS X consist of standards-based technologies fully integrated into the operating system. Quartz 2D is a high-performance graphics rendering library based on Adobe's cross-platform Portable Document Format (PDF) standard. OpenGL is the industry standard for visualizing 3D shapes and textures. QuickTime digital media software provides a fully standards-based environment for creating, playing, and delivering video (MPEG-4), audio (AAC), and images (JPEG 2000 and other formats). **Darwin** lies beneath the user interface and graphics of Mac OS X. It's an Open Source UNIX-based foundation built on technologies such as FreeBSD, Mach, and Apache. Darwin represents a complete operating system, and is comparable to Linux, and provides kernel, libraries, networking, and a rich command-line environment.

While programming may be a discipline that few consider, the open architecture of the OS X environment makes it something within the reach of any serious Macintosh user.

What You'll Do

Understand UNIX and Mac OS X

View Man Pages for a Command

List Directory Contents

Move Around Directories

Get the Directory Location

Create a New Directory

Use Wildcards in File Names and Directories

View File Contents

Copy and Move Files

Remove Files or Directories

Create and Edit Files with Pico

Redirect Output

Change UNIX Passwords

Change Permissions for a File or Directory

Understanding UNIX and Mac OS X

When working on a Macintosh, you operate using an easy-to-use interface that guides you though your daily tasks. If you want to open MS Word, and you've placed it in the Dock, all you have to do is move your cursor into the Dock, and click on the MS Word icon. While elegant interfaces are not new to the Macintosh, what's going on in the background has totally changed.

When Apple created an operating system for Macintosh computers, they used UNIX; when they created OS X, they beefed it up, and gave users easier access to the internal system of codes that operate the computer. Bell Labs' Ken Thompson developed UNIX in 1969, and with the help of Dennis Ritchie, the inventor of the "C" programming language, they rewrote UNIX entirely in "C" so it could be ported to different computers. In 1974, UNIX was licensed to universities for educational purposes, and over the years, people added and improved the language, until it spread into the commercial world. Today dozens of different UNIX versions are around; each with unique qualities, yet still staying faithful to the original AT&T version. All of the versions were based on AT&T's System V, Berkeley System Distribution (BSD) UNIX, or a hybrid of both.

Apple's Macintosh operating system was designed from the ground up as graphical OS. But there were no command line shells like MS Windows. This made life easy for people who were new to computers, but was extremely frustrating for UNIX experts. With Mac OS X, a Macintosh/UNIX hybrid, Apple satisfies both new computer users and command line junkies.

What this translates into is that any Macintosh user, with a bit of adventure, can access the UNIX command line through the Terminal utility and directly interface with the operating system. You can use UNIX to create sophisticated searches, create directories; even redirect output. It's a brave new world for all Macintosh users.

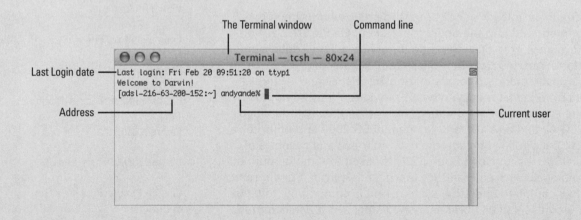

Last Login date — Last login: Fri Feb 20 09:51:20 on ttyp1
Welcome to Darwin!
[adsl-216-63-200-152:~] andyande%

The Terminal window — Terminal — tcsh — 80x24
Command line
Address
Current user

Viewing Man Pages for a Command

The Panther operating system includes hundreds of commands derived from the BSD UNIX operating system, that are accessible using the Terminal utility, and over 900 UNIX based programs. UNIX programs come packaged with their own help files. The help files or man (manual) pages are typically written by programmers for access by other programmers and system administrators. Unlike normal help for Macintosh applications, man pages do not appear in a help window, but in a normal text file format and they contain a wealth of information on the UNIX programs they support. Keep in mind that the instruction tends to be more technical, due to the nature of who they were designed for—other programmers and administrators. For instructions on how to use man pages, type **man man**, and then press Return, to see instructions on viewing text in the Terminal utility.

View Man Pages for a Command

1. Open the Applications folder, double-click the Utilities folder, and then double-click the Terminal icon.

2. Type **man command name**. (where command name is, type the name of the command), and then press Return.

    The man (manual) page appears for that particular command.

3. To move around the screen, press:

    ◆ **Spacebar.** Press the Spacebar to scroll down to the next page.

    ◆ **P.** Press P to scroll up to the previous page.

4. Press Q to quit and return to the command prompt.

5. Click the Close button.

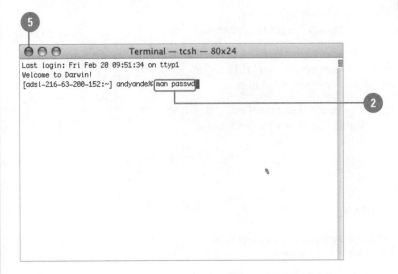

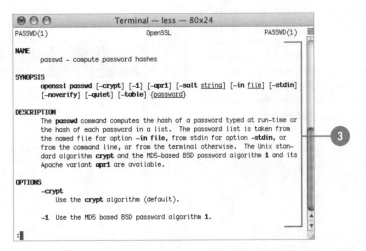

> ### Did You Know?
>
> *You can create a current calendar in the Terminal.* Open the Terminal window, type **cal 08 2005**, and then press Return. The Terminal utility creates a calendar for August, 2005.

Listing Directory Contents

Working in UNIX requires information on the current working directory and it's contents. Both of these commands are simple to execute within the Terminal window. If you want to know where you are, just type **pwd** (print working directory), and then press Return. UNIX does not print anything; instead it displays the path and name of the current working directory, such as Users/andyanderson. To list the contents of that directory type the **ls** (list) command, and then press Return. The terminal window displays the contents of the working directory, i.e. Users/andyanderson. But it doesn't stop here, to list the contents of a specific directory, type **ls** and the directory path—for example, **ls Users/andyanderson/ Documents**. In addition, UNIX allows for paths to specific files, and the use of flags, which instruct the Terminal window what to display.

List Directory Contents

1. Open the Applications folder, double-click the Utilities folder, and then double-click the Terminal icon.

2. Type **pwd**, and then press Return to display the current user.

3. Type **ls**, and then press Return to display the contents of the working directory.

4. Click the Close button.

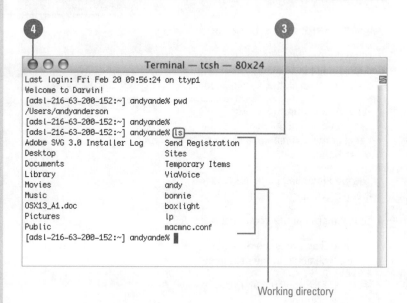

Working directory

Did You Know?

You can cancel out of a command in the Terminal window.

Click the Close button in the middle of a command to cancel the command. An alert message appears, warning you that closing the window terminates the command. Click Cancel to cancel the interruption or click Terminate to stop the command, and close the Terminal window. Any work is lost if you click Terminate, so select wisely.

List Command Flags	
Flag	**Purpose**
-a	Displays a list of all hidden or invisible files.
-F	Displays all files and folders, including hidden UNIX dot (.) files (items ending in a forward slash are folders).
-G	Displays a color-coded view—Blue for directories, red for programs, black for documents.
-R	Displays the directories within each directory in the list.

Moving Around Directories

When you first open the Terminal utility, you're placed within the working directory. This is typically the directory that you logged in as. If you are logged in as the System Administrator, that's your working directory. While this makes it easy to identify exactly where you are, you'll probably want to move into another directory. If you're the System Administrator, you'll have no problem moving anywhere you wish; however, if you don't have Administrator priority, UNIX won't let you look into or access directories that you don't have permission to use. Attempting to access a restricted directory produces the response Access Denied. Changing directories is as easy as using the **cd** (change directory) command. Change to the working directory you need, it'll make it easier to type UNIX commands.

Move Around Directories

1. Open the Applications folder, double-click the Utilities folder, and then double-click the Terminal icon.

2. Type **cd /Users/user account** (where user account is, type the name of the new working folder), and then press Return.

3. Type **ls**, and then press Return to view a list of the directories in the folder.

4. Type **pwd**, and then press Return to display the current working folder.

   TIMESAVER *To return to your home directory, it's not necessary to type cd /Users/home directory (where home directory is the name of your home working directory). Just type* **cd ..**, *and then press Return. The cd .. (double dot) instructs UNIX to back you out of the current directory. If you dig a deeper path such as: cd /Users /bonnie/Library/ColorSync, just type* **cd ...** *the three dots back you out of ColorSync, Library, and bonnie; placing you back into your home directory.*

5. Click the Close button.

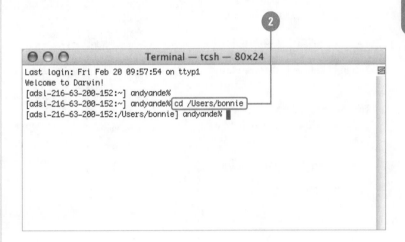

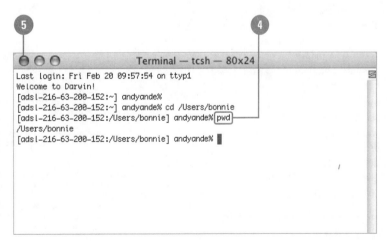

Getting the Directory Location

Sometimes moving into another directory using the Terminal utility is not the hard part, typing in the correct path is. This is where you'll use a combination of the Macintosh Graphical User Interface, and the Terminal window. When you drag a folder, file, or application into the Terminal window, you'll see the exact path to that item. The drag and drop method of identifying location is an excellent way to determine the exact path structure to any item on a Macintosh computer. In addition, if you first type in a command such as **cd** (change directory), you can drag an item into the terminal and execute the command on the selected item.

Get the Directory Location

1. Open the Applications folder, double-click the Utilities folder, and then double-click the Terminal icon.

2. Open a folder window, and drag a file, folder, or application into the Terminal window, and then press Return.

    The Terminal window displays the exact path to the item and shows the command line.

3. Type **ls**, and then press Return.

4. Click the Close button.

Did You Know?

You can first type any UNIX command, and then drag an item into the Terminal window. Drag and drop the item, and then press Return. The command executes on the item.

You can also do the same on a network. If you work on a network, and you have a remote location activated, dragging an item from the remote location window into the terminal window, gives you the exact path back to the remote network.

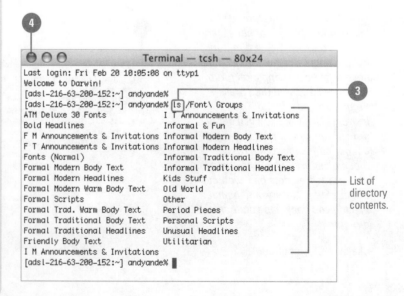

List of directory contents.

Creating a New Directory

UNIX lets you do more than just search for files, folders, and applications; it lets you create directories which you can then move files and folders into. Actually, the process is simple and can be incorporated with other commands. You could instruct UNIX to create a new directory, using the **mkdir** command, and then move or copy some files or folders into the directory. In addition, you can save UNIX commands and execute them over and over again. That's the real power of UNIX; the ability to create a complex command, save it, and then use it over again.

Create a New Directory

1. Open the Applications folder, double-click the Utilities folder, and then double-click the Terminal icon.

2. Type **mkdir 'directoryname'**

   In our example, UNIX makes a directory named productions.

   By entering single quotes around the directory name, you avoid having to use the forward slash to identify blank spaces between words.

3. Press Return.

   UNIX creates a new directory in the current working directory. The mkdir command creates a directory in whatever directory is active.

4. To see the new directory, type **ls**, and then press Return.

5. Click the Close button.

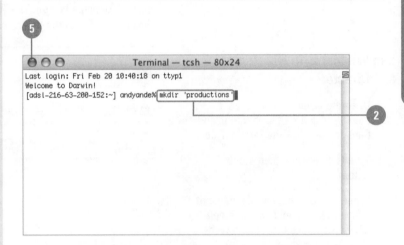

Newly created productions directory.

Did You Know?

You can create a directory and nest another directory inside using the -p option. Type the following command:

mkdir -p 'documents/newdirectory /nestdirectory'

UNIX creates a new directory named newdirectory, inside the documents folder, and then nest a second directory named nestdirectory.

Using Wildcards in File Names and Directories

You've probably noticed that some of the folders contain dozens, if not hundreds of files. If your intention is to locate a specific file, you could type its name. Something like: **ls /Users/bonnie/Applications/file-name** (where "filename" is, type the exact name of the file you're looking for). That's great, but what if you're looking for a file, and you only know part of the name, or you're looking for files that have the .mov extension? When that happens, UNIX lets you incorporate wildcards into the search statement. **Wildcards** let you add special characters into the search string that instruct UNIX to look for similar files. To list all file names ending with on, type **ls *on**. The Terminal window displays a listing of all the files that end with the letters *on*.

Use Wildcards in File Names and Directories

① Open the Applications folder, double-click the Utilities folder, and then double-click the Terminal icon.

② Type **ls file***, and then press Return.

Where *file* is, type a partial name of a file or extension. In our example, UNIX lists all files that begin with NU.

③ Click the Close button.

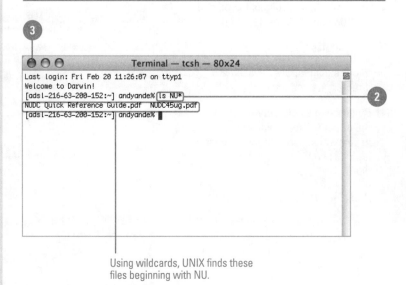

Using wildcards, UNIX finds these files beginning with NU.

Wildcard Uses	
Wildcard	**Purpose**
*ed	List all files that end with the letters ed.
me*	List all files that begin with the letters me.
audio	List all files that have the letters, audio somewhere in the file name.
?an*	List all files where the second and third letters of the file name are an. Files such as **sa**ndy.doc and **sa**nderson.txt would be listed. The Question mark character counts as a space in the file name.

Viewing File Contents

The **more** command is used to view the contents of files. If the file fits one screen of the display, the **more** command displays the whole file. Otherwise, **more** displays one screen of data at a time and then pauses. At the pause, you can press the Return key to advance the data one line at a time, or the Spacebar key to advance the data a full screen.

View File Contents

1. Open the Applications folder, double-click the Utilities folder, and then double-click the Terminal icon.

2. Type **more filename.doc**, and then press Return.

   Where *filename* is, type a file name. In our example, UNIX shows the contents of OSX13_A1.doc.

   TIMESAVER *You typed in a long UNIX command, and you want to use it again, but you don't want to have to retype the whole line. Press the Up and Down arrow keys to display the last five hundred commands typed at the Terminal prompt.*

3. Click the Close button.

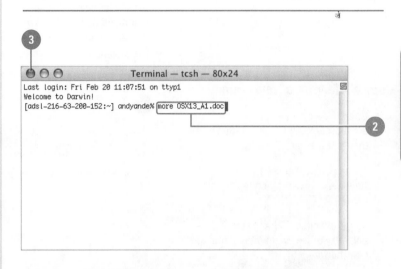

View the contents of the file named: OSX13_A1.doc

Did You Know?

You can view a set number of lines in a file using the head or tail command. To view the first ten lines of a long file, type **(head ~/directory/filename.doc)**.

To view the last ten lines of a long file, type **(tail ~/directory/filename.doc)**. You may need to type more than one directory name, but you get the idea.

Copying and Moving Files

Copying files is almost as easy as creating a new folder. All you have to do is know the name of the file that you want to copy (and it's path), and the name and path you want it copied to. Moving files works the same way. The difference is when you copy a file, the original item stays put, and a copy is placed somewhere else. You can also create a copy of a file and leave it in the same location, you'll just need to rename the file. When you move a file, you are removing it from its original location and placing it somewhere else. Copying files uses the **cp** (copy) command, and moving files uses the **mv** (move) command.

Copy a File with a New Name

1. Open the Applications folder, double-click the Utilities folder, and then double-click the Terminal icon.

2. Type **cp filename.ext newfilename.ext**, and then press Return.

   In our example, UNIX makes a copy of the file with a new name of macOldConf.

3. Click the Close button.

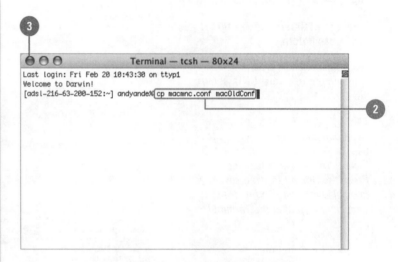

Did You Know?

You can copy a file from one location to another with the same name. Type the following code on the command line, and then press Return.

cp document.doc ~/Movies

The file is copied into the Movies folder with the same name. The ~ symbol is used to represent the home directory.

You can copy a file from one location to another with a different name. Type the following code on the command line, and then press Return:

cp document.doc ~/Movies/ document2.doc

The file is copied into the Movies folder with the name documents2.doc. The ~ symbol is used to represent the home directory.

Original file
New file

Move Files

1. Open the Applications folder, double-click the Utilities folder, and then double-click the Terminal icon.

2. Type **mv filename.ext ~/location,** and then press Return.

   In our example, UNIX moves the file to the Desktop.

3. Click the Close button.

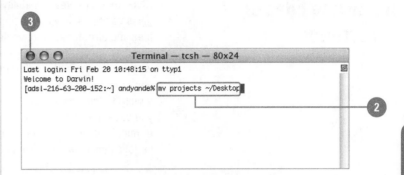

Did You Know?

You can rename a file or directory.
Type the following code on the command line, and then press Return:

mv Fall Winter

The folder named Fall is renamed to Winter.

You can move and rename a file or directory at the same time. Type the following code on the command line, and then press Return:

mv ~/Documents/Fall.doc ~/Movies/Winter.doc

The file Fall.doc, located in the Documents folder is moved into the Movies folder and renamed Winter.doc.

Projects has been moved to the Desktop.

Move Command Flags	
Command	**Purpose**
mv -i	Instructs the terminal to stop and ask before replacing a file with the same name.
mv -f	Instructs the terminal to overwrite files with the same name without asking.
mv -n	Instructs the terminal to skip files with the same name.
mv -v	Instructs the terminal to display verbose code, a line-for-line display of exactly what was moved.

Removing Files or Directories

UNIX not only gives you ability to create items such as directories, it also gives you the ability on the opposite side of the coin, to remove (delete) files and directories. You would expect to see a word of caution at this point. When you remove files using UNIX commands there are no pre-warning boxes or other alert messages, which you can say No to. When you remove a file or folder, it's permanent, there's no undo operation. So a word to the wise—be careful when using the **rm** (remove) command. If you use the **srm** (secure removal) command without the **s** or **m** flags, the terminal performs a strong removal by erasing over the deleted data with various junk data thirty five times.

Remove Files

1. Open the Applications folder, double-click the Utilities folder, and then double-click the Terminal icon.

2. Type **rm ~/filename.ext**, and then press Return.

   In our example, UNIX removes the file macOldConf.

3. Click the Close button.

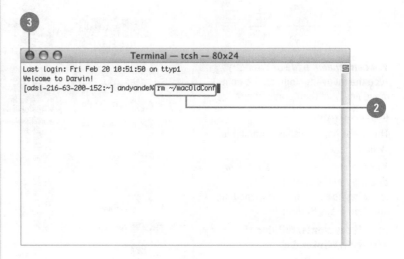

Did You Know?

You can remove a directory the same way you remove a file. Type the following code on the command line, and then press Return:

rm -r ~/Movies/TestFiles

The directory TestFiles, located in Movies is removed along with all of its contents. Remember, there is no undo once you've applied the rm command.

You can perform a secure removal of a file or directory. Type the following code on the command line, and then press Return:

srm private.doc

The file private.doc is securely deleted.

Remove Command Flags

Command	Purpose
rm -r	Instructs the terminal to erase a directory and contents.
rm -d	Instructs the terminal to delete empty directories.
rm -i	Instructs the terminal to ask for conformation before removing a file or directory.
srm -s	Instructs the terminal to perform a simple removal by overwriting the deleted material with random data once.
srm -m	Instructs the terminal to perform a simple removal by overwriting the deleted material with random and not random data.

Creating and Editing Files with Pico

Pico is a full-screen UNIX text editor. Although it doesn't operate much differently than TextEdit, it contains features that help you work with UNIX based code. The Pico text editor lets you create and edit any type of text file. In addition, you can use Pico to change your account configuration files or write a computer program source code file. For example, to create a file and name it accounting.txt, type **pico accounting.txt**. If the file already exits, Pico opens it for you; if it doesn't exist, Pico creates it. Pico displays a menu bar of commonly used commands at the bottom of the window. Pico accepts commands from your keyboard only, and not from your mouse.

Create and Edit Files with Pico

1. Open the Applications folder, double-click the Utilities folder, and then double-click the Terminal icon.

2. Type **pico filename.ext**, and then press Return.

   UNIX retrieves the file for editing or if it can't find the name, creates a new file.

   In our example, UNIX opens the file *OSX13_A1.doc*.

3. Make your changes using the command keys at the bottom of the window.

4. To save the file, press Control+O.

   Pico displays the current file name. (To save the file under a different name, delete the filename that Pico displays and type a new one).

5. To Exit pico, press Control+X.

6. Click the Close button.

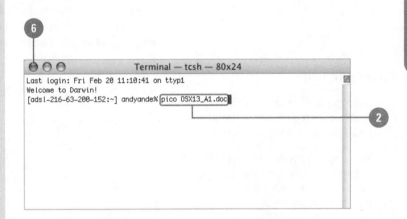

File is retrieved for editing.

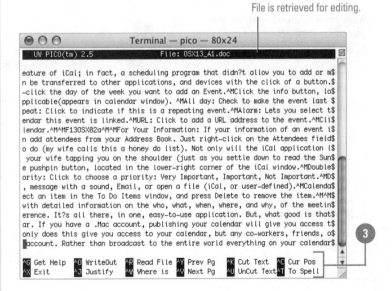

Redirecting Output

Another useful UNIX command is redirection. Re-direction allows the users to store the output of a process to a file (output re-direction). **Output Re-direction** is a useful feature, that lets you store the output of a process into a file so that it may be used in some way later. For example, you're starting a program and receive an error message; however, it disappears before you can see it. By redirecting the output to a file you are able to view it at your leisure. **Input Re-direction** allows the user to prepare processes input ready for later use. Think of it this way, when you type the **ls** (list) command, the Terminal displays a listing of the files and folders in the working directory. When you use the redirect command, the list command can be redirected to another output such as a text file. The redirect command uses the greater than sign to perform the redirect. A single greater than sign (>) instructs UNIX to create a new file, while a double greater than sign (>>) creates a new file.

Redirect Output

① Open the Applications folder, double-click the Utilities folder, and then double-click the Terminal icon.

② To redirect the ls (list) command to create a file, type the following code on the command line, and then press Return.

ls > listing.txt

A file named listing.txt is created, and the ls (list) command is written to the file.

③ To redirect the ls (list) command to append the list onto an existing file, type the following code on the command line, and then press Return.

ls >> lists.txt

An existing file named lists.txt is used, and the ls (list) command is appended to the end of the file.

④ Click the Close button.

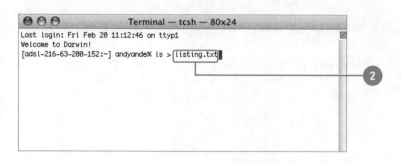

Redirect the output of the ls (list) command to a text file named listing.txt

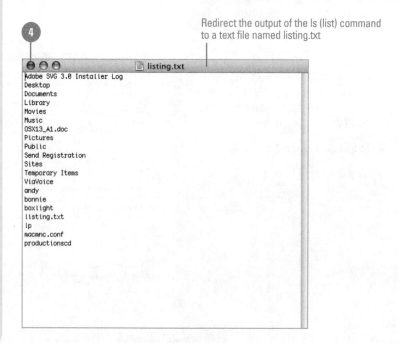

Changing UNIX Passwords

Passwords are an important part of computers. They essentially protect your account and prevent other users from accessing information that you deem as important. When you log into a secure computer, you're asked for your password and user account name. After typing the correct information, you're logged into the computer. Passwords can be changed in the Account area of System Preferences, or they can be quickly changed using the passwd command in the Terminal window. When evoking the passwd command, it's important to understand that your password is permanently changed, and the next time you log in you'll be required to type the new password. In addition, when you're typing and verifying you new password, no keystrokes appear in the Terminal window; not even little dots. There's nothing wrong with your computer, that's just the Terminal window's way of keeping your password safe and secure.

Change UNIX Passwords

1. Open the Applications folder, double-click the Utilities folder, and then double-click the Terminal icon.

2. Type **passwd** at the terminal prompt, and then press Return.

3. Type in your old password (nothing shows in the terminal), and then press Return.

4. Type in your new password, and then press Return.

   IMPORTANT *No keystrokes show in the Terminal window, so be sure that you accurately type your password, and then retype it to verify.*

5. Verify your new password by retyping, and then press Return.

6. Click the Close button.

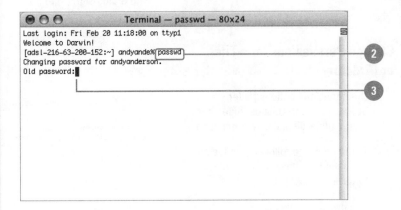

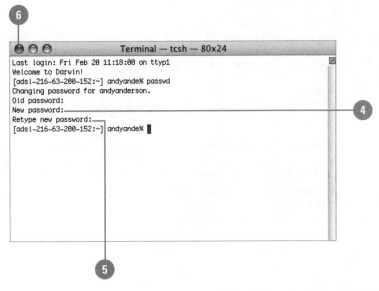

Changing Permissions for a File or Directory

A file's **permissions** are what allow it to open when you double-click applications to use and folders to open. They're the little security guards that instruct the file what it can and can't do. In general, the files that you create aren't accessible to other users. However, UNIX allows you to explicitly make your files available to others. Each file in UNIX has an owner—normally the user who creates the file. The file also belongs to a particular group. A **group** in UNIX is a set of users. Type the command **groups** to see what groups you are a member of. Each user can have read, write, or execute permissions to the file (r, w, or x). These permissions are set and modified by the owner of the file. **Read** permission allows users to view the contents of a file and to copy it. **Write** permission allows users to modify the file. **Execute** permission allows users to run the file if it is executable. The current permissions for a file can be listed using the **ls -l** (lower case L) command. To modify the permissions of a file or directory, use the **cmod** command. Commands are connected with a plus sign (+) to add permission, or the minus sign (-) to remove permission.

Change Permissions for a File or Directory

1. Open the Applications folder, double-click the Utilities folder, and then double-click the Terminal icon.

2. Type one of the following codes on the command line, and then press Return.

   - **File**
     chmod ug+r filename.doc

     The owner (u) and group (g) have permission to read the filename.doc file, located in the active user's directory.

   - **Directory**
     cd /Users/username
     chmod a+rx *

     The **cd** command moves the user to the username directory, and the **chmod** command allows all users (the letter a can be used to replace the u, g, and o attributes), the ability to read and execute all files (* equals all) in the active directory.

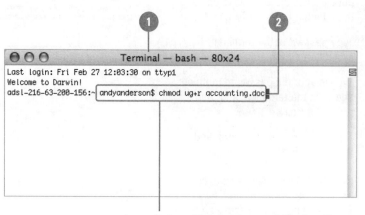

Command for changing permission for a file.

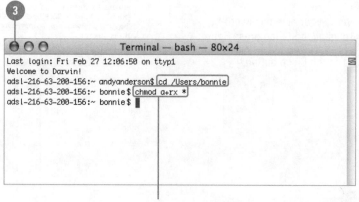

Command for changing permission for a directory.

Allow Access to an Application

1. Open the Applications folder, double-click the Utilities folder, and then double-click the Terminal icon.

2. Type **chmod g+x modular.cpp**, and then press Return.

   The group can now execute the application named modular.cpp.

3. Click the Close button.

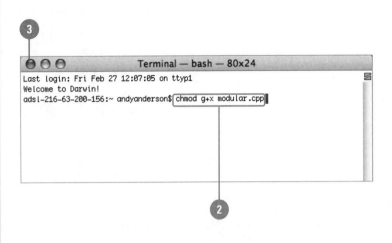

Deny Access to an Application

1. Open the Applications folder, double-click the Utilities folder, and then double-click the Terminal icon.

2. Type **chmod g-x modular.cpp**, and then press Return.

   The group cannot execute the application named modular.cpp.

3. Click the Close button.

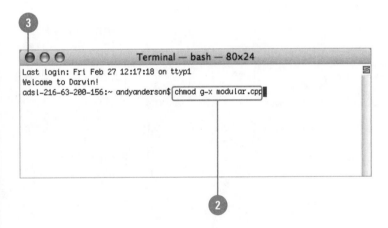

Did You Know?

You can give permissions for everyone to read and execute all files in the working directory. To give everyone the ability to read files and execute applications, type the following code on the command line, and then press Return.

chmod o=rx *

The group can now read and execute all files in the working directory. The **o** (others) command is connected to multiple permissions with the equal sign (=), and the asterisk(*) is a wild card for all items in the working folder.

20

Appendix:
Using the Classic Environment

Introduction

Now that you're using Mac OS X Panther, why do you need to know about using Mac OS 9, the Classic environment? You upgraded your system to Mac OS X, but unless you upgraded all your applications to Mac OS X compatible versions, you'll need to run them in Mac OS 9. When all your applications are upgraded to Mac OS X, you'll have no need for this material, so upgrade as soon as you can.

If you need to use Mac OS 9 to run an older application, you'll need to install it on your Mac OS X system, which means you'll have two operating systems on your computer. Don't worry, Mac OS X Panther can manage them both. Apple only asks that you have at least 128K of memory on your Macintosh to run both operating systems. If you purchased a new Macintosh with Mac OS X, or upgraded your old Macintosh from Mac OS 9.1 or later to Mac OS X, you don't need to install a thing. If you erased your hard disk when you installed Mac OS X, you need to install Mac OS 9.1 or later. However, version 9.2.2 or later is the best.

Mac OS X uses the **Classic environment**, or Classic mode, to automatically run Mac OS 9. The Classic environment uses the Mac OS 9 System Folder and retains the same look and feel as well as the old functionality, which means you need to know two operating systems. When you double-click a Mac OS 9 application, Classic mode automatically starts, where you can run applications and work with files as if you were working in Mac OS 9. Classic mode is actually a simulator for Mac OS 9, which supports only a limited number of external hardware devices; Mac OS X is still running in the background. If you want to run Mac OS 9 in pure form, you can restart your computer in Mac OS 9. When your Mac starts in Mac OS 9, it's just as though Mac OS X is not there.

Installing Mac OS 9

In order to use Mac OS 9 in the Classic environment, you need to install the Mac OS 9.1 or later operating system. You can install and use Mac OS 9.1, but it's recommended by Apple that you use Mac OS 9.2. Depending on the type of installation you need to perform, either an upgrade from Mac OS 9.0 or earlier, or a clean install with no prior version of Mac OS 9, your installation steps may differ from the ones provided here. Since you are running Mac OS 9 on a Mac OS X system, you can install more than one Mac OS 9 system (separate System Folders). You might use one for Classic mode (a slim down version) and another for dual-booting (a maximized version); each system can have different settings based on your usage.

Install Mac OS 9 on a Panther System

1. Start your computer from the Mac OS 9 installation CD. Insert the CD, and then hold down the c key while restarting your computer.

2. Double-click the Mac OS Install icon to the launch the installer.

   TROUBLE? If you need to restore an archived zip, double-click it's icon.

3. Click Continue in the Welcome window.

4. Select the disk on which you want to install Mac 9.2.

   ◆ **Mac OS 9.0.** Click Select to update the system.

   ◆ **Mac OS X.** Click Options, select the Perform Clean Installation check box, click OK, and then click Select to install a new system for Mac OS 9.

5. Read the important information, and then click Continue.

6. Read the Software License Agreement, and then click Continue.

7. Click Agree to continue.

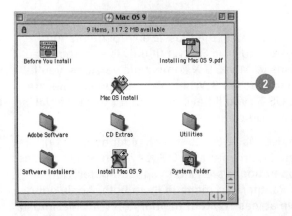

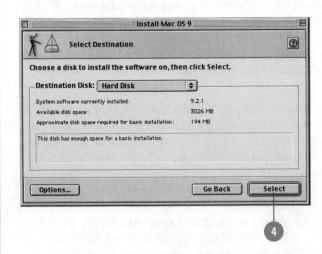

8 Click Start in the Install Software window.

9 When the installation is done, click Quit.

10 Click the Special menu, and then click Restart.

The Mac OS Setup Assistant Introduction window appears when you start your computer for the first time with Mac OS 9.

11 Read the instructions that appear in each screen, and then click the right-point arrow button in the bottom right-corner to move from screen to screen.

Did You Know?

You can install Mac OS 9.2 from Software Restore CDs. Insert the first Software Restore CD, open the CD, double-click the SoftwareRestore.pkg icon to launch the installer, and then follow the onscreen instructions. The steps are similar to an install from the Installation CD with additional authentication and security.

You can optimize Mac OS 9 performance. Turning off extensions maximizes Mac OS 9 performance in Classic mode. While Mac OS 9 starts, hold down the Spacebar to open the Extensions Manager, where you can turn off extensions you don't need, because Mac OS X does it better. Some not to turn off are General, Startup Disk, Apple Guide, CarbonLib, Classic RAVE, Open Transport, Open Transport ASLM Modules, Classic Support, Classic Support UI, and ProxyApp. If you turn the important ones off, the Mac will let you know about it. Classic mode also requires QuickTime version 6.0.3 or later for best results.

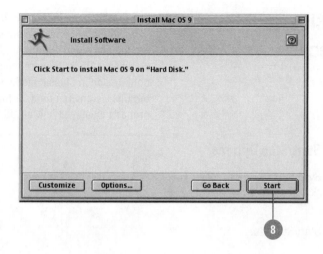

Mac OS X System folder

Mac OS 9 folders

A

Setting Classic Preferences

The Classic pane in System Preferences gives you options to start and stop the Classic environment within Mac OS X, setup Mac OS 9 system startup and sleep options, and view status and memory information about Mac OS 9. If you're having problems with Mac OS 9 or an application running in Classic mode, you can use the Classic pane to also restart the Classic environment, or force an immediate quit. If icons are not properly displayed in Mac OS 9, you can rebuild the desktop to fix it.

Set Classic Start/Stop Options

1. Click the System Preferences icon in the Dock, and then click the Classic icon.

2. Click the Start/Stop tab.

3. Select the System Folder for the Mac OS 9 system.

4. Select the start options you want:

   ◆ **Start Classic When You Login.** Check to automatically start Mac OS 9 when you login to Mac OS X.

   To start and hide it, select the Hide Classic While Starting check box.

   ◆ **Warn Before Starting Classic.** Check to display an alert before Mac OS 9 automatically starts.

   ◆ **Show Classic Status In Menu Bar.** Check to start/stop Mac OS 9 and change options from the menu bar.

5. If you want, use buttons to manually start, restart, and quit:

   ◆ **Start.** Click to start Mac OS 9. While the system is starting, you can click Stop to halt it.

   ◆ **Restart.** Click to save changes and restart Mac OS 9.

   ◆ **Force Quit.** Click to quit now.

6. Click the Close button.

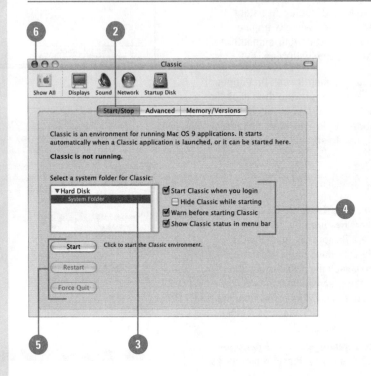

Set Classic Startup Options and Show Memory Usage & Versions

1. Click the System Preferences icon in the Dock, and then click the Classic icon.

2. Click the Advanced tab.

3. Click the Startup And Other Options pop-up, and then select from the following options:

   ◆ **Turn Off Extensions.** Select to turn off all extensions when Classic starts; same as holding the Shift key during startup.

   ◆ **Open Extensions Manager.** Select to automatically open Extensions Manager when Classic starts; same as holding the Spacebar during startup.

   ◆ **Use Key Combinations.** Select to enter up to five keys to start or restart Classic.

4. To set up Classic for multiple users, select the Use Mac OS 9 Preferences From Your Home check box.

5. If you want, click Start Classic or Restart Classic to start or restart Classic with your startup options.

6. To put Classic mode to sleep when it's inactive (no Classic applications are running), drag the slider to specify inactivity before it sleeps.

7. To rebuild the Classic desktop, click Rebuild Desktop, select the disk to rebuild, and then click Rebuild.

8. Click the Memory/Versions tab to display application memory usage and versions.

9. To include background applications in the list, select the Show Background Applications check box.

10. Click the Close button.

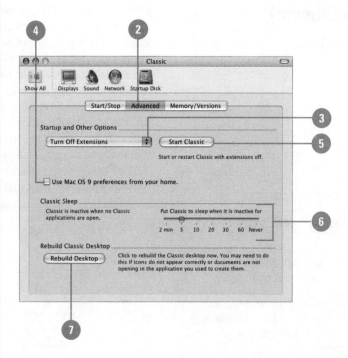

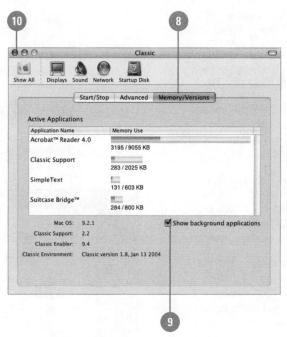

Using Classic Applications

After you start the Classic environment with Mac OS 9, you can use applications as if you were actually in Mac OS 9. In fact, Mac OS 9 applications actually launch faster in Classic than they do on a pure Mac OS 9 system. However, not all applications work in Classic mode; you might get an alert message when you launch it. If an application fails, turn off the virus protection in the Control Panel for Mac OS 9, and then try again. When you start a Mac OS 9 application, the Classic environment starts, and the Classic application icon appears in the Dock, just like Mac OS X ones. Be aware that only one person at a time can use the Classic environment on a shared computer. In the Classic application, you use Mac OS 9 commands and features. I've noted some main differences between Mac OS 9 and Mac OS X that you'll quickly come across.

Use a Classic Application

① In Mac OS X, open the Finder window with the Mac OS 9 application you want to open.

② Double-click a Mac OS 9 Classic application icon, or a document created with the Classic application.

The Classic environment starts with Mac OS 9 along with an application and document.

③ Be aware of differences between Classic Mac OS 9 and Mac OS X:

◆ **Menus.** The Classic Apple and File menu contain different commands and the Application menu doesn't exist.

◆ **Printing and Networking.** Use the Chooser to set up and select a printer or networked computer. Click the Apple menu, and then click Chooser.

◆ **System Preferences.** Use the Control Panel to set system preferences. Click the Apple menu, point to Control Panel, and then select one.

④ When you're done, click the File menu, and then click Quit.

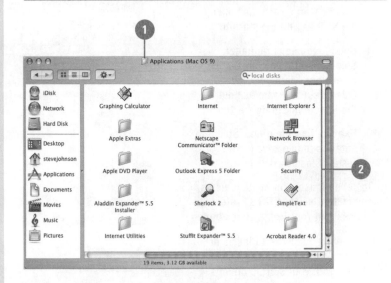

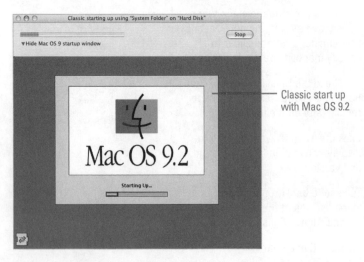

Classic start up with Mac OS 9.2

Switch Between Classic and Mac OS X

After you start a Classic application, you can quickly switch between Classic and Mac OS X using the following methods:

◆ **Dock.** Click a Mac OS X application icon in the Dock to switch to it, or double-click a Mac OS 9 application icon in the Dock to switch to Classic mode.

◆ **Classic status in menu bar.** Click the Classic icon on the menu bar to select .

If the Classic environment is running, the Classic icon contains a half-filled black background. If not, the icon is gray.

◆ **Activate.** Click the window of the application to activate the associated operating system.

See Also

See "Setting Classic Preferences" on page 472 for information on turning on the Classic status menu on the menu bar using System Preferences in Mac OS X.

Did You Know?

You can quit Classic mode several ways. Click the Classic icon on the menu bar, and then click Stop Classic. In the Classic pane (Start/Stop tab) in System Preferences, click Stop or Restart.

Classic application; click to activate.   Mac OS X application; click to activate.

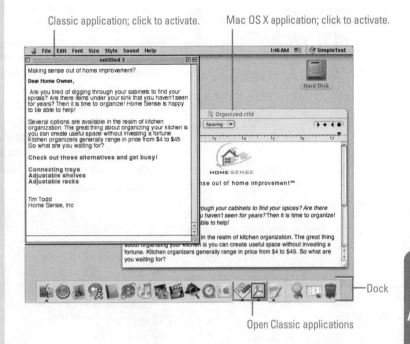

Dock

Open Classic applications

Classic status in menu bar

A

Starting Your Computer with Mac OS 9

Using Classic mode doesn't actually use Mac OS 9, Mac OS X simulates it, so working with hardware devices typically creates problems. Instead of using Classic mode, you can avoid these problems and start your computer in Mac OS 9, the real thing. You can use the Startup Disk pane in System Preferences to set Mac OS 9 as your startup disk. When you restart your computer, Mac OS 9 starts. In Mac OS 9, you need to use the Startup Disk control panel in the Apple menu to switch back to your Mac OS X startup disk and use Mac OS X features. If Mac OS 9 is not available in the Startup Disk preference pane, your computer only starts in Mac OS X, which happens on some newer computers (typically 2003 or later). In that case, you can use the Classic environment instead.

Restart with Mac OS 9

1. Click the System Preferences icon in the Dock, and then click the Startup Disk icon.

2. Click the Mac OS 9 icon system folder you want to use as the startup disk.

   An alert message appears, asking for confirmation.

3. Click Restart, and then click Restart again as confirmation.

   TIMESAVER *Hold down the Option key while you restart your computer, select a startup disk, and then click Restart.*

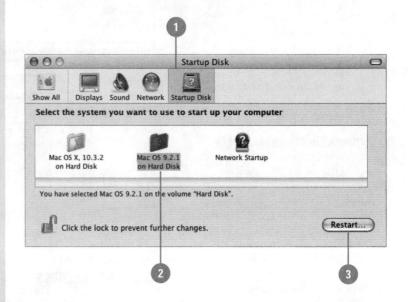

Did You Know?

You can quickly restart with Mac OS X. In Mac OS 9, click the Apple menu, point to Control Panel, and then click Startup Disk. In the control panel, select the folder icon for the Mac OS X System folder, and then click Restart.

For Your Information

Fast Startup Switch in Mac OS X or Mac OS 9

If you have both Mac OS X and Mac OS 9 installed on the same hard disk or partition (divide one hard disk into two sections), while the Mac is starting up, hold down the X key to start up in Mac OS X. If you have installed Mac OS X and Mac OS 9 on different hard disks or partitions (where the Mac OS 9 system is on the internal disk or first partition, and Mac OS X is the startup disk), you can hold down the D key while the Mac starts up to start up in Mac OS 9. With the same set up, you can also hold down the Option key to display the Startup Manager, where you can select the OS you want to start.

Appendix:
Installing Mac OS X Panther

Introduction

If you're upgrading to Mac OS X panther from a previous version of Mac OS, this appendix describes how to prepare and install Mac OS X 10.3. The temptation is to insert the Installation CD and start the installation, but you can avoid problems by making sure your computer is ready for Mac OS X Panther. Before you install Panther, you need to check your computer hardware and software and make several setup decisions that relate to your computer. The Mac OS X Panther Installer walks you through the installation process.

Mac OS 9 Upgrade for Classic

If you are upgrading from Mac OS 9 to Mac OS X Panther and want to run Mac OS 9 compatible applications in Panther, you need to have Mac OS 9.1 or later installed on your computer. However, Mac OS 9.2.2 is recommended. It's a good idea to upgrade your Mac OS 9 installation to the latest and greatest before you install Mac OS X Panther. See Appendix A, "Using the Classic Environment," on page 469 for more details.

What You'll Do

Prepare to Install Mac OS X Panther

Determine the Current Mac OS Version

Install Mac OS X 10.3

Configure Mac OS X 10.3

Download Mac OS X Tools from Apple

Preparing to Install Mac OS X Panther

The Apple Installer guides you through many of the choices you need to make, but there are some decisions and actions you need to make before you start the installation. In order to run Mac OS X, you'll need at least 128MB of physical RAM, and at least 3.0GB of available space on your hard disk for the installation. And your Mac needs to be one of the models that can run Mac OS X.

Confirm that your hardware can run Mac OS X Version 10.3 Panther

Mac OS X Version 10.3 requires a Macintosh with a PowerPC G3, G4, or G5 processor, built-in USB; at least 128MB of physical RAM and a built-in display or a display connected to an Apple-supplied video card supported by your computer. Mac OS X does not support processor upgrade cards. Verify your hardware is supported from the list below.

Power Mac. Power Mac G5, Power Mac G4 (Dual Processor or Quicksliver), Power Mac G4 Cube, Power Mac G4, or Power Mac G3.

PowerBook. Power Book G4 (12, 15, 17-inch aluminum), Power Book G4 (DVI video) PowerBook G4 (400, 500, 550, 667), or PowerBook (Bronze keyboard).

iMac. iMac (flat panel), iMac (slot loading), iMac (5 flavors tray loading), or iMac (Blondi Blue).

eMac. eMac (ATI Graphics), or eMac.

iBook. iBook (12.1" & 14.1"), iBook SE, or iBook SE (FireWire).

Verify you have enough hard drive space.

While the amount of disk space required depends on your computer and the way you are installing Mac OS X, you are recommended to have at least 2.0 GB of available space on your hard drive, or 3.5GB of disk space if you install developer tools.

Check out third party hardware and software compatibility

Third Party Hardware. Mac OS X Version 10.3 Panther includes out-of-the-box functionality for many hardware devices. Mac OS X will automatically configure itself to support most Canon, HP and Epson USB inkjet printers. Mac OS X Image Capture will work with USB digital still cameras that support mass storage, PTP and Digita, plus an array of cameras from Canon, Kodak and Nikon. However, some devices may need additional driver support from the manufacturer. Please check with the manufacturer of your product to see if Mac OS X Version 10.3-compatible drivers are available.

Third Party Software. The Classic environment in Mac OS X is based upon an installation of Mac OS 9.1 or later (9.2.2 recommended). Most Mac OS 9-compatible applications will run in the Classic environment. If you have any questions, contact the vendor of your product.

Uninstall Mac OS X 10.3. Unfortunately, there isn't any clean way, like an uninstall application, to uninstall Mac OS X10.3. The only real way is to backup your Home folder, Applications folder, Library folder, and anything else you want to save, and then erase the hard drive and install the operating system you want to use.

Determining the Current Mac OS Version

If you're not sure what version of the Mac operating system you've currently installed on your computer, you can use the Startup Disk utility to find out. If you're upgrading from Mac OS 9, you can access the utility from the Control Panel on the Apple menu. If you're using Mac OS X, you can access the utility from System Preferences on the Apple menu. A quick visual way to determine which operating system, either Mac OS 9 or X, is installed on your computer is to check the Apple icon on the left side of the menu bar. If a six color apple appears, you're using Mac OS 9.2 or earlier. If a blue 3-D apple appears, you're using Mac OS X or later.

Check the Startup Disk on Mac OS 9.2 or Earlier

1. Click the Apple menu, point to Control Panels, and then click Startup Disk.

2. If necessary, click the triangle next to your hard disk to display the system folders.

   The OS version appears in the Version column.

3. Click the Close button.

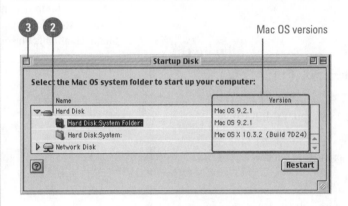

Check the Startup Disk on Mac OS X or Later

1. Click the Apple menu, and then click System Preferences.

2. Click the Startup Disk icon.

   The OS versions for Mac OS 9 (if installed) and Mac OS X appear in the pane.

3. Click the Close button.

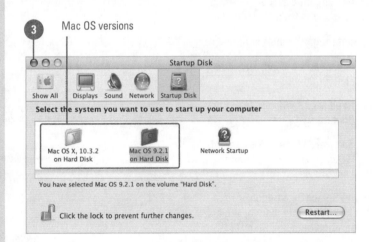

B

Installing Mac OS X 10.3

There are four different kinds of installation: clean (new or erased disk), upgrade from Mac OS 9, upgrade from Mac OS 10.0 through 10.2, and reinstall Mac OS 10.3. The Installer guides you step-by-step through the process of installing Mac OS X Panther no matter what the installation type. However, a clean install or Mac OS X upgrade to Panther requires you to select additional options as you step through the installation, but the steps are basically the same. You insert the installation CD, restart your computer from the CD, and then follow the on-screen instructions (read the instructions, select options, and then click Continue) to complete the process. As you go through the installation process, you can click the Go Back button at any time to change option in previous screens. The installation process takes about an hour if all goes well. When the installation is finished, you are ready to login to Panther.

Install Mac OS X 10.3

1. Insert the Mac OS X Panther CD Disc 1 into your CD-ROM drive.

2. Double-click the Install Mac OS X icon in the CDs window.

3. Click Restart.

4. If an Authenticate dialog appears, enter the administrator name and password, and then click OK.

5. In the Language screen, select a language, and then click Continue.

6. Step through the intro screens:

   ◆ **Introduction.** Read, and then click Continue.

   ◆ **Read Me.** Read, and then click Continue.

   ◆ **Software License Agreement.** Read, click Continue, and then click Agree.

7. In the Select Destination screen, click to select the icon for the disk or partition to install Mac OS X.

   A green arrow appears on the disk or partition. If a yellow exclamation appears, the drive probably has a newer version of Mac X 10.3.

8 To set advanced options, click Options. You can select install-ation options, and then click OK:

◆ **Upgrade Mac OS X.** Upgrades an existing Mac OS X installation to Panther.

◆ **Archive and Install.** Creates a fresh clean installation. The Installer moves existing system files to a new folder named Previous System, and then installs Mac OS X from scratch.

Select the Preserve Users And Network Settings check box to automatically save all existing system settings, and skip the Setup Assistant.

◆ **Erase and Install.** Erases the destination disk and installs Mac OS X from scratch with the format you choose.

9 Click Continue.

10 To perform a custom install, click Customize, and then select or clear the components you want or don't want.

IMPORTANT *This is the last step in which you can back out of the installation. Click the Installer menu, click Quit Installer, and then click Quit to confirm. Hold down the mouse button to eject the Mac OS X CD.*

11 Click Install or Upgrade, and then wait for the Installer to copy files.

12 Follow the on-screen instructions to insert additional installation CDs and complete the process.

Your computer restarts and displays the first screen for the Setup Assistant.

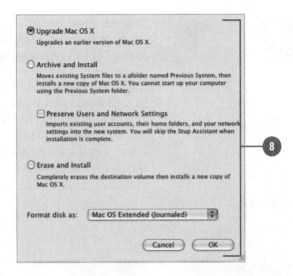

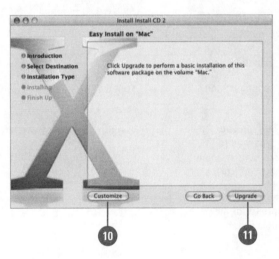

B

Configuring Mac OS X 10.3

After you install Mac OS X Panther, your computer restarts and displays the Setup Assistant, which helps you configure Panther to your specific needs. The Setup Assistant is a program that steps you through the process using a simple question and answer format. The information you enter is automatically used in System Preferences to customize your Mac OS X environment. The Setup Assistant allows you to configure options for personal identification, Internet account, telephone or DSL modem connection, network usage, e-mail account, and the date & time. Unfortunately, there is not a way to take screen shots of the configuration process, so illustrations are not available for the configuration parts.

Configure Mac OS X 10.3

① Install Mac OS X 10.3.

Your computer restarts and displays the first screen for the Setup Assistant.

② In the Personalize Your Settings window, select a keyboard layout, and then click Continue.

③ Specify the basic configuration options:

◆ **My Apple ID is.** Type your Apple user name and password (if you registered for a .Mac account or on the Apple Web site), and Apple ID.

◆ **Create an Apple ID for me.** Creates an Apple ID for you durin g registration.

◆ **Don't create an Apple ID for me.** Skips getting an Apple ID.

④ Step through the following screens:

◆ **Registration.** Read, and then click Continue.

◆ **A Few More Questions.** Read, and then click Continue.

◆ **Thank You.** Read, click Continue, and then click Agree.

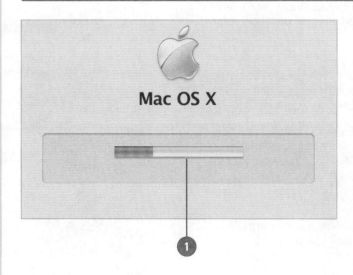

5. Specify one of the following Internet options:

   ◆ **EarthLink account.** Select an option, follow the on-screen set up, and then click Continue.

   ◆ **Existing account.** Select an option, follow the on-screen set up, and then click Continue.

   Select an Internet connection option (cable or DSL, telephone, or network).

   ◆ **Not ready to connect to the Internet.** Skips getting an Apple ID.

6. To set up an e-mail account, select an option, follow the on-screen set up, and then click Continue.

7. To set up the time zone, date & time, select an option, follow the on-screen set up, and then click Continue.

8. When the Thank You window appears, click Go to complete the process.

9. The Software Update utility may automatically start after installing Mac OS X 10.3 if there are any software updates available from Apple. Select the items you want to install, and then click Install *X* Items.

See Also

See "Automating Software Updates" on page 417 for information on using the Software Update utility.

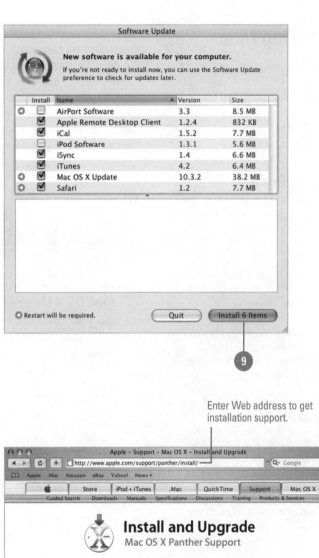

Enter Web address to get installation support.

Downloading Mac OS X Tools from Apple

Mac OS X provides additional programs and tools you can download from the Web that may not be included in the Automatic Software Update. These programs include the non essentials that are not required by the system, but make computer life easier and much more fun. You can download screen savers, icons, system/disk utilities, productivity tools, games, and much more. Developers are continually upgrading applications, utilities, and games, so check the Apple Web site from time to time for the latest and greatest stuff.

Download and Install Mac OS X Tools, Etc.

1. Open your Web browser.

2. Go to *www.apple.com*.

3. Click the Mac OS X tab.

4. Click the Downloads subtab.

> **TIMESAVER** *Click the Apple menu, and then click Mac OS X Software to access this Web page directly.*

5. Click a category link to narrow down the list of downloads.

6. Explore the page, and then click any of the links to find out more about a product and download it to your computer.

7. When you're done, quit your Web browser.

See Also

See *"Downloading and Installing Software" on page 414 for information on downloading software from the Web and installing it on your computer.*

New! Features

Mac OS X Panther

Each new release of the Macintosh Operating System (OS) brings with it new features, improvements, and added sophistication. With Mac OS X Panther there are many. When you examine the over 150 new features... yes, that's right, Panther contains over 150 new features, all designed to make your computing experience, easier, faster, and painless, you'll see why.

While creating new features for Mac OS X Panther, some older features were taken out. These features include Extension conflicts (no longer needed), Memory controls (no longer needed), Rebuilding the desktop (no longer needed), the Apple menu and Application menu for switching between applications (replaced with the Dock), and the Control Strip (replaced with Menu status icons).

General

- **Context Sensitive Help Icon (p. 20)** Get help by clicking the purple help icon on many system panels.

- **Switch Between Help Libraries (p. 20)** Switch between the different help libraries using the Library menu.

- **Fast User Switching (p. 22-23, 384)** Switch to another user account without logging out and quitting current applications.

- **Windows-compatible DVD Burning (p. 54)** Burn data DVDs that are compatible with Windows without any hassle.

- **Finer LCD Font Antialiasing (p. 82)** Read text more easily on flat panel displays.

- **Smooth Scrolling (p. 82)** Enjoy refined and smoother scrolling for drag and page scrolling.

- **Desktop Picture Selection From iPhoto Library (p. 84)** Choose photographs from any iPhoto Album directly from the Desktop system preference.

- **Higher Quality Text-to-Speech Voice (p. 102-103)** Listen to text-to-speech applications with higher quality.

◆ **Application Switcher (p. 111)** View active application icons semi-transparently, heads-up style when using ⌘+Tab.

◆ **Accounts Preferences (p. 377-380, 382-384)** Set up your Mac for multiple users more easily.

◆ **Software Update Activation (p. 414)** Activate Software Update directly from the Apple menu or About This Mac window.

◆ **Install and Keep Package (p. 414)** Retain a software update package to install on another Mac without re-downloading.

◆ **Download Updates in Background (p. 415)** Download important software updates in the background.

◆ **Journalled File System (p. 420)** Ensure superior reliability of drives with journalled HFS+ file system.

◆ **Keyboard Shortcut Preferences (p. 435)** Customize keyboard shortcuts for the system and applications.

◆ **Recent Display Resolution Changes (p. 440)** Access recent display resolutions from Displays Status Menu.

Finder

◆ **Sidebar (p. 17, 66)** Navigate Finder windows displaying volumes, network and favorite folders in left column.

◆ **Action Menu (p. 18)** Convenient access to context specific Finder commands based on selection.

◆ **Local iDisk (p. 37, 280)** Access the contents of your iDisk quickly on a local hard drive mirror with automatic sync to Internet servers. You can open the iDisk from the Go menu or the Sidebar in a Finder window.

◆ **Network Browsing (p. 37, 399)** Browse AFP, NFS, SMB, managed and ad-hoc network servers directly in the Finder using the Sidebar.

◆ **Color Labels (p. 38-39)** Organize and search for files and folders using customizable color labels (a new feature back from Mac OS 9). Assign color labels with customized names to any file or folder.

◆ **Fast Searching (p. 40-41)** Enjoy super fast filename searching with smart refined search capability. Use the Magnifying Glass icon to choose where you want to search, and then type part of the name you want to find.

◆ **Search Locations (p. 40-41)** Narrow Finder searches via pop-up with Local Disks, Home, Everywhere and Selection options.

◆ **Secure Empty Trash (p. 51)** Completely erases the files you put in the Trash; you can no longer recover the files.

- **Eject Controls (p. 56)** Eject CDs and DVDs using a button next to their names.

- **Announce the Time (p. 86)** Have the computer announce the time at intervals you set in the Date & Time pane in System Preferences.

- **New Open and Save Panels (p. 136-137, 158)** Open and save documents using the Sidebar, and List and Columns views.

- **Archive Files and Folders (p. 416-417)** Compress and expand files and folders directly in the Finder using the standard gzip format.

Address Book

- **Speakable Address Book (p. 100-101, 116)** Use Speech Recognition to look up phone numbers, place calls or start iChats.

- **Related Contacts (p. 112-113)** Keep track of family members or assistants for your contacts.

- **iChat AV Presence (p. 112-113)** View iChat AV Buddy status while browsing contacts.

- **Auto-merge (p. 113)** Reconcile conflicts and updates when importing vCards.

- **Label Printing (p. 115)** Print labels using more than 250 different Avery label templates.

- **Mail List Printing (p. 115)** Print a copy of your Address Book to use when you are away from your Mac.

- **Change of Address Notification (p. 116-117)** Notify a group of contacts when public info in your "My Card" changes.

- **Auto-phone Number Formatting (p. 116-117)** Display phone numbers in consistent format without typing the format yourself on every card.

- **Customized Contact Template (p. 116-117)** Choose which contact fields are displayed by default for all contacts.

- **Exchange Contact Synchronization (p. 116-117)** Synchronize Address Book contacts with Microsoft Exchange servers.

- **Private My Card Info (p. 116-117)** Keep info about yourself private when sharing vCards.

- **Add Theaters (p. 225)** Add the address of a movie theater to your Address Book directly from the Sherlock 3 Movies channel.

- **AutoFill Contact Info** Save time when entering contact info, such as a company name, that you already entered for another contact.

Exposé

◆ **Instant Access Any Open Window (p. 16)** Access any open window.

◆ **Instant Access to Any Application Window (p. 16)** Access any open window for only the current application.

◆ **Instant Access to Desktop (p. 16)** Clear away all open windows to show files and folders on the desktop.

◆ **FKEY, Mouse Button, Screen Corner Customization (p. 72)** Customize Exposé activation including function keys and mouse buttons.

Font Book

◆ **Font Installation (p. 129)** Install fonts by clicking a single command in Font Book.

◆ **New Fonts - Hoefler, Skia, Apple Symbol, Plantagenet Cherokee (p. 129)** Spice up your documents with additional fonts that support advanced typography and other languages.

◆ **Font Character Variations (p. 130-131)** Quickly see all variations of a specific character glyph in all available fonts

◆ **Underline, Strike-through and Shadow Controls (p. 130-131)** Create strike-throughs, underlines and elegant shadows.

iCal 1.5.2

◆ **Set Alarms For To Do Items (p. 307)** Set a reminder alarm for To Do items.

◆ **Edit Events Using the Info Drawer (p. 309)** Edit event information using the Info Drawer.

◆ **Publish or Subscribe to Calendars on Servers (p. 310-311)** Publish or subscribe to calendars located behind a firewall.

◆ **Choose a Time Zone For Events (p. 312)** Select a time zone for different events.

iChat AV 2.1

◆ **AOL Instant Messenger 5.5 for Windows (p. 283)** iChat AV 2.1 supports video conferencing with PC users using AIM 5.5 for Windows.

◆ **Buddy Groups (p. 292-293)** Filter and organize buddies in different groups.

◆ **Two-way video Conferencing (p. 298-299)** Chat with high quality two-way video conferencing over any broadband Internet connection.

- ◆ **Audio Conferencing (p. 298-299)** Talk with full duplex (two-way) audio conferencing over any 56k dialup or better connection.

- ◆ **Resizable and Full-Screen Video (p. 298-299)** iChat AV lets you size your video window from the large default of 352 x 288 to full screen with great quality, thanks to Quartz Extreme. You can even resize a window during a video conference.

- ◆ **Video and Audio Buttons (p. 298-299)** iChat AV includes intuitive status buttons that both indicate your buddies conferencing capabilities and provide a convenient way to initiate a conference.

iMovie 3.03

- ◆ **Specify PAL or NTSC Format (p. 360)** A new preference that lets you specify PAL or NTSC format for new projects.

- ◆ **Integration with iPhoto (p. 363)** Drag photos directly from an iPhoto library into iMovie. Crop stills from an iPhoto library.

- ◆ **Integration with iTunes (p. 363)** Create chapter markers in iMovie and turn your movie into an iDVD project.

- ◆ **Sound Effects (p. 363)** New sound effects, which includes Skywalker Sound.

- ◆ **Ken Burns Effect (p. 369)** Add pan and zoom motion to photographs.

- ◆ **QuickTime Support (p. 370)** Import and export video formats supported by QuickTime.

- ◆ **Volume Controls** Improved volume controls that give you tighter control over the sound in a movie.

iPhoto 2

- ◆ **Share and Exhibit Pictures (p. 352-353)** Share and exhibit your pictures using controls in the Organize pane.

- ◆ **Slideshow Preferences (p.353)** Set and save slideshow preferences for individual albums.

- ◆ **Burn Slideshow on iDVD (p. 353)** Copy a slideshow to iDVD with the click of a button.

- ◆ **Share Slideshow (p. 353)** Share slideshows over the Internet with Mac OS X 10.2 users.

- ◆ **Create CDs (p. 353)** Create a CD to archive pictures or share them with others.

- ◆ **Retouch a Picture (p. 354-355)** Retouch a photo to remove blemishes, wrinkles, shadows, and other marks.

- ◆ **Printing Templates (p. 357)** Choose from new templates when printing photos.

- ◆ **E-mail Photos (p. 357)** E-mail your photos using Mac OS X mail, entourage, Eudora, and AOL.

- ◆ **View and Copy CD Libraries** View and copy CD libraries while you work in a library.

- ◆ **Use ActionScript** Use ActionScript to automate tasks.

International

- ◆ **Keyboard Viewer Palette (p. 88-89)** View keyboard layout and enter text with mouse clicks via system floating palette.

- ◆ **Unicode 4 Support (p. 88-89)** Take advantage of support for new languages as defined by the latest Unicode standard.

Mail 1.3.2

- ◆ **Exchange Mail (p. 237)** Set up Exchange e-mail accounts simply using the IMAP protocol.

- ◆ **Always Show BCC (p. 241)** Choose to permanently add a BCC field for newly composed e-mails.

- ◆ **Drag and Drop Addressing (p. 242)** Mail allows you to drag e-mail addresses between the address fields in a Compose window or in the Address Book. E-mail addresses can appear as an address or simply a name to make addressing easier.

- ◆ **Attachment Interface (p. 250-251)** Manage attachments directly from the message header/Mail Viewer window.

- ◆ **Attachments for Windows Users (p. 250)** E-mail attachments are compressed using the standard GNU Zip (gzip) format, so Windows users can open attachments you send from the Mac.

- ◆ **View Message Threads (p. 252-253)** Mail includes the option to group and view all messages in an e-mail thread, which is a group of related messages and replies. Viewing messages by thread makes it easy to view and manage e-mail. You can group messages together, collapse and expand all the messages in a thread, and highlight threads in color.

- ◆ **Junk Mail Filtering (p. 260-261)** Mail improves junk mail filtering, offering advanced options to help you take control of your mail and reduce the amount of junk mail you receive.

- **Junk Mail Privacy (p. 260-261)**   Prevent spammers from knowing you received their junk mail.

- **Erase All Junk Mail (p. 260-261)**   Erase all accumulated Junk Mail in one fell swoop.

- **HTML Rendering**   Mail uses Safari's HTML rendering engine to display messages in HTML format.

iTunes 4.2

- **Share Music Between Macintosh and Windows (p. 323)**   Use iTunes on Windows 2000 and Windows XP computers.

- **Burn Large Playlists to Multiple CDs or DVDs (p. 330)**   Burn large playlist on multiple CDs or DVDs when it doesn't fit on one.

- **Buy Audible Spoken Content (p. 332)**   Buy audible spoken word content from the iTunes Music Store using your Apple or AOL account.

- **Drag Web Page to a Document or E-mail (p. 333)**   Drag a Web page from the iTunes Music Store to a document or e-mail.

- **Synchronize Playlists or Voice Notes (p. 336)**   Sync On-The-Go playlists or voice notes that you create on your iPod with iTunes.

Networking and Security

- **Simplified Network Preferences (p. 184)**   View current status of all network connections via Network preference summary.

- **Authenticate on Wake (p. 385)**   Ensure maximum security of system by prompting user name and password when system wakes from sleep.

- **FileVault Master Password (p. 385)**   Create backup or master password for administrators to access FileVault home directories.

- **Log out Based on Inactivity (p. 385)**   Set your system to log out automatically when idle.

- **FileVault Home Directory Encryption (p. 389)**   Secure the contents of your home directory with powerful AES-128 encryption.

- **Virtual Private Network (VPN) Support (p. 404)**   Supports PPTP and L2TP over IPSec to create secure connections to popular VPN servers, including Windows.

- **V.92 Incoming Call Notification**   Optionally answer incoming voice calls on V.92 modems while connected to Internet.

Preview

◆ **PDF Fast Searching (p. 124)**   Enjoy PDF search with indexed results.

◆ **PDF Rendering Performance (p. 124)**   Use the fastest PDF reader on any platform.

◆ **Text and Image Selection and Copy (p. 124)**   Select PDF text and graphics to copy and paste to other applications.

◆ **FAX Display (p. 124)**   View multi-page TIFF fax documents with high fidelity.

◆ **Full Screen PDF (p. 124)**   Display any PDF full screen for easy cross platform presentations.

◆ **PDF Table of Contents (p. 124)**   View table of contents for a PDF.

◆ **URL Support (p. 124)**   Navigate PDFs via PDF links and Internet URLs.

Printing and Faxing

◆ **Printing to Windows Shared Printers (p. 164)**   Print directly to Windows shared printers over the SMB protocol.

◆ **Drag and Drop Printing Proxies (p. 174)**   Manage print jobs easily via individual printer icons accessible on the Desktop, in folders, and the Dock.

◆ **Fax Sending From any Application (p. 167, 178-179)**   Print any Mac OS X document as a fax through a built-in internal modem.

◆ **Fax Receive via Folder, E-Mail or Printer (p. 167, 180-181)**   Receive a fax from the built-in fax modem as a file, in e-mail or printed to any printer.

◆ **Fax Cover Page (p. 177)**   Create customized cover page for sending faxes.

◆ **Faxing using the Address Book (p. 182)**   Send a fax to contacts in your Address book for any application in which you can print.

Safari 1.2

◆ **Using SnapBack Buttons (p. 197)**   When you browse from a starting Web page, click the SnapBack button in the address box to quickly return to that Web page. Similarly, when you browse from your Goggle search results, click the SnapBack button in the Google Search bar to return to them.

◆ **Browsing the Internet (p. 198-199)**   Browsing Web pages is easy with Safari. You can browse multiple pages using tabs instead of separate windows to cut down on window clutter. If you always want to open a collection of bookmarks in the Bookmarks bar in tabs, you can click the AutoTab check box next to the collection in the Bookmarks Library.

◆ **Working with Bookmarks (p. 203-205)** To add a bookmark, open a Web page and click the Add Bookmark button (+) in the toolbar. You can name the bookmark and add it to the Bookmarks bar. You organize your bookmarks in the Bookmarks Library. You can create collections of bookmarks and add the collections to the bookmarks bar for quick access. Safari maintains a history of Web pages you open so you can easily return to them. You can also use Safari to browse Web sites available with Rendezvous or entered in your Address Book. Use iSync to synchronize your bookmarks so that you can have the same bookmarks on all the computers you use.

◆ **Filling Out Forms (p. 206-207)** Safari can automatically fill out forms for you using information in your Address Book or that it stores from forms you filled out previously. It can also store account names and passwords for secure Web sites you visit regularly.

◆ **Finding Web Pages Using Google (p. 208)** Google searching is built into Safari. Just click the Google Search bar in the toolbar, type a word or phrase, and press Return. To repeat a search, click the magnifying glass and choose the search from the pop-up.

◆ **Downloading Files (p. 212-213)** When you download files from the Internet, Safari cleans up after itself so you only have to see the decompressed file you're interested in.

◆ **Blocking Pop-Up Windows (p. 217)** As you browse Web pages, you may notice lots of windows opening. These pop-up windows can get in the way of your Web experience. Safari can block these pop-up windows for you, making it easier to navigate the Internet.

◆ **Deleting Personal Information from Safari (p. 218)** If you use Safari on a public computer to access your personal data, you can select Reset Safari from the Safari menu to delete all your personal information.

◆ **Based on Standards** Safari is based on Internet standards so pages that use advanced HTML, XML, XHTML, DOM, CSS, Javascript, and Java specifications look right and work correctly. You can view content in QuickTime, Macromedia Flash and Shockwave Players, and RealNetwork Real Player.

TextEdit

◆ **Word Documents (p. 136)** Open and create Microsoft Word Format files (.doc).

◆ **Word Search (p. 146)** Search for full words or parts or words.

◆ **Create Styles (p. 154-155)** Save font style attributes as a named Style which can be applied later to other text in TextEdit.

◆ **Fine-tune Editing (p. 152-153)** Set line height, inter-line spacing, and paragraph spacing. You can also set base writing direction.

Utilities

- **Calculator (p. 120-121)** Use recent conversions across multiple launches of Calculator.

- **Image Capture (p. 122)** Automatically enhance images while scanning with Image Capture.

- **Preview (p. 124)** Preview PDF files quickly with Preview. In addition, you can preview an EPS file or Postscript file as a PDF file.

- **DVD Player 3 (p. 126)** Set bookmarks so you can start a DVD from where you left off or use favorite scenes. You can also view closed captioning over video or in a separate window, and select the text color you want. Watch your video in Full Screen mode while you work on or dim another display.

- **Sherlock 3.6 (p. 220, 223, 226, 232)** Search the Internet more quickly with integrated Sherlock channels and a third-party channel listing that makes it easy to find Web services. You can also organize and manage channels in collections. You can now use the Phone Book channel to get location information from your Address Book.

- **iSync 1.4 (p. 271, 313-316)** Sync more devices, including the iPod mini, and your Safari bookmarks to .Mac. You can also sync your calendar and contact information on a wider variety of Symbian OS smart phones.

- **Bluetooth (p. 396-398, 412)** Use secure connections between Bluetooth devices and your Mac and use Bluetooth input devices, mouse and keyboard.

Keyboard Shortcuts

If a command on a menu includes a keyboard reference, known as a keyboard shortcut, to the right of the command name, you can perform the action by pressing and holding the first key, and then pressing the second key to perform the command quickly. In some cases, a keyboard shortcut uses one key or three keys. For three keys, simply press and hold the first two keys, and then press the third key. Keyboard shortcuts provide an alternative to using the mouse and make it easy to perform repetitive commands. If you don't like a global shortcut key combination, you can change it. See "Changing Keyboard Settings," on page 435 for details.

Finding a Keyboard Shortcut

The Mac OS X Panther contains keyboard shortcuts for many commands and tasks in the different applications and utility programs. To find a keyboard shortcut for a menu command, click the menu with the command to display the keyboard shortcut keys. See the illustration below for key symbols on menus. To find a keyboard shortcut for a common task, use the list provided here. To help you locate the keyboard shortcut you're looking for in the list, the shortcuts are organized by Mac OS X Panther system or application and listed with page numbers.

Mac OS X System

Mac OS X Applications

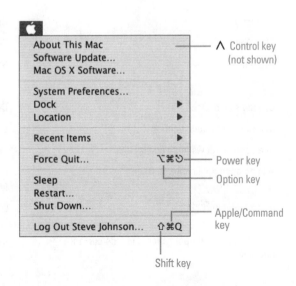

Keyboard Shortcuts

Task/Application	Shortcut
STARTING UP	
Prevent automatic login	Hold down Left Shift key and mouse button when you see progress bar
Close open Finder windows	Shift
Start up from CD	C
Start up from default NetBook image	N
Start up computer connected using FireWire in Target Disk Mode	T
Select startup disk (on some computers)	Option
Open CD tray when selecting startup disk (on some computers)	⌘+. (period)
Prevent startup items from opening	Hold down Shift when you see progress bar
Start up using Mac OS X rather than Mac OS 9 (if both on same volume)	⌘+X
Eject removable disks	Hold down mouse button
Reset Parameter RAM	⌘+Option+P+R
Show console messages (verbose mode)	⌘+V
Start up in single user mode	⌘+S
Start up in Safe Mode	Hold down Shift immediately after startup tone, and release when you see progress bar
SHUTTING DOWN	
Sleep	Control+Eject or Control+F12
Restart	Control+⌘+Eject
Shut Down	Control+Option+⌘+Eject
Log Out	Shift+⌘+Q
DOCK	
Change size of Dock	Drag dividing line in Dock
See Dock shortcuts menu	Control+click Dock background
See open windows in an application	Press application's icon
Add an open application to Dock	Press its icon and select Keep In Dock from pop-up menu
See an item in Finder	⌘+click item's icon in Dock, press its icon and select Show In Finder from pop-up menu
Switch to another application and hide current application	Option+click icon in Dock

Keyboard Shortcuts *(continued)*

Task/Application	Shortcut
Switch to another application and hide all other applications	⌘+Option+click icon in Dock
Quit an open application	Press its icon and select Quit from pop-up menu
Force quit an application	Option+press application icon in Dock, then select Force Quit from pop-up menu
Force an application to open a document	⌘+Option+drag document icon to icon in Dock
FINDER	
Jump to search field in a Finder window	⌘+Option+F
Define a search using multiple criteria	⌘+F
Open your home folder	⌘+Shift+H; ⌘+Up Arrow (in some cases)
Open iDisk	⌘+Shift+I
Open Desktop folder	⌘+Shift+D
Open Computer area	⌘+Shift+C
Open Network browser	⌘+Shift+K
Open Applications folder	⌘+Shift+A
Open Utilities folder	⌘+Shift+U
Select next icon	Arrow keys
Select icon by first letter of its name	Letter keys
Select next alphabetic item in a window	Tab
Select previous alphabetic item in a window	Shift+Tab
Select group of icons	Drag pointer across icons
Add icon to selection	Shift+click
Select adjacent icons in list	Shift+click
Select or deselect non-adjacent icons in list	⌘+click
Select name of icon	Return
Align icons as you drag them	⌘+drag
Copy file instead of moving it	Option+drag file's icon to new location
Make an alias to file instead of moving it	⌘+Option+drag file's icon
See path name of current window	⌘+Option+click window's title; select item from pop-up menu to open it
Open folder in separate window	⌘+double-click
In List view, open selected folder	Right Arrow

Task/Application	Shortcut
In List view, open each level within selected folder	⌘+Option+Right Arrow
In List view, open all folders within selected folder	Option+click disclosure triangle
In List view, close selected folder	Left Arrow
In List or Icon view, open selected folder	⌘+Down Arrow
In List or Icon view, show folder containing current folder	⌘+Up Arrow; If no Finder windows are open, opens window showing Home folder
Open new window showing folder that contains current folder and close current window	⌘+Option+Up Arrow
Open new window showing contents of current folder and close current window	⌘+Option+Down Arrow
Make desktop active	⌘+Option+Shift+Up Arrow
Move selected item to Trash	⌘+Delete
Empty Trash	⌘+Shift+Delete
Empty Trash without a warning or with locked files	⌘+Shift+Option+Delete
FREEZES	
Stop process	⌘+. (period)
Force application to quit	⌘+Option+Esc (Escape)
Turn off computer	Power key
Force some computers to shut down or restart	⌘+Option+Shift+Power key
Force computer to restart	⌘+Control+Power key
SYSTEM	
Use Exposé to show all open windows	F9 (default setting)
Use Exposé to show all open windows in application	F10 (default setting)
Use Exposé to hide all open windows and show desktop	F11 (default setting)
Switch to previous application	⌘+Tab
Switch to open application	Hold down ⌘+Tab until application is selected, then release keys; to reverse order, also hold down Shift
See shortcut (contextual) menu for item	Control+click item
Make window active and hide current program	Option+click window; Option+click Dock icon
Select folder that contains current folder or document	⌘+click window title, then select Folder from pop-up menu
Arrange status menus	⌘+drag status menu icon
Change alert volume	Option+drag sound volume slider in menu bar

Keyboard Shortcuts *(continued)*

Task/Application	Shortcut
DIALOGS	
Select next area of dialog	Tab
Click default button	Press Return
Close dialog	Esc (Escape) or ⌘+. (period)
Scroll list up or down	Page Up or Page Down
Open Go To Folder dialog to specify path	⌘+Shift+G
WINDOWS	
Make next window in current application active	⌘+' (single quote)
Make previous window in current application active	⌘+~ (tilde)
Minimize window	Double-click title bar
Drag a window without making it active	⌘+drag window
Close all windows in active application	Option+click Close button
Minimize all windows in active application	Option+click Minimize button
Enlarge all windows in active application	Option+click Zoom button
Hide previous program	Option+click window; Option+click Dock icon
Move window without making it active	⌘+drag window
Select folder that contains current folder or document	⌘+click window title, then select Folder from pop-up menu
File path name of document in window	⌘+click window's title
Scroll quickly through long document	Press and hold in scroll bar
Switch between "Scroll to here" and "Jump to page"	Option+click in scroll bar
TAKING SCREEN PICTURES	
Picture of whole screen	⌘+Shift+3
Picture of part of screen	⌘+Shift+4, then drag to select area you want
Picture of a window, menu bar, Dock, or other area	⌘+Shift+4, then press Spacebar; move pointer over area you want, then click
iCAL	
Calendar	
Go to next day, week, or month	⌘+Right Arrow
Go to previous day, week, or month	⌘+Left Arrow
Move calendar view up or down	Up Arrow or Down Arrow
Check or uncheck selected calendar in Calendars list	Press Spacebar
Check or uncheck all selected calendars in Calendars list	⌘+click any calendar's check box

Task/Application	Shortcut
Check or uncheck only selected calendar in Calendars list	⌘+Option+click calendar's check box
View only events on selected calendar	⌘+Option+~ (tilde)
Event	
Select next event or To Do item in main calendar view	Press Tab
Select previous event or To Do in main calendar view	Tab+Shift
Move an event to another calendar	Control+click event, then select Calendar from pop-up menu
Move selected event to next day	Control+Right Arrow
Move selected event to previous day	Control+Left Arrow
Move selected event 15 minutes earlier; all-day events move one week earlier (only in Month view)	Control+Up Arrow
Move selected event 15 minutes later; all-day events move one week later (only in Month view)	Control+Down Arrow
In Day or Week view, make selected event end 15 minutes sooner	Shift+Control+Up Arrow
In Day or Week view, make selected event end 15 minutes later	Shift+Control+Down Arrow
In Month view, move selected all-day event one week later	Down Arrow
In Month view, move selected all-day event one week earlier	Up Arrow
Make selected all-day event last one more day	Shift+Control+Right Arrow
Make selected all-day event start one day sooner	Shift+Control+Left Arrow
iMOVIE	
Navigation	
Play/Stop and Start/Stop capture	Press Spacebar
Move playhead to beginning of movie	Home (not available on some keyboards)
Move playhead to end of movie	End (not available on some keyboards)
Forward one frame; Forward ten frames	Right Arrow; Shift+Right Arrow
Roll playhead forward	Hold down Right Arrow
Fast forward	⌘+] (right bracket)
Back one frame; Back ten frames	Left Arrow; Shift+Left Arrow
Roll playhead backward	Hold down Left Arrow
Rewind	⌘+[(left bracket)

Keyboard Shortcuts (continued)

Task/Application	Shortcut
Selection	
Select multiple items	Shift+click items
Select range of items (in clip viewer or timeline viewer)	Click first item, then Shift+click last item
Moving/Cropping	
Move audio clip	Click clip, then Left Arrow or Right Arrow
Move audio clip ten frames	Click clip, then Shift+Left Arrow or Right Arrow
Move video clip to create black frames	Click clip in timeline viewer, then Control+Left Arrow or Right Arrow
Move video clip to create ten black frames	Click clip timeline viewer, then Control+Shift+Left Arrow or Right Arrow
Move crop marker	Click marker+Left Arrow or Right Arrow
Move crop marker ten frames	Click marker, then Shift+Left Arrow or Right Arrow
iPHOTO	
Import	
Import photos	Shift+⌃⌘+I
Organize	
Show or hide titles	Shift+⌃⌘+T
Show or hide keywords	Shift-⌃⌘+K
Show or hide film rolls	Shift+⌃⌘+F
Assign, edit, or search by keywords	⌃⌘+K
Show photo's image and camera information	⌃⌘+I
Duplicate photo	⌃⌘+D
Move photo to Trash from photo library, or remove photo from album	Delete
Switch between book and organize view when selecting album	Option+click album
Open photo in its own window or in edit view (depends on double-click preference you set)	Double-click photo
Reverse double-click preference when opening photo	Option+double-click photo
Selecting and Deselecting photos	
Select all photos	⌃⌘+A
Select all photos between current selection and non-adjacent photo	Hold down Shift and click non-adjacent photo

Task/Application	Shortcut
Select photos that are non-adjacent to each other	Select first photo, then hold down ⌘ and click additional photos
Select several photos located together	Click outside photos and drag to enclose them within selection rectangle
Select all photos in film roll	Click film roll icon
Deselect specific photos in group of selected photos	Hold down ⌘ and click photos you want to deselect
Deselect all photos	Shift+⌘+A or click outside photo
Slideshow	
Stop a slideshow	Press mouse button
Pause and resume playing	Press Spacebar
Adjust speed	Up and Down Arrows
Move through slideshow manually	Right and Left Arrows
Edit	
Rotate photo	⌘+R
Reverse rotate direction	Shift+⌘+R or press Option while clicking Rotate button
Go to next photo	Right Arrow
Go to previous photo	Left Arrow
Disable constrain setting when selecting area	⌘ while dragging
Switch between portrait and landscape constrain setting when selecting area	Press Option while dragging
Return to organize view	Double-click photo
Book	
Apply page design through end of book	Select first page and press Option when selecting Design from Page Design pop-up menu
Show fonts	⌘+T
Copy font	⌘+3
Paste font	⌘+4
Spelling	⌘+: (colon)
iTUNES	
Playback	
Play selected song immediately	Press Return

Keyboard Shortcuts *(continued)*

Task/Application	Shortcut
Listen to next or previous album in list	Option+Right Arrow or Left Arrow
Rewind or fast-forward to next song in list	⌘+Left Arrow or Right Arrow
Library and Playlist	
Create playlist from selection of songs	Shift+click Add button (+)
Create new Smart Playlist	Option+click Add button (+)
Reshuffle current playlist	Option+click Shuffle button
Delete selected playlist from Source list (no confirmation)	⌘+Delete
Delete selected playlist and all songs it contains	Option+Delete
Delete selected song from your library and all playlists	Option+Delete
File and window	
Check or uncheck all songs in a list	⌘+click check box next to song
Change song information columns you see	Control+click column heading
Expand or collapse all triangles in Radio's Stream list	⌘+click triangle
Shrink iTunes window to show only playback controls	Click Zoom control in upper-left window corner
Zoom window to ideal size	Option+click Zoom control in upper-left window corner
In Get Info window, see info for next or previous song	⌘+N or ⌘+P
See more options when visual effect is showing	Press ?, then press indicated key to use option
iPod	
Prevent iPod from automatically updating when you connect it to your computer	⌘+Option as you connect iPod to your computer (hold keys down until iPod appears)
MAIL	
Mail application	
Create new compose window	⌘+N
Get new mail	⌘+Shift+N
Open new viewer window	⌘+Option+N
Open Activity Viewer	⌘+0 (zero)
Open Page Setup dialog	⌘+Shift+P
Add senders to Address Book	⌘+Y
Apply rules to selection	⌘+Option+L
Use selection for Find	⌘+E
Find text in single message body	⌘+F

Keyboard Shortcuts *(continued)*

Task/Application	Shortcut
Find previous	⌘+Shift+G
Find next	⌘+G
Minimize window	⌘+M
Display pop-up menu with commands for Mail	Press and hold Mail icon in Dock
Switch between different display settings in toolbar	Hold down ⌘+click toolbar button in upper-right corner

Mailboxes

Open In mailbox	⌘+1
Open Out mailbox	⌘+2
Open Drafts mailbox	⌘+3
Open Sent mailbox	⌘+4
Open Trash mailbox	⌘+5
Open Junk mailbox	⌘+6
Show/hide mailboxes	⌘+Shift+M
Select search field	⌘+Option+F
Erase junk mail	⌘+Option+J
Move to last mailbox you moved or copied message to	⌘+Option+T
Display pop-up menu that lets you quickly perform several actions on item you click	Control+click message or mailbox

Sending messages

Add Bcc header	⌘+Option+B
Add Reply-To header	⌘+Option+R
Show/hide long headers	⌘+Shift+H
Attach file to message	⌘+Shift+A
Append selected messages to new message	⌘+Option+I
Paste as quotation	⌘+Shift+V
Increase quote level	⌘+' (single quote)
Decrease quote level	⌘+Option+' (single quote)
Save as draft	⌘+S
Send message	⌘+Shift+D
Redirect message	⌘+Shift+E
Forward message	⌘+Shift+F

Keyboard Shortcuts *(continued)*

Task/Application	Shortcut
Prevent next message from being selected/marked as read	Hold down Option when deleting message
Receiving messages	
Select all highlighted messages	⌘+Shift+K
Mark as junk mail	⌘+Shift+J
Mark as flagged/unflagged	⌘+Shift+L
Mark as read/unread	⌘+Shift+U
Reply with iChat	⌘+Shift+I
Reply to sender	⌘+R
Reply to all	⌘+Shift+R
Bounce to sender	⌘+Shift+B
Show/hide deleted messages	⌘+L
Show raw source/original content	⌘+Option+U
Compact/empty deleted messages	⌘+K
Show plain text alternative	⌘+Option+P
Show previous alternative (in multi-part message)	⌘+[(left bracket)
Show next alternative (in multi-part message)	⌘+] (right bracket)
Jump to selected text in message	⌘+J
Copy message to different mailbox	Hold down Option when dragging message
Fonts, formatting, and spelling	
Show Font panel	⌘+T
Convert message to rich/plain text	⌘+Shift+T
Make font larger	⌘++ (plus)
Make font smaller	⌘+- (minus)
Show Colors panel	⌘+Shift+C
Align left	⌘+{ (open bracket)
Align center	⌘+I
Align right	⌘+} (close bracket)
Check spelling of email message	⌘+: (colon)
Flag misspelling of selected word	⌘+; (semi-colon)
Copy style	⌘+Option+C
Paste style	⌘+Option+V

Keyboard Shortcuts *(continued)*

Task/Application	Shortcut
Collapse thread containing selected message	Left Arrow
Expand currently selected thread	Right Arrow
Move to next message in thread	Down Arrow
Move to previous message in thread	Up Arrow

SAFARI

Web pages

Scroll up, down, left, or right	Arrow keys
Scroll larger increment	Option+Arrow key
Scroll down screen	Page Down; Spacebar
Scroll up screen	Page Up; Shift+Spacebar
Open page in new window, if tabbed browsing is off	⌘+click link or bookmark
Open page in new window behind current window, if tabbed browsing if off	⌘+Shift+click link or bookmark
Open all bookmarks in older in bookmarks bar in tabs	⌘+click folder in bookmarks bar
Close all tabs except one	Option+click Close button on tab you want open
See list of recent pages by name	Hold down Back or Forward button
See list of recent pages by address	Hold down Option+Back or Forward button
See downloaded file in Finder	Click icon next to file in Download window

Bookmarks

Add bookmark to Bookmarks menu	Open page, press ⌘+Shift+D
Add bookmark to bookmarks bar	Drag page icon from address box to bar
Move bookmark on bookmarks bar	Drag bookmark left or right
Remove bookmark from bookmarks bar	Drag bookmark off top of bar

Bookmarks Library

Open Bookmarks Library	⌘+Option+B
Select next bookmark or folder in collection	Up or Down Arrow
Open folder in collection	Right Arrow
Close folder in collection	Left Arrow
Open folder in collection and all folders it contains	Option+Right Arrow
Close folder in a collection and all folders it contains	Option+Left Arrow
Change name or address of bookmark	Select bookmark, press Return, then type
Delete bookmark in Bookmarks Library	Select it, press Delete

Troubleshooting

Index

A

Abstracts backgrounds, 84
accessories, list of, 106
access privileges. *See* privileges
Action pop-up menu, 8, 18
Activity Monitor, 426-427
address bar in Safari window, 194
Address Book, 106. *See also* Mail; Safari
  archiving data, 113
  Calendar events, adding attendees to, 309
  change of address notification, 112
  creating, 112-113
  editing, 114-115
  enhancements in, 112
  exchanging contacts with other users, 117
  faxes, addressing, 182
  groups, creating, 116-117
  iChat AV buddies, adding, 290-2912
  images, adding, 118
  importing vCards, 113
  instant snapshots, adding, 118
  iSync, adding to, 314
  .MAC Address Book, 270-271
  managing, 116-117
  moving contacts in, 117
  printing, 115
  undoing mistakes, 115
Adobe
  Acrobat Reader, 125, 173
  GoLive, 274
  InDesign, 337
Adobe Photoshop
  Color Picker, accessing, 443
  iPhoto and, 354
Advanced preferences, 58
  Finder Preferences, 58
  for iTunes, 335

Safari, setting for, 215
airlines and Sherlock Flights channel, 228
AirPort Admin Utility, 410
AirPort connection, 184, 391
  computer-to-computer networks, creating, 188
  iChat AV with, 300
  Internet Connect for, 191-192
  multiple connections, creating, 185
  setting up, 188
    for network, 395
alarms in To Do list, 307
albums in iPhoto, 352-353
alerts
  iChat AV alerts, 304
  modem options, 437
  spoken user interface options, 103
aliases, 70-71
ambient light and monitor brightness, adjusting, 440
amr files, QuickTime supporting, 127
animation of Dock application icon, 68
antialiasing with System Preferences, 82
AOL Instant Messenger (AIM). *See* iChat AV
Apache, 451
Appearance preferences
  for iChat AV chats, 302-303
  Safari, setting for, 215
  System Preferences for changing, 78
Apple Backgrounds, 84
AppleCare channel, Sherlock, 229
Apple Computer Web site, 20
Apple Exchange, 282
Apple Knowledge Base, 229
Apple Music Store, 332
Apple Remote Desktop, 393

buttons. *See also* toolbars
- for iDVD projects, 339-340
- in windows, 12

C

cache
- Mail cache, setting, 236
- Safari, emptying, 202

Calculator, 106
- conversions with, 121
- working with, 120-121

calendar. *See also* iCal
- iSync, adding to, 314

CandyBar utility, 76

Carbonized versions of applications, 418

case-sensitivity of passwords, 3

CD-R disks, 27
- erasing, 348

CD-ROM disks, 27

CD-RW disks, 27
- erasing, 348

CDs. *See also* burning CDs/DVDs; iTunes
- adding/removing files and folders to, 55
- data CD, duplicating, 422
- desktop, icons on, 59
- erasing, 348
- Finder, creating with, 54-55
- image, creating CDs from, 422
- mounting/ejecting disks, 56
- Sidebar, burning CD with, 17
- start settings, changing, 95
- System Preferences settings, 78
- System Profiler checking on, 429
- uneven CDs, loading, 27

Cellos voice, 102

center tab stops, setting, 150

change of address notification, 112

channels. *See* Sherlock

Character Map, 106

check boxes in dialogs, 9

check marks on menu, 7

Chess, 119

Chooser, 77

circle opening/closing, adding to iMovie, 368

Claris Emailer, importing e-mail from, 235

Classic environment, 78-79

applications, using, 474-476
- fast startup in, 476
- installing Mac OS 9, 470-471
- preferences, setting, 472-473
- Show Memory Usage & Versions, 473
- starting computer with, 476
- Start/Stop options, 472-473
- Startup Disk, selecting, 94
- switching between Mac OS X and, 475
- upgrades, 477
- working with, 469-476

Clean Up
- command, 32
- files and folders, sorting, 33
- Macaroni utility, 76

clicking with mouse, 6

Clipboard, editing and, 138

Close button, 12

closing
- documents, 159
- windows, 13

color labels
- files and folders, organizing, 38-39
- Finder Label preferences, 58
- Find window, searching with, 42-43
- List view, sorting in, 39
- names, changing, 39

Color Picker, selecting colors with, 443

colors. *See also* color labels; color text; iChat AV; monitor
- desktop background colors, 84
- hexadecimal value of, 442
- for iDVD projects, 339
- scroll bar colors, changing, 82

ColorSync utility
- for faxes, 179
- monitor colors, matching, 444-445
- for printing, 171

color text, 148
- e-mail text, 244
- for instant messages, 295

columns
- headings in windows, 12
- List view, working in, 35
- Search bar columns, adjusting, 41
- Sidebar column, adjusting, 17, 66

Q